Web Services Research and Practices

Liang-Jie Zhang
IBM T.J. Watson Research, USA

Cybertech Publishing

Hershey • New York

Acquisition Editor:	Kristin Klinger
Senior Managing Editor:	Jennifer Neidig
Managing Editor:	Jamie Snavely
Assistant Managing Editor:	Carole Coulson
Development Editor:	Kristin Roth
Copy Editor:	Maria Boyer
Typesetter:	Larissa Vinci
Cover Design:	Lisa Tosheff
Printed at:	Yurchak Printing Inc.

Published in the United States of America by
CyberTech Publishing (an imprint of IGI Global)
701 E. Chocolate Avenue
Hershey PA 17033
Tel: 717-533-8845
Fax: 717-533-8661
E-mail: cust@igi-global.com
Web site: http://www.cybertech-global.com

and in the United Kingdom by
CyberTech Publishing (an imprint of IGI Global)
3 Henrietta Street
Covent Garden
London WC2E 8LU
Tel: 44 20 7240 0856
Fax: 44 20 7379 0609
Web site: http://www.eurospanbookstore.com

Library of Congress Cataloging-in-Publication Data

Zhang, Liang-Jie.
 Web services research and practices / Liang-Jie Zhang.
   p. cm.
  Summary: "This book provides researchers, scholars, and practitioners in a variety of settings essential up-to-date research in this demanding field, addressing issues such as communication applications using Web services; Semantic services computing; discovery, modeling, performance, and enhancements of Web services; and Web services architecture, frameworks, and security"--Provided by publisher.
  ISBN 978-1-59904-904-5 (hardcover) -- ISBN 978-1-59904-907-6 (e-book)
 1. Web sites. 2. Web services. I. Title.

  TK5105.888.Z47 2008
  006.7--dc22

British Cataloguing in Publication Data
A Cataloguing in Publication record for this book is available from the British Library.

All work contributed to this book is original material. The views expressed in this book are those of the authors, but not necessarily of the publisher.

Adances in Web Services Research Book Series (AWSR)

ISBN: 1935-3685

Editor-in-Chief: Liang-Jie Zhang, IBM Research, USA

Modern Technologies in Web Services Research Vol. I
Liang-Jie Zhang IBM, USA

CyberTech Publishing · copyright 2007 · 284pp · H/C (ISBN: 978-1-59904-280-0) · US $85.46 (our price)

Web service technologies are constantly being recreated, continuously challenging Web service professionals and examiners. Modern Technologies in Web Services Research facilitates communication and networking among Web services and e-business researchers and engineers in a period where considerable changes are taking place in Web services technologies innovation.

Modern Technologies in Web Services Research provides mathematic foundations for service oriented computing, Web services architecture and security, frameworks for building Web service applications, and dynamic invocation mechanisms for Web services among other innovative approaches.

Web Services Research and Practices Vol. II
Liang-Jie Zhang, IBM Research, USA

CyberTech Publishing · copyright 2008 · 278pp · H/C (ISBN: 978-1-59904-904-5) · US $89.96 (our price)

Web services is rapidly becoming one of the most valued aspects of information technology services, as Web-based technological advancements continue to grow at an exponential rate.

Web Services Research and Practices provides researchers, scholars, and practitioners in a variety of settings essential up-to-date research in this demanding field, addressing issues such as communication applications using Web services; Semantic services computing; discovery, modeling, performance, and enhancements of Web services; and Web services architecture, frameworks, and security.

The Advances in Web Services Research (AWSR) Book Series features only the latest research findings and industry solutions dealing with all aspects of Web services technology. The overall scope of this book series will cover the advancements in the state of the art, standards, and practice of Web services, as well as to identify the emerging research topics and define the future of Services computing, including Web services on Grid computing, Web services on multimedia, Web services on communication, etc. AWSR provides an open, formal series for high quality books developed by theoreticians, educators, developers, researchers and practitioners for professionals to stay abreast of challenges in Web services technology.

Web services are network-based application components with services-oriented architecture using standard interface description languages and uniform communication protocols. Due to the importance of the field, standardization organizations such as WS-I, W3C, OASIS and Liberty Alliance are actively developing standards for Web services. Considering these developments, the Advances in Web Services Research (AWSR) Book Series seeks to further emphasize the importance of web services research and expand the availability of comprehensive resources in the advancing field.

Hershey · New York
Order online at www.igi-global.com or call 717-533-8845 x 10 –
Mon-Fri 8:30 am - 5:00 pm (est) or fax 24 hours a day 717-533-8661

Web Services Research and Practices

Table of Contents

    Christian Werner, University of Lübeck, Germany
    Carsten Buschmann, University of Lübeck, Germany
    Stefan Fischer, University of Lübeck, Germany

    Shahram Ghandeharizadeh, University of Southern California, USA
    Christos Papadopoulos, University of Southern California, USA
    Min Cai, University of Southern California, USA
    Runfang Zhou, University of Southern California, USA
    P. Pol, University of Southern California, USA

    Xiang Fu, Georgia Southwestern State University, USA
    Tevfik Bultan, University of California – Santa Barbara, USA
    Jianwen Su, University of California – Santa Barbara, USA

Preface

I am pleased to bring you *Web Services Research and Practices*. Web services technology has been widely admitted as the future technology for Internet computing and distributed computing. As the second volume in the IGI Advanced Book Series, this book provides researchers, practitioners, and educators with the most current research results in the field in 10 chapters.

Chapter I is titled "Efficient Encodings for Web Service Messages" by Christian Werner, Carsten Buschmann, and Stefan Fischer. The chapter discusses the overhead of network bandwidth using SOAP for service integration. The authors explore compression strategies through a detailed survey and evaluation of state-of-the-art binary encoding techniques for SOAP. The chapter also introduces an experimental concept for SOAP compression based on differential encoding, which makes use of the commonly available WSDL description of a SOAP Web service.

Chapter II is titled "NAM: A Network Adaptable Middleware to Enhance Response Time of Web Services" by Shahram Ghandeharizadeh, Christos Papadopoulos, Min Cai, Runfang Zhou, and P. Pol. The chapter presents a network adaptable middleware that strikes a compromise between the encoding/decoding and associated overhead of data compression to enhance response time of Web services.

Chapter III is titled "Realizability Analysis of Top-Down Web Service Composition Specifications" by Xiang Fu, Tevfik Bultan, and Jianwen Su. The chapter presents "conversation protocol," a top-down specification approach to study the realizability problem of conversation protocols.

Chapter IV is titled "Efficient Transport Bindings for Web Service Messages" by Christian Werner, Carsten Buschmann, Tobias Jäcker, and Stefan Fischer. The chapter introduces PURE, a UDP-based transport binding method that significantly reduces the protocol overhead while featuring low latency. The authors prove the resulting reduction of network traffic, and discuss how the data rate efficiency and latency can be enhanced further by transport-level considerations.

Chapter V is titled "A Framework Supporting Context-Aware Multimedia Web Services Delivery" by Jia Zhang, Liang-Jie Zhang, Francis Quek, and Jen-Yao Chung. The chapter presents a componentization model to support quality of service (QoS)-centered, context-aware multimedia Web services delivery. A multimedia Web service is divided into control flow and data flow, each being delivered via different infrastructures and channels. The authors also propose enhancements to Simple Object Access Protocol (SOAP) and Composite Capability/Preference Profiles (CC/PP) protocols to improve their flexibility to serve multimedia Web services.

Chapter VI is titled "Adaptive Search- and Learning-Based Approaches for Automatic Web Service Composition" by Nikola Milanovic and Miroslaw Malek. The chapter models automatic service composition as a search problem. Basic heuristic search, probabilistic, learning-based, backwards (decomposition), and bidirectional (hybrid) automatic composition mechanisms are presented and compared, and the state space and equality of abstract machines are defined.

Chapter VII is titled "XWRAPComposer: A Multi-Page Data Extraction Service" by Ling Liu, Jianjun Zhang, Wei Han, Calton Pu, James Caverlee, Sungkeun Park, Terence Critchlow, David Buttler, Matthew Coleman, and Lawrence Livermore. The chapter presents XWRAPComposer, a wrapper code generation toolkit built on service-oriented architecture to facilitate semi-automatically generating WSDL-enabled wrapper programs.

Chapter VIII is titled "An SLA-Based Auction Pricing Method Supporting Web Services Provisioning" by Jia Zhang, Ning Zhang, and Liang-Jie Zhang. The chapter presents a formal model for Web services-based auctions. The authors examine the specific features of Web services towards applying auctions and establish a Web services-oriented auction model, focusing on investigating and mathematically proving how service providers can decide different service auction strategies to obtain higher profit. The chapter also proposes to utilize the technique of service level agreement (SLA) documents as resources to deduce service requestors' preferences.

Chapter IX is titled "Dynamic, Flow Control-Based Information Management for Web Services" by Zahir Tari, Peter Bertok, and Dusan Simic. The chapter presents a model of information flow control using semi-discretionary label structures. A set of rules are identified to increase the flexibility of information flow control, while exploiting labels as a practical component to ensure security control. A centralized model for dynamic label checking is also proposed to theoretically verify the presented model.

Chapter X is titled "Model-Driven Semantic Web Services" by Gerald C. Gannod, John T.E. Timm, and Raynette J. Brodie. The chapter proposes a suite of automated software tools for facilitating the construction of OWL-S specifications. The authors introduce an approach for specifying OWL-S specifications (OWL-S profiles and process models) through the use of model-driven architecture and user interaction to describe OWL-S groundings.

In summary, this book accumulates some of the most recent research results in the field of Web services. Enjoy the reading of the book!

Liang-Jie (LJ) Zhang, PhD

Editor-in-Chief, Advances in Web Services Research Series

Chapter I

Efficient Encodings for Web Service Messages

Christian Werner, University of Lübeck, Germany

Carsten Buschmann, University of Lübeck, Germany

Stefan Fischer, University of Lübeck, Germany

Abstract

A major drawback of using SOAP for application integration is its enormous demand for network bandwidth. Compared to classical approaches like Java-RMI and Corba, SOAP messages typically cause more than three times more network traffic. In this chapter we will explore compression strategies and give a detailed survey and evaluation of state-of-the-art binary encoding techniques for SOAP. We also introduce a new experimental concept for SOAP compression based on differential encoding, which makes use of the commonly available WSDL description of a SOAP Web service. We not only conduct a detailed evaluation of compression effectiveness, but also provide the results of execution time measurements.

Introduction

Like all other XML protocols, SOAP suffers from the fact that only a very small part of the transmitted message contains real payload. The rest of it is XML markup and protocol overhead. Comparisons on different approaches for realizing remote procedure calls (RPCs) have shown that SOAP over HTTP uses significantly more bandwidth than competitive technologies (Tian, Voigt, Naumowicz, Ritter, & Schiller, 2003; Marahrens, 2003). For our experiments, we implemented a simple RPC server and client on different platforms (MS .Net, Apache Axis, Corba, Java-RMI, RMIIIOP). Then we measured the resulting network traffic for each case using the Ethereal network analyzing utility.

Figure 1 summarizes the results. For all implementations the number of transmitted bytes increases with the number of transmitted RPC messages in an almost linear way (all values do not include overhead for protocols on network layer and below). There is virtually no difference in the number of transmitted bytes between Microsoft's SOAP Implementation and Apache Axis. Both cause more than three times more network traffic than Java-RMI and Corba.

For the case of only one message (n = 1), the SOAP Implementations cause the smallest amount of traffic: 1,972 bytes (Java), 1,976 bytes (SOAP .Net), 2,626

Figure 1. Transmission of random strings (l = 250 bytes)

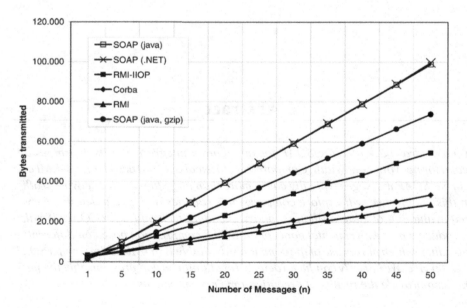

bytes (RMI), and 2,887 bytes (Corba). For all cases with more than one message, the two SOAP implementations perform worse than RMI, RMIIIOP, and Corba. The reason for this is that, unlike SOAP, these implementations exchange information about naming service before sending the first RPC message, causing a relative high-traffic offset.

Though today's wired networks are powerful enough to provide sufficient bandwidth even for very demanding applications like media streaming, there are still some fields of computing where bandwidth is costly. In cellular phone networks (GPRS, UMTS) for example, it is quite common to charge according to the transmitted data volumes. Also dialup connections via modem or ISDN are still rather common in enterprise networks. Third, communication in energy-constrained environments such as sensor networks calls for economical use of resources such as bandwidth. In these domains powerful compression strategies for SOAP could be useful to minimize costs and ensure best possible performance by saving bandwidth.

The SOAP specification does not explicitly define strategies for compressing SOAP documents, but states that there is no need for the underlying transport protocol to use the XML 1.0 serialization of the SOAP message's XML information set for transporting SOAP documents "on the wire." Also compressed representations are allowed. So compression is generally out of focus of SOAP, but is rather located on transport level.

Since HTTP is by far the most widely used protocol for transporting SOAP messages, it is no surprise that nearly all practically used approaches for compressing SOAP documents are based on HTTP's compression mechanisms. Well-known SOAP toolkits (respectively their underlying HTTP implementations) like Apache Axis and Microsoft .NET already offer support for the gzip HTTP-Content-Encoding, as defined in Deutsch (1996) and Fielding et al. (1999).

By using gzip compression for HTTP requests, as well as for responses, we could reduce the network traffic by roughly 26% for all cases (illustrated in Figure 1). This is still worse than Java-RPC, RPCIIOP, and Corba.

In this chapter we will discuss different strategies for compressing SOAP messages more efficiently than gzip does. Since SOAP messages are always written in XML, we can—as a first step—make use of advanced strategies for compressing XML rather than using general compression approaches like gzip.

Binary representations of XML data have gained a lot of interest in the last two years. Therefore, the W3C XML Binary Characterization Working Group (*http://www. w3.org/XML/Binary/*) was founded in March 2004. Its members conducted a detailed requirement analysis for binary XML representations and created a survey of the existing approaches in this field (W3C, 2006). This working group has specified a set of properties that are important for binary XML representations. Besides compactness, the main aspects that have been evaluated are support for directly reading and writing the binary XML data, independence of transport mechanisms, and processing efficiency. As a major outcome, the XML Binary Characterization Working Group created a set of 18 typical use cases for binary XML representations and analyzed their requirements. It is notable that in all use cases, the property "compactness," which will be in the focus of this chapter, has been rated at least as a nice-to-have feature. In 10 use cases this property was even rated as mandatory.

In December 2005 another W3C working group has been established to focus on the interoperability of binary XML: the Efficient XML Interchange Working Group (*http://www.w3.org/XML/EXI/*).

Up to now both of the W3C working groups in this field have not drafted any recommendations. Currently they are still discussing the requirements of interoperable binary XML representations.

In this chapter we will introduce a highly specialized mode of XML compression that is custom tailored for SOAP: differential SOAP encoding. The idea behind this is the following: rather than transmitting the whole SOAP message, we only transmit the differences between the SOAP message and a SOAP skeleton which is generated out of the service's WSDL description.

The remainder of this chapter is structured as follows: After an introduction on the theoretical basics of data compression, we will give a survey of XML compression, with a focus on SOAP. Then we will present our approach of differential SOAP compression. We will finally make a conclusion and discuss some future work.

Theoretical Background

There are basically two different approaches for data compression. The first one is entropy encoding. Compression algorithms using this approach exploit the fact that not all symbols of a message have the same frequency. Short codes are assigned to symbols with high frequencies, and longer codes are assigned to symbols with lower frequencies. Shannon (1948) found that there is a fundamental limit for the gain of this encoding scheme. Each symbol has certain information content, called *entropy,* which is determined by its frequency.

The idea behind entropy encoding is to minimize the redundancy of a message by coding all symbols according to their entropy. It is crucial for entropy encoding that no other characteristics of the data source are taken into account than the statistical characteristics of its symbols. Entropy encoding is always lossless.

In computer science practice, it is common to use octets as symbols. Due to the different probabilities of the 256 different octets in binary files, we can compress all kinds of binary data with various entropy encoding algorithms. A very well-known approach is the Huffman-Algorithm (Huffman, 1952), which is used in many compression programs including gzip.

Another way for data compression is called *source encoding*. Here certain characteristics of the data source are exploited. Example: If we know that a binary file is a black-and-white image where every black pixel is encoded as "0" and every white pixel as "1," we can use the fact that a "0" is normally followed by other "0"s and vice versa (because a black-and-white image has normally large areas which are solid black or white). So we can encode a block of n "0"s as "n times 0" instead of writing n "0"s into the output file.

Beside the technique explained in this example, which is known as *run length encoding,* there are many other occurrences of source encoding. Some of them, like motion compression and spectral encoding, are limited to applications in signal and image processing, but others are more universal. One very important concept here is called "differential encoding." Here we do not transmit the message itself, but only the difference between this message and a previous one. If a block of similar messages is sent, the resulting compression rates are very high. In computer networking, differential encoding is used, for example, for compressing RTP headers (Casner & Jacobson, 1999). Source encoding can be lossy or not and commonly achieves much higher compression rates than plain entropy encoding.

In practice it is quite common to use combinations of entropy and source encoding for even better compression rates.

Survey on XML Compression

Since XML finds wide use today as a general data format for storing semi-structured information, many authors proposed algorithms for compressing XML. Especially in the field of XML databases, researchers investigated strategies for storing very large XML documents efficiently. We will not discuss these approaches here in detail, but will give a short overview with a strong focus on the specific advantages and disadvantages in conjunction with SOAP. SOAP documents are special in the way that they are typically:

- Not larger than a few kilobytes; and
- Not described by XML Schema instances or DTDs, but by WSDL documents (which may however contain XML Schema definitions).

Text Compression

The first idea for XML compression that comes to mind is to use general text file compressors, because XML documents can be stored as text files, and pure entropy encoding mechanisms such as those implemented in gzip do perform quite well here. Unfortunately, this approach has bad side effects. The XML file is compressed and uncompressed as a whole (or at least in fixed size blocks) ignoring the XML structure completely. This makes it impossible to parse or change a compressed XML file without uncompressing and recompressing it completely.

Using SAX Events

A first thing that is important to understand when talking about XML compression is that there is usually no need for encoding the XML text file, but only the underlying XML information set (W3C, 2001). In almost all cases there is no need for preserving indentations and thus they should not be encoded. Also most of the CR (carriage return) and LF (line feed) characters might be unnecessary.

A smart way of separating the significant parts from unimportant ones is to use a SAX (Simple API for XML) parser. It interprets the XML structure and fires events which can be interpreted by the compressor. This approach has been taken for all implementations of XML-specific compressors. It obviously leads to a kind of source encoding, because it relies on the specific property of XML documents to be SAX-parsable. Also, encoding using SAX events can be seen as lossy if we think of compressing text representations of XML documents, since things like indentations might be lost.

XMILL

Liefke and Suciu (2000) introduced XMILL as a universal XML compressor. Here, SAX events are evaluated by a so-called path processor. This processor separates the XML document's structure from its content and stores all isolated tokens in separate containers. There is one special container exclusively for the document's structure, which holds integer-encoded references to start and end tags, as well as to attributes and text node values. These references point to other containers which hold the actual data. The big advantage of this approach is that values in the data containers do not have to be stored as strings but can be encoded with respect to their specific characteristic using semantic compression. For example, IP addresses can be stored as a sequence of four bytes. Such encoding rules are not determined automatically by XMILL, but must be specified manually using command line options. Each container is entropy encoded using gzip compression and is then stored in the binary output file.

XMILL is probably the most versatile of all currently available XML compressors, its behavior being adaptable to special use cases. XMILL performs quite well also on very small files, which is very important when compressing SOAP messages. Versions of XMILL (newer than the one described in Liefke & Suciu, 2000) also have support for entropy encoders other than gzip which lead to even better results. Nevertheless, one major drawback of using XMill for encoding SOAP is that for best results (with semantic compressors), compressing options must be adjusted for each service. This is probably not feasible in practice.

In Ghandeharizadeh, Papadopoulos, Cai, and Chintalapudi (2002), the benefits of using binary encoding for XML network messages instead of plain text encoding are discussed. The authors compare zip and XMILL compression. XMILL is slower than zip, but achieves better compression rates even without semantic compression. The authors propose an adaptive middleware that is capable of determining which encoding style is the best one with respect to parameters like message size or available network capacity. XMILL is available as open source at *http://sourceforge. net/projects/xmill.*

ESAX and Multiplexed Hierarchical Modeling

Cheney (2001) introduced the concept of ESAX, which stands for "Encoded SAX" events. Here a symbol table is maintained that translates SAX events directly into binary format. Then, the resulting binary stream is passed to an entropy encoder for eliminating remaining redundancy. This simple approach works surprisingly well. The author compared the ESAX compressor with XMILL and found out that compression rates are only 1% to 7% worse, depending on the used entropy encoder.

Cheney also discussed the use of Prediction by Partial Match (PPM) in conjunction with ESAX for further improvements. PPM is a generic algorithm for text compression and was introduced by Cleary and Witten (1984). It makes use of the fact that a symbol in a text often occurs in the same context of preceding symbols. The algorithm maintains statistics of which symbol has been seen in what contexts and uses this information for finding optimal encoding rules for each symbol.

Cheney conjectured that this approach can be used for XML compression more effectively if the hierarchical structure of an XML document is taken into account when applying the PPM algorithm. This technique is called Multiplexed Hierarchical Modeling (MHM). He implemented different algorithms for identifying suitable context symbols for the PPM. One important result of his experiments is that it is very efficient to keep separate symbols statistics for elements, attributes, and (text node) characters.

This approach is also very efficient for compressing small XML files. A free XML compressor called *xmlppm,* which makes use of Multiplexed Hierarchical Modeling, is available at *http://sourceforge.net/projects/xmlppm/.*

WBXML and Millau

Another approach for binary XML encoding is WBXML (WAP Binary XML). It was standardized by the W3C in 1999 and was originally meant for use in narrow-band wireless networks, especially in conjunction with WML (Wireless Markup Language). WML is comparable to HTML but custom tailored for mobile devices. Unlike HTML, WML is well-formed XML and thus parsable with any XML parser. In order to reduce WML file sizes for transmission over wireless phone networks, WML documents are recoded on the Web server to a much more compact binary WBXML representation. To ensure high performance on the server side and low usage of computing resources on the mobile clients, WBXML encoding is not based on sophisticated entropy and source encoding strategies such as those in XMILL and xmlppm. Instead, WBXML encoders split up the XML document in predefined tokens that are binary encoded using standardized coding tables (called *code spaces*). As an example, the token `charset="UTF8"` is encoded as the byte value `0x6A`. There is no need to include the coding tables when transmitting the WBXML message, because all WBXML parsers are aware of these encoding rules.

In fact, WBXML is not limited to being used for encoding WML, but is a general approach for all XML languages. However, to implement WBXML encoding rules for other languages, language-specific tag and attribute code spaces are needed. Currently there are implementations for various languages used in the field of mobile communication—for example, SyncML (2001) and Digital Rights Management Rights Expression Language (DRMREL, 2002).

Characters that cannot be found in the predefined coding tables (e.g., text node values) are always encoded inline—that is, they are directly written to the binary file, enclosed by a predefined I_STRING escape token and a termination symbol specific to the character set.

A major benefit is that a WBXML-aware SAX parser can interpret the binary encoded file directly and very quickly. Decoding is basically done by using lookup tables; no expensive arithmetic computations are needed. Girardot and Sundaresa (2000) introduced the Millau compression approach, which is based on WBXML but adds two further improvements.

The first additional feature is that in Millau, character data is not encoded inline, but in a separate stream. This is comparable to what is done in xmlppm and XMILL. This separation makes it possible to apply entropy encoding mechanisms efficiently in order to achieve higher compression ratios for files with a high amount of character data.

The second improvement concerns the code spaces. In WBXML the number of entries in the codespaces for tags and attributes is very limited. For complex languages these value ranges might be too small, and so the WBXML grammar was slightly modified in Millau, enabling more table entries.

We are not aware of any publicly available Millau implementation. Thus we could not make any performance evaluations for Millau. Since it is an improved version of WBXML, it should achieve even higher compression rates than WBXML. As we will see in the next section, the compression results of WBXML on small files are very promising. For WBXML there are several implementations. In addition to various versions for mobile devices, there is a free WBXML library that also includes some conversion tools for WBXML experiments on Windows and Unix Systems.

The authors are not aware of a SOAP compressor based on the WBXML or similar approaches. It is surely impossible to adopt WBXML or Millau directly for SOAP compression, because in SOAP it is common to use custom data types, which cannot be predicted when defining coding tables. In this way SOAP is much more dynamic than languages with a quite limited number of possible elements such as SyncML.

Compression Performance on Small Files

Many authors already evaluated the compression techniques described above in different contexts (Cheney, 2001; Liefke & Suciu, 2000). Nevertheless, most of these experiments were done with rather large files (> 100k bytes), and the efficiency of a compressor can vary for smaller files. Here it is very important that the compression algorithms do not reserve much space in the output stream for large tables mapping symbols to their bit codes. For very small files these coding tables might need more space than the encoded data itself, whereas for larger files, the added overhead for symbol tables becomes more and more irrelevant. Hence, compression results for large files are not necessarily transferable to small files which are typical for SOAP messages.

In order to evaluate the compression techniques described above with small files, we set up a test bed with 182 files of eight different languages. All files were taken from the test suite of a freely available WBXML library at *http://wbxmllib.sourceforge. net/*. We used these files because we want to include WBXML in our evaluation, and as described above, WBXML only works for some selected languages.

The results of this experiment are shown in Table 1. We compared the compression characteristics of two generic text compressors (gzip and bzip2) and three XML

Table 1. Compression results for small XML files

Encoding	S_{total} [Bytes]	$S_{smallest}$ [Bytes]	$S_{largest}$ [Bytes]	$S_{average}$ [Bytes]	λ_{best}	λ_{worst}	$\lambda_{average}$	s_{λ}
XML (text, uncompr.)	191,856	129	6,645	1,054.15	1.00	1.00	1.00	0.00
XML (text. bzip2)	80,296	157	1,253	441.19	0.16	1.22	0.62	0.31
XML (text, gzip)	73,439	153	1,202	403.51	0.16	1.19	0.58	0.30
XMILL (bzip2)	87,646	195	1,282	481.57	0.18	1.51	0.73	0.43
XMILL (gzip)	72,720	153	1,085	399.56	0.16	1.19	0.58	0.32
XMILL (ppm)	68,981	145	1,064	379.02	0.15	1.12	0.55	0.30
xmlppm	62,598	75	1,099	343.95	0.14	0.70	0.43	0.14
wbxml	28,664	7	1,164	157.49	0.05	0.25	0.14	0.03

compressors (XMILL, xmlppm, and WBXML). As described above, XMILL has support for different entropy encoders for compressing the different XMILL containers. This, of course, also affects compression results. Hence we made different test series with gzip, bzip2, and a ppm compressor in the backend of XMILL. The performance of the different compressors is compared to the values within the line "XML (text, uncompressed)" in Table 1, which represents the normal, uncompressed XML encoding as a text file.

For all encoding variants, we measured the total size of all 182 files stored in that encoding (S_{total}). The values for $S_{smallest}$ and $S_{largest}$ indicate the sizes of the smallest/ largest file (also separately for each encoding). $S_{average}$ is the average file size (which is simply $S_{total}/182$). We then compared the file size of each file with its size encoded as text (uncompressed). The quotient $S_{text}/S_{encoding}$ yields the compression ratio λ. Table 1 shows the best, the worst, and the average compression rate. The average compression rate is not weighted by file size and thus different from the quotient of the S_{total} values for text and compressed encoding. The standard deviation s_{λ} indicates if the compression rates are more or less constant for all files (small values for s_{λ}) or if they are spread over a wider range (larger values for s_{λ}).

The two text compressors perform quite well, their compression rates on small files are comparable with the XMILL compressor. In all test cases the gzip compression is more effective than bzip2, but XMILL (ppm) outperforms both. Nevertheless xmlppm compresses even better. Using this tool, even very small files could be further compressed ($\lambda_{worst} < 1$). Also s_{λ} is very small for xmlppm's compression algorithm. That means that it performs well on most of the files, irrespective of certain file characteristics like a high amount of markup or repetitive structures.

This comparison shows clearly that WBXML is the most effective compressor for small files available. As outlined above there is no need to include the coding tables in the WBXML binary output, because for supported XML languages, these tables are static and thus an identification tag for the compressed language is enough to find the right decoding rules for decompression or parsing. This makes WBXML compression more than twice as effective as xmlppm compression, and also the s_λ value of 0.03 is very good. Enhanced variants of this approach, like Millau, should even perform better.

The drawback of WBXML compression is of course that only selected XML languages can be compressed, and hence, this compression technique is not directly relevant for compressing SOAP. Nevertheless these results are surely important for future work in this research area.

Differential SOAP Compression

Unlike the compression approaches described in the last section, which are usable for various kinds of text and XML files, we will now have a look at a new source encoding technique specifically designed for SOAP messages. We developed this approach out of the observation that SOAP messages that are sent by or sent to a Web service are in most cases very similar. In such cases, it is quite common to use differential encoding, which basically means that only the difference between a message and a previous one is sent over the wire. The documents, describing only the differences, are typically much more compact.

Architecture

When applying differential encoding to SOAP messages, there is one major problem. Since commonly used transport protocols like HTTP and also SOAP itself are stateless, we cannot use previously sent messages to calculate the difference. Hence we use the commonly available WSDL description of a Web service to generate skeleton SOAP messages for all service operations (input and output). Then, the differences between a SOAP message and its corresponding skeleton file are calculated and sent over the wire. Each skeleton file contains a "generic" SOAP request or response in the sense that there are no data values in it, but only markup. These skeleton files are then used for SOAP differencing (sender side) and SOAP patching (receiver side). SOAP patching here means to patch the SOAP difference file into the SOAP skeleton to reconstruct the original message. To ensure that the original SOAP message can be reconstructed at the receiver side, it is important that the service consumer and service provider apply the same algorithm for skeleton generation and work with the same WSDL service description.

Figure 2. Differential encoding and decoding of SOAP requests

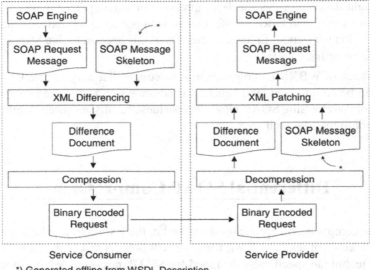

*) Generated offline from WSDL Description

A prototypical architecture for differential SOAP encoding and decoding is illustrated in Figure 2. Here a service consumer sends a SOAP request to a service provider. At first, its SOAP engine produces a SOAP request message. Then the difference between this message and a previously generated SOAP request skeleton is calculated. The resulting difference document is then passed to an entropy encoding stage in order to remove the remaining redundancy. It produces a binary representation of the difference document, which is finally sent to the service provider. Here the request skeleton is patched with the (previously decompressed) difference document. The patching process reconstructs the original SOAP message, which is then passed to the service provider's SOAP engine. For SOAP response messages this process would work vice versa.

The effectiveness of this approach depends on one important factor: the better the generated skeletons match with the SOAP messages generated by the used SOAP implementation, the smaller are the resulting difference documents. A fundamental issue here is that a WSDL description (unlike pure XML Schema) does not describe exactly one valid SOAP document structure for the input and output messages of a certain service operation. Hence, the SOAP document structure may vary between different SOAP implementations, resulting in varying compression rates.

Fortunately it is not important for the overall performance that the document structure predicted by the algorithm for SOAP skeleton generation and the structure of the SOAP message to be sent *always* match very closely. The better the matching, the smaller the resulting difference files are: it is important that this prediction works reliable in *the common cases* resulting in a good overall compression performance.

It is also important that the calculation of a difference document is always possible, even if the SOAP message document is completely different from the predicted skeleton. This happens, for example, if a SOAP Fault element is returned in the body of a SOAP response. In such cases the differential encoding does not of course provide any benefits in comparison with directly encoded SOAP messages.

Implementation

For implementing a differential SOAP compressor as outlined in the previous section, three main components are needed:

- A tool generating SOAP skeletons from WSDL files,
- Tools for differencing and patching SOAP documents, and
- A common data format for representing differences between two SOAP documents.

For generating the SOAP skeletons, we are currently using an XSLT program. It is currently limited to work with RPC-encoded services and provides only support for simple data types like strings and integers.

For the last two items listed above, we can again make use of the fact that SOAP messages are written in XML and that such components have already been developed for XML in general.

In recent years, tools for XML differencing became more and more popular. But not all implementations are suitable for SOAP differential encoding, because most tools only provide functionalities for XML differencing, but not for patching. A main aspect here is that a machine-readable output format must be produced instead of just highlighting the differences between two files.

The authors tested two free implementations of XML differencing tools which provide output in a machine-readable format that can be interpreted by a patching utility.

The first one, diffxml (Mouat, 2002), uses the so-called Delta Update Language (DUL) as an output format. DUL is an XML-based, proprietary language, which is currently exclusively used for this project. In this project, also a patch utility for processing DUL documents has been developed. Diffxml is available at *http://diffxml.sourceforge.net/*.

The second tool, xmldiff, provides functionalities only for differencing and is available at *http://www.logilab.org/projects/xmldiff*. It can output the differencing results in two formats: a proprietary non-XML text format (no patching processor is available), and XUpdate, which is an industry standard developed by the XML:db initiative (Laux & Martin, 2000). For patching XML files with XUpdate documents, we used another utility called 4xupdate. It is based on the programming language python and included in the free XML processing library 4Suite (*http://sourceforge. net/projects/foursuite/*).

Example

To illustrate how SOAP differencing and patching works, we will demonstrate the whole process with a simple example. We implemented an RPC Web service providing a `concatString(String0, String1, String2)` procedure that returns a concatenation of the three input parameters. Both the SOAP server and the according client were implemented with the Apache Axis SOAP engine.

In a first step the automatically generated WSDL description is processed with a short XSLT program for generating SOAP skeleton messages. This program generates two skeletons: one for `concatString` request messages and one for responses. The request skeleton is exemplarily shown in Figure 3(a). If the Web service would provide any other operations than this, the XSLT program would also produce input and output skeletons for them. This process must be done only once at the client and the server side.

For each RPC the client's SOAP engine generates a SOAP request document; an example is shown in Figure 3(b). This document and the request skeleton are compared and the differences are written to a file.

The output format depends on the used differencing utility. Figure 3(c) shows an example for DUL output, which can be compared to output in XUpdate format shown in Figure 3(d). But of course other formats might also be used here.

The output document in text format is obviously not much smaller than the original SOAP message. Hence, a compression utility (e.g., xmlppm) is used to create a smaller binary representation of this difference document. As we will see in the next section, the regular structure of XUpdate and DUL documents can be compressed very effectively.

This binary representation is then transmitted to the service provider. In practice, additional information must be transmitted: an unambiguous reference to the used WSDL instance for skeleton generation and also an unambiguous reference to the service's operation for identifying the correct skeleton to be used for patching. With these parameters, the service provider can restore the original SOAP request. Their encoding depends on the used transport protocol and is not in the focus of our work.

Figure 3. (a) Request skeleton, (b) SOAP request, (c) DUL, and (d) XUpdate difference documents

```
        <?xml version="1.0" encoding="UTF8"?>
        <soapenv:Envelope
          xmlns:soapenv="http://schemas.xmlsoap.org/soap/envelope/"
          xmlns:xsd="http://www.w3.org/2001/XMLSchema"
          xmlns:xsi="http://www.w3.org/2001/XMLSchemainstance">
          <soapenv:Body>
a)          <ns1:concatString
              xmlns:ns1="http://somename.test/concat"
              soapenv:encodingStyle=
              "http://schemas.xmlsoap.org/soap/encoding/">
              <in0 xsi:type="xsd:string"/>
              <in1 xsi:type="xsd:string"/>
              <in2 xsi:type="xsd:string"/>
            </ns1:concatString>
          </soapenv:Body>
        </soapenv:Envelope>

b)      <?xml version="1.0" encoding="UTF8"?>
        <soapenv:Envelope
          xmlns:soapenv="http://schemas.xmlsoap.org/soap/envelope/"
          xmlns:xsd="http://www.w3.org/2001/XMLSchema"
          xmlns:xsi="http://www.w3.org/2001/XMLSchemainstance">
          <soapenv:Body>
            <ns1:concatString
              soapenv:encodingStyle=
              "http://schemas.xmlsoap.org/soap/encoding/"
              xmlns:ns1="http://somename.test/concat">
              <in0 xsi:type="xsd:string">foo</in0>
              <in1 xsi:type="xsd:string">bar</in1>
              <in2 xsi:type="xsd:string">foo</in2>
            </ns1:concatString>
          </soapenv:Body>
        </soapenv:Envelope>

c)      <?xml version="1.0" encoding="UTF8"?>
        <delta>
          <insert charpos="1" childno="1" name="#text" nodetype="3"
            parent="/node()[1]/node()[2]/node()[2]/node()[2]">foo</insert>
          <insert charpos="1" childno="1" name="#text" nodetype="3"
            parent="/node()[1]/node()[2]/node()[2]/ node()[4]">bar</insert>
          <insert charpos="1" childno="1" name="#text" nodetype="3"
            parent="/node()[1]/node()[2]/node()[2]/ node()[6]">foo</insert>
        </delta>

d)      <?xml version="1.0"?>
        <xupdate:modifications version="1.0"
          xmlns:xupdate="http://www.xmldb.org/xupdate">
          <xupdate:append select="/soapenv:Envelope[1]/
            soapenv:Body[1]/ns1:concatString[1]/in0[1]" child="first()">
            <xupdate:text>foo</xupdate:text>
          </xupdate:append>
          <xupdate:append select="/soapenv:Envelope[1]/
            soapenv:Body[1]/ns1:concatString[1]/in1[1]" child="first()">
            <xupdate:text>bar</xupdate:text>
          </xupdate:append>
          <xupdate:append select="/soapenv:Envelope[1]/
            soapenv:Body[1]/ns1:concatString[1]/in2[1]" child="first()">
            <xupdate:text>foo</xupdate:text>
          </xupdate:append>
        </xupdate:modifications>
```

As already shown the compressed difference document is then unpacked at the server side, merged with the request skeleton during a patching process and then passed to the server's SOAP engine. The SOAP response is then returned to the client—possibly also differentially encoded.

Compression Effectiveness

In order to compare the effectiveness of differential encoding with other compression approaches, we implemented a SOAP RPC test server and a client with three different remote procedures, which yield SOAP messages with different amounts of payload: `void doNothing()`, `String echoString(String)`, and `String concatString(String0, String1, String2, String3, String4)`. We saved SOAP requests (using random strings with five characters as request parameter) and responses for each operation to files. Then, we compressed these SOAP files using xmlppm, the most effective encoder for such small files. We also created skeleton messages for all operations and generated difference documents by using diffxml (for DUL output) and xmldiff (for XUpdate output). These documents were also compressed with xmlppm.

The results are shown in Figure 4. The skeletons generated for `doNothing` requests and responses match the SOAP request and response nearly perfectly (because no request or response values are exchanged with void `doNothing(void)`). There are only a few differences at the syntactical level (different positions for parameters and namespace declarations in the XML file), but the semantics are the same. Hence, we get an empty XUpdate document without any update instructions. File size is 133 bytes as text file and 79 bytes when compressed with xmlppm. The difference document for encoding the request in DUL format is much larger here. This is because the diffxml did not detect the semantic equivalence of SOAP request and skeleton file for some reasons, and various update actions are unnecessarily encoded here.

As for `echoString` and `concatString`, requests and responses carry real payload in the form of string parameters. These cannot be predicted during skeleton generation, and therefore the difference files are bigger compared to `doNothing` messages. In the XUpdate and DUL documents for the `concatString` request, the insertion of five strings is encoded. The DUL document for the `concatString` response is again much larger than needed. Probably this is due to certain heuristics in diffxml for speeding up the differencing process but decreasing the accuracy (which might be useful with much larger files).

In all cases the xmlppm compressed difference documents are not only significantly smaller than the text encoded, but also more compact than the xmlppm compressed SOAP messages. The advantage of using differential encoding is largest if the SOAP messages are only predictable markup (`doNothing`). If the amount of payload increases, the sizes of compressed difference documents get closer to directly compressed SOAP messages.

Of course, these promising results cannot be generalized. We measured these values for SOAP messages generated with Apache Axis and an XSLT program that generates optimized skeletons for Axis-style messages. We also experimented with .Net-style messages, and here we measured nearly no advantages over directly compressed SOAP messages. So in practice quite complex adaptation mechanisms might be needed. Other problems occur if this approach is extended to complex data types, like arrays or vectors. Here, the structure of SOAP messages cannot be predicted precisely, because the structure's length is unknown at the time the skeleton is generated.

Another issue is that in some cases the available differencing and patching utilities produce unexpected and unwanted results. In some cases it was not possible to restore the original SOAP message by applying the patch. Hence, we decided not to implement any components for the integration of XML differencing into a SOAP engine at the moment. Differencing and patching of SOAP messages is possible, but only with user interaction. But we expect the needed tools to become more reliable in the near future. We are also exploring possibilities to integrate differencing components specially adapted to SOAP directly into the transport handler chain of the SOAP engine.

Algorithmic Complexity and Execution Speed

As already stated in the architecture section, the proposed scheme consists of the four steps:

1. Differencing
2. Compression   } at the sender side
3. Decompression
4. Patching   } at the reciever side

Compared to the SOAP communication commonly known, these steps are additional ones that do not have to be taken if no differential encoding is employed. Thus the time it takes to execute them must be considered as overhead. Especially at servers answering many requests per time unit, fast execution is important.

First we want to shed light on the theoretical algorithmic complexity of the involved algorithms. Considerations on runtime complexity of these kinds of algorithms are commonly based on tree structures because XML and SOAP are generalized to hierarchically structured information.

Figure 4. Effectiveness of different encoding techniques

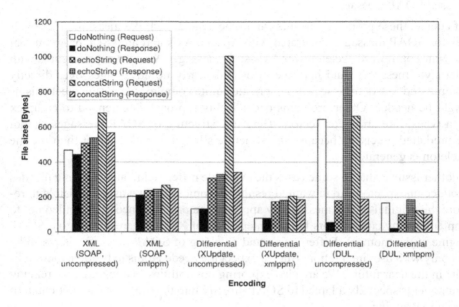

As for the step of differencing, implementations for two different algorithms are publicly available (Mouat, 2002). Whereas the Fast Match Edit Script (FMES) algorithm uses a heuristic to find a compact difference document, the Extended Zhang and Shasha Algorithm (EZS) always finds a minimum difference document. This accuracy is paid by taking a runtime of $O(n^2 log^2 n)$, where n is the number of leaves in a balanced tree, while FMES is done in $O(ne+e^2)$, where n is the number of leaves, and e is a constant representing the degree of difference between the two trees. Even though SOAP documents are typically not balanced, we believe that this assumption is still close to the average case because total disequilibrium is extremely rare.

As for compression and decompression, we experimentally evaluated the runtime complexity of xml(un)ppm. Experiments showed that it exhibits linear behavior with regard to the number of nodes regardless of tree disequilibrium for both.

Patching is possible in $O(m\ log\ n)$, where m is the number of patching operations applied to a balanced tree with n nodes. We experimentally confirmed the linear dependence on m by measuring insertion time into documents of constant size. With regard to a single insertion, $\frac{1}{2}h$ comparisons are needed to find the position where to insert the new node, with h being the height of the tree ($log\ n$).

Apart from these theoretical considerations, we also conducted runtime measurements using the SOAP messages resulting from doNothing, echoString,

Table 2. Execution time results of different tools in milliseconds

		doNothing		echoStr		concatStr	
		Req.	Resp.	Req.	Resp.	Req.	Resp.
1. Differencing	FMES Java	3.6	3.1	3.6	4.0	4.9	3.6
	FMES Java Native	2.3	2.0	2.4	2.7	3.5	2.5
	FMES Python	3.1	3.1	3.8	3.8	6.5	3.8
	EZS Python	∞	∞	40.8	41.7	180.8	40.2
2. Compression	xmlppm(DUL)	1.3	1.2	1.5	2.0	1.9	1.5
	xmlppm(Xupdate)	1.4	1.4	2.0	2.0	2.6	2.0
	gzip(DUL)	1.0	1.0	1.0	1.0	1.0	1.0
	gzip(Xupdate)	1.0	1.0	1.0	1.0	1.0	1.0
3. Decompression	xmlunppm(DUL)	1.1	1.1	1.3	1.7	1.6	1.3
	xmlunppm(Xupdate)	1.2	1.2	1.7	1.7	2.2	1.7
	gzip(DUL)	0.9	0.9	0.8	0.9	0.8	0.8
	gzip(Xupdate)	0.9	0.9	0.9	0.9	0.8	0.9
4. Patching	Java	2.8	3.2	6.2	17.2	15.3	6.4
	Python	3.6	3.7	4.8	4.9	9.1	4.9

and `concatString`. Table 2 depicts the results in milliseconds. We explored the different available alternatives for all four steps on a machine powered by an Intel Xeon 3GHz HT CPU with 1.5 gigabytes of memory, running a Debian 3 Linux. Runtime measurements were carried out by calculating the average over 5,000 executions.

We compared three differencing implementation variants of the FMES algorithm with the EZS algorithm using the tools referenced in the implementation section. Two major conclusions can be drawn: First of all, the EZS algorithm is hardly suitable for real-world SOAP differencing due to its extremely low execution speed. For the `doNothing` messages, the algorithm did not terminate at all, which hints at implementation errors. The FMES algorithm works between 10 and 50 times faster; the Java implementation runs fastest if static linking into native code is used (*http://gcc.gnu.org/java/*).

For compression as well as decompression, g(un)zip runs up to three times faster than xml(un)ppm, but yields significantly lower compression rates. Because difference documents expressed in XUpdate are larger than the DUL ones, compression takes longer due to more expensive I/O operations.

We finally compared two patching tools implemented in Java and Python (described in the implementation section), finding that the Java variant runs faster for the short messages corresponding to doNothing but slower for the longer messages generated by echoString and concatString. This hints that the Python tool needs longer for initialization, but is more effective with regard to document length.

In total, differentially encoded doNothing requests can be processed on the server side in 7.9 milliseconds if xmlunppm(DUL) decompression and Python patching are used for the request and FSME Java Native differencing and xmlppm(DUL) are used for the response. This combination is also optimal in terms of compression effectiveness (see Figure 4). echoString and concatString take 10.8 milliseconds and 14.7 milliseconds respectively. On the client side, processing takes 8.4 milliseconds, 10.5 milliseconds, and 11.6 milliseconds. However, we are convinced that a significant speedup can be achieved if differential encoding is implemented directly into the input and output streams of servers and clients, saving I/O operations due to not having to read and write the message from and to the hard disk.

Conclusion and Future Work

For clients with poor network connectivity, the high network traffic caused by encoding SOAP messages as text is a severe issue. In such environments application performance can be improved by using binary encoding styles for SOAP message transport. This is totally transparent to the SOAP engine, and therefore the typical benefits of XML Web services are not affected.

Today the most common approach for binary encoding SOAP messages is gzip in conjunction with HTTP. Nevertheless, gzip is not always the best choice for SOAP compression, because it is designed as a generic text compressor unaware of the hierarchical XML structure found in SOAP messages.

The contribution of this chapter is two fold. In an evaluation study of state-of-the-art XML compressors with focus on small files as they are typical for SOAP, we showed that WBXML produces the best results, but is too limited in its applicability. Thus, currently the best available solution for SOAP compression is to use xmlppm.

Second, we presented a new compression approach based on differential encoding. Instead of sending the entire SOAP message, only the difference between the message and a skeleton, which is previously generated from the WSDL service description, is transmitted. First tests presented by the authors indicate that it yields promising performance. Thus this approach might be interesting for future work, especially including the development of more robust tools for SOAP message differencing resulting in compact binary output.

We are currently working on another approach that veers more towards WBXML. Here encoding rules are generated from the WSDL description (so that they are not generally static for SOAP, but static per service). First results of this compression approach were presented in Werner, Buschmann, Brandt, and Fischer (2006b).

Another important issue concerns the transport protocol itself. As mentioned by Tian et al. (2003), not only SOAP but also HTTP adds significant overhead to the payload. Hence, the development of lightweight transport mechanisms for mobile Web services might also be very interesting. A first prototype of such a specialized transport binding for SOAP was presented in Werner, Buschmann, Jäcker, and Fischer (2006a).

All in all SOAP compression is a field with a lot of open problems. We think that it is possible to improve compression rates if we take the step from generic XML compressors to language-specific ones. As shown in this chapter, the step from generic text compressors to XML-aware encoders has already considerably improved compression results.

References

Casner, S., & Jacobson, V. (1999). *RFC 2508: Compressing ip/udp/rtp headers for low-speed serial links.*

Cheney, J. (2001, March 27-29). Compressing XML with multiplexed hierarchical PPM models. *Proceedings of the Data Compression Conference* (DCC'01) (pp. 163-173), Snowbird, UT.

Cleary, J.G., & Witten, I.H. (1984). Data compression using adaptive coding and partial string matching. *IEEE Transactions on Communications, 32*(4), 396-402.

Deutsch, L.P. (1996). *RFC 1952: GZIP file format specification version 4.3.*

DRMREL. (2002). *Digital Rights Management Rights Expression Language version 1.0.* Retrieved from *http://xml.coverpages.org/OMA-DRMRELv10-20020628p.pdf*

Fielding, R., Gettys, J., Mogul, J.C., Frystyk, H., Masinter, L., Leach, P.J., & Berners-Lee, T. (1999). *RFC 2616: Hypertext transfer protocol–HTTP/1.1.*

Ghandeharizadeh, S., Papadopoulos, C., Cai, M., & Chintalapudi, K.K. (2002). Performance of networked xml-driven cooperative applications. *Concurrent Engineering: Research and Applications, 12*(3), 195-204.

Girardot, M., & Sundaresan, N. (2000, May 15-19). Millau: An encoding format for efficient representation and exchange of XML over the Web. *Proceedings of the 9th International World Wide Web Conference on Computer Networks* (pp.747-765), Amsterdam, The Netherlands.

Huffman, D.A. (1952). A method for the construction of minimum-redundancy codes. *Proceedings of the Institute of Radio Engineers, 40*(9), 1098-1101.

Laux, A., & Martin, S. (2000). *XUpdate working draft.* Retrieved from *http://xmldb-org.sourceforge.net/xupdate/xupdate-wd.html*

Liefke, H., & Suciu, D. (2000). *XMill: An efficient compressor for XML data.* Technical Report MSCIS-99-26, University of Pennsylvania, USA.

Marahrens, I. (2003). *Performance- und effizienz-analyse verschiedener RPC-varianten.* Diploma Thesis, Institute of Operating Systems and Computer Networks, Technical University of Braunschweig, Germany.

Mouat, A. (2002). *XML diff and patch utilities.* Cs4 Dissertation, Heriot-Watt University, Scotland.

Shannon, C.E. (1948). A mathematical theory of communication. *Bell System Technical Journal, 20,* 379-423.

SyncML. (2001). *SyncML specification version 1.0.1.* Retrieved from *http://www.openmobilealliance.org/syncml/*

Tian, M., Voigt, T., Naumowicz, T., Ritter, H., & Schiller, J. (2003, July 3-4). Performance considerations for mobile Web services. *Proceedings of the IEEE Communication Society Workshop on Applications and Services in Wireless Networks,* Berne, Switzerland.

W3C. (2001, October 24). *W3C recommendation: XML information set.* Retrieved from *http://www.w3.org/TR/2001/REC-xml-infoset-20011024/*

W3C. (2006, March 31). *W3C working group note: XML binary characterization.* Retrieved from *http://www.w3.org/TR/2005/NOTE-xbc-characterization-20050331/*

Werner, C., Buschmann, C., Jäcker, T., & Fischer, S. (2006a). Bandwidth and latency considerations for efficient SOAP messaging. *International Journal of Web Service Research, 3*(1), 49-67.

Werner, C., Buschmann, C., Brandt, Y., & Fischer, S. (2006b, September 18-22). Compressing SOAP messages by using pushdown automata. *Proceedings of the IEEE International Conference on Web Services* (ICWS'06), Chicago.

Chapter II

NAM:
A Network Adaptable Middleware
to Enhance Response Time of
Web Services

Shahram Ghandeharizadeh, University of Southern California, USA

Christos Papadopoulos, University of Southern California, USA

Min Cai, University of Southern California, USA

Runfang Zhou, University of Southern California, USA

P. Pol, University of Southern California, USA

Abstract

Web Services is an emerging software technology that is based on the concept of software and data as a service. Binary and XML are two popular encoding/decoding mechanisms for network messages. A Web Service may employ a loss-less compression technique (e.g., Zip, XMill, etc.) in order to reduce message size prior to its transmission across the network, minimizing its transmission time. This saving might be outweighed by the overhead of compressing the output of a Web Service at a server and decompressing it at a client. The primary contribution of this paper is NAM, a middleware that strikes a compromise between these two factors in order to enhance response time. NAM decides when to compress data, based on the available client and server processor speeds and network characteristics. When compared with today's common practice to transmit the output of a Web Service uncompressed always, our experimental results show NAM either provides similar

or significantly improved response times (at times, more than 90% improvement)
with Internet connections that offer bandwidths ranging from 80 to 100 Mbps.

Introduction

Many organizations envision Web services as an enabling component of Internet-scale computing. A Web service is either a computation or an information service with a published interface. Its essence is a remote procedure call (RPC) that consumes and processes some input data in order to produce output data. It is a concept that renders Web applications extensible: By identifying each component of a Web application as a Web service, an organization may combine these Web services with others to rapidly develop a new Web application. The new Web application may consist of Web services that span the boundaries of several (if not many) organizations. A final vision of Web services is to realize a dynamic environment that identifies, composes, and integrates Web services in response to a query (Ghandeharizadeh et al., 2003a). This is similar to how a relational database management system identifies and composes the appropriate relational algebra operator into a query plan to process an SQL command.

The eXtensible Markup Language (XML) produces human-readable text and is emerging as the standard for data interoperability among Web services and cooperative applications that exchange data. XML is predicted to rise from 3% of global network traffic in 2003 to 24% by 2006 and to at least 40% by 2008 (Geer, 2005). Well-formed XML documents consist of elements, tags, attributes, and so forth and satisfy precise grammatical rules. The major commercial vendors (e.g., Microsoft, IBM, etc.) employ XML to publish, invoke, and exchange data among Web services. A Web service publishes its interface using the Web Service Description Language (WSDL). An Internet application may invoke a remote Web service using the Simple Object Access Protocol (SOAP). Typically, an invoked Web service produces an XML-formatted response.

Binary encoding is an alternative encoding mechanism that produces compact streams for efficient parsing, which are not human readable. A binary formatted message is typically smaller than its XML formatted counterpart. This is because XML encoding includes repeated tags, labels, and attributes. One may employ compression in order to reduce the size of both XML and binary formatted messages.

In this study, we first quantify the performance tradeoff associated with binary and XML formatters for a decision support benchmark. Next, we analyze the role of compression in reducing the number of transmitted bytes with each encoding mechanism. With XML, we analyze two compression schemes: Zip/GZip library and XMill (Liefke & Suciu, 1999). Both employ techniques based on Lempel-Ziv algorithm (Ziv & Lempel, 1977). Our results demonstrate that without compression, the XML encoder results in message sizes that at times are five times larger than their binary representation. With Zip, compressed XML messages at most are twice the size of their compressed binary representation. With XMill, compressed XML messages at times are smaller than their Zip compressed binary representation. This trend holds true for large messages (more than one megabyte). Otherwise, Zip-compressed binary messages are smaller. The key difference is that XMill employs the semantic information provided by XML tags to group data items with related meaning into containers and compresses each container independently (Liefke & Suciu, 1999). This column-wise compression generally is better than row-wise compression (Iyer & Wilhite, 1994) for large message sizes.

The primary contribution of this paper is Network Adaptable Middleware (NAM) designed with the objective to enhance response time[2] by trading CPU time for network transmission time. NAM is divided into a client and a server component and is designed to scale in environments consisting of millions of clients that invoke a single Web service. If a Web service is stand-alone and does not depend on another Web service, denoted WS_s, it is configured with NAM's server component. Otherwise, a Web service plays dual roles of being a client of one or more Web services and a server for others, denoted WS_{sc}, and is configured with both the client and server components. NAM's components might be included as libraries of a software development environment such as Microsoft's .NET in order to be deployed seamlessly when a Web service is deployed.

Compression techniques are a plug-in module for NAM's components. In addition to Zip/GZip and XMill, NAM may employ other XML compression techniques, such as multiplexed hierarchical PPM (Cheney, 2001) and differential encoding (Werner & Buschmann, 2004). This study does not compare alternative compression techniques. Instead, it strives to demonstrate feasibility of a middleware (i.e., NAM) to selectively use a compression technique to enhance response time of Web services that employ primitives of a programming language. The last section discusses attachments such as images.

Our experimental results from both Internet and intranet deployments of NAM demonstrate its feasibility. NAM readily adapts to its environment to use the appropriate transmission paradigm to minimize response time. Experimental results in the section "Performance Results of NAM" demonstrate that NAM provides significant savings compared with uncompressed transmission, which is representative of today's deployments, with bandwidths in the order of 10s of Mbps.

The rest of this paper is organized as follows. The next section presents alternative encoding mechanisms. In the third section, we provide an overview of NAM and its components. The fourth section presents an experimental evaluation of NAM. We survey related research in the fifth section. Brief conclusions and future research directions are contained in the final section.

Binary and XML Formatters with Alternative Compression Techniques

In this section, we analyze the performance of alternative compression techniques for binary and XML formatters. We quantified the performance of alternative transmission protocols using TPC-H benchmark (Poess & Floyd, 2000), because it is a standard that provides documented queries and data sets. This enables others to recreate our experiments. TPC-H includes both retrieval and refresh queries. The refresh commands generate large requests and small responses. The retrieval queries offer a mix of commands that generate either (1) large requests and small responses or (2) large requests and large responses. This motivated us to focus on retrieval queries and ignore refresh queries from further consideration. We report on 21 out of 22 queries, because we could not implement query 15 in a timely manner.

Our hardware platform consists of two PCs. One is a server, and the other is a client. (We analyze results with PCs configured with four different processor speeds: 450 MHz, 1 GHz, 2 GHz, and 3.06 GHz.) The client and server were connected using a LINKSYS Ethernet (10/100 megabit per second, mbps) switch. Each machine is configured with a 20-gigabyte internal disk, 512 megabytes of memory (unless specified otherwise), and a 100 mbps network interface card. The server is configured with Microsoft Windows 2000 Server, SQL Server 2000, and Visual Studio .NET Beta 2 release. The client is configured with Microsoft Windows 2000 Professional and Visual Studio .NET Beta 2 release. The server implements a Web service that accepts one TPC-H retrieval query, processes the query using ADO.NET, and returns the obtained results to the client. The client employs a TPC-H-provided component that generates SQL retrieval query strings, invokes the server's Web service, and receives the obtained results.

The communication between the client and server uses the .NET Remoting framework. For transmission, we use the TCP and HTTP channels provided with the .NET framework. For message formatting, we use the SOAP (Box et al., 2000) and binary formatters provided with the .NET framework. We extended this framework with two new formatters: (1) compression using Zip/GZip library written entirely in $C^\#$ and (2) XMill compression scheme (Liefke & Suciu, 1999). XMill employs zlib, the library function for gzip. We modified XMill to consume its input from buffers (instead of a file). This framework configures channels and encoders without requiring modification of the application code. When performing our experiments, our system reconfigures at runtime to repeat a query workload while communicating over different channels with different encoders. All of our experiments were conducted in a single user mode with no background load on the underlying hardware. The client was configured to invoke the Web service in an asynchronous manner.

A Comparison

We used a 1-gigabyte TPC-H database for evaluation purposes. The presented results ignore the query execution time. They pertain only to the encoding, transmission, and decoding times for processing a query. Different TPC-H queries produce a different amount of data. With the binary formatter, the message sizes vary from a few hundred bytes to a few megabytes. With the XML formatter, the message varies from a few hundred bytes to tens of megabytes. The server produces the largest volume of data for Query 10, approximately 25 megabytes of data with XML.

A compression scheme such as Zip can be applied to both the binary and XML formatters. XMill compresses XML data using its semantics. Figure 1 shows a comparison of these alternatives using Zip-compressed binary (Zip-Binary) messages as a yardstick. The y-axis of this figure shows the ratio in size between a technique such as XMill-XML and Zip-Binary. For example, with Query 1, Zip-XML messages are 1.5 times larger than their Zip-Binary counterparts. A y-axis value less than 1.0 implies a smaller message size relative to Zip-Binary. Xmill-compressed XML (XMill-XML) produce smaller messages than Zip-Binary (i.e., 0.84 times the size with Query 2). In our experiments, in the worst-case scenario, Zip-compressed XML (Zip-XML) messages are twice the size of Zip-Binary messages (see Figure 1). In the best case, they are approximately the same size. This is because a lossless compression technique can effectively compress the repeated XML tags. To illustrate, Figure 2 shows the compression factor for Zip-XML and XMill-XML. In general, compression factor is higher with XML. With binary, compression factor ranges from 1.4 to 5.5. With XML, the Zip compression factor ranges from 2.1 to 19.6. With XMill, the compression factor is as high as 26 with query 16.

Figure 1 shows that XMill-XML messages at times are smaller than Zip-Binary messages (see Query 2). This is because XMill groups data items with related meaning into containers and compresses each independently (Liefke & Suciu, 1999). This column-wise compression generally is better than row-wise compression (Iyer & Wilhite, 1994). At the same time, Figures 1 and 2 show that XMill is not always superior to Zip compression technique for XML messages (see Queries 1, 4, 5, 6, 7, 8, 12, 13, 14, 17, 18, 19, and 22). Generally speaking, when compared with Zip, XMill is more effective with large messages. The aforementioned queries transmit fewer than 9,000 bytes. With the remaining queries that produce XML messages that are tens of thousands of bytes in size, XMill outperforms Zip.

We analyzed the performance of Zip and XMill with these query classes as a function of different processor speeds: 450 MHz, 1 GHz, 2 GHz, and 3.06 GHz. Table 1 shows these numbers for all TPC-H queries (1 gigabyte database size) with a 3.06 GHz PC. (We refer the interested reader to Cai, et al. (2002) (Ghandeharizadeh et al., 2002) for tables showing these numbers for different processor speeds.) Table 1 shows three important observations. First, the compression factor does not neces-

Figure 1. Comparison of XML and binary message sizes with and without compression

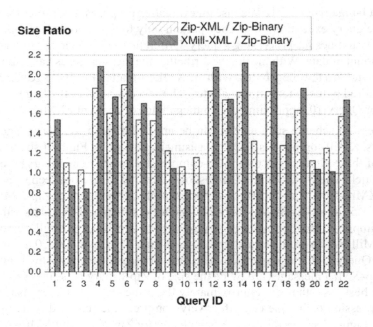

Figure 2. Impact of compression on each encoding scheme

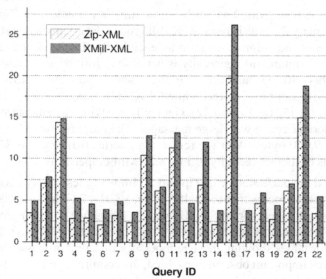

sarily increase as a function of message size. Second, XMill yields more compact messages when compared with Zip for messages larger than 1 KB. Third, XMill is more time consuming than Zip.

It also is important to note that compression and decompression times do not scale linearly as a function of processor speeds. In Figure 3, we show the speedup observed with one TPC-H query (Q_{13}) as a function of different processor speeds. The breakdown is applied to both compression and decompression times of Zip and XMill. Similar trends hold for other TPC-H queries. In particular, no query observes a linear speedup as a function of processor speed.

Table 1. Compression and decompression times using a 3.06 GHz processor. The query ID in parentheses denotes the TPC-H query used as a representative of a category. The granularity of reported message size and times are in bytes and ms, respectively.

Query	MSG Size	MSG Size	Zip Compression Comp Factor	Comp Time (ms)	Decomp Time (ms)	Msg Size	XMill Compression Comp Factor	Comp Time (ms)	Decomp Time (ms)
Q_{14}	591	254	2.3	0.66	0.07	314	1.88	1.76	0.68
Q_{19}	594	257	2.3	0.66	0.08	316	1.88	1.73	0.66
Q_{17}	595	258	2.3	0.68	0.07	318	1.87	1.73	0.66
Q_6	596	259	2.3	0.67	0.08	319	1.87	1.74	0.63
Q_8	819	282	2.9	0.68	0.08	344	2.38	1.78	0.64
Q_S (Q_{12})	929	303	3.1	0.68	0.07	358	2.6	1.78	0.7
Q_4	1509	373	4	0.71	0.09	421	3.59	1.84	0.67
Q_5	1618	405	4	0.72	0.09	460	3.52	1.83	0.68
Q_7	1848	395	4.7	0.72	0.09	455	4.07	1.86	0.69
Q_{22}	2172	428	5.1	0.74	0.1	481	4.52	1.9	0.76
Q_1	2863	600	4.8	0.82	0.13	643	4.45	2.04	0.78
Q_{18}	4315	669	6.5	0.82	0.15	714	6.05	2.08	0.83
Q_{13}	8067	765	10.6	0.93	0.16	701	11.51	2.42	0.98
Q_M (Q_{20})	46,219	6,766	6.8	2.8	0.85	5,962	7.75	9.54	3.04
Q_9	49209	4172	11.8	2.73	0.77	3425	14.37	10.24	3.22
Q_{21}	90861	5427	16.7	4.07	1.77	4121	22.05	14.63	6.06
Q_{11}	186133	16104	11.6	8.68	3.35	12106	15.38	23.75	11.51
Q_2	329086	45949	7.2	23.53	9.23	36032	9.13	53.17	22.52
Q_L (Q_3)	3,513,484	243,912	14.4	146.4	55.32	199,671	17.6	356.54	173.1
Q_{16}	6020556	305290	19.7	237.41	92.6	226890	26.54	629.44	308.27
Q_H (Q_{10})	25,927,167	4,166,404	6.2	1,493.00	569	3,259,501	7.95	2,916.60	1273.3

By studying the performance of alternative compression techniques, we found we can design a middleware, which serves as an intermediary between the underlying network protocol and the cooperative applications to enhance response time for Web services. This middleware analyzes the characteristics of the underlying network and the transmitted data to render intelligent decisions. We present this Network Adaptable Middleware in the next section.

NAM

NAM consists of a server and a client component, denoted NAM_s and NAM_c, respectively. NAM_c constructs and maintains (1) a profile of messages processed by a client; namely, the time required to decompress a message and (2) a profile of network round-trip time-and-loss rate for each contacted server. NAM_s maintains a profile of the time required to compress a message. Profiles gathered by both NAM_s and NAM_c are maintained in a persistent manner to ensure their cumulative growth in the presence of shutdowns, power failures, and so forth.

Figure 3. Speedup of compression and decompression times for TPC-H Query 13 as a function of processor speed

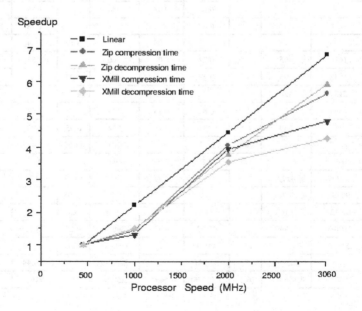

The primary advantages of maintaining the profile at the client are that (1) the client may customize its estimator based on the characteristics of its hardware and statistical peculiarities of its requested data and (2) the server is freed to support millions of clients without incurring the overhead of maintaining a decompression profile on behalf of each client. A drawback of this approach is the extra CPU overhead and storage required for a client to maintain the profile, which may be significant for small, mobile devices. As detailed in the following subsection, one may use regression in order to maintain a compact representation of these profiles in the order of tens of bytes. Moreover, the CPU overhead is negligible for clients that perform decompression and retrieve and process tens of thousands of bytes of data. Experimental results of the fourth section show that the benefits of NAM significantly outweigh these overheads.

A Web service configured with NAM (acting either as a WS_s or WS_{sc}) continues to interoperate with legacy clients and Web services not configured with NAM. This is supported as follows. When a client configured with NAM_c (say a WS_{sc}) invokes a remote Web service, its SOAP header includes a flag (along with several other tagged data items required by NAM) denoting the presence of NAM. If the referenced Web service is not configured with NAM_s, it ignores this flag and always provides an uncompressed output. If the service is configured with NAM (say a WS_s), it utilizes this flag to transmit its output in either a compressed or an uncompressed manner.

If a NAM Web service receives a SOAP header without the NAM flag, it assumes that the client is not configured with NAM and produces an uncompressed reply. To simplify the discussion and without loss of generality, we assume an environment that consists of two Web services, a WS_s and a WS_{sc}, is configured with NAM. The WS_{sc} invokes remote methods published by WS_s.

Figure 4 shows the pseudo-code for NAM_s. It consists of a collection of estimation techniques in order to render a decision quickly. When WS_s produces a response M to a request issued by a WS_{sc}, it invokes this pseudo-code with the byte array corresponding to M and WS_{sc}'s SOAP header. NAM_s estimates (1) the size of this message once compressed, (2) the time required to compress this message, (3) the time to decompress this message at the client, WS_{sc}, and (4) the network characteristics.

Next, NAM_s employs an analytical model of the underlying network protocol to estimate transmission time with the estimated network characteristics for a given a message size. If the estimated response time using a compression technique is better than an uncompressed transmission, then NAM compresses the message and transmits it. Otherwise, the message is transmitted in uncompressed format. If NAM_s includes several compression techniques, then it must estimate response time with each and choose the one with the best response time. This trivial extension is not shown in Figure 4.

In the following subsection, we describe a general purpose technique to estimate compressed message size, compression time, and decompression time as a func-

Figure 4. Pseudo-code of NAM, a network adaptable middleware

```
NAM_S (byte[ ] M, Client WS_SC) {
    S = M.Length();
    S_C = Estimate size of M in compressed form;
    T_Comp = Estimate time to compress M at server;
    T_Decomp = Estimate time to decompress M at WS_SC;
    Estimate network round-trip time RTT and loss rate p for network connection between server
    and WS_SC;
    RT_U = transmission time (S, RTT, p);
    RT_C = transmission time (S_C, RTT, p) + T_Comp + T_Decomp;
    if (RT_U < RT_C) then "transmit uncompressed";
    else "compress and then transmit";
}
```

tion of message size. Next, the subsection "Network Models" describes how NAM estimates network transmission time. This model is specific to the TCP protocol (Postel, 1981). The overall performance of NAM is dependent on the accuracy of these estimation techniques.

Regression to Estimate Compression Time and Compressed Message Size

This section describes a generic technique to estimate compression time, decompression time, and compressed message size for a given message. Of course, there are many ways to perform this estimation, and one may develop and deploy an application-specific approach. NAM is envisioned as a collection of different plug-and-play components, enabling an application developer to replace our generic technique with his or her own specific model. The fourth section shows the tradeoff associated with using our generic approach and how it impacts NAM's decisions.

We utilize a generic polynomial regression technique to detect a curvilinear function between a message size and (1) its compressed message size, (2) compression time, and (3) decompression time. In the following, we provide an overview of polynomial regression and its alternative models. The key advantage of regression is that it represents a large sample set with a finite set of variables. NAM_c computes the coefficients of a regression model for decompression time and transmits it to NAM_s to estimate the decompression time of a message at the client.

Table 2. Terms and their definitions

Term	Definition
NAM_S	Server component of NAM.
NAM_C	Client component of NAM.
WS_S	A Web service that is not dependent on other Web services, configured with NAM_S only.
WS_{SC}	A Web service that depends on other Web services, configured with both NAM_S and NAM_C.

Polynomial regression computes the relationship (e.g., linear, exponential, logarithmic, etc.) between a dependent variable (e.g., y) and an independent variable (e.g., x). Based on Taylor approximation, if the original functions are difficult or impossible to evaluate directly, the partial sums of the corresponding infinite series is polynomials and can be evaluated as follows:

$$y = f(x) = a_i \times x^i = a_0 + (a_1 \times x) + ... + (a_n \times x^n) + ...$$

Linear, quadratic and cubic regressions are special cases of this general equation:

Linear regression: $y = f(x) = a_0 + (a_1 \times x)$ \hfill (1)

Quadratic regression: $y = f(x) = a_0 + (a_1 \times x) + (a_2 \times x^2)$ \hfill (2)

Cubic regression: $y = f(x) = a_0 + (a_1 \times x) + (a_2 \times x^2) + (a_3 \times x^3)$ \hfill (3)

Given n observed samples: $\{x_1, y_1\}$, ..., $\{x_n, y_n\}$, a regression model solves for a_i values with the objective to minimize the sum of difference between the estimated value y'_i and its observed value y_i (i.e., minimize $\sum_{i=1}^{n}(y_i - y'_i)^2$). Conceptually, this is accomplished by computing the partial derivatives at every point of x_i and by setting its result to zero. With cubic regression, this is realized by maintaining three matrices (see Figure 5, where $Y = X \times A$). One may solved for matrix A to obtain the coefficients by computing the inverse of X (i.e., $A = X^{-1} \times Y$).

At run time, the system may accumulate m new samples by maintaining separate X' and Y' matrices. The system may add these into the existing X and Y matrices and solve for a new A matrix. The space complexity of this approach is the size of matrices and independent of the total number of samples. Its time complexity is to solve for matrix A: compute the inverse of matrix X and multiply it by matrix Y.

Network Models

The network characteristics have a significant impact on the response time associated with transmitting the output of a Web service. The response time depends on network bandwidth, transmission and propagation delays, loss rate, and the interaction of the transport protocol with loss. In this paper, we focus on the TCP (Postel, 1981) transport protocol because of its wide spread use.

The main challenge for NAM is to devise mechanisms to estimate the response time of a server, based on information such as round-trip time (RTT), bandwidth, output size, and loss rate. Of these, only the response size is known; thus, the remaining variables either must be measured or estimated. NAM builds on existing work on TCP modeling. Accurately modeling TCP over a wide range of network conditions is a challenging issue, and most existing models are constrained with a strict set of assumptions. TCP modeling is also complicated due to the existence of several TCP variants, but not all of them are widely deployed. Such variants include TCP SACK (Mathis et al., 1996), which speeds up loss recovery with selective retransmission, and TCP Vegas (Brakmo & Peterson, 1977), which proposes enhanced techniques for congestion detection. The dominant TCP variant today is TCP Reno (Fall & Floyd, 1996) and thus is the focus of NAM. As other TCP variants become popular, NAM must be enhanced to accommodate them.

Several analytical models exist to estimate response time with TCP Reno. These include models that consider both network loss (Padhye et al., 1998) and no loss (Sikdar et al., 2001), termed LM (Loss-estimation Model) and NLM (No-Loss estimation Model), respectively. We evaluated these two models with both simulation using ns2 (Fall & Vardhan, 2002) and experimentation using in a testbed with NIST Net (Carson, 1997). Some of these results are presented next. In summary, each model has its own strengths and weaknesses: LM is accurate with long flows but inaccurate with short flows (such as those frequently produced by Web services). NLM is accurate at modeling both short and long flows but inaccurate when flows experience loss. Finally, both models become less accurate when response time is

Figure 5. Matrices maintained in support of cubic regression

$$X = \begin{bmatrix} n & \sum_{i=1}^{n} x_i & \sum_{i=1}^{n} x_i^2 & \sum_{i=1}^{n} x_i^3 \\ \sum_{i=1}^{n} x_i & \sum_{i=1}^{n} x_i^2 & \sum_{i=1}^{n} x_i^3 & \sum_{i=1}^{n} x_i^4 \\ \sum_{i=1}^{n} x_i^2 & \sum_{i=1}^{n} x_i^3 & \sum_{i=1}^{n} x_i^4 & \sum_{i=1}^{n} x_i^5 \\ \sum_{i=1}^{n} x_i^3 & \sum_{i=1}^{n} x_i^4 & \sum_{i=1}^{n} x_i^5 & \sum_{i=1}^{n} x_i^6 \end{bmatrix} \quad Y = \begin{bmatrix} \sum_{i=1}^{n} y_i \\ \sum_{i=1}^{n} x_i y_i \\ \sum_{i=1}^{n} x_i^2 y_i \\ \sum_{i=1}^{n} x_i^3 y_i \end{bmatrix} \quad A = \begin{bmatrix} \sum_{i=1}^{n} a_0 \\ \sum_{i=1}^{n} a_1 \\ \sum_{i=1}^{n} a_2 \\ \sum_{i=1}^{n} a_3 \end{bmatrix}$$

dominated by CPU time to transfer data from the user to the kernel space. The two models are presented next in more detail.

In order to understand TCP's contribution to response time, we first summarize the behavior of TCP. A TCP connection begins with a three-way handshake, which takes up one round-trip time (RTT).

For data larger than a single packet, TCP enters the slow-start phase, where it increases its transmission window by one for each received acknowledgment (ACK). In the absence of delayed ACKs, the receiver sends an ACK for each new packet. If there is no loss, the sender's window doubles every Round-Trip Time (RTT) until it reaches a pre-specified limit, termed maximum window size W_{max}, typically bounded by the receiver's socket buffer size. At this point, the sender enters a steady state and continues to transmit W_{max} packets every RTT, until the entire message is transmitted. Therefore, in the absence of loss, we can use the model described by NLM (Sikdar et al., 2001) to estimate the transfer time of a message consisting of N packets, denoted by T_{tr}, as follows:

$$T_{tr} = \begin{cases} RTT \times \lfloor \log_2 N \rfloor & \text{if } N \leq N_{exp} \\ RTT \times (\lfloor \log_2 W_{max} \rfloor + \left\lceil \dfrac{N - N_{exp}}{W_{max}} \right\rceil + 2 & \text{otherwise} \end{cases}$$

(4)

where N_{exp} is the number of packets transmitted during slow start phase, and

$$N_{exp} = 2 \lceil \log_2 W_{max} \rceil + W_{max} - 1$$

NAM_C maintains a history of measurements with all the recently contacted servers. This history is kept in a local database, which is consulted before a request is sent to a server. If past experience has shown the network path to be relatively free of loss, or if the response size is small (a few packets), then using this model is reasonable. In our framework, NAM_C maintains an estimate of RTT for each of the corresponding servers. When communicating with a specific server, NAM_C provides its RTT estimate to NAM_S as a part of its request (e.g., in a SOAP header). Note that having NAM_C communicate this information to NAM_S is more scalable, because it frees the server from maintaining a potentially large database for all its clients. NAM_C might estimate the RTT to NAM_S either off-line by using PING, by monitoring the RTT on recent transactions with the server, or a combination of these. With PING and low bandwidth connections (e.g., DSL, cable modem, etc.), where transmission time of data dominates RTT, we must ensure that the transmitted ECHO request is padded to the size of a full packet; otherwise, the estimates of Equation 4 will be inaccurate.

NAM needs additional parameters to estimate response time, such as the maximum TCP window size and the loss rate. Both reside in the kernel in the TCP protocol control block (a control block maintains the state the protocol requires for each connection). Currently, there is no interface that provides these parameters to the application. Work such as Congestion Manager (Andersen et al., 2000), however, aims to remedy this problem by allowing congestion information to be shared among all protocols residing on a machine. For our NAM prototype, we modified the Linux kernel to return such information to the application via the *getsockopt()* system call. This was a simple modification requiring just a few lines of code.

NLM works well if there is no packet loss. Packet loss in TCP may lead to a timeout, and the impact on response time is dramatic, because it adds idle time and causes the protocol to enter slow start again. When history indicates that loss is likely during the transmission of a particular large message, we estimate the network transmission time of message M by using its size, *M.length()*, and an estimation of network bandwidth, $\beta(p)$: *M.Length()* / $\beta(p)$. Using the models of (Padhye et al., 1998), the network bandwidth is estimated as:

$$\beta(p) \approx \min(\frac{W_{max}}{RTT}, RTT\sqrt{\frac{2p}{3}} + T_0 \min(1, 3\sqrt{\frac{3p}{8}})p(1+32p^2))$$

(5)

where p is the loss probability. Equation 5 is appropriate for bulk transmissions that send a large amount of data.

Figure 6 shows the accuracy of both models with different latencies. These experiments were conducted using three machines: a client, a server, and a dedicated NISTNet router. These machines were connected using a 100 Mbps Ethernet switch. The x-axis shows the message size. The y-axis shows the percentage difference between the observed and estimated network transmission times, $100 \times$ [(Observed - Estimated)/Observed]. With high network latency and no loss (see Figure 6(a)), NLM performs very well. In the presence of loss, this model becomes inaccurate (and eliminated from this presentation). LM does well for large messages (long flows) with and without loss. With short messages (less than 100 Kilobytes), LM exhibits a high percentage of error (Padhye et al., 1998).

Figure 6(b) shows the accuracy of each model when network latency is low. With no packet loss, the observed error was high. The reason is that we estimate RTT using PING. This estimation is inaccurate, because it ignores the time required to transfer data from user space to kernel space (see Figure 7). This time becomes significant with large message sizes (100 Kilobyte), resulting in a high percentage of error. One may enhance the accuracy of these models by requiring NAM_c to maintain the observed RTT for the previous connections with a server. It is important to note that this correction in RTT will enhance the quality of decisions

Figure 6. A comparison of analytical models with a 100 Mbps ethernet switch using NIST Net

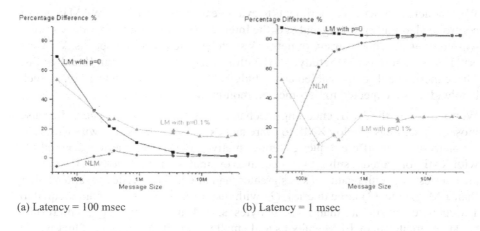

(a) Latency = 100 msec   (b) Latency = 1 msec

rendered by NAM, but it does not impact it greatly, because it is almost always appropriate to transmit messages uncompressed for environments where RTT is so low that the CPU time or memory transfers become significant. When the RTT is underestimated, NAM underestimates the total transmission time, motivating it to transmit data uncompressed.

In light of these results, NAM employs a hybrid model, building on the strengths of both models. This hybrid model works as follows. For connections where the expected loss is zero (based on previous statistics), NAM employs NLM. If previous statistics reveal a high likelihood of loss, then NAM employs LM.

Figure 7. PING does not take into account the transfer time from user space to kernel space

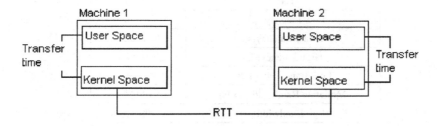

Performance Results of NAM

We conducted numerous experiments to evaluate the effectiveness of NAM in both a controlled laboratory setting and over the Internet. The controlled laboratory setting was configured with a variety of network switches and processor speeds. We used NISTNet (Carson, 1997) to study NAM with a variety of packet loss and bandwidths. This experimental setup enabled us to study NAM with speeds up to 1 Gbps. Such bandwidths are expected to become common in the near future.

We focused on the XML encoding mechanisms in the rest of the paper, because most Web services employ XML to share and exchange data. As shown in Table 1, we analyzed four different queries representative of (1) small queries, denoted Q_S, with XML formatted result set sizes equal to or smaller than 1 Kilobyte, (2) moderate queries, Q_M, with result set sizes greater than or equal to 1 Kilobyte and smaller than 1 Megabyte, (3) large queries, Q_L, with result set sizes greater than or equal to 1 Megabyte and smaller than 10 Megabytes, and (4) huge queries, Q_H, with results set sizes greater than 10 Megabytes and smaller than 50 Megabytes. Queries 12, 20, 3, and 10 were chosen for each category, respectively.

The Internet experiments were conducted using connections between USC and clients at different academic institutions as well as home clients connected using either DSL/Cable modems or 56 Kbps dial-up modems. These experiments offered a variety of network bandwidths and latencies. A connection might offer either a low ($\downarrow$ L), moderate ($\leftrightarrow$ L), or high ($\uparrow$ L) latency. With a given latency, a connection may offer either a low ($\downarrow$ B), moderate ($\leftrightarrow$ B), or high ($\uparrow$ B) bandwidth (see Table 3). This yields nine combinations. This paper describes our observations with five of these, which were selected to show that NAM is a general-purpose technique that adapts to its target environment and application. NAM's overall behavior is determined by how well regression model of the section "Regression to Estimate Compression Time and Compressed Message Size" and analytical models of the section "Network Models" perform their estimations.

Table 3. Bandwidth/latency terms and their ranges

Term	Range
Low Latency($\downarrow$ L)	< 20 ms
Moderate Latency($\leftrightarrow$ L)	20-100 ms
High Latency(L)	> 100 ms
Low Bandwidth($\downarrow$ B)	< 10 Mbps
Moderate Bandwidth($\leftrightarrow$ B)	10-100 Mbps
High Bandwidth(B)	> 100 Mbps

The five reported experiments are:

- Southern California, $SC_{\downarrow L,\leftrightarrow B}$: An Internet deployment with a Linux server at USC and a client at University of California, San Diego. This connection offers typical bandwidth of 90 to 96 Mbps and latency of 3.5 ms (RTT = 7 ms). This is a low latency, moderate bandwidth experiment.

- $US_{\leftrightarrow L,\downarrow B}$: An Internet deployment with a Linux server at USC (West Coast) and ISI at Washington, D.C. (East Coast). The ISI connection is a T1 with typical bandwidth of 1-1.2 Mbps and 45 ms latency (RTT = 90 ms). This experiment represents a moderate latency, low bandwidth connection.

- $US_{\leftrightarrow L,\leftrightarrow B}$: A coast-to-coast Internet deployment consisting of one machine at the University of Massachusetts at Amherst and another at USC in Los Angeles. The bandwidth between USC and the University of Massachusetts is approximately 87 to 96 Mbps with 45 ms latency (RTT = 90 ms). This experiment represents a moderate latency, moderate bandwidth connection.

- Trans-Atlantic$_{L,\leftrightarrow B}$: An Internet deployment with a Linux server at USC and a Sun OS 5.8 client at the University of Saarlandes in Germany. We observed 90 to 97 Mbps network bandwidth for connections USC and Saarlandes with 89 ms latency (RTT = 178 ms). This represents a high latency, moderate bandwidth connection.

- Gbps$_{\downarrow L, B}$: An intranet configuration consisting of two machines connected using a Gigabit Ethernet switch. The bandwidth is limited by the processor speed and varies from 300 to 500 Mbps. Latency is a low 0.15 ms (RTT = 0.3 ms), because the machines are physically located in the same room at USC's database laboratory. This represents a high bandwidth, low latency connection.

The Internet is a shared resource, and we did not want to impose am unnecessary load that might interfere with existing network application. Thus, we used the controlled environment of Figure 8 to analyze the impact of alternative estimation techniques on NAM. The details of this environment are as follows. We stored the result of each TPC-H queries in a file and registered the compression and decompression time of each data set with alternative processor speeds. These times exclude the time to read the file into memory. These correspond to the compression profiles box of Figure 8. Next, we performed an experiment consisting of an Internet application configured with a NAM_c invoking a remote server with the identity of a query. The query id uniquely identifies the data set size that must be transmitted from the server to NAM_c. The server employs NAM to determine if the referenced data set should be transmitted compressed or uncompressed and logs this information. Next, it transmits the data set in uncompressed, Zip compressed, and XMill compressed

Figure 8. Experimental framework

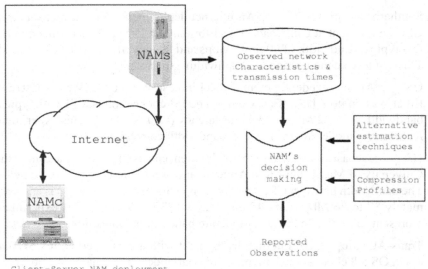

to *NAM_c* and registers the observed response time and network characteristics in a log file. An off-line program, NAM's decision-making box of Figure 8 processes these logs and emulates different processor speeds. In addition, it computes the percentage improvement provided by NAM when compared with (1) uncompressed transmission always, corresponding to how Web services are deployed today, termed *uncompressed*, (2) Zip transmission always, a simple improvement on today's status that would employ Zip always, and (3) XMill transmission always, an environment that employs XMill at all times.

Figure 9 shows the percentage improvement with NAM when configured with a 3.06 GHz processor speed for five different deployments. For each, the y-axis shows the percentage improvement of NAM when compared with XMill compression always, Zip compression always, and uncompressed always. We observed a zero loss rate in these experiments. NAM employs an uncompressed transmission for Q_s always because the message is smaller than a TCP packet (a packet is 1480 bytes between two Linux machines and 1460 bytes between a Linux machine and a Sun OS 5.8 machine). Its model assumes TCP must transmit at least one packet worth of data and attributes zero benefits to using either Zip or XMill. The results show the superiority of this decision with the low latency connections that offer moderate to high bandwidths (1-Gbps, SC). With a low bandwidth, moderate la-

Figure 9. Percentage improvement with NAM for QS with 3.06 GHz processors

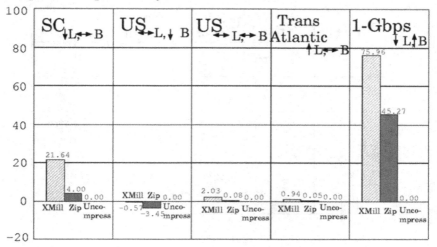

% Improvement provided by NAM

tency connection, $US_{\ll L,^-B}$, compression provides marginal benefits (1% to 3%) with a 3.06 GHz processor, because the model's assumption is violated (transmitting fewer than one packet worth of data does provide savings in network transmission times). With a 2-GHz processor speed, this marginal benefit disappears. With both 1 GHz and 450 MHz processor speeds, use of either Zip or XMill is inferior to an uncompressed transmission.

Figure 10 shows the percentage savings for Q_M and a 2 GHz processor speed. With the 1-Gbps$_{\downarrow L,B}$ environment, NAM continues to transmit data uncompressed, providing substantial savings when compared with environments configured to use either Zip or XMill always. With Trans-Atlantic$_{L,\leftrightarrow B}$ and $US_{\leftrightarrow L,\leftrightarrow B}$, NAM employs XMill for 77% of queries, Zip for 14% of queries, and uncompressed transmission for the remaining 9% of queries. An environment that would employ XMill compression always outperforms NAM by approximately 19% for Trans-Atlantic$_{L,\leftrightarrow B}$. This drops to 2% with a 1-GHz processor. With a 450-MHz processor, NAM is superior to XMill always. Note that NAM provides substantial savings when compared with today's common practice to transmit uncompressed always.

The results observed with both $US_{\leftrightarrow L,\downarrow B}$ and $SC_{\downarrow L,\leftrightarrow B}$ demonstrate the importance of estimating network characteristic and data compression times accurately. Consider each experiment in turn. With $US_{\leftrightarrow L,\downarrow B}$, NAM employs XMill for 68% of queries,

Figure 10. Percentage improvement with NAM for QM with 2 GHz processors

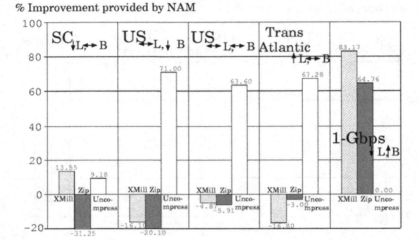

Zip for 22% of queries, and uncompressed transmission for the remaining 10%. This is partly because cubic regression cannot estimate the compressed message size, compression, and decompression times accurately with samples from both the 1 and 10 gigabyte databases. If perfect estimates were provided, NAM would employ Zip and XMill 81% and 19% of the time, respectively, providing savings when compared with XMill. The same would hold true if NAM were provided with samples from 1-gigabyte database. The $US_{\leftrightarrow L, \downarrow B}$ results demonstrate the importance of estimating compression and decompression times accurately.

With $SC_{\downarrow L, \leftrightarrow B}$, NAM employs XMill for more queries than desired, resulting in inferior performance when compared with an environment that employs Zip always. This is partly due to inaccurate estimates provided by regression. However, even with perfect knowledge of compressed message size, compression and decompression times, an environment that employs Zip always will continue to outperform NAM by 7%. This is because NAM observes a loss from a prior transmission and uses this to estimate response times with different compression techniques. However, the observed transmission does not encounter the expected loss rate, causing the Zip compressed response times to appear superior.

Figure 11 shows the percentage savings for the Q_L and a 1-GHz processor speed. With low latency connections that offer moderate to high bandwidths (1-Gbps$_{\downarrow L, B}$ and $SC_{\downarrow L, \leftrightarrow B}$), NAM transmits data uncompressed, producing significant savings. With Trans-Atlantic $_{L, \leftrightarrow B}$, $US_{\leftrightarrow L, \leftrightarrow B}$ and $US_{\leftrightarrow L, \downarrow B}$, NAM switches to Zip compression,

Figure 11. Percentage improvement with NAM for QL with 1 GHz processors

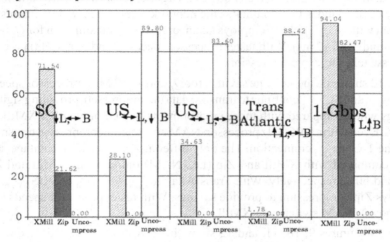

Figure 12. Percentage improvement with NAM for QH with 450 MHz processors

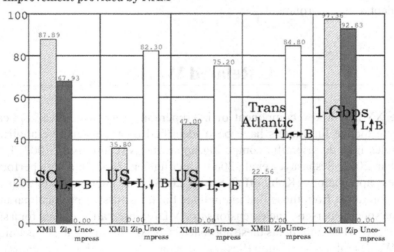

providing savings when compared with an uncompressed transmission. With Trans-Atlantic$_{\uparrow L, \leftrightarrow B}$, NAM's savings when compared with an environment that employs XMill always is marginal. This is due to a larger RTT between USC and the University of Saarlandes that dominates the network response time. It is interesting to note that with SC$_{\downarrow L, \leftrightarrow B}$, NAM employs an uncompressed transmission for Q_L because of the small RTT (7 ms). With faster processor speeds (2 and 3.06 GHz) processors, NAM switches to Zip compression.

Figure 12 shows the percentage savings for Q_H and a 450 MHz processor speed. The 1-Gbps$_{\downarrow L, B}$ and SC$_{\downarrow L, \leftrightarrow B}$ continue to transmit data uncompressed, providing significant savings when compared with those environments that employ either XMill or Zip always. Even with a 3.06 GHz processor, NAM employs uncompressed transmission with the 1-Gbps$_{\downarrow L, B}$ connection. The only difference is a lower percentage savings when compared with XMill and Zip (i.e., NAM) outperforms XMill and Zip by 82% and 60%, respectively. With Trans-Atlantic$_{L, \leftrightarrow B}$, US$_{\leftrightarrow L, \leftrightarrow B}$ and US$_{\leftrightarrow L, \downarrow B}$, NAM employs Zip compression to provide savings. With faster processor speeds (1 GHz and above), NAM switches to XMill.

Results of Figures 9, 10, 11, and 12 show that NAM adapts to enhance response time across different output XML data set sizes, processor speeds, and network conditions. It may not provide a superior response time for every single transmission; however, it significantly improves the average response time across many transmissions. Of course, given a specific processor speed and query output size, one may tailor the system to outperform NAM. Results of Figure 10 for US$_{\leftrightarrow L, \downarrow B}$ is a demonstration of this claim. However, NAM is designed to be general purpose and adapt to its environment.

Related Work

While XML is a key component of interoperability for wide-area applications, its performance limitations have been identified by time-sensitive applications. Examples include scientific computing applications (Chiu et al., 2002; Davis & Parashar, 2002; Seshasayee et al., 2004; van Engelen, 2003) and high performance business applications (Kohlhoff & Steele, 2003). The approaches to address this limitation range from those that manipulate the transmission protocol parameters, schema specific parsers, and extensions to XML representation of data for a specific domain. NAM complements these approaches. Next, we survey these techniques in turn. We describe SOAP-binQ (Seshasayee et al., 2004) as the closest approach to NAM and how it is different. We end this section with a comparison to our earlier published study on NAM.

Davis et al. (2002) evaluated the latency performance of several implementations of SOAP with HTTP and compared the results with the performance of JavaRMI and CORBA using HTTP and TCP (Davis & Parashar, 2002). Similar to our findings, their study also shows that binary XML encodings improve the response time of SOAP. They found that two large sources of inefficiency in SOAP implementation are the use of multiple system calls to send one logical message and the XML parsing and formatting time. They suggested using different capabilities of the HTTP protocol, such as HTTP chunking, to improve the SOAP performance.

Chiu et al. (2002) analyzed the limitations of SOAP for high-performance scientific computing and recommended several optimizations for using SOAP in scientific computing applications.. They showed that the performance of SOAP can be improved significantly by using optimization techniques, including schema-specific parser mechanisms for arrays, trie data structure for matching tags, efficient memory management as well as persistent connections, and chunking in HTTP. They also recommended a multi-protocol approach that uses SOAP to negotiate faster binary protocols among messaging participants.

The SOAP (van Engelen, 2003) exploits XML schema extensibility for defining optimized XML representations of numerical data in scientific applications. It also improved the performance of SOAP by using several message-passing optimization techniques such as chunking, compression, multi-hop routing, and the streaming of Direct Internet Message Encapsulation (DIME).

To apply XML and SOAP in time-sensitive business applications, Kohlhoff, et al. (2003) compared the performance of SOAP in real-time trading systems with both binary CDR and a domain-specific protocol (i.e., Financial Information eXchange [FIX] protocol). Their results show that SOAP did fare poorly when compared to both binary CDR and native FIX, although the difference is less than that measured for scientific computing applications.

Our NAM approach differs from these studies in the sense that it proactively measures the characteristics of underlying communication channels and adaptively chooses different messaging formatters to minimize the response time of Web services applications. The closest approach to NAM is the SOAP-binQ protocol recently proposed by Seshasayee, et al. (2004). The SOAP-binQ protocol associates run-time quality management functions with SOAP parameters. It can dynamically adjust data volumes to available clients by using application-specific data manipulations, such as data down-sampling. However, the SOAP-binQ protocol relies on developers or end users to provide a quality file accompanying the WSDL information that indicates the data precision to be used under different resource availabilities. In contrast, our NAM approach can intelligently choose an optimal message formatting decision based on current network condition without the participation of developers or end users.

This paper is a comprehensive version of our earlier study that introduced NAM (Ghandeharizadeh et al., 2003). There are two key extensions. First, we have included an in-depth discussion of the alternative formatters and their impact on message size (see the second section). Second, the experimental section has been extended to present results from additional queries (see Table 1).

Conclusion and Future Research Directions

This paper investigates the performance of XML and binary formatters and the role of compression to reduce the number of transmitted bytes. Our primary contribution is NAM, a middleware to enhance response time of Web services using compression techniques when appropriate. Our performance results demonstrate how NAM switches from using XMill compression to Zip and uncompressed transmission selectively to improve response time. We analyzed the performance of this middleware with TPC-H queries that produce data set sizes ranging from a few hundred bytes to tens of Megabytes. This was done in the context of different Internet and intranet settings.

NAM is designed to adapt, based on the data characteristics of an application, available client and server processor speeds, and network characteristics. It exchanges profile information between a client (NAM_c) and a Web service (NAM_s) in support of intelligent decisions. This distributes the overhead of NAM between the client and the Web service in order to free the Web service to scale to a large number of clients. It is important to note that NAM is not appropriate for multimedia content such as still images, audio and video clips, and so forth. This is because these data types are compressed using a lossy compression technique. A lossless compression technique, such as Zip, reduces the size of these files by only a few percentages (instead of several factors, as with XML) (see Table 1).

An immediate research direction is to extend NAM to maintain a history of its decisions and their quality. This would enable it to detect when its estimates are inaccurate. Moreover, it is possible to attribute this error either to the regression models or the observed network characteristics. Based on this, NAM may start to modify its models in order to enhance the quality of its decisions. A challenge here is the division of this activity between NAM_c and NAM_s. Another research direction is to extend NAM to streaming architectures. In its present form, NAM assumes that a Web service produces its output in its entirety prior to its transmission. While this assumption matches today's practices, we anticipate the emergence of XML streaming architectures in support of integrated Web services. These will incrementally produce and transmit their XML-formatted output in a pipelined manner, overlapping the server's production of output with the client's consumption and processing of this output. We intend to explore extensions of NAM to these architectures in the near future.

Acknowledgment

We wish to thank the anonymous referee for his valuable comments that helped refine this manuscript. This research is supported in part by an unrestricted cash gift from Microsoft and a grant from the National Science Foundation IIS-0307908.

References

Andersen, D., Bansal, D., Curtis, D., Seshan, S., & Balakrishnan, H. (2000). *System support for bandwidth management and content adaptation in Internet applications* (technical report LCS-TR-808). MIT.

Box, D. et al. (2000). Simple object access protocol (SOAP). In *Proceedings of the World Wide Web Consortium (W3C)*, May.

Brakmo, L., & Peterson, L. (1977). TCP Vegas: End to end congestion avoidance on a global Internet. *IEEE Journal on Selected Areas in Communications, 13*(8), 1465-1480.

Cai, M., Ghandeharizadeh, S., Schmidt, R., & Song, S. (2002). A compression of alternative encoding mechanism for Web services. In *Proceedings of the DEXA Conference.*

Carson, M. (1997). NIST Net. Internetworking Technologies Group. Retrieved from *http://snad.ncsl.nist.gov/itg/nistnet/*

Cheney, J. (2001). Compressing XML with multiplexed hierarchical PPM models. In *Proceedings of the Data Compression Conference.*

Chiu, K., Govindaraju, M., & Bramley, R. (2002). Investigating the limits of SOAP performance for scientific computing. In *Proceedings of the 11th IEEE International Symposium on High Performance Distributed Computing HPDC-11 20002 (HPDC'02)*, Washington, D.C.

Davis, D., & Parashar, M.P. (2002). Latency performance of SOAP implementations. In *Proceedings of the Second IEEE/ACM International Symposium on Cluster Computing and the Grid*, Washington, D.C.

Fall, K., & Floyd, S. (1996). Simulation-based comparisons of Tahoe, Reno, and SACK TCP. *Computer Communications Review, 26*(3), 5-21.

Fall, K., & Varadhan, K. (2002). *The NS manual*. The VINT Project. Retrieved April 2002, from *http://www.isi.edu/nsnam/ns/index.html*

Geer, D. (2005). Will binary XML speed network traffic? *IEEE Computer, 38*(4).

Ghandeharizadeh, S. et al. (2003a). Proteus: A system for dynamically composing and intelligently executing Web services. In *Proceedings of the First International Conference on Web Services (ICWS)*, Las Vegas, Nevada, June (pp. 17-21).

Ghandeharizadeh, S., Papadopoulos, C., Cai, M., & Chintalapudi, K. (2002). Performance of networked XML-driven cooperative applications. In *Proceedings of the Second International Workshop on Cooperative Internet Computing*.

Ghandeharizadeh, S., Papadopoulos, C., Pol, P., & Zhou, R. (2003b). NAM: A network adaptable middleware to enhance response time of Web services. In *Proceedings of the 11th IEEE/ACM International Symposium on Modeling, Analysis and Simulation of Computer and Telecommunication Systems (MASCOTS)*, Orlando, Florida, October (pp. 136-146).

Iyer, B.R., & Wilhite, D. (1994). Data compression support in databases. In *Proceedings of the 20th International Conference on Very Large Data Bases*.

Kohlhoff, C., & Steele, R. (2003). Evaluating SOAP for high performance business applications: Real-time trading systems. In *Proceedings of the 12th World Wide Web Conference*, Budapest, Hungary.

Liefke, H., & Suciu, D. (1999). *XMill: An efficient compressor for XML data* (technical report MSCIS-99-26). University of Pennsylvania.

Mathis, M., Mahdavi, J., Floyd, S., & Romanow, A. (1996). *TCP selective acknowledgment options* (technical report 2018). Network Working Group RFC.

Padhye, J., Firoiu, V., Towsley, D., & Krusoe, J. (1998). Modeling TCP throughput: A simple model and its empirical validation. In *Proceedings of the ACM SIGCOMM '98 Conference on Applications, Technologies, Architectures, and Protocols for Computer Communication*, Vancouver, Canada (pp. 303-314).

Poess, M., & Floyd, C. (2000). New TPC benchmarks for decision support and Web commerce. *ACM SIGMOD Record, 29*(4), 64-71.

Postel, J. (1981). *Transmission control protocol* (technical report 793). Network Working Group RFC.

Seshasayee, B., Schwan, K., & Widener, P. (2004). SOAP-binQ: High-performance SOAP with continuous quality management. In *ICDCS*, (pp. 158-165).

Shek, E.C., Muntz, R.R., & Fillion, L. (1996). *The design of the FALCON framework for application level communication optimization* (technical report CST-TR-960039). Los Angeles, CA: UCLA.

Sikdar, B., Kalyanaraman, S., & Vastola, K.S. (2001). An integrated model for the latency and steady-state throughput of TCP connections. *Performance Evaluation, 46*(2-3), 139-154.

van Engelen, R.A. (2003). Pushing the SOAP envelope with Web services for scientific computing. In *Proceedings of the International Conference on Web Services (ICWS)*.

Werner, C., & Buschmann, C. (2004). Compressing SOAP messages by using differential encoding. In *Proceedings of the IEEE International Conference on Web Services*, July (pp. 540-547).

Ziv, J., & Lempel, A. (1977). A universal algorithm for sequential data compression. *IEEE Transactions on Information Theory, 23*(3), 337-343.

Endnotes

[1] This research was supported in part by an unrestricted cash gift from Microsoft research.

[2] One also may employ NAM as a stack layer in frameworks such as FALCON (Shek et al., 1996).

This work was previously published in International Journal of Web Services Research, edited by Zhang, pp. 1-21, 2(4), copyright 2005 by IGI Publishing, formerly known as Idea Group Publishing (an imprint of IGI Global).

Chapter III

Realizability Analysis of Top-Down Web Service Composition Specifications

Xiang Fu, Georgia Southwestern State University, USA

Tevfik Bultan, University of California – Santa Barbara, USA

Jianwen Su, University of California – Santa Barbara, USA

Abstract

A conversation protocol specifies the desired global behaviors of a Web service composition in a top-down fashion. Before implementing a conversation protocol, its realizability has to be determined—that is, can a bottom-up Web service composition be synthesized so that it generates exactly the same set of conversations as specified by the protocol? This chapter presents three sufficient conditions to restrict control flows of a conversation protocol for achieving realizability. The model is further extended to include data semantics of Web services into consideration. To overcome the state-space explosion problem, symbolic analysis techniques are used for improving the accuracy of analysis. The realizability analysis can effectively reduce the complexity of verifying Web services with asynchronous communication.

Introduction

To construct a mission-critical Web service composition (also called "composite Web service") is a very challenging task, as any design or implementation fault could lead to great losses. Recently, automated verification and testing of Web services have attracted attention in both academia and industry (Bultan, Fu, Hull, & Su, 2003; Foster, Uchitel, Magee, & Kramer, 2003; Narayanan, & Mcllraith, 2003; Betin-Can, Bultan, & Fu, 2005; Canfora & Di Penta, 2006). However, before any automatic verification technique can be applied, a formal model must be defined to describe behaviors of Web services. This chapter presents a top-down specification approach called "conversation protocol" and studies the realizability problem of conversation protocols. It is an extension of the work by Fu, Bultan, and Su (2004c, 2005b) and covers other results by Fu et al. (2003, 2004a, 2004b, 2004d, 2004e, 2005a) in the area.

Background

In general, there are two different ways of specifying a Web service composition: (1) the bottom-up approach, favored by many industry standards such as WSDL (W3C, 2001), in which each participant of the composition is specified first and then the composed system is studied; and (2) the top-down approach, such as Message Sequence Charts (ITU-T, 1994), conversation policies (Hanson, Nandi, & Kumaran, 2002a), WSCI (W3C, 2002), and WSCL (Banerji et al., 2002), in which the set of desired message exchange patterns is specified first and detailed specification of peer implementation is left blank.

In this chapter we concentrate on the top-down specification approach due to its simplicity and the potential benefits in verification complexity (Bultan et al., 2003). One natural idea for top-down specification of Web services is to use finite state machines (FSAs) to represent some aspects of the global composition process. The state machines can involve two parties (Hanson, Nandi, & Levine, 2002b) or multi-parties (Bultan et al., 2003), and may describe the global composition process directly (Hanson et al., 2002b) or may specify its local views (Banerji et al., 2002).

A top-down conversation protocol must be realized by a bottom-up Web service composition. In studying the composition behaviors, asynchrony usually complicates analyses. Asynchronous communication is one of the benefits provided by the Web service technique. It is supported by many industry platforms such as Java Message service (Sun, n.d.) and Microsoft Message Queuing service (Microsoft, n.d.). In an asynchronous communication environment, the receiver of a message does not have to synchronize its action with the send action by the sender. However, asynchrony may significantly increase the complexity of many verification problems. Fu et al. (2003) proved that the general problem of verifying a Linear Temporal Logic property on a bottom-up specified Web service composition is undecidable, which is essentially caused by the undecidable nature of communicating finite state machines (Brand & Zafiropulo, 1983).

Asynchronous communication is usually modeled by equipping participating services with FIFO queues. For example, Bultan et al. (2003) established a conversation-oriented framework where each participating Web service (called a "peer") of a composition is characterized using a finite state automaton, with the set of input/output message classes as the FSA alphabet. To capture asynchronous communication, each peer is equipped with a FIFO queue to store incoming messages. The behaviors generated by a composition of peers can be characterized using the set of message sequences (conversations) exchanged among peers. Linear Temporal Logic (Clarke, Grumberg, & Peled, 2000) can be naturally extended to this conversation-based framework. Desired system properties such as "a cancel request always results in a confirmation message" can be expressed using Linear Temporal Logic, and the Web service composition can then be verified using automatic verification tools such as the Web Service Analysis Tool (Fu et al., 2004d).

A conversation protocol is not always realizable—that is, there exists conversation protocols which do not have any peer implementations whose composition generates exactly the same set of conversations as specified by the protocol. Hence, before implementing a conversation protocol, its realizability must first be studied. Fu et al. (2003) proposed three sufficient conditions that can guarantee the realizability of conversation protocols. Later the realizability analysis technique is extended to a model with data semantics (Fu et al., 2004c).

Related Work

Realizability of software systems has been investigated for decades in different branches of computer science. In the late 1980s, researchers proposed the realizability problem of open systems (Abadi, Lamport, & Wolper, 1989; Pnueli, & Rosner, 1989). It studies whether a peer has a strategy to cope with the environment no matter how the environment moves. A closer notion to the realizability problem studied in this chapter is the concept of "weak/strong realizability" on the Message Sequence Chart Graphs (MSCG) model by Alur, McMillan, and Peled (2000) and Alur, Etessami, and Yannakakis (2001). In the MSCG model, each peer is also equipped with a message buffer to simulate the asynchronous communication environment. The difference is that the MSCG model includes both send and receives events, while the conversation model used in this chapter studies the send events only. This leads

Figure 1. Three non-realizable conversation protocols, adapted from the Büchi autumata protocol examples by Fu et al. (2003)

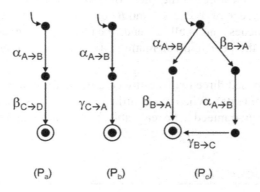

to a delicate difference in the analysis complexity and the realizability conditions on the two models. A detailed comparison of the two models can be found in Fu et al. (2005b).

Basic Realizability Analysis
without Message Contents

Consider the three conversation protocols presented in Figure 1, and let them be P_a, P_b, and P_c. Each conversation protocol is expressed using a finite state machine. In a finite state machine, the initial state is denoted using an incoming edge without source, and a final state is denoted using a double cycle. Each of these three protocols involves four peers A, B, C, and D.

Conversation protocol P_a is not realizable. It specifies one single conversations $\alpha\beta$, where message α is sent from A to B and message β is sent from C to D. Clearly any implementation of the four peers which generates a conversation $\alpha\beta$ can also generate the conversation $\beta\alpha$. Similarly P_b is not realizable because there is no way for peer C to learn about the time message α that is sent. Hence, any peer implementation which generates $\alpha\gamma$ will also generate $\gamma\alpha$.

Protocol P_c defines a conversation set: $\{\alpha\beta, \beta\alpha\gamma\}$. This protocol is more interesting in the sense that peers might have "confusion" when executing the protocol. It is possible that peers A and B take the left and the right branches of the protocol (respectively), unaware that the other peer is taking a different branch. For example, the following execution sequence can generate a conversation not specified by the protocol, although each peer is executing the protocol faithfully. Peer A first sends a message α, which is then stored in the queue of B; then B sends a message β, which is then stored in the queue of A. Peers A and B consume (i.e., receive) the messages in their respective queues, and finally B sends the message γ. Hence a conversation $\alpha\beta\gamma$ is produced by the peer implementations. However, this conversation is not specified by P_c.

Fu et al. (2003) proposed three realizability conditions for conversation protocols (without message contents). When these sufficient conditions are satisfied, a conversation protocol is guaranteed to be realizable. In the following we briefly present these conditions.

Lossless Join Condition

A conversation protocol is said to be lossless join if its conversation set is equal to the join of its projections to all peers. Here, the terms "join" and "projection" are borrowed from relational database theory.

The projection of a conversation to a peer i generates a message sequence by removing all the messages that are not related to peer i from the given conversation. For example, consider the conversation $\alpha\beta$ defined by P_a in Figure 1. Its projection to peer A is α (where message β is removed from the conversation because A is neither its sender nor its receiver); similarly, the projection of $\alpha\beta$ to C is β.

Given a set of languages (one language for each peer), their join is a set which includes all conversations whose projection to each peer is included in the corresponding language for that peer. For example, suppose message α is sent from A to B and message β is sent from C to D. The join of four languages $\{\alpha\}$, $\{\alpha\}$, $\{\beta\}$, $\{\beta\}$ (for A, B, C, and D respectively) results in the set $\{\alpha\beta, \beta\alpha\}$.

A conversation protocol is said to be a lossless join if its conversation set is the join of its projections to all peers. For example, the join of the projections of P_a to all peers is $\{\alpha\beta, \beta\alpha\}$, which is a strict superset of the conversation set specified by P_a. Hence, P_a is not lossless join. However, it can be verified that P_b and P_c in Figure 1 satisfy the lossless join condition.

Lossless join condition is actually a necessary condition of realizability. It is not hard to see that it reflects the requirement that a conversation protocol should be complete in the sense that the relative order of messages should not be restricted if they do not have a causal relationship.

Synchronous Compatibility Condition

Intuitively a conversation protocol is synchronous compatible if its straightforward implementation (by projecting the protocol to each peer) can work without conflicts using synchronous communication semantics. Formally, a conversation protocol satisfies the synchronous compatibility condition if it can be implemented using synchronous communication semantics without generating a state in which a peer is ready to send a message while the corresponding receiver is not ready to receive that message.

The synchronous compatibility condition is checked as follows:

1.   Project the protocol to each peer by replacing all the transitions labeled with messages for which that peer is neither the sender nor the receiver with ε-transitions (empty moves).
2.   Determinize the resulting automaton for each peer.
3.   Generate a product automaton by combining the determinized projections based on the synchronous communication semantics (i.e., each pair of send and receive operations are taken simultaneously at the sender and receiver).
4.   Check if there is a state in the product automaton where a peer is ready to send a message while the corresponding receiver is not ready to receive that message.

Consider the conversation protocol P_b in Figure 1. Its projection to peer A returns the same FSA. However, its projection to B replaces γ transition with an ε-transition, and its projection to C replaces the α transition with an ε-transition. After the determinization, the automaton for peer C consists of one initial and one final state, and a single transition labeled γ from the initial state to the final state. When we generate the automaton, which is the product of the projections in the initial state of the product automaton, peer C is ready to send the message γ but the receiver (i.e., A) is not yet ready to receive the message. Hence, P_b in Figure 1 does not satisfy the synchronous compatibility condition. It can be verified that P_a and P_c in Figure 1 satisfy the synchronous compatibility condition.

Autonomy Condition

A conversation protocol satisfies the autonomy condition if at every state each peer is able to do exactly one of the following: send a message, receive a message, or terminate.

Note that a state may have multiple transitions corresponding to different send operations for a peer, and this does not violate the autonomy condition. Similarly, a peer can have multiple receive transitions from the same state. However, the autonomy condition is violated if there are two (or more) transitions originating from a state such that one of them is a send operation and another one is a receive operation for the same peer. For example, consider the conversation protocol P_c in Figure 1. The two transitions labeled α and β originating from the initial state violate the autonomy condition, because at the initial state, peer A can either send or receive. However, notice that the conversation protocols P_a and P_b in Figure 1 satisfy the autonomy condition.

We have the following results concerning the three conditions introduced above.

Theorem 1. If a conversation protocol (without message contents) satisfies the lossless join condition, synchronous compatibility condition, and autonomy condition, it is realized by its projections to each peer.

The key proof idea of Theorem 1 (Fu et al., 2003) is that when a conversation protocol satisfies the realizability conditions, the composition of its projections to peers has a property called "eager consumption," which ensures that during any execution (interleaving) of the peers, whenever a peer sends out a message, it is not in a final state and its input queue is always empty—that is, each incoming message is consumed "eagerly" before any send action is taken by its receiver. When a composition satisfies the "eager consumption" property, for any conversation generated by the composition (using the asynchronous communication semantics), its projection to a peer is an accepted word by that peer FSA. This naturally leads to the conclusion that the conversation set is in the join of the languages accepted by all peers. If the conversation protocol is lossless join, the conversation set generated using the asynchronous semantics is the same as the one generated using the synchronous communication. Therefore a conversation protocol is realizable if the three sufficient conditions are satisfied.

The Guarded Automata Model

The abstract model of conversation protocol presented in the previous section is still not sufficient for real-world practice, because messages exchanged among Web services are simply abstract "message classes" without contents. In this section we present a formal model, called the "guarded automata" (GA) model, which takes message contents into consideration. We begin this section by defining the composition schema (i.e., the structure of a Web service composition). Then we present

Figure 2. The composition schema and the conversation protocol for a simplified warehouse example

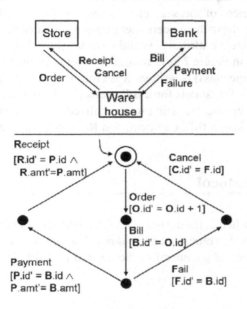

the formal models for both the top-down and bottom-up specification approaches, namely, conversation protocols and Web service compositions.

Composition Schema

A composition schema entails the information about peers, message classes, and the message domains for each message class. Formally, a composition schema is defined as follows:

Definition 1 (Composition Schema): *A composition schema is a tuple (P, M, Σ) where P is the finite set of peers, M is the finite set of message classes, and Σ is the set of messages. Each message class c ∈ M has a finite set of attributes and each attribute has a static data type. Each message m ∈ Σ is an instance of a message class. Thus the message alphabet Σ can be defined as follows:*

$$\Sigma = \bigcup_{c \in M} \{c\} \times DOM(c)$$

where DOM(c) is the domain of the message class c. Notice that Σ may be a finite or an infinite set, which is determined by the domains of the message classes.

Shown in Figure 2 is a composition schema that consists of three peers: Store, Bank, and Warehouse. Instances of message classes, such as **Order**, **Bill**, and **Payment**, are transmitted among these three peers. Let us assume that each of **Bill**, **Payment**, and **Receipt** has two integer attributes *id* and *amount* (shortened by "amt"), and all other message classes in Figure 2 have a single integer attribute *id*. A message (i.e., an instance of a message class) is written in the following form: "class(contents)." For example, **B**(100, 2000) stands for a **Bill** message whose id is 100 and amount is 2000. Here **Bill** is represented using its capitalized first letter **B**. Note that, the domains of message classes **Bill**, **Payment**, and **Receipt** are $Z \times Z$, where Z is the set of integers.

Conversation Protocol

Given a composition schema, the design of a Web service composition can be specified using a conversation protocol, in a top-down fashion. A conversation protocol is a guarded automaton, which specifies the desired global behaviors of the Web service composition.

Definition 2 (Conversation Protocol): *A conversation protocol is a tuple R = ((P, M, Σ), A), where (P, M, Σ) is a composition schema, and A is a **guarded automaton** (GA). The guarded automaton A is a tuple (M, Σ, T, s, F, δ) where M and Σ are the set of message classes and messages respectively, T is the finite set of states, s $\in$ T is the initial state, F $\subseteq$ T is the set of final states, and δ is the transition relation. Each transition $\tau \in \delta$ is in the form τ = (s, (c, g), t), where s, t $\in$ T are the source and the destination states of τ, c $\in$ M is a message class, and g is the guard of the transition. A guard g is a predicate on the attributes of the message that are being sent (which are denoted by the attribute names with apostrophe) and the attributes of the latest instances of the message classes (which are denoted by the attribute names without apostrophe) that are received or sent by the peer involved.*

During a run of a guarded automaton, a transition is taken only if the guard evaluates to true. For example, in Figure 2, the guard of the transition that sends an **Order** is:

Order.id' = Order.id+1.

The guard expresses that the id attribute of an **Order** message is incremented by 1 after executing the transition. Notice that in the above formula "id'" refers to the

Figure 3. A realization of the conversation protocol in Figure 2

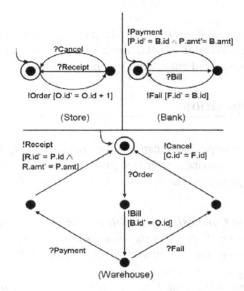

(Warehouse)

value of the next **Order** message being sent, and "id" refers to the value of the id attribute of the latest **Order** message. With the use of primed forms of variables, the symbol "=" in guards stands for the "equality" instead of "assignment." The declarative semantics (instead of procedural semantics) used here are more convenient for symbolic analysis.

By studying the semantics of transition guards in Figure 2, it is not hard to see that the conversation protocol in Figure 2 describes the following desired message exchange sequence of the warehouse example: an **Order** is sent by the Store to the Warehouse, and then the Warehouse sends a **Bill** to the Bank. The Bank either responds with a **Payment** or rejects with a **Fail** message. Finally the Warehouse issues a **Receipt** or a **Cancel** message. The guards determine the contents of the messages. For example, the id and the amount of each **Payment** must match those of the latest **Bill** message.

The language accepted by a guarded automaton can be naturally defined by extending standard finite state automaton semantics. Given a GA $A = (M, \Sigma, T, s, F, \delta)$, a *run* of A is a path that starts from the initial state s and ends at a final state in F. A message sequence $w \in \Sigma$ is accepted by A if there exists a corresponding run. For example, it is not hard to infer that the following is a message sequence accepted by the GA in Figure 2:

O(0), **B**(0, 100), **P**(0, 100),**R**(0, 100),**O**(1), **B**(1, 200), **F**(1),**C**(1).

Given a conversation protocol $R = ((P, M, \Sigma), A)$, its language is defined as $L(R) = L(A)$. In other words, the conversation set defined by a conversation protocol is the language accepted by its guarded automaton specification.

Web Service Composition

Bottom-up Web service compositions can also be specified using the GA model. However, the GA used to describe a peer is slightly different than the one used to describe a conversation protocol. The formal definition is as follows:

Definition 3 (Web Service Composition): *A Web service composition is a tuple S = ((P, M, Σ), A₁, ..., Aₙ), where (P, M, Σ) is the composition schema, n = |P|, and for each i ∈ [1..n], Aᵢ is the peer implementation for pᵢ ∈ P. Each Aᵢ is a tuple (Mᵢ, Σᵢ, Tᵢ, sᵢ, Fᵢ, δᵢ) where Mᵢ, Σᵢ, Tᵢ, sᵢ, Fᵢ, and δᵢ denote the set of message classes, set of messages, set of states, initial state, final states, and transition relation, respectively. A transition τ ∈ δᵢ can be one of the following three types: a send transition (t, (!α, g₁), t'), a receive transition (t, (?β, g₂), t'), and an ε-transition (t, (ε, g₃), t'), where t, t' ∈ Tᵢ, α ∈ Mᵢᵒᵘᵗ, β ∈ Mᵢⁿ, and g₁, g₂, and g₃ are predicates.*

The send and receive transitions are denoted using symbols "!" and "?", respectively. In an ε-transition, the guard determines if the transition can take place based on the contents of the latest message for each message class related to that peer. For a receive transition $(t, (?\beta, g_2), t')$, its guard determines whether the transition can take place based on the contents of the latest messages as well as the class and the contents of the message at the head of the queue. For a send transition $(t, (!\alpha, g_1), t')$, the guard g_1 determines not only the transition condition, but also the contents of the message being sent. For example, Figure 3 shows a Web service composition which realizes the conversation protocol in Figure 2. Note that, if the guard for a transition is not shown, then it means that the guard is "true."

The conversations produced by a Web service composition can be defined similarly as the language accepted by a guarded automaton. However, one important difference is that the effect of queues must be taken into account. To characterize the formal semantics of a conversation, we need to define the notion of *global configuration* of a Web service composition. A global configuration is used to capture a "snapshot" of the whole system. A global configuration contains the information about the local state and the queue contents of each peer, as well as the latest sent and received copies for each message class (so that the guards can be evaluated). The *initial configuration* of a Web service composition is obviously the one where each peer is in its initial state, each FIFO queue is empty, and the latest copies for each message class are the constant "undefined value." Similarly, a *final global configuration* is a configuration where each peer is in a final state, and each peer queue is empty. Then a *run* of a Web service composition can be defined as a sequence of global configurations, which starts from the initial configuration and ends with a final configuration. Between each pair of neighboring configurations c_i and c_{i+1} in a complete run, c_i evolves into c_{i+1} by taking one action by a peer. This action can be a send, receive (from queue), or ε-action which corresponds to a transition in that peer GA. Obviously, for this action to take place, the associated guard of that transition must be satisfied. A *conversation* is a message sequence, for which there is a corresponding run.

Now given both the definitions of conversation protocols and Web service compositions, we can define the notion of *realizability* that relates them. Let $C(S)$ denote the set of conversations of a Web service composition S. We say S *realizes* a conversation protocol R if $C(S) = L(R)$.

Conversion Between Top-Down and Bottom-Up Specifications

One interesting question concerning the specification of Web service compositions is if it is possible to convert a specification from top-down specification to bottom-up, and vice versa. This section introduces two operations to achieve this goal, namely "projection" and "product" operations. The projection of a conversation protocol produces a Web service composition, and the product of a Web service composition produces a conversation protocol. However, the projection of a conversation protocol is not guaranteed to generate exactly the same set of conversations as specified by the protocol. Similarly, the product of a bottom-up Web service composition is not guaranteed to specify all the possible conversations that can be generated by that Web service composition. Only when additional conditions (such as the ones presented in the skeleton analysis in later sections) are satisfied, can the projection and the product operations be used to convert from one specification approach to the other while preserving the semantics (i.e., the set of conversations).

Product

Intuitively, the product operation is to construct the synchronous composition of a set of guarded automata. In synchronous composition, each send operation and the corresponding receive operation must be executed simultaneously. Formally, the product operation is defined as follows:

Definition 4 (Production): *Leg $S = ((P, M, \Sigma), A_1, ..., A_n)$ be a Web service composition, where for each $i \in [1..n]$, A_i is a tuple $(M_i, \Sigma_i, T_i, s_i, F_i, \delta_i)$. The product of all peers in S is a GA $A' = (M, \Sigma, T', s', F', \delta')$, where each state $t' \in T'$ is a tuple $(t_1, ..., t_n)$, such that for each $i \in [1..n]$, t_i is a state of peer A_i. The initial state s' of A' corresponds to the tuple $(s_1, ..., s_n)$, and a final state in F' corresponds to a tuple $(f_1, ..., f_n)$ where for each $i \in [1..n]$, f_i is a final state of A_i. Let ρ map each state $t' \in T'$ to the corresponding tuple, and further let $\rho(t')[i]$ denote the i'th element of $\rho(t')$. For each pair of states t and t' in T', a transition $(t, (m, g'), t')$ is included in δ' if there exists two transitions $(t_i, (!m, g_i), t'_i) \in \delta_i$ and $(t_j, (?m, g_j), t'_j) \in \delta_j$ such that:*

1. (Sending and receiving peers take the send and receive transitions simultaneously)
    - $\rho(t)[i] = t_i$ and
    - $\rho(t')[i] = t'_i$ and
    - $\rho(t)[j] = t_j$ and
    - $\rho(t')[j] = t'_j$ and
    - for each $k \neq i \wedge k \neq j$, $\rho(t')[k] = \rho(t)[k]$, and

2. (Both guards need to hold) Let $g' = g_i \wedge g_j$, then g' must be satisfiable.

Clearly, by the above definition, the construction of the product can start from the initial state of the product (which corresponds to the tuple of initial states of all peers), then iteratively include new transitions and states. From a state in the product, a transition is added to point to another destination state, only if there is a pair of peers which execute the corresponding send and receive actions from the source state simultaneously. Obviously, the construction can always terminate because the number of transitions and the states of each peer are finite. However, the algorithm requires that none of the peer implementations should have ε-transitions. We will present the algorithm to remove ε-transitions later in this section.

Figure 4. The Infinite Content (IC) conversation protocol, which does not have an accurate projection to each peer

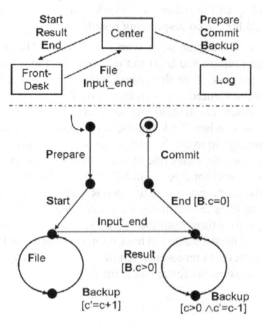

Projection

Projection of a GA conversation protocol is complex and interesting. For example, a GA conversation protocol with an infinite message alphabet may not always have an "exact" projection. However, if its message alphabet is finite, a GA conversation protocol is always guaranteed to have an exact projection. For GA conversation protocols with infinite message alphabet, several "coarse" approximation algorithms exist. We start our discussion with the following classification of conversation protocols.

Definition 5 (FC and IC Protocol): *A conversation protocol $R = ((P, M, \Sigma), A)$ is called an Infinite Content (IC) conversation protocol if Σ is an infinite set; otherwise R is called a Finite Content (FC) conversation protocol. Similarly, a guarded automaton is either an IC-GA or FC-GA, and a Web service composition is either an IC composition or a FC composition.*

An IC conversation protocol may not have an exact projection, as shown in the following example. Figure 4 presents an IC conversation protocol (call it R) which involves three peers Front-Desk, processing Center, and Log center. The processing Center processes files from Front-Desk in a batch sequential mode. For each incoming file, a backup of the request is recorded in the Log center and another backup is also created for the corresponding result.

The interaction between the three peers works as follows. The processing Center first sends a message **Prepare** and **Start** to the Front-Desk and Log center respectively to initiate the process. Then the Front-Desk sends a collection of **Files** one by one to the processing Center. For each incoming **File**, a corresponding **Backup** copy is sent to Log center. The **Backup** message has a counter named "c" to count the number of messages. When the Front-Desk has sent out all the cases, it sends out an **Input_end** message to mark the end of the data input process. The processing Center then processes the cases one by one, sends out a corresponding **Result** message to Front-Desk, accompanied with a **Backup** message for each **Result**. The counter attribute of the **Backup** message for each **Result** is decremented by one each time until its values reaches zero. Finally, the processing Center sends out the **End** and **Commit** message to inform both the Front-Desk and Log center to complete the interaction. Here all messages do not have contents except the **Backup** message. If we use the first character to represent each message, obviously the conversation set can be represented using the following formula:

Figure 5. Algorithm of coarse projection from a Guarded Automaton A to peer i

```
Procedure ProjectGA (((P, M, Σ), A), i): GA
Begin
   Let A' = (M, Σ, T, s₀, F, δ) be a copy of A.
   Substitute each (q₁, (a, g₁), q₂)
       where a ∉ Mᵢ with (q₁, (ε, g₁'), q₂).
   Substitute each (q₁, (a, g₂), q₂)
       where a ∈ Mᵢⁱⁿ with (q₁, (?a, g₂'), q₂).
   Substitute each (q₁, (a, g₃), q₂)
       where a ∈ Mᵢᵒᵘᵗ with (q₁, (!a, g₃'), q₂).
   // Generate g₁', g₂' and g₃' using Coarse Processing 1 or 2
   // Coarse Processing 1:
   //   g₁' = g₂'= "true", and g₃' = g₃.
   // Coarse Processing 2:
   //   g₁', g₂' are the predicates generated from g₁, g₂ (resp.),
   //   by eliminating unrelated message attributes
   //   via existential quantification, e.g., g₁' ≡ ∃₍ₘ|ₘ∉Mᵢ₎ g₁
   //   g₃' = g₃.
   return A'.
End
```

PS(FB)^{n}I(RB)^{n}EC

If we project this conversation set to peer Log center, it is not hard to see that the projection is the following set $\{\mathbf{PB^nB^nC} \mid n \geq 0\}$, which is obviously a context-free language. However, since none of the messages (sent or received) by peer Log center has message contents, any GA with the alphabet of Log center is essentially a standard FSA, and it cannot accept the projection language, which is not regular.

On the contrary, for FC conversation protocols, it is always possible to construct a corresponding projected composition S_P^{PROJ} where each peer implementation of S_P^{PROJ} is an "exact" projection of P. Given a conversation protocol $R = ((P, M, \Sigma), A)$, where $n = |P|$, since Σ is finite, we can easily construct a standard FSA A' from A such that $L(A') = L(A)$, where the alphabet of A' is the message alphabet Σ of A. The construction of A' is essentially an exploration of all reachable global configurations of A. Note that since Σ is finite, the number of global configurations of A is finite; hence, the size of A' is finite. Let the projection of A' to each peer be A_1, ..., A_n, respectively. Obviously, each of the standard FSA A_1, ..., A_n can be converted into an equivalent GA by associating dummy guards with each transition.

The construction of S_R^{PROJ}, however, can be very costly—it requires essentially a reachability analysis of the state space of the FC conversation protocol. In Figure

Figure 6. Elimination of ε-transitions for guarded automata

```
1.  Procedure ElimGA(A): GA
2.  Begin
3.    Let A' = ⟨M, Σ, T, s, F, δ⟩ be a copy of A.
4.    For each t ⊂ T Do
5.      insert each t' reachable from t via ε-paths into ε-closure(t).
6.    End For
7.    // let Υ(t, t') be the set of non-redundant ε-paths from t to t'.
8.    // each transition in δ appears at most once
          //in a non-redundant path.
9.    // let cond(μ) be the conjunction of
          //all guards along a non-redundant path μ.
10.   For each transition (t, (m, g), t') ∈ δ do
11.     insert transition (t, (m, g'), t') into δ for each t'' in ε-closure(t'),
12.     where g' = g ∧ g'' and
            g'' = ⋁_{μ∈Υ(t',t'')} cond(μ)
13.   End For
14.   eliminate all ε-transitions from δ.
15.   return A'
16. End
```

5, we present a lightweight projection algorithm, which is not "exact" but works for both FC and IC conversation protocols.

Given a GA protocol and a peer to project, the *coarse projection* algorithm in Figure 5 simply replaces each transition that is not related to the peer with ε-transitions, and adds "!" and "?" for send and receive transitions respectively. The algorithm provides two different levels of "coarse processing." In Coarse Processing 1, the guards of the ε-transitions and the receive transitions are essentially dropped (by setting them to "true"), and the guards of the send transitions remain the same. In Coarse Processing 2, *existential quantification* is used to eliminate the unrelated message attributes from the guards. The following example illustrates the existential quantification operation.

Given a GA conversation protocol on three peers p_1, p_2, and p_3, let $\tau = (t, (m_1, g), t')$ be a transition in the protocol, where $m_1 \in M_3^{out} \cap M_1^{in}$, $m_2 \notin M_1$, and $g \equiv m_1.\text{id} + m_2.\text{id} < 3 \wedge m_2.\text{id} > 0$.

We assume that $m_1.\text{id}$ and $m_2.\text{id}$ are both of integer type. During the projection to peer p_1, if τ is being processed using Coarse Processing 1, the corresponding transition would be $(t, (?m_1, true), t')$; if Coarse Processing 2 is used, the corresponding transition would be $(t, (?m_1, g'), t')$ where $g' \equiv \exists\, m_2.\text{id } g$, and after simplification, $g' \equiv m_1.\text{id} < 2$.

Given a GA conversation protocol R, the Web service composition generated using coarse-1 and coarse-2 processing algorithms are denoted as $S_R^{PROJ,C1}$ and $S_R^{PROJ,C2}$ respectively. Clearly $S_R^{PROJ,C1}$ and $S_R^{PROJ,C2}$ have the following relationship.

Given a conversation protocol $R = ((P, M, \Sigma), A)$, and its projections $S_R^{PROJ,C1}$ and $S_R^{PROJ,C2}$ for each $1 \leq i \leq |P|$, let A_i^{C1} and A_i^{C2} be the peer implementation of p_i in $S_R^{PROJ,C1}$ and $S_R^{PROJ,C2}$(respectively). Then the following holds: $\pi_i(L(R)) \subseteq L(A_i^{C2}) \subseteq L(A_i^{C1})$—that is, the actual projection language is contained by the resulting set produced by the approximation algorithms.

Determinization of Guarded Automata

We now introduce a "determinization" algorithm for guarded automata which is useful in the decision procedures for realizability conditions. The determinization process consists of two steps: (1) to eliminate the ε-transitions, and (2) to determinize the result from step 1.

The ε-transition elimination algorithm is presented in Figure 6, which is an extension of the ε-transition elimination algorithm for standard FSA. It first collects a set of nodes that are reachable via ε-paths for each node. Then for each pair of nodes that are connected by an ε-path plus one normal transition, the algorithm packs the guards associated with the ε-path to the non-ε-transition so that the ε-path can be

Figure 7. Determinization of guarded automata

```
1.  Procedure DeterminizeGA(A): GA
2.  Begin
3.    Let A' = (M, Σ, T, s, F, δ) be a copy of ElimGA(A).
4.    Mark all states in T as "unprocessed".
5.    For each "unprocessed" state t ∈ T Do
6.      For each message class m ∈ M Do
7.        Let {τ₁, ..., τᵢ} include each τᵢ = (t, (m, gᵢ), tᵢ')
              which starts from t and sends m.
8.        mark each τᵢ as "toRemove"
9.        For each c = μ₁ ∧ ... ∧ μₖ where μⱼ is gⱼ or ¬gⱼ
            (however c ≠ ¬g₁ ∧ ¬g₂ ... ∧ ¬gₖ) Do
10.          If c is satisfiable Then
11.            Let s' be a new state name, include s' in T.
12.            include (t, (m, c), s') in δ.
13.            For each j ∈ [1..k] s.t. gⱼ appears in c Do
14.              For each transition τ' = (tⱼ', (m', g'), tⱼ'')
                  from tⱼ' and each τ'' = (s'', (m'', g''), tⱼ') to tⱼ' do
15.                include (s', (m', g'), tⱼ'') in δ
                   include (s'', (m'', g''), s') in δ
16.                mark τ', τ'' as "toRemove".
                   mark tⱼ' as "toRemove".
17.              End For
18.            End For
19.          End If
20.        End For
21.      End For
22.    End For
23.    remove all states and transitions marked as "toRemove".
24.    return A'
25. End
```

eliminated. This operation is accomplished at line 11 of Figure 6. The transition $(t, (m, g'), t'')$ is a replacement for a set of paths, where each path is a concatenation of the transition $(t, (m, g), t')$ and an ε-path from t' to t''. The guard g' has to be the conjunction of g and g'' where g'' is the disjunction of the conjunctions of guards along each ε-path from t' to t''. Note that for each ε-transition, its guard is only a "transition condition" which does not affect the message instance vector in a GA configuration, according to the guarded automata model. Hence it suffices to consider those non-redundant paths. Since the number of non-redundant paths is finite, the algorithm in Figure 6 will always terminate.

Figure 7 presents the determinization algorithm for a guarded automaton, which is rather different than the determinization algorithm for a standard FSA. The key idea is the part between lines 9 and 20, where for each state and each message class, we collect all the transitions for that message class, enumerate every combination of guards, and generate a new transition for that combination. For example, suppose at some state t, two transitions are collected for message class m, and let their guards be g_1 and g_2 respectively. Three new transitions $g_1 \wedge g_2$, $g_1 \wedge \neg g_2$, and $\neg g_1 \wedge g_2$ will be generated, and the two original transitions are removed from the transition relation. It is not hard to see that for each word $w \in L(A')$, where A' is the resulting GA, there exists one and only one run for w, due to the enumeration of the combinations of guards. Since the procedure of enumerating guards and reassembling states does not deviate from the semantics of the original guards, for example, $g_1 \wedge g_2 \vee g_1 \wedge \neg g_2 \vee \neg g_1 \wedge g_2 = g_1 \vee g_2$, each A is equivalent to its determinization A' (after applying DeterminizeGA)—that is, $L(A) = L(A')$.

Figure 8. Two examples that demonstrate the relationship between a conversation protocol and its skeleton. (a) is an example where the GA conversation protocol is not realizable but its skeleton is. (b) is an example of realizable GA conversation protocol which has a non-realizable skeleton.

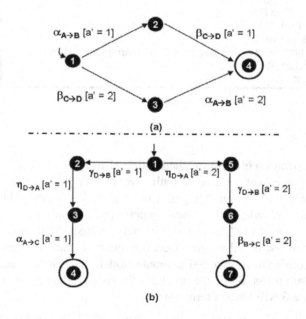

Skeleton Analysis

One interesting question concerning the GA model is: Can the realizability analysis of a GA protocol be conducted using the techniques available on the standard FSA model? This section answers this question and shows that an abstract analysis method called *skeleton analysis* works for both FC and IC conversation protocols. We start with the definition of a skeleton.

Definition 6 (Skeleton): *Given a GA $A = (M, \Sigma, T, s, F, \delta)$, its skeleton, denoted as skeleton(A), is a standard FSA (M, T, s, F, δ') where δ' is obtained from δ by replacing each transition $(s, (c, g), t)$ with (s, c, t).*

Note that $L(skeleton(A)) \subseteq M$, while $L(A)$ is a subset of Σ. For a conversation protocol $R = ((P, M, \Sigma), A)$, we can always construct an FSA conversation protocol $((P, M), skeleton(A))$. We call this protocol the *skeleton protocol* of P. Now, one natural question is the following: If the skeleton protocol of a conversation protocol is realizable, does this imply that the GA protocol is realizable?

We can easily find counter examples against the above conjecture. As shown in Figure 8a, four peers A, B, C, and D are involved in a guarded conversation protocol. Message α is from A to B and β is from C to D. Both message classes have an attribute a. The protocol specifies two possible conversations $\alpha(1)\beta(1)$ and $\beta(2)\alpha(2)$, where the "1" and "2" are values of attribute a in messages. Obviously, the skeleton protocol, which specifies the conversation set $\{\alpha\beta, \beta\alpha\}$, is realizable because it satisfies all three realizability conditions. However, the guarded protocol itself is not realizable, because any implementation that generates the specified conversations will also generate the conversation $\beta(1)\alpha(1)$.

Interestingly, there exist examples where the skeleton is not realizable but the guarded conversation protocol is. In addition, the lossless join and synchronous compatibility conditions of a guarded conversation protocol are not implied by the corresponding properties satisfied by its skeleton, and vice versa.

For example, the GA protocol in Figure 8a is not lossless join, however its skeleton is. The guarded protocol in Figure 8b is lossless join, however its skeleton is not. As shown in Figure 8b, there are four peers A, B, C, and D, and all message classes contain a single attribute a. In the beginning, peer D informs peers A and B about which path to take by the value of the attribute a (1 for left branch, 2 for right branch). Then A and B know who is going to send the last message (α or β), so there is no ambiguity. It can be verified that the protocol is lossless join. However the skeleton is obviously not lossless join, because $\eta\gamma\alpha$ is included in its join closure.

The counter examples in Figure 8 seem to suggest pessimistic results—we cannot tell if a conversation protocol is realizable or not based on the properties of its skeleton protocol. However, in the following, we will show that with an additional condition, we can use the properties of a protocol's skeleton to reason about its realizability. We now introduce a fourth realizability condition to restrict a conversation protocol so that it can be realized by $S_R^{\text{PROJ}}, S_R^{\text{PROJ},\mathbb{C}}$, and $S_R^{\text{PROJ},\mathbb{C}}$ when its skeleton satisfies the three realizability conditions discussed above.

Definition 7 (Deterministic Guard Condition): *Let $R = ((P, M, \Sigma), A)$ be a conversation protocol where $A = (M, \Sigma, T, s, F, \delta)$. R is said to satisfy the deterministic guard condition if for each pair of transitions $(t_1, (m_1, g_1), t_1')$ and $(t_2, (m_2, g_2), t_2')$, g_1 is equivalent to g_2 when the following conditions hold:*

1. $m_1 = m_2$, *and*
2. *Let p_i be the sender of m_1. There exists two words w and w' where a partial run of w reaches t_1, and a partial run of w' reaches t_2, and $\pi_i(\pi_{TYPE}(w)) = \pi_i(\pi_{TYPE}(w'))$.*

Here the operation π_{TYPE} projects a conversation to a sequence of message classes by replacing each message in the conversation with its message class. Intuitively, the deterministic guard condition requires that for each peer, according to the conversation protocol, when it is about to send out a message, the guard that is used to compute the contents of the message is uniquely decided by the sequence of message classes (note, not message contents) exchanged by the peer in the past.

The decision procedure for the deterministic guard condition proceeds as follows:

Given a conversation protocol R, obtain its coarse-1 projection $S_R^{\text{PROJ},\mathbb{C}}$, and let $S_R^{\text{PROJ},\mathbb{C}}$ $= ((P, M, \Sigma), A_1, ..., A_n)$. For each $i \in [1..n]$, regard A_i as a standard FSA, and get its equivalent deterministic FSA (let it be A_i'). Now each state t in A_i' corresponds to a set of states in A_i, and let it be represented by $T(t)$. We examine each state t in A_i'. For each message class $c \in M$, we collect the guards of the transitions that start from a state in $T(t)$ and send a message with class c. We require that all guards collected for a state/message class pair (t, c) should be equivalent.

Running the algorithm on Figure 8a leads to the result that Figure 8a violates the deterministic guard condition, because (intuitively) peer A has two different guards when sending out α at the initial state. Formally, to show that the deterministic guard condition is violated, we can find two transitions $(t_1, (\alpha, [a' = 1]), t_2)$ and $(t_3, (\alpha, [a' = 2]), t_4)$, and two words $w = \varepsilon$ and $w' = \beta(2)$ that lead to the states t_1 and t_3, respectively. Since a run of w reaches t_1, a run of w' reaches t_3, and $\pi_A(\pi_{\text{TYPE}}(w)) = \pi_A(\pi_{\text{TYPE}}(w')) = \varepsilon$. By Definition 7, the guards of the two transitions should be equivalent. However, they are not equivalent, which violates the deterministic guard condition.

Theorem 2. *A conversation protocol R is realized by S_R^{PROJ}, $S_R^{\text{PROJ,C}}$, and $S_R^{\text{PROJ,C}}$ if it satisfies the deterministic guard condition, and its skeleton protocol satisfies the lossless join, synchronous compatibility, and autonomy conditions.*

The main proof idea of Theorem 2 is as follows. First, we argue that if the skeleton protocol satisfies the synchronous compatibility and autonomy conditions, then during any (complete or partial) run of $S_R^{\text{D PROJ,C}}$, each message is consumed "eagerly"—that is, when the input queue is not empty, a peer never sends out a message or terminates.

The "eager consumption" argument can be proved using proof by contradiction (Fu et al., 2003). Assume that there is a partial run against this argument—that is, we can find a corresponding partial run of the skeleton composition of $S_R^{\text{D PROJ,C}}$ (which consists of the skeletons of each peer of $S_R^{\text{D PROJ,C}}$) where a message class is not consumed eagerly (without loss of generality, suppose this is the shortest one). Then there must be a pair of consecutive configurations where a peer i has a message at the head of its queue and it sends a message rather than receiving the message. Due to synchronous compatible condition, we know that peer i should be able to receive

Figure 9. Alternating bit protocol

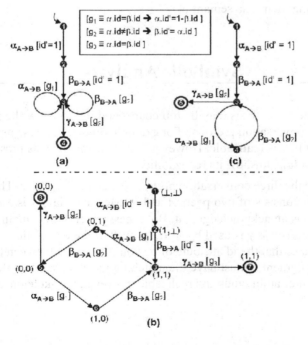

the message at the head of the queue immediately after it was sent. We also know that due to autonomy condition, peer i can only execute receive transitions if it has one receive transition from a configuration. Then, sending a message will violate these conditions and create a contradiction. Hence we conclude that each message class is consumed eagerly.

Now it suffices to show that $C(S_R^{D,PROJ,C1}) \subseteq L(R)$, as $L(R) \subseteq C(S_R^{D,PROJ,C1})$ is obvious. Let $R = ((P, M, \Sigma), A)$ and let $S_R^{D,PROJ,C1} = ((P, M, \Sigma), A_1, ..., A_n)$. Given a word $w \in C(S_R^{D,PROJ,C1})$, and γ being the corresponding run, we can always construct a run γ' of A to recognize w. Since $\pi_i(w)$ is accepted by each peer A_i, $\pi_i(\pi_{TYPE}(w))$ is accepted by $skeleton(A_i)$. Because $skeleton(A)$ is lossless join, it follows that $\pi_{TYPE}(w)$ is accepted by $skeleton(A)$, and let $T : \tau_1 \tau_2 ... \tau_{|w|}$ be the path of $skeleton(A)$ traversed to accept $\pi_{TYPE}(w)$. Since each transition in $skeleton(A)$ is the result of dropping the guard of a corresponding transition, we can have a corresponding path T' in A by restoring message contents. Notice that we can always do so because in each step, the global configuration allows the guards to be evaluated as if it is executed synchronously. This results from the fact that whenever a message is to be sent, its contents always depend on the latest copies of arrived messages, because queue is empty and every input message which causally happens before it has already been consumed.

Based on Theorem 2, we obtain a lightweight realizability analysis for conversation protocols. We check the first three realizability conditions on the skeleton of a conversation protocol (i.e., without considering the guards), and then examine the fourth realizability condition by syntactically checking the guards (but actually without analyzing their data semantics).

Symbolic Analysis

Sometimes skeleton analysis may be too coarse and fail to show the realizability of a realizable conversation protocol. For example, Figure 9a presents an alternating bit protocol that is realizable. However, the skeleton analysis presented in the previous section fails to show its realizability.

Let A_a, A_b, A_c be the three conversation protocols shown in Figure 9. The conversation protocol A_a consists of two peers A and B. Message class α is a request, and message class β is an acknowledgment. Both message classes contain an attribute called id. Message class γ is used by A to notify B of the end of the conversation. The protocol states that the id attribute of α should alternate between 0 and 1, and every acknowledgment β must have the matching id. It is clear that the conversation protocol is non-ambiguous and realizable; however, the skeleton analysis fails to recognize it.

Clearly the projection of *skeleton(A_a)* to peer A does not satisfy the autonomy condition, because at state 3, there are both input and output transitions. However, A_a is actually autonomous. If we explore each configuration of A_a, we get A_b, the "equivalent" conversation protocol of A_a. The pair of values associated with each state in A_b stands for the id attribute of α and β. It is obvious that A_b satisfies the autonomy condition, and hence A_a should satisfy autonomy as well. In fact, to prove that A_a is autonomous, we do not even have to explore each of its configurations like A_b. As we will show later, it suffices to show A_c is autonomous.

Analysis of Autonomy Using Iterative Refinement

The examples in Figure 9 motivate the analysis of the autonomous condition using iterative refinement (Fu et al., 2004c, 2005a) as follows: Given a conversation protocol A, we can first check its skeleton. If the skeleton analysis fails, we can refine the protocol (e.g., refine A_a and get A_c), and apply the skeleton analysis on the refined protocol. We can repeat this procedure until we reach the most refined protocol which actually plots the transition graph of the configurations of the original protocol (such as A_b to A_a). In the following, we first present the theoretical background for the analysis of the autonomy condition using iterative refinement. This analysis is based on the notion of *simulation*, which is defined below.

A transition system is a tuple (M, T, s, Δ) where M is the set of labels, T is the set of states, s the initial state, and Δ is the transition relation. Generally, a transition system can be regarded as an FSA (or an infinite state system) without final states. On the other hand, a standard FSA (M, T, s, F, Δ) can be regarded as a transition system of (M, T, s, Δ); and a GA $(M, \Sigma, T, s, F, \Delta)$ can be regarded as a transition system of the form $(\Sigma, T', s', \Delta')$ where T' contains all configurations of the GA, and Δ' defines the derivation relation between configurations.

Definition 8 (Simulation): *A transition system $A' = (M', T', s', \Delta')$ is said to simulate another transition system $A = (M, T, s, \Delta)$, written as $A \leq A'$, if there exists a mapping $\rho : T \rightarrow T'$ and $\xi : M \rightarrow M'$ such that for each (s, m, t) in Δ there is a $(\rho(s), \xi(m), \rho(t))$ in Δ'. Two transition systems A and A' are said to be equivalent, written as $A \cong A'$, if $A \leq A'$ and $A' \leq A$.*

Intuitively a transition A' simulates A if we can find a corresponding action in A' for every action of A—that is, A' can subsume the set of actions of A. For example, the following is true for the three conversation protocols A_a, A_b, A_c in Figure 9:

$$skeleton(A_b) \leq skeleton(A_c) \leq skeleton(A_a)$$

For example, in the simulation relation $skeleton(A_c) \leq skeleton(A_a)$, ρ maps states 1, 2, 3, 4, 5 in $skeleton(A_c)$ to states 1, 2, 3, 3, 4 of $skeleton(A_a)$ respectively, and ξ is the identity function which maps each message class to itself. For another example, $A_a \leq skeleton(A_a)$, and $A_a \leq A_b \leq A_c$.

It is not hard to infer the following properties of simulation relation; detailed proof can be found in Fu et al.'s (2004c) work:

- For any GA A, $A \leq skeleton(A)$. In others word, the skeleton of a conversation protocol simulates the protocol.

Figure 10. The algorithm which examines the autonomy condition of a guarded conversation protocol using iterative refinement

```
Procedure AnalyzeAutonomy(A): List
Begin
   A' = DeterminizeGA(A)
   While true do
      If skeleton of A' is autonomous Then return null
      Find a pair (s, (m₁, g.), t.), (s, (m₂, g₂), t₂) violating autonomy
      (A', trace) = Refine(A', (s, (m₁, g.), t₁), (s, (m₂, g₂), t₂))
      If trace ≠ null Then return trace
   End While
End


Procedure Refine(A, (s, (m₁, g₁), t₁), (s, (m₂, g₂), t₂)) : (GA, List)
Begin
   If (Pre(g.) ∧ Pre(g₂)) is satisfiable then
      Path = FindPath(A, s, Pre(g₁) ∧ Pre(g₂))
      If Path ≠ null then
         return (null, Path)
      End If
   End If
   Let A' = (M', T', s_c', F', Δ') be a copy of A
   T' = T' − {s} + {s., s₂}, F' = F' − {s} + {s., s₂} if s ∈ F'
   Substitute each (t, (m_j, g_j), s) in Δ' s.t. m_j ≠ m₁ and m_j ≠ m₂
      with (t, (m_j, g_j), s₁) and (t, (m_j, g_j), s₂)
   Substitute each (s, (m_j, g_j), t) in Δ' s.t. m_j ≠ m₁ and m_j ≠ m₂
      with (s., (m_j, g_j), t) and (s₂, (m_j, g_j), t)
   Substitute (s, (m., g₁), t₁) in Δ' with (s., (m., g₁), t₁)
   Substitute (s, (m₂, g₂), t₂) in Δ' with (s₂, (m₂, g₂), t₂)
   Remove all unreachable transitions
   return (A', null)
End
```

- For each GA $A = (M, \Sigma, T, s, F, \Delta)$ on a finite alphabet Σ, there is a standard FSA on alphabet Σ such that $A \cong A'$. This can be easily achieved by exploring the configuration space of the GA protocol, which is finite.

- If $A \leq A'$ and A' is autonomous, then A is autonomous. The proof follows directly from the fact that each run of A has a corresponding run in A'. If during each run of A', autonomy condition is not violated, obviously any run of A will not violate it either.

Figure 11. Generation of a concrete error trace

```
Procedure FindPath(A, s, g₀): List
Begin
  Let A = (M, T, s₀, F, Δ)
  Let T be
```

$$\bigcup_{(s_i, (m_j, g_k), s_i') \in \Delta} g_k \wedge \mathit{state} = s_i \wedge \mathit{state}' = s_i'$$

```
  Stack path = new Stack()
  Let g = state = s ∧ g₀
  g' = false
  stack.push(g)
  While g ≠ g' and g ∧ state = s₀ is not satisfiable do
    g' = g
```

$$g = (\exists M' (g_{M'/M} \wedge T)) \vee g'$$

```
    path.push(g-g')
  End While
  If g ∧ state = s₀ is not satisfiable Then
    return null
  Else
    path = reverse order of path
    List ret = new List()
    cvalue = a concrete value of path[1]
    For i =1 to |path| do
      ret.append(cvalue)
      cvalue = a concrete value in
```

$$(\exists M \text{ cvalue} \wedge T)_{M/M'} \wedge \text{path}[i+1]$$

```
    End For
    return ret
  End If
End
```

From the above results, we can immediately infer the following:

Theorem 3. *A GA conversation protocol is autonomous if its skeleton is autonomous.*

Based on Theorem 3 we have an error-trace guided symbolic analysis algorithm, presented in Figure 10. If the input GA is autonomous, procedure AnalyzeAutonomy returns null; otherwise it returns the error trace which is a list of configurations that eventually leads to the violation of the autonomy condition. AnalyzeAutonomy starts from the input GA, and refines it incrementally. During each cycle, it analyzes the skeleton of the current GA A'. If the skeleton is autonomous, by Theorem 3, the procedure simply returns and reports that the input GA is autonomous; otherwise, it identifies a pair of input/output transitions violating autonomy. For example, the two transitions starting at state 3 of Figure 9a will be identified. Then the Refine procedure is invoked to refine the current GA. This refinement process continues until the input GA is proved to be autonomous or a concrete error trace is found.

The bottom part of Figure 10 presents the algorithm of the Refine procedure. Its input includes two transitions (with guards g_1 and g_2 respectively) which lead to the violation of the autonomy condition on the skeleton. The Refine procedure will try to refine the current GA by splitting the source state of these two transitions. If refinement succeeds, the refined GA is returned; otherwise, a concrete error trace is returned to show that the input GA is not autonomous.

The first step of Refine is to compute the conjunction of the precondition of the two guards—that is, $\mathrm{Pre}(g_1) \wedge \mathrm{Pre}(g_2)$. If the conjunction is satisfiable, there is a possibility that at some configuration, both transitions are enabled. Then we call the procedure FindPath to find a concrete error trace, which will be explained later. If the conjunction is not satisfiable, we can proceed to refine the GA. The basic idea is to split the source state of the two transitions into two states; each corresponds to the precondition of one guard in the input. The transitions are re-wired correspondingly. Finally the procedure eliminates transitions that cannot be reached during any execution of the GA.

For example, if Refine is applied to Figure 9a and the two transitions starting at state 3, it first computes the conjunction of the two preconditions: $\alpha.id \neq \beta.id \wedge \alpha.id = \beta.id$. Obviously the conjunction is not satisfiable. Then state 3 is split into two states (states 3 and 4 in Figure 9c), and transitions are modified accordingly. Finally, unreachable transitions are removed, which results in the GA in Figure 9c.

The precondition operator Pre is a standard operator in symbolic model checking in which all primed variables are eliminated using existential quantifier elimination. For example, given a constraint g as "$a = 1 \wedge b' = 1$", its precondition is $\mathrm{Pre}(g) \equiv \exists a' \exists b' (a = 1 \wedge b' = 1)$, which is equivalent to "$a = 1$".

Figure 11 presents the algorithm to locate a concrete error trace. FindPath has three inputs: a GA A, a state s in A, and a symbolic constraint g_0. FindPath computes an error trace (a list of configurations) which starts from the initial state of A, and finally reaches s in a configuration satisfying constraint g_0.

The algorithm of FindPath is a variation of the standard symbolic backward reachability analysis used in model checking. It starts with the construction of a symbolic transition system T based on the control flow as well as the data semantics of A. Then given the target constraint g_0, the main loop computes the constraint which generates g_0 via transition system T. The loop terminates when it reaches the initial configuration, or it reaches a fixed point.

We use the following example to illustrate the symbolic backward analysis. In the example of Figure 9a, if we redefine the guard g_2 as $\alpha.\text{id} = \beta.\text{id} \wedge \beta.\text{id'} = \alpha.\text{id}$, when procedure Refine is called on Figure 9a, the conjunction of preconditions of g_1 and g_2 (i.e., $\alpha.\text{id} = \beta.\text{id}$) is satisfiable. Then procedure FindPath is called with inputs Figure 9a, state 3, and constraint $\alpha.\text{id} = \beta.\text{id} \wedge \text{state} = 3$. The while loop of FindPath eventually includes in variable path the following constraints:\

1. $\alpha.\text{id} = \beta.\text{id} \wedge \text{state} = 3$.

2. $\alpha.\text{id} = 1 \wedge \text{state} = 2$.

3. $\text{state} = 1$.

For example, given formula 1, $\alpha.\text{id} = \beta.\text{id} \wedge \text{state} = 3$ at state 3, the guard of the transition from state 2 to state 3 is $\alpha.\text{id}' = \alpha.\text{id} \wedge \beta.\text{id}' = 1 \wedge \text{state}' = 3 \wedge \text{state} = 2$, using the formula $(\exists M'\ (g_{M'/M} \wedge T)$ to compute its backward image at state 2 (where $g_{M'/M}$ means to substitute every message in M with its corresponding primed form) we have:

$(\exists M'\ (g_{M'/M} \wedge T))$

$\equiv (\exists M'\ ((\alpha.\text{id} = \beta.\text{id} \wedge \text{state} = 3)_{M'/M} \wedge (\alpha.\text{id}' = \alpha.\text{id} \wedge \beta.\text{id}' = 1 \wedge \text{state} = 2 \wedge \text{state}' = 3)))$

$\equiv (\exists M'\ (\alpha.\text{id}' = \beta.\text{id}' \wedge \text{state}' = 3 \wedge \alpha.\text{id}' = \alpha.\text{id} \wedge \beta.\text{id}' = 1 \wedge \text{state} = 2 \wedge \text{state}' = 3))$

$\equiv \alpha.\text{id} = 1 \wedge \text{state} = 2$

Then the order of path is reversed, and cvalue is randomly generated which satisfies constraint state = 1 and each message attribute has an exact value in cvalue. For example, let cvalue be $\alpha.\text{id} = 1 \wedge \beta.\text{id} = 0$, then the list ret will record the following constraints:

1. $\alpha.\text{id} = 1 \wedge \beta.\text{id} = 0 \wedge \text{state} = 1$.
2. $\alpha.\text{id} = 1 \wedge \beta.\text{id} = 0 \wedge \text{state} = 2$.
3. $\alpha.\text{id} = 1 \wedge \beta.\text{id} = 1 \wedge \text{state} = 3$.

It is not hard to see that the above list of system configurations captures an error trace leading to state 3 which violates the autonomy condition.

Complexity of the algorithms in Figures 10 and 11 depends on the data domains associated with the input GA. When the message alphabet is finite, they are guaranteed to terminate. For infinite domains, a constant loop limit can be used to terminate algorithms by force; however, the analysis is still conservative.

Symbolic Analysis of Other Realizability Conditions

It is interesting to ask: Are there similar iterative analysis algorithms for the lossless join and synchronous compatibility conditions? The answer is negative, because the lossless join and synchronous compatibility of a GA conversation protocol do not depend on those of its skeleton. In other words, there exists a GA conversation protocol which is lossless join and whose skeleton is not. There also exists a GA conversation protocol which is not lossless join, however its skeleton is. Similar observation holds for synchronous compatibility.

In the following we introduce "conservative" symbolic analyses for these two conditions. We introduce the analysis for synchronous compatibility first. Recall the algorithm to check synchronous compatibility of an FSA conversation protocol. The protocol is projected to each peer and determinized (including ε-transition elimination). Then the Cartesian product is constructed from the deterministic projection to peers. Each state in the Cartesian product is examined. A state is called an illegal state if at the state some peer is not ready to receive a message that another peer is ready to send. Note that the determinization of each peer projection is a necessary step. The analysis of synchronous compatibility for a GA conversation protocol follows a same procedure. However, we must discuss two different cases on GA conversation protocols with finite or infinite domains. Given an FC conversation protocol R, we can always construct its exact equivalent FSA conversation protocol (let it be R') and use the synchronous compatibility analysis for standard FSA protocols to analyze R'. However, for IC conversation protocols we might not be able to do so, because there may not exist projections for IC conversation protocols. In the following, we introduce a "conservative" symbolic analysis for the synchronous compatible condition.

Given an IC (or FC) conversation protocol R, we can project it to each peer using coarse projection (either Coarse Processing 1 or Coarse Processing 2 in Figure 5).

Then we determinize each peer in $S_R^{\text{PROJ,C1}}$ (or $S_R^{\text{PROJ,C2}}$) using the DeterminizeGA in Figure 7. We construct the product of those determinized GAs. If no illegal state is found, the IC conversation protocol R is synchronous compatible. The method is conservative—that is, if an illegal state is found, R might still be synchronous compatible, because a coarse projection accepts a superset of the language accepted by the exact projection. However, if a conversation protocol is identified as synchronous compatible by the approximation algorithm, it is guaranteed to be truly synchronous compatible.

The analysis of lossless join condition is similar. Recall that each GA A can be regarded as a transition system and can be represented symbolically. Let $T(A)$ denote the symbolic transition system derived from A. From the initial configuration of A, we can compute all the reachable configurations of $T(A)$, and let the set of reachable configurations be S^A. Given A_1 and A_2, the following statement is true:

$$(S^{A1} \wedge T(A_1) \Rightarrow S^{A2} \wedge T(A_2)) \Rightarrow (L(A_1) \subseteq L(A_2)).$$

Intuitively, the equation means that if A_2 as a transition system is a superset of A_1—that is, for any reachable configuration, there are more enabled transitions in $T(A_2)$ than $T(A_1)$—then $L(A_2)$ should be a superset of $L(A_1)$. The equation naturally implies a symbolic analysis algorithm. Given a conversation protocol R (with finite or infinite domains), let its GA specification be A. We can project A using coarse projection. Then construct the product of $S_R^{\text{PROJ,C1}}$ (or $S_R^{\text{PROJ,C2}}$), and let it be A'. Then we construct $T(A)$ and $T(A')$, and compute S^A and $S^{A'}$. It is not hard to see that if $(S^{A'} \wedge T(A')) \Rightarrow (S^A \wedge T(A))$, we can conclude that R is lossless join. The above symbolic analysis algorithm is decidable when the domain is finite. When R has an infinite domain, we can simply use the approximate closure of S^A and $S^{A'}$, and it is still a conservative algorithm.

Conclusion

This chapter presents Bultan et al.'s (2003) discovery on the realizability problem of conversation protocols. The analysis can be conducted on two levels: the abstract level without data semantics and the concrete level with message contents. The chapter reveals the relationship between the realizability analyses on the two models. It is shown that realizability of the "skeleton" of a conversation protocol does not imply the realizability of the conversation protocol itself. Only by enforcing an additional condition are we able to identify some classes of realizable conversation protocols. When skeleton analysis is not precise enough, refined symbolic realizability analyses can be used to improve both the accuracy and efficiency of the analysis.

The skeleton realizability analysis presented in this chapter has been implemented as a part of the Web Service Analysis Tool (*WSAT*) (Fu et al., 2004d). The front-end of WSAT accepts industry Web service standards such as WSDL and BPEL. The core analysis engine of WSAT is based on the intermediate representation GA. The back-end employs model checker *SPIN* (Holzmann, 1997) for verification. At the front-end, a translation algorithm from BPEL to GA is implemented. Then at the core analysis part, realizability analysis and another similar analysis called "synchronizability analysis" are implemented to avoid the difficulty of verification in the presence of asynchronous communication. At the back-end, translation algorithms are implemented from GA to Promela, the input language of SPIN. Based on the results of the realizability and the synchronizability analyses, LTL verification at the back-end can be performed using the synchronous communication semantics instead of asynchronous communication semantics. WSAT is applied to verify a wide range of examples, including conversation protocols converted from IBM Conversation Support Project (IBM, n.d.), five BPELS services from BPEL4WS standard and Collaxa.com, and the SAS example (Fu et al., 2004d). The empirical experiences suggest that the realizability conditions presented in this chapter can capture a large class of real-world Web service designs.

References

Abadi, M., Lamport, L., & Wolper, P. (1989). Realizable and unrealizable specifications of reactive systems. *Proceedings of the 16th International Colloquium on Automata, Languages and Programming* (pp. 1-17).

Alur, A., Etessami, K., & Yannakakis, M. (2001). Realizability and verification of MSC graphs. *Proceedings of the 28th International Colloquium on Automata, Languages, and Programming* (pp. 797-808).

Alur, R., McMillan, K. , & Peled, D. (2000). Model-checking of correctness conditions for concurrent objects. *Information and Computation, 160,* 167-188.

Andrews, T., Curbera, F., Dholakia, H., Goland, Y., Klein, J., Leymann, F. et al, (2003). *Business Process Execution Language for Web services (BPEL) 1.1.* Retrieved from http://www.ibm.com/developerworks/library/wsbpel

Banerji, A., Bartolini, C., Beringer, D., Chopella, V. , Govindarajan, K., Karp, A., Kuno, H. , Lemon, M. , Pogossiants, G., Sharma, S., & Williams, S. (2002). *Web Services Conversation Language (WSCL) 1.0.* Retrieved from http://www. w3.org/TR/2002/NOTE-wscl10-20020314/

Betin-Can, A., Bultan, T., & Fu, X. (2005). Design for verification for asynchronously communicating Web services. *Proceedings of the 14th International Conference on World Wide Web* (WWW).

Brand, D., & Zafiropulo, P. (1983). On communicating finite-state machines. *Journal of the ACM, 30*(2), 323-342.

Bultan, T., Fu, X., Hull, R., & Su, J. (2003). Conversation specification: A new approach to design and analysis of e-service composition. *Proceedings of the 12th International World Wide Web Conference* (WWW) (pp. 403-410).

Canfora, G., & Di Penta, M. (2006). Testing services and service-centric systems: Challenges and opportunities. *IT Professional, 8*(2), 10-17.

Clarke, E.M., Grumberg, O., & Peled, D. A. (2000). *Model checking.* Cambridge, MA: MIT Press.

Foster, H. , Uchitel, S., Magee, J. , & Kramer, J. (2003). Model-based verification of Web service compositions. *Proceedings of the 18th IEEE International Conference on Automated Software Engineering Conference* (ASE) (pp. 152-161).

Fu, X., Bultan, T., & Su, J. (2003). Conversation protocols: A formalism for specification and verification of reactive electronic services. *Proceedings of the 8th International Conference on Implementation and Application of Automata* (CIAA) (pp. 188-200).

Fu, X., Bultan, T., & Su, J. (2004a). Analysis of interacting Web services. *Proceedings of the 13th International World Wide Web Conference* (WWW) (pp. 621-630).

Fu, X., Bultan, T., & Su, J. (2004b). Model checking XML manipulating software. *Proceedings of the 2004 International Symposium on Software Testing and Analysis* (ISSTA) (pp. 252-262).

Fu, X., Bultan, T., & Su, J. (2004c).Realizability of conversation protocols with message contents. *Proceedings of the 2004 IEEE International Conference on Web Services* (ICWS) (pp. 96-103).

Fu, X., Bultan, T., & Su, J. (2004d). WSAT: A tool for formal analysis of Web service compositions. *Proceedings of the 16th International Conference on Computer Aided Verification* (CAV) (pp. 510-514).

Fu, X., Bultan, T., & Su, J. (2004e). Conversation protocols: A formalism for specification and analysis of reactive electronic services. *Theoretical Computer Science, 328*(1-2), 19-37.

Fu, X., Bultan, T., & Su, J. (2005a). Realizability of conversation protocols with message contents (extended version of the ICWS'04 paper). *International Journal of Web Services Research, 2*(4), 68-93.

Fu, X., Bultan, T., & Su, J. (2005b). Synchronizability of conversations among Web services. *IEEE Transactions on Software Engineering, 31*(12), 1042-1055.

Hanson, J.E., Nandi, P., & Kumaran, S. (2002a). Conversation support for business process integration. *Proceedings of the 6th IEEE International Enterprise Distributed Object Computing Conference* (EDOC) (pp. 65-74).

Hanson, J.E., Nandi, P., & Levine, D.W. (2002b). Conversation-enabled Web services for agents and e-business. *Proceedings of the 2002 International Conference on Internet Computing* (IC) (pp. 791-796).

Holzmann, G.J. (1997) The model checker SPIN. *IEEE Transactions on Software Engineering, 23*(5), 279-295.

IBM. (n.d.). *Conversation support project.* Retrieved February 14, 2007, from *http://www.research.ibm.com/convsupport/*

ITU-T. (1994). *Message Sequence Chart (MSC).* Geneva Recommendation Z.120, ITU-T.

Microsoft. (n.d.). *Microsoft message queuing service.* Retrieved February 14, 2007, from *http://www.microsoft.com/msmq/*

Narayanan, S., & McIlraith, S.A. (2002) Simulation, verification and automated composition of Web services. *Proceedings of the 11th International World Wide Web Conference* (WWW) (pp. 77-88).

Pnueli, A., & Rosner, R. (1989). On the synthesis of a reactive module. *Proceedings of the 16th ACM Symposium on Principles of Programming Languages* (pp. 179-190).

Sun. (n.d.). *Java message service.* Retrieved February 14, 2007, from *http://java.sun.com/products/jms/*

W3C (World Wide Web Consortium). (2001, March). *Web Services Description Language (WSDL) 1.1.* Retrieved February 14, 2007, from *http://www.w3.org/TR/wsdl*

W3C. (2002). *Web Service Choreography Interface (WSCI) 1.0.* Retrieved February 14, 2007, from http://www.w3.org/TR/2002/NOTE-wsci-20020808

Chapter IV

Efficient Transport Bindings for Web Service Messages

Christian Werner, University of Lübeck, Germany

Carsten Buschmann, University of Lübeck, Germany

Tobias Jäcker, EVES Information Technology AG, Germany

Stefan Fischer, University of Lübeck, Germany

Abstract

Although Web service technology is being used in more and more distributed systems, its areas of application are inherently limited by high latencies and high amounts of protocol overhead. For messaging in environments with user interaction, like Web platforms for business or multimedia applications, the response time of the whole system needs to be kept in tight boundaries. In other scenarios comprising mobile communication and battery-powered devices, bandwidth-efficient communication is imperative. In this chapter we address both of these issues. First we conduct a detailed latency analysis of different transport mechanisms for SOAP and then we thoroughly investigate their protocol overhead. For both aspects we present a theoretical analysis as well as experimental measurement results. We then will introduce a new transport binding called PURE that significantly reduces the protocol overhead while featuring low latency. Furthermore it enables interesting additional features such as point-to-multipoint communication via IP multicast and broadcast.

Introduction

A major drawback of using Web services for application integration is its enormous demand for network bandwidth. Like all other XML protocols, SOAP suffers from the fact that only a very small part of the transmitted message contains real payload. The rest of it is XML markup and protocol overhead. Comparisons on different approaches for realizing Remote Procedure Calls (RPCs) have shown that SOAP over HTTP uses significantly more bandwidth than competitive technologies (Werner, Buschmann, & Fischer, 2005; Werner, Buschmann, Brandt, & Fischer, 2006; Tian, Voigt, Naumowicz, Ritter, & Schiller, 2003; Marahrens, 2003). Though today's wired networks are powerful enough to provide sufficient bandwidth even for very demanding applications like media streaming, there are still some fields of computing where bandwidth is costly. In cellular phone networks (GPRS, UMTS) for example; it is quite common to charge according to the transmitted data volumes.

Another problem, which might become even more severe in the future, is the comparably high latency of SOAP-based communication. Since not all service operation can be processed in parallel, the response time of the whole systems increases with the number of involved services. Especially when using several intermediaries between SOAP endpoints, a single services call might take considerable time. Hence, if an operation with user interaction needs a number of subsequent calls to complete, the responsiveness of the whole system decreases below an acceptable level.

Typical application domains, in which low latency is particularly important, include high-performance application in the field of grid computing, as well as all kinds of real-time applications like controlling industrial devices and plants. But also all Web services which are used in applications with user interaction have to meet certain latency restrictions: Shneiderman (1984) found that the acceptable response time depends on the user's perception of the complexity of the task the computer system has to solve. For easy tasks, like login procedures, delays up to 200 milliseconds are acceptable. For more complex tasks, for example search operations on large databases, a computer system should respond within a time interval of two seconds. Higher response times lead to decreased usability and unsatisfied users.

Allman (2003) conducted a detailed survey on Web service response time using RPC-style Web service calls. Under local area network conditions he measured latencies between 50 and 70 milliseconds for a single Web service call. For more complex test cases, where we have several SOAP intermediaries that are connected over the Internet, the overall response time can easily go up over values larger then two seconds. These results show that the optimization of Web service latency is a very important issue. In the past, approaches for improving the response time performance of SOAP services mainly concentrated on the optimization of the used XML parser (van Engelen, 2004; Chiu, Govindaraju, & Bramley, 2002), the SOAP engine (Marahrens, 2003), or the used Web server (Tian et al., 2003; Ghandeharizadeh, Papadopoulos, Cai, & Chintalapudi, 2002). But as we will show in the remainder of this chapter, also the used transport binding can have a significant impact on the Web service performance with regard to its latency.

Bearing the "talkative" nature of XML in mind, our recent work focused on strategies for compressing SOAP messages. First we will summarize our approach and present the resulting reduction of network traffic. Here we will also discuss how the data rate efficiency and latency can be enhanced further by transport-level considerations. Next we will present a survey on existing transport protocol bindings, again with a strong focus on both data rate efficiency and latency. The following section introduces a new binding based on UDP, which is extremely efficient and versatile at the same time. Furthermore, we will discuss the results of a thorough evaluation of this new binding. Finally we will draw a conclusion and discuss some future work.

Problem Analysis

Overhead

In our past efforts to enhance Web service efficiency with regard to the generated network traffic, we concentrated on SOAP compression. We found that xmlppm (*http://sourceforge.net/projects/xmlppm/*) is the most effective compressor that can be applied to arbitrary XML documents. It achieves an average compression ratio of 1:2.3. WBXML (*http://libwbxml.aymerick.com/*) produces even more compact XML representations, but is limited to documents sticking to certain predefined XML languages. Hence, it cannot be applied to SOAP documents.

To further improve compression performance, we proposed a concept that combines differential SOAP encoding with xmlppm compression (cf. Chapter 1, "Efficient Encodings for Web Service Messages"). We use the commonly available WSDL description of a Web service to generate skeleton SOAP messages for all service operations (input and output). Each skeleton file contains a "generic" SOAP request or response in the sense that there are no data values in it, but only markup. The basic idea here is that only the differences between a SOAP message and its corresponding skeleton file need to be transmitted over the wire.

Figure 1. Effectiveness of different encoding techniques

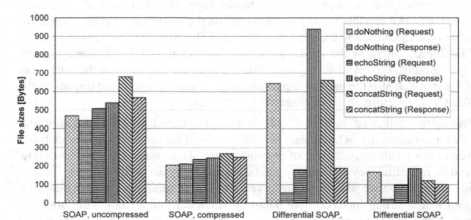

A prototypical implementation for differential SOAP encoding and decoding works as follows: When a service consumer sends a SOAP request to a service provider, its SOAP engine produces a SOAP request message. Then the difference between this message and a previously generated SOAP request skeleton is calculated using diffxml (Mouat, 2002). The resulting difference document is then passed to an entropy encoding stage in order to remove the remaining redundancy. It produces a binary representation of the difference document, which is finally sent to the service provider. Here the request skeleton is patched with the previously decompressed difference document. The patching process reconstructs the original SOAP message, which is then passed to the service provider's SOAP engine. For SOAP response messages this process works vice versa.

In order to compare the effectiveness of differential encoding to other compression approaches, we implemented a SOAP RPC test server and a client with three different remote procedures, which yield SOAP messages with different amounts of payload: `void doNothing()`, `String echoString(String)`, and `String concatString(String0, String1, String2, String3, String4)`. We then compared the sizes of the resulting uncompressed SOAP messages, their compressed representations, and the sizes of the corresponding compressed and uncompressed differential messages. The results are shown in Figure 1. Although mere compression already showed to be quite effective, it is obvious that the differential encoding technique performs best.

With regard to the compression effectiveness, three factors are important: How well does differencing work with a particular message/skeleton pair, how much (unpredictable) data does the SOAP message carry, and what compression ratio can be achieved on the difference document? Depending on these three, the original SOAP messages could be compacted by factors varying between about 3 and 20 employing differencing and compression. Note that for all six cases, the compressed differential messages are smaller than the compressed original SOAP messages. This is remarkable because the uncompressed differential documents are not necessarily smaller than the SOAP messages themselves.

While all of the aforementioned considerations are based on the size of the involved SOAP messages only, we then extended our view to the generated overall network traffic. If a standard HTTP-POST transport binding is used, the SOAP message is enveloped into an HTTP request, which results in additional overhead. Protocol information exchanged by TCP, IP, and link layer protocols when transporting these HTTP messages also adds to network traffic.

To evaluate the overhead generated by the different transport protocols on the different layers, we analyzed the data packets in our test setup using the Ethereal Network Analyzer (*http://www.ethereal.com/*). We ignored the link layer and below because they depend on the employed network type and measured only the traffic produced by protocols on layer three and above. Another factor of influence is the setting of the Maximum Transfer Unit (MTU). It determines the maximum size a layer 2 packet may have in the underlying network and into how many IP packets the original message is fragmented, each carrying overhead in the form of packet headers. For our measurements the MTU was set to 1,300 bytes.

Figure 2. Network traffic resulting from SOAP and transport protocol overhead

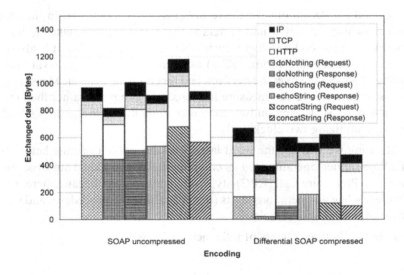

Figure 2 depicts the results differentiated by protocol, based on the uncompressed and differentially compressed SOAP documents also visible in Figure 1. For simplicity, we regarded the TCP connection setup as part of the Web service request, and the disconnection as part of the response. While for uncompressed SOAP the message constitutes about 50% or more of the generated network traffic, the situation is pretty disillusioning for compressed SOAP. The traffic resulting from protocols is between 2 and 18 times as voluminous as the actual SOAP payload. It is easy to see that HTTP contributes most to the overhead. Its share varies between 60 and 70%; the rest must be imputed to TCP/IP.

The measurement showed that about 50% of the TCP/IP traffic is due to connection and disconnection; the other half results from actually transporting HTTP. While the former is independent of the transported SOAP message, the latter potentially varies with the SOAP message and the underlying network. SOAP influences the HTTP request and response with regard to size.

It is clear that these results must lead to a discussion of how transport protocol efficiency can be increased. The obvious starting point is HTTP, producing the most traffic. Later we will discuss whether it could be replaced by something else, and whether an application layer protocol is necessary at all.

Latency

Besides the data rate efficiency of a Web service, its performance in terms of latency becomes more and more important. If a SOAP massage is routed via several intermediaries or if a Web service makes subsequent calls to other Web services, the overall execution time may exceed an acceptable level.

There are multiple definitions for the term "latency" in literature. In the area of computer networks, latency usually refers to the time a message takes to traverse the network from its sender to its receiver, also called "delay." But it is also common to denote the round-trip-time (RTT) as latency. That is the interval between the sending of a message over the network and receiving an answer. Measuring the RTT is easier because we can measure it on a single computer rather than on two different systems. Measuring on two computers would lead to the problem of accurately synchronizing two clocks.

In the following we will use the word latency as the amount of time between the start of a Web service operation and its completion. We conducted our experiments using Remote Procedure Call (RPC)-style SOAP messaging, because here it is absolutely clear when an operations starts (time of calling the procedure) and when it ends (time of returning the result).

There are basically three factors of influence for latency:

1. *Processing Delay* t_{proc}: The time a network node needs to process the message. For the SOAP RPC scenario, we have at least four different values for t_{proc}—the time for generating the request message, processing the request, generating a response, and processing the response. In a network with active components like SOAP intermediaries, routers, or bridges, their processing times also add to t_{proc}.

2. *Transmission Delay* t_{trans}: The transmission delay is the message size S [*bits*] divided by the network data rate C [*bits/sec*]. The values for transmitting the request and the response may differ.

3. *Propagation Delay* t_{prop}: The propagation delay is the time that a network message takes to travel from its sender to its receiver. The value for t_{prop} primarily depends on the physical characteristics of network—that is, the velocity of propagation in the network media and the distance between sender and receiver.

The total latency S is a composition of all three delay types. Depending on the used hardware setup and the chosen software components, the weight of each delay type varies.

One could now start to evaluate all three types of delay in separate experiments. This approach seems not very gainful because each parameter is strongly dependent on the chosen test setup. Furthermore, in practice only the weighted sum of all delays S affects the perceived Web service latency. Furthermore, t_{trans} and t_{prop} can be analytically predicted with high accuracy if the message sizes and the used network type are known.

Although we will not keep the different delay types separated in our experimental evaluation, this classification is useful to identify different approaches for reducing the overall latency: Techniques for reducing the size of a network message, either by applying data compression (Tian et al., 2003; Ghandeharizadeh et al., 2002; Werner et al., 2005, 2006) or reducing the protocol overhead, will improve t_{trans}. Approaches that are targeting at better performance of the involved software components (van Engelen, 2004; Chiu et al., 2002), such as efficient parsers, are reducing t_{proc}. The propagation delay t_{prop} cannot be influenced directly, because it depends on the physical characteristics of the network media.

Up until now the influence of the used transport binding has not been discussed in literature, but obviously there are several impacts: First, the used transport binding affects t_{trans} by causing a certain protocol overhead. Furthermore, it also affects t_{proc}: The transport binding protocol implementation needs some processing time for maintaining data structures as well as doing various I/O tasks and computations. However, depending on the protocol implementation and the used hardware, these values are usually quite small. A more important factor that adds to t_{proc} is the time needed for connection establishment and teardown if the binding is based on connection-oriented transport protocols like TCP.

In the following section we will first give an overview of existing SOAP bindings. Then we will present an evaluation study of both protocol overhead and latency.

Survey on Existing SOAP Bindings

A very important feature of the Web service technology is that SOAP can be bound to virtually any transport mechanism. The used binding affects the way in which SOAP messaging takes place in an important aspect: The SOAP specification (W3C, 2003a) defines the concept of message exchange patterns (MEPs). An MEP is a template that defines in what way messages are exchanged between SOAP nodes.

In this section we will first give an overview of the advantages and disadvantages of six different protocol bindings: HTTP, SMTP, FTP, MSMQ, TCP, and UDP. We will discuss the supported SOAP message exchange patterns in each case and give an overview of protocol-specific benefits, such as point-to-multipoint messaging or reliable message transport. Second, we will present a summary on the protocol overhead for these bindings.

We originally planned also to include SOAP-over-JMS (Du & Liu, 2004) and SOAP-over-Beep (O'Tuathail & Rose, 2002) in our evaluation, but it was very difficult to find working implementations that can be set up in a comparable way to the other bindings. Therefore we excluded these two bindings until now. It is not expected that these bindings will perform significantly better than HTTP because both are TCP-based application-layer protocols.

Overview

HTTP

The most popular binding by far is SOAP-over-HTTP because HTTP is ubiquitously available and its built-in addressing and error-handling functionalities are fully covering SOAP's needs. SOAP-over-HTTP is the only binding that is available as a W3C recommendation (W3C, 2003b). The recommended version to use with SOAP is HTTP/1.1, which is specified in RFC 2616 (Fielding et al., 1999). Even though the HTTP binding is not mandatory, virtually all SOAP implementations do provide HTTP bindings.

The HTTP binding provides two MEPS (W3C, 2003b): the Request-Response MEP and the Response MEP. The first one is based on the HTTP-POST command. The SOAP node A is operating as an HTTP client and sends out a POST request that carries a SOAP document to the other SOAP node B, which is running an HTTP server. Node B processes this request and sends out an HTTP response, carrying the answer to that request in the form of another SOAP document. In contrast to that the Response MEP is based on HTTP-GET. Node A sends out a GET request, where the desired information is directly encoded in the HTTP request URI. Node B sends back a SOAP document in the HTTP response. So here SOAP is only used in the response, not in the request.

With the Request-Response MEP, HTTP is perfectly suitable for the RPC-style SOAP messaging. Unfortunately the use of HTTP also has a number of disadvantages. HTTP is a client-server protocol and has not been designed for transferring messages between SOAP nodes in a peer-to-peer manner. Asynchronous messaging, where SOAP nodes can communicate independently from a fixed request-response-cycle, is not supported. But more and more Web service applications, especially in the field of grid computing, are demanding peer-to-peer messaging.

Like all bindings on top of TCP, HTTP provides reliable message transport, flow, and congestion control.

SMTP

A SOAP-over-E-Mail binding is described in Mountain, Kopecky, Williams, Daniels, and Mendelsohn (2002). Because e-mail has not been designed for request/response message exchange, it supports only one-way messaging. But a Request-Response MEP can be added by associating requests and responses according to their Message-ID mail header or by using WS-Addressing (W3C, 2004). This binding directly supports point-to-multipoint messaging by using multiple To: header fields.

Although the SOAP-over-E-Mail specification is not limited to a certain mail transport protocol, we only evaluated SOAP-over-SMTP because SMTP is the natural choice for our RPC test case described below. Still, SOAP messaging over POP3 or IMAP might be interesting alternatives in scenarios with asynchronous messaging. SMTP works on top of TCP and therefore it provides reliable message transport and flow/congestion control in the sense of TCP.

FTP

Although SOAP-over-FTP is a common example for alternative SOAP bindings in literature, the authors are not aware of a specification or implementation. Due to FTP's purpose of transferring files between an FTP client and server, it supports one-way messaging only. Of course, if WS-Addressing is used, a Request-Response MEP can be realized by associating request and response messages according to their WS-Addressing headers. FTP is also based on TCP and provides the corresponding features.

MSMQ

SOAP-over-MSMQ is a reliable and asynchronous store-and-forward communication mechanism based on TCP. With the MSMQ binding (Kiss, 2004), messages can be sent even if the receiving SOAP node application is not running. MSMQ has been mainly designed for one-way messaging but also provides a Request-Response MEP through WS-Addressing. It supports application layer multicast, enabling unidirectional point-to-multipoint messaging as well as an enhanced Request-Response MEP (multicast request, unicast responses).

TCP

SOAP-over-TCP has been specified by Microsoft, and an implementation is included in the Web Service Enhancements (WSE) package (*http://msdn.microsoft.com/webservices/building/wse*) since version 2.0. The basic idea here is to remove the application layer protocol completely and put the required addressing information directly into the SOAP header using WS-Addressing. The WSE provides two versions of TCP-based messaging: synchronous and asynchronous. With synchronous TCP the request and response messages are exchanged over a common TCP connection realizing a Request-Response MEP. In the asynchronous mode, the TCP connection is torn down after a single message has been sent, realizing one-way messaging. Asynchronous TCP messaging increases flexibility but leads to more protocol overhead at the same time.

UDP

Gudgin (2004) introduced a SOAP-over-UDP binding specification that supports one-way messaging over unicast, multicast, and broadcast, providing the greatest flexibility of all evaluated bindings. It is notable that in contrast to the multicast features of SMTP and MSMQ, the UDP multicast uses IP multicast, which significantly increases efficiency.

As a major drawback of this binding, the size of a SOAP message is limited to about 64 kilobytes in order to fit into a single UDP datagram. Unlike TCP, UDP does not provide any congestion or flow control mechanisms. Furthermore, it is an unreliable transport protocol and messages might get lost.

Summary on Data Rate Efficiency

In order to evaluate the data rate efficiency of the different bindings with respect to varying message sizes, we implemented a test case with two RPC operations: `void doNothing(void)` and `byte[] getImage(String)`. The first one generates very small SOAP messages with 1,128 bytes for the request and 1,021 bytes for the response. These can be transported in a single IP Datagram. The `byte[] getImage(String)` returns a jpg-file as byte array. The message size here is 1,161 bytes for the request and 143,501 bytes for the response. The response message exceeds the maximum datagram size by far; therefore the message must be fragmented for all bindings.

For HTTP and TCP we used the binding implementations provided by the .NET platform with the WSE 2.0 SP2 package installed. The TCP binding was used in synchronous mode, which is a natural choice for our RPC test cases. For SMTP, MSMQ, and UDP, we used the bindings provided in Maine (2004), Kiss (2004), and Wilson (2004). Because of the message size limitation with the UDP binding, we could not analyze this binding with the `byte[] getImage(String)` operation. Since we are not aware of a working SOAP-over-FTP implementation, we measured the traffic for FTP manually by saving the SOAP request and response messages to files and transferring these files to a FTP server.

It must be taken into consideration that SOAP bindings like TCP or UDP, which are lacking SOAP node addressing capabilities, require some extras for realizing addressing. We decided to use WS-Addressing (W3C, 2004) here. Instead of using

Table 1. Protocol overhead of different SOAP bindings [bytes]

Operation	doNothing						getImage					
Binding	HTTP	SMTP	FTP	MSMQ	TCP	UDP	HTTP	SMTP	FTP	MSMQ	TCP	UDP
App. Layer	560	2,535	576	2,959	-	-	558	2,581	577	2,996	-	-
Trans. Layer	276	992	1,301	493	538	16	3,716	4,792	4,744	3,855	4,052	-
IP Layer	260	960	1,300	480	320	40	3,700	4,760	4,680	3,880	3,820	-
Overall	1,096	4,487	3,177	3,932	858	56	7,974	12,133	10,000	10,732	7,872	-

transport-level features, WS-Addressing puts the addressing information directly into the SOAP header. In order to get comparable results for all bindings, we used WS-Addressing also for bindings like HTTP which do provide basic addressing capabilities.

As already stated, another factor that affects protocol overhead is the setting of the Maximum Transfer Unit (MTU). For all overhead measurements the MTU was set to 1,300 bytes. If a larger IP datagram needs to be transported, it is automatically fragmented at the sender-side IP implementation and reassembled at the receiver side. For a detailed discussion of this topic, see Shannon, Moore, and Claffy (2002).

Our results are summarized in Table 1. All application layer protocols add a significant amount of overhead. Moving to plain TCP reduces the overhead but leaves room for further improvements. UDP might be a possible solution. Unfortunately its limitations with regard to message size and reliability restrict conceivable application scenarios.

Summary on Latency

As when measuring the resulting overhead, we used the RPC methods doNothing() and getImage(String) for analyzing the corresponding latencies. In addition to client and server, we used a third machine in between that functioned as a router. On it we ran the *Nistnet Network Emulator (NNE)* (*http://snad.ncsl.nist.gov/itg/nistnet/*), which allows emulating transport networks with given parameters such as link overload, packet drop rate, or latency. For both test operations we preset latencies of 0, 10, 50, and 500 ms. Since latency occurs on the way to the server and back, it accumulates to 0, 20, 100, and 1,000 ms respectively. To make the measurements insensitive to network performance variations, we averaged results over 1,000 measurements (i.e., 10 series of 100 RPC calls). For all latency measurements the MTU was set to 1,500 bytes.

As already mentioned in the introduction, the latency is heavily influenced by layer-4 connection setup. To take that into account, we analyzed both persistent and non-persistent connections. Persistent connections enable transmission of multiple RPC calls over one lasting connection, whereas new setup for each call is required otherwise.

We analyzed the MSMQ and JMS bindings for persistent connections only because non-persistent connections could not be simulated with the implementations we used.

For the TCP binding we experimented with both the synchronous and asynchronous modes provided by the Web Service Enhancements (WSEs). Synchronous TCP uses the connection that was set up for the transmission of the request also for trans-

Table 2. Latencies of different SOAP bindings [ms] using non-persistent connections

Operation	doNothing				getImage			
Delay (NNE)	0	10	50	500	0	10	50	500
HTTP	10.57	71.24	311.95	3,011.64	84.43	281.64	1,073.24	9,082.84
Syn. TCP	14.68	55.02	215.69	2,015.29	87.05	304.79	1,185.76	10,081.13
Asyn. TCP	15.21	75.95	316.03	3,015.03	74.03	293.63	1,172.10	10,069.80
UDP	8.40	28.72	109.05	1,009.25	-	-	-	-

mitting the response. Asynchronous TCP instead sets up a new connection for the response and can hence send it to an address different from the source address. For the persistent test case, two connections are used: one for transmitting all requests, and another one for all responses.

SMTP and FTP were not taken into account for the latency measurements. The used SOAP-over-SMTP implementation exhibits disproportionately long processing delays due to implementation issues. Hence latency increases heavily without SMTP itself bearing responsibility for that. Since FTP, as described above, could only be simulated manually for lack of an implementation, latency measurements would not have yielded sensible results either.

The measurement results for non-persistent connections are summarized in Table 2. The column "0 ms" can be interpreted as an approximation of processing times. The other columns show the latencies that roughly accumulate from this processing time and multiples of the latency set in NNE. For each binding, particular reasons for the occurrence of multiple "delay periods" set in NNE can be determined. Since RPC-style Web services use the request-response communication pattern, at least two delay periods occur. All TCP-based bindings feature two extra delay periods for connection setup: The client sends a TCP segment with the SYN flag set, the server answers with another one having the SYN and ACK flags set. The client again sends a segment with ACK set, but can transfer the request payload with that segment already. At least another segment by the server is needed for transmitting the response. For asynchronous TCP, two extra delay periods occur due to the second connection setup. UPD causes only two delay periods due to request-response communication without connection setup.

When HTTP is used as a transport binding, the request is sent via HTTP POST. With the used implementation, POST first only sends the message header to the server, which answers with a CONTINUE message. After the client received this,

Table 3. Latencies of different SOAP bindings [ms] using persistent connections

Operation	doNothing				getImage			
Delay (NNE)	0	10	50	500	0	10	50	500
HTTP	9.48	50.24	210.79	2,011.66	83.33	182.59	585.52	5,118.61
MSMQ	64.74	68.44	146.32	1,431.22	182.04	182.47	344.35	3,580.18
JMS	47.82	286.64	1,220.53	12,039.94	276.89	471.53	1,786.03	1,7165.06
Syn. TCP	9.79	30.23	110.55	1,011.42	81.53	180.99	569.37	4,840.72
Asyn. TCP	8.91	29.22	110.09	1,011.76	68.05	142.43	449.58	3,853.07
UDP	8.40	28.72	109.05	1,009.25	-	-	-	-

it sends over the message body of the request message. Hence two additional delay periods are added compared to synchronous TCP. This mechanism is efficient if the sender wants to check whether the receiver is ready for reception before sending large messages. For small messages, this mechanism should be omitted for the benefit of latency.

For all TCP-based bindings, the response message sent by the server as a result of calling getImages(String) causes multiple segments. Hence the slow start mechanism affects the overall delay.

All in all, UDP causes the lowest latencies, but has the disadvantage that it cannot transport SOAP messages of more than 64 kilobytes of size. Hence it cannot be used for getImage(String).

The use of persistent connections reduces latencies because the delay for connection setup occurs only once. The corresponding measurement results are depicted in Table 3. However, it assumes a rather uncommon application scenario: client and server are in a longer-lasting communication relationship. Hence it can be used for saving latency in special cases, but not as a general solution to the latency problem. For this reason, comparisons with persistent connections will be omitted in the remainder of this chapter.

This analysis proved that latency is mainly resulting from blocking protocol steps in the transport layer such as TCP connection setup or slow start. Hence, moving to connectionless transport protocols can reduce latency significantly.

PURE: A Multi-Packet UDP Binding

The specification introduced by Gudgin (2004) provides a very efficient and flexible approach for SOAP messaging over UDP. However, as stated in the previous section, its major drawback is that the SOAP message size is limited to a fixed value (about 64 kilobytes). As discussed in Werner et al. (2005), SOAP messages are rather small in most cases, but for many applications it is impossible to predict a maximum value. A simple search operation of a bookstore Web service for example could easily produce SOAP messages with more than 64 kilobytes for some queries. So if there is a fixed message size constraint for a binding, the Web service developer must take care of this limitation. But if we think of SOAP transport via intermediaries, a Web service developer might not even know that some intermediaries are using bindings that are limiting the maximum message size. So in the SOAP world this message size constraint is definitely a severe problem.

In order to overcome this limitation, the authors developed a very lightweight application layer protocol on top of UDP called PURE. It has been custom tailored for transporting SOAP messages. As well as the single packet UDP binding described in Wilson (2004), PURE employs SOAP extensions like WS-Addressing (W3C, 2004) for endpoint addressing and WS-ReliableMessaging (Ferris & Langworthy, 2004) for ensuring transport reliability instead of using transport level features.

One could now argue that we are adding a lot of protocol overhead to the SOAP header while removing the HTTP overhead. In fact such SOAP extensions are not replacing transport level features but are significantly adding value for future Web service applications. If we think of SOAP messaging via intermediaries, the use of such extensions is crucial (Davis, 2004)—even if we are using full-scale application protocols like HTTP. So the overhead imposed by employing SOAP extensions will occur independently of the transport protocol overhead and should therefore be discussed separately. Furthermore we have already developed effective strategies to reducing SOAP overhead by applying advanced data compression strategies (Werner et al., 2005). From this point of view, shifting the overhead from the binding into the SOAP message is a promising solution.

Of course the use of such high-level SOAP extensions is not always adequate. The motivation behind our work is to use SOAP everywhere, even on very tiny battery-powered devices. Therefore, we are providing some optional low-level features in PURE which can be used in scenarios where basic transport reliability is needed but mechanisms like WS-ReliableMessaging are oversized.

Although PURE is a best-effort protocol that does not provide any guaranties concerning reliability or speed, we are very confident that it covers the needs of a wide range of Web service applications.

Architecture

PURE is an application layer protocol based on UDP (Postel, 1980). In contrast to the single packet UDP binding of Gudgin (2004) which inserts the serialized XML

Figure 3. Structure of PURE packets. The lower four bits of the Flags field are indicating "Last Message (END)," "Automatic Repeat Request (ARQ)," "Acknowledgment Requested (AKR)," and "Reception Acknowledged (ACK)."

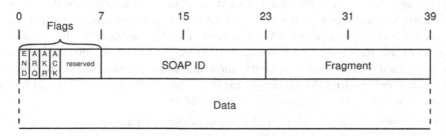

representation of the SOAP message directly into the data field of an UDP datagram, PURE adds an additional 5 bytes header in front of the payload. Its basic features are variable message fragmentation, selective Automatic Repeat Request (ARQ) with negative acknowledgments, and optional positive acknowledgments (ACKs).

The structure of a PURE packet is depicted in Figure 3. The first octet of the message header is the *Flags* field. As illustrated, this field is interpreted as a set of bit flags, which are used for various signaling tasks. Currently only the lower four bits are used; the remaining bits are reserved for future use.

The *SOAP ID* field contains a 16-bit unsigned integer value. Before the PURE implementation on a sending SOAP node fragments a SOAP message, it assigns a unique SOAP ID to it. Each fragment carries this ID in its *SOAP ID* field. The receiving SOAP node uses this information to identify PURE packets that belong to a certain SOAP message. The sending SOAP node generates this ID by incrementing a counter.

The *Fragment* field is used for numbering single SOAP Fragments. Since UDP does not prevent out-of-order delivery, the receiver uses this field for reordering incoming PURE messages if needed. Furthermore, duplicate messages can be detected when a SOAP node receives multiple messages which carry identical *SOAP ID* and *Fragment* values within a certain time interval.

Finally, the *Data* field carries the SOAP message or a fragment of it as payload.

Theoretically, each PURE message including header can have a maximum size of 65,507 bytes. The maximum possible size for an IP packet is 65,535 bytes (Postel, 1981), and at least 20 bytes are needed for the IP header and another 8 bytes are needed for the UDP header (Postel, 1980). In practice this maximum possible value leads to serious IP fragmentation, because the Maximum Transfer Unit (MTU) for usual network technologies is something between 1,200 and 1,500 bytes. When a single IP fragment is lost, for example due to Ethernet collisions, the receiving

IP implementation cannot reassemble the UDP Datagram and drops it as a whole. In some scenarios it might be a good choice to set the maximum size of a PURE fragment to MTU minus 28 bytes for IP and UDP headers in order to avoid fragmentation on IP level.

The PURE header format does not provide any fields for the message length or a checksum, because these are already included in the enclosing UDP header.

Below we will give some typical examples that demonstrate the meaning of the different header fields instead of covering all special cases that may occur when using PURE.

Message Fragmentation Example

In order to overcome the message size limitation of 64 kilobytes, PURE supports splitting up a SOAP message into smaller chunks that are transmitted in separate fragments. An example is shown in Figure 4. Node A wants to send a large SOAP message to node B. At first, node A fragments the serialized SOAP message into three chunks, simply by cutting the byte stream into three parts. The last part is tagged by setting the *END* flag.

In the first message no signaling bits are set. In this example the value for *SOAP ID* is 0. Also in the second message, no signaling bits are set and the value for *SOAP ID* is 0, indicating that this fragment belongs to the previous one. The *Fragment* field has the value 1 (counting 0, 1, 2, ...).

The third message contains the last fragment for the SOAP message with ID 0. Hence the *END* flag is set. The *Fragment* field has the value 2. Node B can now reassemble the whole SOAP message by concatenating the data parts from all three PURE messages. Even if they arrive in a different order, node B can restore the original message using the *END* flag and the incremental *Fragment* values.

Figure 4. Message fragmentation with PURE

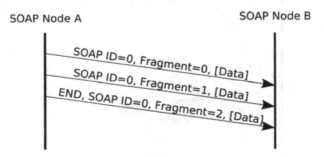

Since the *Fragment* value is limited to 16 Bits, a SOAP-Message can be split up into 65,536 fragments at most, resulting in a theoretical maximum SOAP message size of $2^{16} \cdot 65,502$ bytes ≈ 4 GB, where 65,502 is the maximum size of the *Data* field.

Automatic Repeat Request Example and Duplicate Detection

Since UDP does not guaranty that a sent datagram will reach its receiver, it is possible that some PURE messages get lost, for example due to frame loss on layer-2 or overloaded routers. A receiving node buffers all incoming PURE messages until all fragments for a certain *SOAP ID* are received. For each *SOAP ID* the PURE implementation maintains a receiver timer. If a fragment with this *SOAP ID* comes in, this timer is reset. If the timer expires, the SOAP node sends a PURE message with the *ARQ* flag set back to the other node, indicating that some messages are still missing. The *SOAP ID* of this ARQ message has the same value as in the missing messages. The *Data* field contains the missing Fragment IDs as a sequence of 16 Bit values. The *Fragment* field has no meaning if the *ARQ* flag is set, and it must be set to 0.

Figure 5. Retransmission of lost packets using the ARQ flag

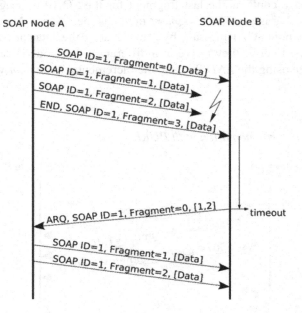

Figure 5 shows an example. SOAP node A splits up its SOAP message into four fragments. It sends them out, but fragments 1 and 2 get lost. After receiving the message with the *Fragment* value 3, the receiver timer expires. Node B assumes that the two missing messages got lost and sends back a PURE message with the *ARQ* flag set. By putting the values 1 and 2 into the *Data* field, it indicates which packets are missing (negative acknowledgment). SOAP node A then retransmits the lost messages.

The problem of message duplication is directly related with the retransmission algorithms of PURE. Messages can be duplicated due to routing errors on ISO/OSI layer-3 or due to unnecessary retransmission. The latter case can occur if a PURE message is not lost, but takes a very long time to reach its destination. Meanwhile the receive timer on the receiving PURE implementation runs out, resulting in the generation of an ARQ message and finally in a copy of the delayed message.

PURE can detect both types of duplicates by keeping a record of the received messages in a certain time interval and identifying those with equal values for *SOAP ID* and *Fragment*. If a duplicate is detected, the message that comes in last is dropped.

Positive Acknowledgment Example

For some applications it is important to know that a sent message reaches its receiver. The natural way of implementing this is the use of acknowledgment messages. Even though transport layer acknowledgments are only of limited use with SOAP and it is better to rely on appropriate extensions like WS-ReliableMessaging (Ferris & Langworthy, 2004), for some applications, especially in cases without SOAP intermediaries, transport layer acknowledgments are sufficient. Therefore, PURE provides a simple mechanism for positive acknowledgments on transport layer.

As illustrated in Figure 6, the sending PURE implementation can use the *AKR* flag to indicate that it wants to get an acknowledgment for this PURE message. Node B issues a new PURE message with the *ACK* flag set, the same values for *SOAP ID* and *Fragment* but no *Data*. In this example the acknowledgments get lost and after a certain timeout node A repeats its message. Node B sends the acknowledgments again, but then drops the incoming message because it is a duplicate.

Node A can be sure that node B has successfully processed the acknowledged message. As shown in this example, the *AKR* flag can be used to protect only selected messages. Protecting only one fragment per SOAP message is enough in most cases: if node A knows that at least one fragment of its SOAP message has reached node B, it can rely on the ARQ mechanism of PURE, which will induce the retransmission of lost SOAP fragments.

Figure 6. Using positive acknowledgments with PURE

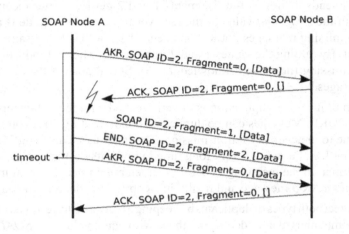

Security Considerations

PURE currently does not include any security-related features. One reason for this is that we can make use of extensions like WS-Security (Nadalin, Kaler, Hallam-Baker, & Monzillo, 2004). Such high-level security measures do provide security services between SOAP endpoints and not just security on a transport level like PURE could.

However, the risk of denial-of-service attacks needs to be addressed on a transport level. Since the PURE implementation needs to keep track of incoming SOAP messages in order to re-request missing fragments, an attacker could easily send a lot of messages with random values for *SOAP ID* and very high values for *Fragment*. This would lead to large memory allocations and the generation of huge *ARQ* messages. In another scenario an attacker could use IP spoofing to infiltrate the fragment buffer of a PURE node with faked SOAP fragments. This could lead to a large number of illegal SOAP messages that must be processed by the receiving SOAP engine. A lot of other denial-of-service attacks are conceivable.

Our current implementation does not take any measures for preventing such attacks, but we are confident that we can rather easily reduce the risk of denial-of-service by implementing reasonable limits for the number of retransmissions and realizing additional plausibility checks for incoming PURE messages. However, in addition to this, it is surely useful to protect PURE services with classical security measures like firewalls.

Overhead Evaluation

The authors have implemented a prototype of PURE for the Microsoft .NET platform. It is fully functional and has been tested with the .NET SOAP engine. The authors have successfully exchanged SOAP messages between PURE-enabled SOAP nodes within the local area network as well as over the Internet.

Figure 7. Overhead of different transport bindings for different RPC calls: void doNothing(void) (a) and byte[] getImage(String) (b)

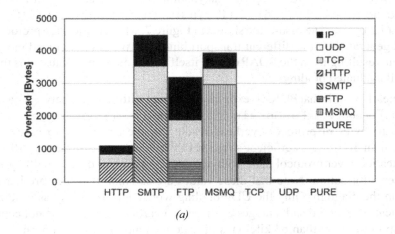

(a)

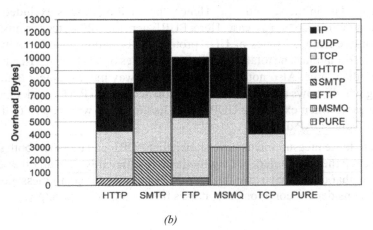

(b)

Currently there is only rudimentary support for limiting the number of retransmissions. Also the buffers and timers are not working with optimized values.

Anyhow, our current implementation is stable enough to run tests in scenarios with no or very little packet loss. Also point-to-multipoint messaging based on IP multicast and broadcast have been implemented and tested.

We evaluated the data rate efficiency of our PURE implementation by measuring the protocol overhead on the different network layers by including PURE into the test series described earlier. We tested our implementation using two 2.4 GHz Intel PCs running Windows XP Professional (SP2) which were directly connected using a 100 Mbit Ethernet crossover cable. Of course we used the same setup for all bindings. For these tests we also used the Ethereal Network Analyzer for measuring the overhead in the different layers of the TCP/IP protocol stack. We experimented again with two RPC-style SOAP operations yielding SOAP messages of different sizes: `void doNothing(void)` (2,149 bytes) and `byte[] getImage(String)` (144,662 bytes). The results are shown in Figure 7, which depicts the protocol overhead generated by the different transport bindings. We have excluded the amount of data resulting from the SOAP engine itself in this diagram because it is the same for all evaluated bindings.

It is clearly visible that PURE is extremely efficient with regard to network bandwidth usage. For both `void doNothing(void)` and `byte[] getImage(String)`, the least bytes of protocol overhead result. For the `doNothing` case, it works more than 16 times as efficient as the HTTP binding, generating only 10 bytes of application layer protocol data, 16 bytes of UDP protocol data, and 40 bytes of IP header information. Note that these values are so small that they are hardly visible in the diagram. Only the UDP binding works approximately as efficient, but implicates several disadvantages as discussed earlier. Because it is not capable of transporting more than 64 kilobytes of data, it cannot be used to return the resulting image data in the second case. Hence, the UDP binding is excluded from the depiction of the `getImage` case. Here, PURE generates 20 bytes of transport layer protocol overhead, 32 bytes of UDP protocol information, and 2,300 bytes of IP header information. The total amount of 2,352 bytes outperforms HTTP by a factor of more than three. Also note that PURE works way more efficient than the TCP binding which shows about the same performance as HTTP. TCP ranks second best in both cases when excluding UDP due to its limitation with regard to the size of transportable SOAP data.

All in all, these measurements have shown that PURE can transport both small and large SOAP message orders of magnitude more efficiently than all other evaluated protocols that do not have size limitations. Especially for small messages that the authors consider the common case, it uses bandwidth very sparingly.

Table 4. Latencies of different SOAP bindings [ms] using non-persistent connections

Operation	doNothing				getImage			
Delay (NNE)	0	10	50	500	0	10	50	500
HTTP	10.57	71.24	311.95	3,011.64	84.43	281.64	1,073.24	9,082.84
Syn. TCP	14.68	55.02	215.69	2,015.29	87.05	304.79	1,185.76	10,081.13
Asyn. TCP	15.21	75.95	316.03	3,015.03	74.03	293.63	1,172.10	10,069.80
UDP	8.40	28.72	109.05	1,009.25	-	-	-	-
PURE (1472)	14.87	34.45	113.84	1,012.17	186.23	186.94	266.65	1,160.34
PURE (65,507)	-	-	-	-	141.53	162.68	242.66	1,133.84

Latency Evaluation

We also evaluated our prototypical PURE implementation with regard to latency, using the same measurement setup as described earlier.

The measurement results are summarized in Table 4. For doNothing(), PURE shows nearly the same outstanding performance as UPD. As can be inferred from the "0 ms" column, the slightly higher latency dates back to slower processing times and is thus owed to the experimental implementation. For the other columns, we expected values about the processing time t_{proc} (roughly 14 ms) plus twice the delay time set in *Nistnet* (t_{Nist}). One period is due to the request message, the other to the response. This expectation becomes manifest in the measured data. For all other columns we measured nearly exactly values of $t_{proc} + 2 \, t_{Nist}$. The same facts are true for UDP and can be seen very clearly in the measured values.

With all TCP-based bindings, at least another two times t_{Nist} must be imputed to the TCP three-way handshake: The value of t_{Nist} occurs once for sending the TCP-SYN fragment and a second time for transmitting the TCP-SYN/ACK response. After receiving this TCP segment, the connecting host is ready to send data. So we need another two times t_{Nist} for exchanging the RPC request and response messages. Therefore we can expect at least $t_{proc} + 4 \, t_{Nist}$ for all TCP-based bindings.

The measured values of the synchronous TCP binding are very close to this analytical value. For asynchronous TCP it is clear that we have to add another two times t_{proc} because two TCP connection setups are necessary. So all in all we need $t_{proc} + 6 \, t_{Nist}$ here.

As shown in the measurement results, the same holds for the HTTP implementation due to the exchanged HTTP CONTINUE message (see the above subsection "Summary on Latency"). As already stated, this behavior also adds two times t_{proc} to the overall delay resulting in $t_{proc} + 6\, t_{Nist}$.

For the doNothing() test case, we can summarize that with PURE, latency decreases by up to two-thirds when compared to HTTP or asynchronous TCP. Even in comparison with synchronous TCP, PURE works up to 50% faster.

With the getImage(String) test case, it is not so easy to make an analytical estimation of the experimental results because here the response message is much larger than the MTU and therefore it must be fragmented into several parts. This fragmentation can be either done by IP or by a protocol on a higher level. The number of fragments is hard to estimate because it may vary from one protocol implementation to another. Also with PURE the number of fragments on the application level is variable: For the sake of transparency and fairness, we conducted the analysis using two different settings for the so-called maximum segment size (MSS) of PURE. To avoid IP fragmentation, the MSS was first set to 1,472 bytes (MSS = MTU - IP header - UPD header), leading to message fragmentation only by PURE (instead of by IP) and hence to longer processing times. If the MSS is set to the maximum value of 65,507 bytes, less fragmentation work is done by PURE (and more by IP). In that case, the more efficient implementation of IP leads to shorter processing times.

For all cases comprising network latency, PURE exhibits the shortest overall delays. Compared to HTTP and TCP, it reduces latency up to a factor of roughly 9. It is notable that HTTP in some cases works faster than TCP which is probably owed to implementation details.

All in all, it can be concluded that PURE is the fastest transport binding that is (other than UDP) capable of transferring SOAP messages bigger than 64 kilobytes. For small messages, it is nearly as efficient as UDP and by orders of magnitude more efficient than all other bindings even though its implementation is currently in a prototypical state.

Conclusion and Future Work

Although SOAP has been designed as a protocol that can be bound to various transport mechanisms, the HTTP binding is virtually the only one that is used in practice. HTTP has basically two major disadvantages. First, it causes a serious amount of overhead, and second, it is a request-response protocol, lacking support for asynchronous messaging.

Since Web services are used in more and more fields of application, developers need a larger variety of bindings to choose from.

In addition to that, more and more SOAP extensions like WS-Addressing and WS-ReliableMessaging become available. They are extending—or even obsolescing—certain binding functionalities: there is a trend to put more and more functionalities directly into the SOAP header rather than relying on transport-level features.

In consequence very lean bindings can be designed. They are reducing the protocol overhead, making SOAP messaging more flexible and efficient.

The contribution of this chapter is two-fold. First, we presented an evaluation study of existing SOAP bindings that tend to be more lightweight than HTTP. We showed that in terms of data rate efficiency and flexibility, SOAP-over-UDP clearly performs best. It also imposes the by far lowest latency, due to the missing TCP-style three-way handshake. Unfortunately this binding can handle SOAP messages with less than 64 kilobytes only. This clearly degrades its applicability in practice.

Second, we presented a new UDP-based SOAP binding called PURE. It combines the advantages of SOAP-over-UDP with the ability to transport SOAP messages up to 4 gigabytes. Furthermore it provides lightweight mechanisms for message retransmission using timeouts in combination with negative acknowledgments. Optional positive acknowledgments can be used to increase the transport reliability. This is especially interesting in scenarios where the use of SOAP-level features like WS-ReliableMessaging is out of scope.

We evaluated our current PURE implementation with focus on both data rate efficiency and latency. Our tests showed that it is as efficient as the UDP binding introduced by Gudgin (2004), but can handle large SOAP messages by supporting message fragmentation.

We are currently working on an improved implementation of PURE. A major problem of UDP is the lack of a flow control mechanism. Therefore we are developing a "stop-and-wait" flow control that makes use of the (already existing) *AKR* and *ACK* header flags. Furthermore we are optimizing timer values, buffer sizes, and the back-off algorithm for retransmits.

The next step will be to work out a detailed specification of PURE. This will be the basis for new implementations on other platforms. Possibly this will include a simulation platform like Ns-2 (*http://www.isi.edu/nsnam/ns/*).

Altogether our survey of different transport bindings showed that the time has come for SOAP bindings other than HTTP. Approaches like WS-Addressing and WS-ReliableMessaging are demanding lightweight SOAP transport. Also Web service applications are increasingly taking advantage of point-to-multipoint MEPs and asynchronous messaging. With PURE we could demonstrate how a modern, lightweight SOAP binding might look. Obviously PURE will not be the "standard" SOAP binding of the future, but targets specialized application domains like mobile networks or real-time control application scenarios.

References

Allman, M. (2003). An evaluation of xml-rpc. *ACM SIGMETRICS Performance Evaluation Review, 30*(4), 2-11.

Chiu, K., Govindaraju, M., & Bramley, R. (2002, July). Investigating the limits of soap performance for scientific computing. *Proceedings of the 11th IEEE International Symposium on High Performance Distributed Computing* (HPDC'02) (pp. 246-255), Edinburgh, Scotland.

Davis, D. (2004). *The hidden impact of WS-Addressing on SOAP.* Retrieved February 15, 2007, from *http://www-106.ibm.com/developerworks/library/ws-address.html*

Du, H., & Liu, J. (2004). *Building a JMS Web service using SOAP over JMS and WebSphere Studio.* Retrieved February 15, 2007, from *http://www-106.ibm.com/developerworks/websphere/library/techarticles/0402_du/0402_du.html*

Ferris, C., & Langworthy, D. (2004). *Web services reliable messaging protocol (WS-ReliableMessaging).* Retrieved February 15, 2007, from *ftp://www6.software.ibm.com/software/developer/library/ws-reliablemessaging200403.pdf*

Fielding, R., Gettys, J., Mogul, J., Frystyk, H., Masinter, L., Leach, P., & Berners-Lee, T. (1999). *RFC 2616: Hypertext transfer protocol–HTTP/1.1.*

Ghandeharizadeh, S., Papadopoulos, C., Cai, M., & Chintalapudi, K. (2004). Performance of networked xml-driven cooperative applications. *Concurrent Engineering, 12*(3), 195-203.

Gudgin, M. (2004). *SOAP-over-UDP.* Retrieved February 15, 2007, from *http://msdn2.microsoft.com/en-us/library/ms951224.aspx*

Kiss, R. (2004). *SoapMSMQ transport.* Retrieved February 15, 2007, from *http://www.codeproject.com/cs/webservices/SoapMSMQ.asp*

Maine, S. (2004). *SoapSMTP transport.* Retrieved February 15, 2007, from *http://hyperthink.net/blog/content/binary/Net.Hyperthink.Samples.SoapSmtp.zip*

Marahrens, I. (2003). *Performace- und effizienz-analyse verschiedener RPC-varianten.* Diploma Thesis, TU Braunschweig, Germany.

Mouat, A. (2002). *XML diff and patch utilities.* Cs4 Dissertation, Heriot-Watt University, Scotland.

Mountain, H.M., Kopecky, J., Williams, S., Daniels, G., & Mendelsohn, N. (2002). *SOAP version 1.2 email binding.* Retrieved February 15, 2007, from *http://www.w3.org/TR/2002/NOTE-soap12-email-20020626*

Nadalin, A., Kaler C., Hallam-Baker P., & Monzillo R. (2004). *Web service security: SOAP Message Security 1.0 (WS-Security 2004).* Oasis.

O'Tuathail, E., & Rose, M.T. (2002). *RFC 3288: Using the simple object access protocol (soap) in blocks extensible exchange protocol (beep).*

Postel, J. (1980). *RFC 768: User datagram protocol.*

Postel, J. (1981). *RFC 791: Internet protocol.*

Shannon, C., Moore, D., & Claffy, K.C. (2002). Beyond folklore: Observations on fragmented traffic. *IEEE/ACM Transactions on Networking, 10*(6), 709-720.

Shneiderman, B. (1984). Response time and display rate in human performance with computers. *ACM Computing Surveys, 16*(3), 265-285.

Tian, M., Voigt, T., Naumowicz, T., Ritter, H., & Schiller J. (2003, July). Performance considerations for mobile Web services. *Proceedings of the IEEE Communication Society Workshop on Applications and Services in Wireless Networks,* Bern, Switzerland.

van Engelen, R.A. (2004, July). Constructing finite state automata for high performance Web services. *Proceedings of the IEEE International Conference on Web Services,* San Diego, CA.

W3C. (2003a). *Recommendation: SOAP version 1.2 part 1: Messaging framework.*

W3C. (2003b). *Recommendation: SOAP version 1.2 part 2: Adjuncts.* Author.

W3C. (2004). *Member submission: Web services addressing (WS-addressing).*

Werner, C., Buschmann, C., Brandt, Y., & Fischer, S. (2006, September 18-22). Compressing SOAP messages by using pushdown automata. *Proceedings of the IEEE International Conference on Web Services* (ICWS'06), Chicago, IL.

Werner, C., Buschmann, C., & Fischer, S. (2005). WSDL-driven SOAP compression. *International Journal of Web Services Research, 2*(1), 18-35.

Wilson, H. (2004). *WSE 2.0 transport supporting SOAP-over-UDP v0.1.* Retrieved February 15, 2007, from *http://www.dynamic-cast.com/downloads/WseTransports_0_1.zip*

Chapter V

A Framework Supporting Context-Aware Multimedia Web Services Delivery

Jia Zhang, Northern Illinois University, USA

Liang-Jie Zhang, IBM T.J. Watson Research, USA

Francis Quek, Virginia Tech, USA

Jen-Yao Chung, IBM T.J. Watson Research, USA

Abstract

As Web services become more and more popular, how to manage multimedia Web services provisioning and delivery remains challenging. This chapter presents a componentization model to support quality of service (QoS)-centered, context-aware multimedia Web services delivery, which seamlessly incorporates cutting-edge technologies relating to Web services. A multimedia Web service is divided into control flow and data flow, each being delivered via different infrastructures and channels. We also propose enhancements to Simple Object Access Protocol (SOAP) and Composite Capability/Preference Profiles (CC/PP) protocols to improve their flexibility to serve multimedia Web services. In addition, we present a set of experiments to show how our service-oriented componentization model can support efficient delivery and management of multimedia Web services.

Introduction

A Web service is a programmable Web application that is universally accessible through standard Internet protocols (Ferris & Farrell, 2003). The rapidly emerging technology of Web services exhibits the capability of facilitating business-to-business (B2B) collaboration in an unprecedented way. By means of each organization exposing its software services on the Internet and making them universally accessible via standard programmatic interfaces, this Web services paradigm enables and facilitates the sharing of heterogeneous data and software resources among collaborating organizations (Benatallah, Sheng, & Ngu, 2002). In addition, Web services technology provides a uniform framework to increase cross-language and cross-platform interoperability for distributed computing and resource sharing over the Internet. Furthermore, this paradigm of Web services opens a new cost-effective way of engineering software to quickly aggregate individually published Web services as components into new services. Therefore, the Web services technology has attained significant momentum in both academia and industry.

If the sharable data to be published by a Web service contain multimedia content, which refers to information that seamlessly integrates multiple media types in a synchronized and interactive presentation, the Web service is considered as a multimedia Web service. Multimedia Web services pose new challenges due to the unique characteristics of multimedia data (Khan, Ghafoor, & Paul, 2002). First, the transport of the multimedia information must meet some quality of service (QoS) requirements, such as the synchronization within and among different multimedia data streams or real-time delivery. For example, let us consider a typical video-on-demand (VoD) service, an Internet Kara OK service. It is critical to provide a significant short-response-time service to a VIP customer. In addition, the audio and video information needs to be synchronized on the customer's system. Second, the Simple Object Access Protocol (SOAP, 2004), the core transport technique of Web services, does not support massive message transport that is imperative for multimedia content transport, nor multimedia QoS requirements (Khan et al., 2002). Third, with the advancement of wireless information appliances, Web service interfaces provide a means to enable the content or service to be created once and accessed by multiple SOAP-enabled [4-6] devices, such as wireless phones (NORTEL), personal digital assistance (PDAs), set-top boxes, as well as regular Web browsers. A Web service is thus considered to be device independent if it can be delivered to different devices (Han, Perret, & Naghshineh, 2000). How to deliver a multimedia Web service to users based upon their possessed devices remains challenging.

In summary, the interoperability of multimedia Web services is not without penalty since the value added by this new Web service paradigm can be largely defeated if a multimedia Web service: (1) cannot guarantee QoS attributes, (2) cannot be transported via the Internet in an organized manner, and (3) cannot be effectively adapted to end devices including mobile devices. In this chapter, we aim to present a solution to these existing issues. We accomplish this goal in several ways. First, we propose a separation of control flow and data flow for multimedia Web services, with SOAP used to transport the control flow. Second, we propose enhancements to SOAP to facilitate its flexibility to serve the transportation of multimedia Web services. Third, we propose enhancements to Composite Capability/Preference Profiles (CC/PP) protocol (CCPP) to provide an easy and flexible way to split and adapt multimedia Web services to appropriate composite devices, and increase the flexibility for users to manage multi-devices. Finally, we propose a service-oriented multimedia componentization model to support device-independent multimedia Web services.

The remainder of this chapter is organized as follows. In the next section, we briefly introduce some core techniques of multimedia Web services. We then discuss related work, and present our solution and performance analysis. Finally, we summarize the contributions and innovations, assess limitations, and discuss future work directions.

Core Techniques of Multimedia Web Services

In this section, we will first briefly introduce the core techniques and standards of multimedia Web services to provide readers with some background context.

Web services typically adopt a provider/broker/requester architectural model (Roy & Ramanujan, 2001). A service provider registers Web services at service brokers, a service broker publishes registered services, and a service requester searches Web services from service brokers. The essential aspect of this model is the concept of dynamic invocation: Web services are hosted by service providers, and service requesters dynamically invoke the Web services over the Internet on an on-demand basis.

In order to enable the communications among service providers, service brokers, and service requesters, the paradigm of Web services mainly embraces three core categories of supporting facilities: communication protocols, service descriptions, and service discovery (Roy & Ramanujan, 2001). Each category possesses its own ad hoc standard. SOAP acts as a simple and lightweight protocol for exchanging structured and typed information among Web services. The Web Service Description Language (WSDL, 2004) is an XML-based description language that is used to describe the programmatic interfaces of Web services . The Universal Description, Discovery, and Integration (UDDI, 2004) standard provides a mechanism to publish, register, and locate Web services. It should be noted that here we adopt a narrow definition of Web services that refers to an implicit definition of SOAP+WSDL+UDDI for the purpose of simplicity. This implies a focus on the management of standalone Web services, instead of the compositions of and the interactions between multiple Web services.

As more and more business organizations have been adopting Web services technology to publish their sharable data to make their services accessible to more other organizations, it is possible that the data to be published include multimedia information (e.g., audio and video). Due to the fact that multimedia data exhibits unique features that require specific handling (Khan et al., 2002), it is necessary to examine the existing Web services techniques to better support multimedia Web services. When the SOAP+WSDL+UDDI framework is applied to support a multimedia Web service, two major factors influence the success of a multimedia Web service: (1) the transport of multimedia information over the Web, and (2) the management of composite devices for multimedia contents. Multimedia content caching and streaming are two essential solutions to the first issue (Paknikar, Kankanhalli, Ramakrishnan, Srinivasan, & Ngoh, 2000). Web caching at a service provider site can largely increase the service provider's ability to support a large amount of service requesters. The streaming paradigm enables a media file be played at the service requester's site while it is being transferred over the Web; therefore, the burden of the service provider can be alleviated. Regarding the latter issue, at the service requester side, multimedia data is normally split over multiple devices with appropriate multimedia capabilities (Han et al., 2000).

Due to the rapid advancement of wireless information appliances, a Web service will gain more popularity if it is accessible from mobile devices in addition to normal Web browsers, such as wireless phones and PDAs (Pham, Schneider, & Goose, 2000). A Web service is thus considered to be device independent if it can be delivered to different devices (Han et al., 2000). Several techniques are designed to support the device independence. Based on an Extensible Markup Language (XML) and Resource Description Framework (RDF)-based framework, Composite Capability/Preference Profiles (CC/PP, 2001) are proposed to define device capabilities and user preferences so as to manage composite devices. The combination of XML and Extensible Stylesheet Language (XSL) is usually utilized to realize device independence (Kirda, 2001).

Related Works

With the basic background, we can now examine related work on multimedia Web services.

Paknikar et al. (2000) define a client-side framework for the caching and streaming of Internet multimedia. The architecture consists of a number of caching proxy servers. A central controlling proxy server called a broker handles all of the initial interactions, and then transfers controls to its sibling proxy servers. This hierarchical structure provides scalability for the proxy servers. Their work also defines a layered replacement policy for caching scalably encoded video objects. Paknikar et al. (2000) predicted that the Real Time Streaming Protocol (RTSP) would become the de facto standard for Internet audio/video (A/V) caching and streaming.

Pham et al. (2000) define a Small Screen/Composite Device (SS/CD) architecture that supports small-screen device-focused communication systems. The key component of the architecture is a Smart Gateway (SG) that distributes multimedia information to the most appropriate composite devices to ensure reliable performances. The critical component of SG is a set of algorithms associated with a Selection-Device-Assignment-Matrix. FieldWise (Fagrell, Forsberg, & Sanneblad, 2000) relies on a server engine to adapt multimedia responses according to the capabilities of the client devices and their network connections. However, these two projects do not adopt the most current Web techniques and standards, such as XML/XSL and CC/PP.

WebSplitter (Han et al., 2000) provides a unified XML framework supporting multi-device Web browsing. The framework defines an XML-based metadata policy file based on the CC/PP protocol to enable users to specify their access privilege groups. With WebSplitter, all Web pages are constructed as XML files, with pre-defined tags describing mappings to the corresponding access privileges. A proxy is then adopted to split a Web page to different devices. Corresponding XSL style sheets are attached to devices to transform the customized XML to the suitable device-understandable languages. MyXML (Kirda, 2001) is an XML/XSL-based template engine to solve the issue of device independence, whose idea is to completely separate the content from its layout information. Similar to the WebSplitter, MyXML utilizes the XML/XSL combination to realize device independence. However, MyXML introduces a whole set of syntax elements that requires a learning curve.

All these efforts concentrate on the client site to facilitate multimedia storage and streaming, to assist multimedia distribution, and to support device independence. At this moment, however, it appears that there is still a lack of generic infrastructure for considering both client and server sides of multimedia Web services. An additional limitation is that these methods may or may not integrate easily with the most current Web technologies and standards, since Web service is still an emerging paradigm. Here we seek to provide efficient support of delivery and management of multimedia Web services. In contrast with the previous approaches, we accomplish this objective by seamlessly incorporating the cutting-edge techniques of Web services and providing a SOAP-oriented component-based framework to support device-independent multimedia Web services.

Service-Oriented Compontization Model

In this section, we will introduce our solution to support multimedia Web services. We will first discuss our idea of separation of control flow from data flow to utilize SOAP. Second, we will propose our enhancements to SOAP. Third, we will propose enhancements to CC/PP protocol. Finally, we will propose our service-oriented multimedia componentization model.

Separation of Control Flow and Data Flow

As a core technique, SOAP is used to transport the content of Web services. However, SOAP was not originally designed to support multimedia Web services; therefore, its current version is not appropriate for streaming multimedia content. The reasons are multi-folded:

1. It is usually infeasible to put a large piece of multimedia content (e.g., a video clip) into one message. However, SOAP does not support message boxcarring and batching (SOAP, 2004); therefore, its current version cannot be used to transfer streamed multimedia content.

2. Using SOAP to transport data requires enormous network bandwidth due to its eXtensible Markup Language (XML) markup and protocol overhead (Werner, Buschmann, & Fischer, 2004). Therefore, its performance drawback hinders SOAP from transporting multimedia content that is usually associated with QoS requirements such as response time.

3. Current SOAP specification does not provide the facility to define multimedia QoS requirements (Khan et al., 2002) and multimedia management information such as synchronization signals necessary for time-dependent media. In summary, current SOAP is not suitable to transport massive amount of multimedia content.

Nevertheless, we do not have to use SOAP to transport multimedia content. There are already a wealth of existing infrastructures, channels, and standards to support transport of different multimedia content (e.g., MPEG-21, 2004; SMIL, 2004; JPEG, 2004; HotMedia, 2004). We can still utilize these existing techniques to transport the content of media files. But how about the multimedia control information?

Our solution is to separate the control information from the content information. The control information may include: (1) metadata that depict the synchronization relationship between multiple media files, (2) QoS requirements, and (3) other control information such as the service provider. Thus transporting a multimedia

Web service includes the delivery of both data flow and control flow. The essential advantage is that different transport protocols can be employed to deliver either data flow or control flow—that is, SOAP can be used to transport the control information while traditional multimedia channels can be used to transport the multimedia content in a SOAP-specific environment.

This separation of control flow and data flow promises several merits. First, the separation solves the dilemma of transferring multimedia applications into multimedia Web services. Control information will be delivered by SOAP so that different multimedia Web services can interoperate with each other, while multimedia content information can be delivered by traditional multimedia protocols to achieve acceptable performance. Second, the separation provides a loose coupling between control information and content information; thus, the content information can be reused for different Web services. Third, the separation facilitates the tracking and logging of control information so that we can achieve better management and monitoring of multimedia Web services.

Enhancements to SOAP to Support Multimedia Web Services

SOAP (2004) has been considered to be a de facto communication standard to deliver Web services; however, it was not originally designed particularly to deliver multimedia Web services. First, the nature of multimedia data (Khan et al., 2002) requires the fact that the transportation of the multimedia information normally has to meet some QoS requirements, such as the synchronization within and among different multimedia data streams or real-time delivery. Consequently, a message containing multimedia data should carry over its QoS requirements as the guidance for Internet transportation. Nevertheless, the original SOAP specifications do not support this feature. Therefore, we believe that enhancements to SOAP are compulsory in order to facilitate multimedia Web services.

Second, for simplicity, SOAP does not support boxcarring and batching of messages; also it is a one-way protocol (SOAP, 2004). There are cases where it is difficult to embed a large multimedia file into one SOAP message. On the contrary, it may be more practical to load a big chunk of information into multiple SOAP messages. Of course there should be a way to identify the relationships among these related SOAP messages. In exceptional cases, some of the media files may not even be suitable to be transferred in SOAP messages, for example, a multimedia segment may need to be transferred in one file with specific file extension. Therefore, special attributes should be provided to identify all of these situations. It should be noted that in the last section, we discussed that multimedia information can be transported via different channels other than SOAP. However, for completeness, we still believe that SOAP should be extended with mechanisms to transport multimedia information.

Our enhancements to SOAP can be therefore categorized into two sets: message batching specifications and multimedia QoS specifications. Two sets of attributes are introduced as summarized in Figure 1, and each of them will be discussed in detail in this section. We first propose a simple workaround of boxcarring and batching of messages to bolster large-scaled multimedia data transportation. A service provider can divide a large message into multiple smaller messages, and these smaller messages altogether conceptually constitute a message box. The service provider can then send these messages to the service requester asynchronously.

As illustrated in the first part of Figure 1, several attributes are defined to support this ability: SenderURL, id, index, and total. SenderURL is defined to specify the unique address of the service provider, so that the service requester knows where to fetch further information if so desired; id is defined to uniquely identify the message box in the domain of the service provider; index is defined to identify the index of the message in the corresponding message box; and total is defined to identify the total number of messages in the message box. These attributes can be utilized to uniquely identify a SOAP message and the relationships between messages. In addition, a global attribute MustSendBack is introduced, which can be utilized to specify that the information is required to be sent back to the service provider without any changes. For example, the service requester's profile needs to be sent back along with the result for the proper multimedia distribution.

Employing the metaphor of the envelope in postal delivery, we insert this identification information of the multimedia content into the corresponding SOAP envelope as the first part. Meanwhile, we propose to always have the first message contain the metadata in its body block, which identifies the structure of the message box--that is, the order of the messages in the box. Attributes Metadata and component are defined to specify the metadata information. Let us take a piece of a SOAP message as an example.

```
<SOAP-ENV:Envelope

....

      SOAP-ENV:MustSendBack="RequestId0001, Profile001"

      SOAP-ENV:id="Msg00001"

      SOAP-ENV:index="1"

      SOAP-ENV:total="5"/>

      <SOAP-ENV:Body>

         <m:Metadata>

            <component>Msg00001"</component>

            <component>Msg00002"</component>

            <component>Msg00003"</component>

            <component>Msg00004"</component>
```

```
            <component>Msg00005"</component>
        </m:Metadata>
      </SOAP-ENV:Body>
....
</SOAP-ENV:Envelope>
```

This SOAP message is the response message to the request "RequestId0001." This request id "RequestId0001" and user profile information "Profile001" must be sent back. We can see that the message is identified by its unique id "Msg00001"; it is the first of the total five messages in the message box. Metadata records the message ids of all five messages: "Msg0001," "Msg0002," "Msg0003," "Msg0004," and "Msg0005." Therefore, the requester that receives this message would be aware of the remaining four messages, then could schedule to pre-fetch them with specified ids if so desired.

Second, we introduce five global attributes to the SOAP definition in order to enable a SOAP message to carry on its QoS requirements: reliable, realTime, unicast, multicast, and secure. These five attributes are summarized in the second part of

Figure 1. SOAP attributes introduced

Attribute	Definition
SenderURL	Unique address of the service provider
id	Uniquely identify the message
index	The index in message box
total	The total number of messages in message box
MustSendBack	Required to be sent back without changes
Metadata	Specify the structure of the message box
component	Specify the messages in the message box

Attribute	Definition
reliable	Reliable transportation
realTime	Real-time transportation
unicast	Unicast to specific node
multicast	Multicast to multiple nodes
secure	Secure in the transportation

Figure 1. For an attribute to be set, its keyword-value pair must be present in this envelop block. The reliable attribute can be used to indicate whether the SOAP message requires reliable transportation or not. The value of the reliable attribute is either "1" or "0." The absence of the reliable attribute is semantically equivalent to its presence with a value "0." If a header element is tagged with a reliable attribute with a value of "1," the recipient of that header entry either MUST find a reliable transportation protocol or MUST fail processing the message.

The realTime attribute can be used to indicate whether the SOAP message requires real-time transportation or not. The value of the realTime attribute is either "1" or "0." The absence of the realTime attribute is semantically equivalent to its presence with a value "0." If a header element is tagged with a realTime attribute with a value of "1," the recipient of that header entry either MUST find enough resources to transfer the message right away or MUST fail processing the message.

The unicast attribute can be used to indicate whether the SOAP message is to be unicasted to a specific end point. The value of the unicast attribute is either "1" or "0." The absence of the unicast attribute is semantically equivalent to its presence with a value "0." If a header element is tagged with a unicast attribute with a value of "1," the recipient of that header entry either MUST find a available path to the specified end point node or MUST fail processing the message.

The multicast attribute can be used to indicate whether the SOAP message is to be multicast to multiple users. The value of the multicast attribute is either "1" or "0." The absence of the multicast attribute is semantically equivalent to its presence with a value "0." If a header element is tagged with a multicast attribute with a value of "1," the recipient of that header entry either MUST find available paths to all specified end-point users or MUST fail processing the message.

The secure attribute can be used to indicate whether the SOAP message has to be kept secure in the process of transportation. The value of the secure attribute is either "1" or "0." The absence of the secure attribute is semantically equivalent to its presence with a value "0." If a header element is tagged with a secure attribute with a value of "1," the recipient of that header entry either MUST find secure paths to the destination or MUST fail processing the message.

Following is another example of a piece of a SOAP message containing some multimedia information. This message needs to be transferred reliably, real time, and only transferred to one specific end user. This enhancement provides a way for a SOAP message to delineate its QoS requirements, which can be utilized as a guidance of Internet transportation tools to select different paths and transportation protocols so as to increase performance.

```
<SOAP-ENV:Envelope xmlns:SOAP-ENV="http://schemas.xmlsoap.org/soap/envelope/"
  SOAP-ENV:encodingStyle="http://schemas.xmlsoap.org/soap/encoding/"/>
    SOAP-ENV:reliable="1"
```

```
        SOAP-ENV:realTime="1"
        SOAP-ENV:unicast="1"
...
        <SOAP-ENV:Body>
...
        </SOAP-ENV:Body>
...
</SOAP-ENV:Envelope>
```

Enhancement to CC/PP Supporting Multimedia Web Services

Multimedia Web services normally need to split multimedia data over multiple devices with appropriate multimedia capabilities (Han et al., 2000). CC/PP specifies an XML- and RDF-based framework to help define device capabilities and user preferences so as to manage composite devices (CC/PP, 2001). We adopt CC/PP to support multimedia Web services for two reasons. One is that CC/PP was designed particularly for describing device capabilities and user preferences. The other is that CC/PP is built on top of popular XML technology. Utilizing the CC/PP format, every user can create his or her own profile that declares the list of the user's available resources (devices) and preferences about how each resource would be utilized. However, we found that CC/PP definition is too rigid for device capabilities. For instance, one device may be capable of accepting one kind of media information with some simple transformations, and CC/PP does not support this specification. Therefore we extend CC/PP by enabling transformation description to be added to devices.

With our extension, in a user's profile, every resource is declared as a separate item, such as a WAP phone. Each item comprises two parts: one is the declaration of the hardware, and the other is the declaration of the service, or more directly, multimedia resource files that the device can receive. Following is an example of a piece of an extended CC/PP profile for a WAP phone.

```
<ccpp:component>
        <rdf:Description rdf:about="TerminalHardware">
            <rdf:type rdf:resource="HardwarePlatform"/>
            <DeviceName>Nokia-3360</DeviceName>
            <screen>30X23mm</screen>
            <display>101X52Pixels</display>
            <PixelStretch>1.24</PixelStretch>
```

```
    </rdf:Description>
</ccpp:component>

...

<ccpp:component>
    <rdf:Description rdf:about="Services">
        <rdf:type rdf:resource="SupportedServices"/>
        <rdf:li>HTML</rdf:li>
        <rdf:transform>HTML2WML.xsl</rdf:transform>
    </rdf:Description>
</ccpp:component>
```

As shown, the declaration of this WAP phone contains two parts. The first part defines the hardware, such as the device name, the size of the screen, and resolution. The second part defines its acceptable multimedia information, such as image, text, and WML. However, it can be noticed that the normal HTML code cannot be directly retrieved on this WAP phone. A style sheet named HTML2WML.xsl needs to be used to transform the receiving HTML code to the WAP-enabled WML code. With this extension, CC/PP protocol becomes more powerful in describing device capabilities.

Proposed Model Supporting Multimedia Web Services

As Roy and Ramanujan (2001) summarized, a three-role model is broadly adopted in the field of Web services: service providers, service brokers, and service requesters. From the perspective of a service requester, there are two key questions: how to find a demanded service, and how to get the service effectively. This chapter focuses on the solution to the second question; therefore service brokers and related issues will not be discussed. The starting point of this chapter is that, with the help of service brokers, service requesters have already located the service providers that offer the requested services. Meanwhile, as high-speed local area networks (LANs) have been deployed extensively over the world (Paknikar et al., 2000), users on such LANs normally access the Internet through a proxy server that provides caching facility. Therefore, we make another assumption on such a concept, that users always invoke Web services through their proxy server. In addition, due to the fact that service requesters are normally separated from service providers by the Internet, it is reasonable to assume that a message must pass through multiple networks between them. Based on these three assumptions, the problem can be refined as: how to effectively and efficiently support multiple service requesters, who rely on the same proxy server and require the same Web service from the same service provider that is several networks away.

Figure 2. A component-based framework for multimedia Web services

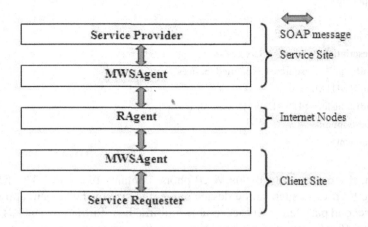

Here we propose a component-based framework as a solution. As illustrated in Figure 2, three types of intelligent agents are introduced as the main components of the framework, and SOAP is adopted as the service transportation protocol. The first agent introduced is the Multimedia Web Service Server Agent (MWSSAgent) that locates at the service provider; the second one is the Multimedia Web Service Agent (MWSAgent) that locates at the proxy server on the clients' LAN; and the third one is the Routing Agent (RAgent) that locates at the intermediate network nodes. Figure 2 also implicates the information path of a multimedia Web service on the basis of this framework. When a service requester submits the request, the MWSSAgent handles the request, invokes the corresponding service backend to get the results, equips return SOAP messages, and sends them to the Internet. The RAgent reads the envelopes of the receiving SOAP messages, analyzes their QoS requirements, and selects the appropriate protocols to send to the next proper RAgent or the proxy server. The MWSAgent finally receives the SOAP messages and propagates to the original requester, as well as distributes the multimedia streams to appropriate media devices, such as Web browsers, audio systems, PDAs, and so forth. We will discuss each of the three agents in detail in the following sections.

Multimedia Web Services Server Agent

A multimedia Web service may generate a complex result including multiple multimedia files. Disregarding the fact that SOAP currently can only bind to HTTP while HTTP was not designed for streaming media data (Paknikar et al., 2000), it is not efficient and practical to encapsulate all information in one SOAP response message

Figure 3. MWSSAgent architecture

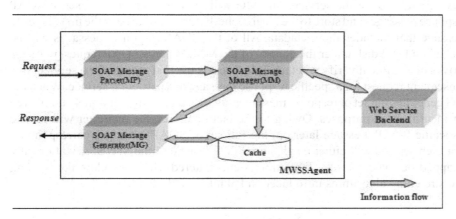

to pass through the Internet, especially when the information may get lost in the process of transportation. With our enhancements to SOAP described in the previous section, a large piece of information can be separated into multiple interrelated SOAP messages, with the first message containing the metadata and specifying the identification of each message. The metadata is completely separated from the real content. Here the metadata includes the structure of the set of the sub-messages, and the relationships between messages. It is one of the main responsibilities of the WMSSAgent to generate the SOAP response message box from the result provided by the service provider. To avoid aggravating Internet traffic, the response philosophy that the MWSSAgent adopts is a lazy-driven norm. That is, it does not always send back to the service requester all of the messages at the same time; some messages may stay on the MWSSAgent until they are requested particularly. Therefore, the caching facility is imperative to support this philosophy. In addition, published Web service providers normally expect a large amount of requests, thus managing and reusing cached messages becomes essential.

Therefore we propose the MWSSAgent as an intelligent agent on the service provider site to facilitate multimedia services. Its architecture is illustrated in Figure 3, together with the interactions among its components. The architecture contains three functional components—SOAP message parser (MP), SOAP message generator (MG), and SOAP message manager (MM)—and a local cache. MP is in charge of parsing incoming SOAP request messages, interpreting the requests, and forwarding them to MM. MM first checks the cache to see whether the result SOAP messages have already been generated and stored. If the results exist, the MM will send back the results through the MG—the MG needs to generate the corresponding return envelopes based on the requests. If the results are not found, the MM will invoke service backend for the service. The MG will then generate the full set of SOAP response messages and store to the local cache, before sending back the first response message that includes the metadata. All of the SOAP response messages will be cached on local disk under the control of the MM. When a SOAP request message arrives, the MP will verify whether the request is the first request for a service, or a subsequent request for a specific response message of a particular service. When the MG generates the set of response messages, all messages will be uniquely numbered for identification purposes. Owing to the fact that a service requester will invoke a specific SOAP message later on, the full set of SOAP messages corresponding to a Web service will either be all stored in the cache of the MWSSAgent or fully swapped out when storage limitation is encountered. Here we adopt the caching and streaming algorithms introduced in Paknikar et al. (2000).

Figure 4. MWSAgent architecture

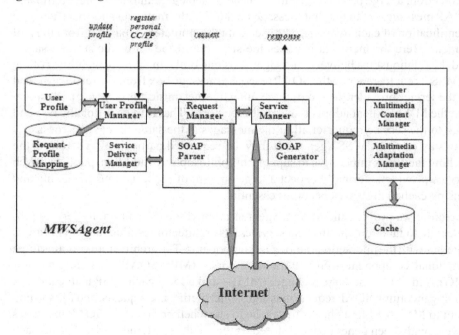

Multimedia Web Services Agent

We propose an MWSAgent as an intelligent agent on the proxy server at the client site to support multimedia Web services. The component-based architecture is illustrated in Figure 4. The MWSAgent comprises four functional components: service broker, user profile manager, service delivery manager, and multimedia manager. Three caches are also contained in an MWSAgent: one for user profiles, one for request-profile mapping, and one for multimedia information.

User Profile Manager (UPM)

UPM registers user profiles and stores them at the user profiles cache. Adopting our extended CC/PP protocol as discussed in the previous section, a user profile declares the list of the user's available resources and the user's preferences about how each resource would be utilized. UPM assigns a unique id to every registered profile, so that one user can possess multiple profiles for the purposes of different Web services. When a user requests a Web service, he or she is required to specify which profile he or she wishes to use to receive the service. The service broker will assign a unique id to each request; and the UPM will store the 2-tuple (request id, profile id) in the cache of request-profile mapping. This 2-tuple will also be included in the SOAP message of the service request as MustSendBack. Therefore, when the response comes in, the UPM will use the sent-back (request id, profile id) pair to pick up the stored corresponding profile from the profile cache. Users are allowed to change their profiles, add new profiles, or delete some profiles. The granularity of the definition of a profile depends on the power of CC/PP and RDF vocabulary.

Multimedia Manager (MManager)

The multimedia manager contains two sub-components: the multimedia content manager (MCM) and the multimedia adaptation manager (MAM). The MCM manages the caching of multimedia SOAP response messages on the local disk of the proxy server. The MAM handles media adaptation if necessary, in order to achieve device independence. In some cases when the destination device is not capable of handling requested multimedia contents, the MAM may convert the media accordingly. In some other cases, the destination device may announce that it is able to receive some media contents after some adaptations are performed. For instance, a WAP phone could accept HTML code; however it needs to be transformed to WML code. In accordance with our extension to the CC/PP, when a user specifies her profile, she can stipulate the transformation algorithm she prefers.

Service Broker

The service broker consists of four sub-components: request manager, service manager, SOAP generator, and SOAP parser, as shown in Figure 4. The SOAP generator generates SOAP request messages; the SOAP parser parses incoming SOAP response messages; and the request manager is a request broker of user requests for Web services. A user may request a Web service that another user from the same LAN has previously requested from the same Web service. Therefore, the request manager will first check the local disk through the MCM. If the result is a hit, the request manager will pass the control to the service manager to send back the information. As a consequence, not only the remote service broker and the service provider will have less traffic, but also the response time may be largely shortened. Otherwise, the request manager will assign a unique id to the request, ask UPM to store to the request-profile mapping, and then call the SOAP generator to generate a SOAP request message and send it to the service provider over the Internet. The unique request id and the user profile id will be marked as MustSendBack and be sent together with the SOAP request.

The service manager is invoked when a SOAP response comes back from Internet. It will first call the SOAP parser to analyze the content of the result message. If the result contains multimedia information not coming together with the first message, the service manager will schedule to pre-fetch the corresponding media files to enhance the streaming of the media data. All the messages will be sent to the MCM to store in a local disk before being sent back to the original requester, so as to achieve caching at the proxy server level. As a result, the service provider might not be even online all the time, but its content can still be available at the cache of the MWSAgent. For persistent multimedia data (e.g., a movie), this cached data may be immediately utilized. For time-varying data, however, a mechanism for determining if the data is stale will have to be employed. Considering scalably encoded or layered video information, for example, such objects have a "base" layer containing essential information, and one or more "enhanced" layers containing higher level information (Paknikar et al., 2000). The service manager will try to download the sub-nodes following the layers. It will attempt to download the lower layers before downloading higher and more enhanced layers. Meanwhile, the service manager will work with the UPM to launch the corresponding user profile. And then the control will be passed to SDM to deliver the result to the original service requester.

Service Delivery Manager (SDM)

The service delivery manager decides the priority and the order of the services to be sent back to the requesters, and decides how to split the returning information to appropriate devices if there are multiple devices. A set of criteria is kept at the SDM to be utilized to optimize the order of the delivery, such as request time, request priority, current available resources, and so forth. The details of the algorithms of the selection and adaptation will not be discussed in this chapter.

Route Agent

SOAP messages are adopted to transfer requests and responses through the Internet between an MWSSAgent and an MWSAgent. A SOAP message in this chapter contains multimedia information that normally possesses QoS requirements. As discussed in the previous section, a SOAP message may have to travel through several heterogeneous intermediate networks before it finally reaches the MWSAgent. Each of these heterogeneous networks could support multiple protocols and the flexibility of selecting protocols dynamically (Banchs, Effelsberg, Tschudin, & Turau, 1998). Therefore, in order to satisfy the performance requirements of the multimedia SOAP message to be transported, each network may need to select the most appropriate network protocol. For example, a NACK-reliable multicast protocol (Floyd, Jacobson, Liu, McCanne, & Zhang, 1997) should be adopted on an ATM network in order to increase performance. We propose the RAgent to achieve this goal. An RAgent resides at intermediate network nodes on the Internet. Generally we suggest that each active network install an RAgent as the high-level director of the network routing. For a legacy system network that does not install RAgent, SOAP messages can be passed without taking a look at the information it carries.

This chapter focuses on the selection of protocols to increase the performance of network transport rather than the selection of path-routing algorithms. The architecture of an RAgent is composed of four sub-components, as illustrated in Figure 5. The SOAP parser is responsible for parsing incoming SOAP messages, determining the QoS requirements, and passing them to the protocol manager (PM). The PM receives QoS requirements, searches the protocol pool (PP), and finds out the appropriate protocol to use. The PP is the interface encapsulating all protocols registered in the corresponding network. The protocol registration manager (PRM) handles the registration of new protocols to the network or removal of some protocols. Under the PP are two sub-components: a cache of the registered protocols, and an abstract matrix that records the protocols and their QoS characteristics, such as reliability, real-time, and security. The PRM maintains the abstract matrix when a new protocol is registered to the PP or removed from the PP.

When the PRM registers a new protocol to the protocol pool, it not only records its QoS properties, but also its cost. The cost here refers to the efficiency of the protocol. The more reliable a protocol is, the more costly it will be. For example, TCP is more costly than UDP because of the acknowledgment requirement. Table 1 is an example of the abstract protocol matrix. Three protocols are registered into the protocol pool: TCP, UDP, and NACKRMP. TCP and NACKRMP are reliable

Figure 5. RAgent architecture

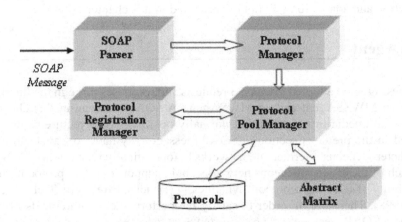

protocols, while NACKRMP is a real-time protocol. TCP and UDP can be used for unicasting to single node, while TCP, UDP, and NACKRMP can all be adopted for the purpose of multicasting. From Table 1 we can also conclude that TCP is more costly than UDP, and NACKRMP costs the most.

Performance Evaluation

The goal of our experiment is to design and conduct a simulation to evaluate the performance of our framework in a typical multimedia Web service application. The application we selected to implement is a distance-learning environment: multiple students request multimedia course information from servers. In such an application, one may assume that the students will be congregated at a set of proxy servers and will be accessing a common set of material. Hence, we want to vary the number of service requesters and proxy servers, holding the other system components constant. To realize this performance analysis, we design the experiment based on the following assumptions. First, we assume that there is only one service provided by the system, and there is only one server machine that provides the service. Second, we assume that multiple students who reside on the same LAN request the service through one common proxy server. Third, we assume that there are three networks between the server and the proxy server: Ethernet and ATM and then Ethernet. A message from the server machine must first pass through these three networks in the

Table 1. Example of abstract protocol matrix

Protocol	TCP	UDP	NACKRMP
Reliability	X		X
Security			
Real-time		X	X
Uni-cast	X	X	
Multi-cast	X	X	
Cost	4	1	5

Figure 6. An example applying framework

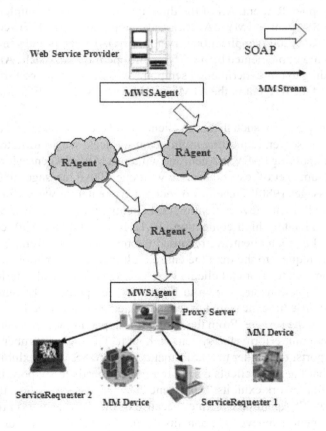

order specified before it hits the proxy server. Ethernet has TCP and is NACK RMP (Floyd et al., 1997) registered, and the ATM network has UDP and is NACK RMP registered. Suppose we require real-time QoS multimedia transportation. Fourth, we assume that the transportation time between a service requester and its corresponding proxy server is ignored due to the fact that they reside on the same LAN. Therefore, the problem is simplified and refined as shown in Figure 6. One server machine stores all of the course information and serves as the service provider, and multiple students request the same course information from this server machine as service requesters. Each student may possess one computer and some multimedia devices, such as speakers or cell phones. All students reside on the same LAN and communicate to the service provider through a proxy server machine.

We set up the experimental environment as shown in Figure 6. The multimedia Web service is implemented as a normal J2EE-compatible Web application on the JRun (2004) application server. One MWSSAgent is installed on the server; and one MWSAgent is installed on the proxy server. Each of the three networks has one machine that applies RAgent. All of the three types of agents are implemented in Java. Both MWSSAgent and MWSAgent are also implemented as J2EE-compatible servers on the JRun (2004) application server. The SOAP parsers and generators on all three agents are implemented by modifying the open source Apache Axis (2004) system. According to our experimental setup, the two RAgents in the Ethernet will choose TCP, and the RAgent in the ATM network will choose UDP to increase the performance.

We design the experiment such that each client would create threads and then communicate with the server, requesting multimedia services. We perform tests on the server machine applying a MWSSAgent and without a MWSSAgent. Moreover, we performed the same set of tests on service with one SOAP message (980KB) and two SOAP messages (980KB each). For our experimentation we performed very low contention (1 client), low contention (2,4 clients), moderately low contention (6,8 clients), moderately high contention (10,12,14 clients), and high contention (16,18 clients). For each client, we recorded the response time, from the time the thread starts the request to the time the entire multimedia information is received. Then the response times from all clients were averaged. The results performed on the four sets of situations are shown in Figure 7. Each point in the figure shows the average response time measured in seconds when there are specific numbers of clients requesting the service. From the figure, it is apparent that the system applying MWSSAgent outperforms the system without it. The higher number of clients the system supports, the higher the performance the MWSSAgent exhibits. Figure 7 also shows that the more clients a service provider needs to support, the higher efficiency our framework exhibits. If only one client requests a service, the system applying the MWSSAgent takes longer because of the extra operation time spent on the MWSSAgent. However, the benefits justify this extra work as long as there are multiple requesters.

Figure 7. One-proxy performance

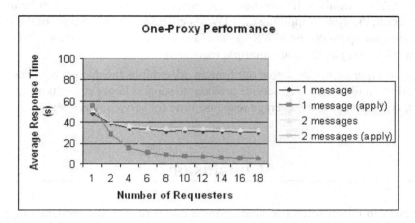

Figure 8. Two-proxy performance

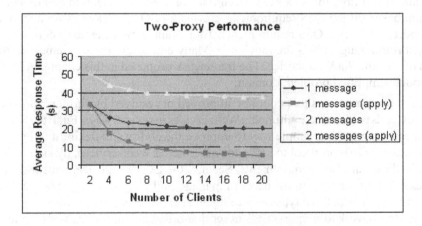

To test the effectiveness and efficiency of applying the MWSAgent, we relax one assumption from the first experiment, so that there are two proxy servers in the experimental system, and clients are averagely distributed behind these two proxy servers. We apply the MWSAgent on each of the proxy servers. The results performed on the same four sets of situations are illustrated in Figure 8. The approach to measure the results is the same as that of the first experiment. The figure shows that the system applying MWSAgent outperforms the system without it. Figure 8 shows that the more clients that share one proxy server, the higher the efficiency the MWSAgent exhibits. It also shows that when there is only one client behind a proxy server, the system applying the MWSAgent takes longer because of the extra operation time spent on the MWSAgent. However, again, the benefits justify this extra work as long as there are multiple requesters.

These two experiments show that our framework exhibits the distinct advantage of facilitating a multimedia Web service provider to support larger amounts of Internet clients, and shortening the average response time for service requesters.

Conclusion

We present in this chapter a service-oriented componentization model to support device-independent multimedia Web services. In the current infrastructure, we adopt caching and replacement algorithms introduced in Paknikar et al. (2000) for both the MWSAgent and the MWSSAgent. Since these two agents serve different purposes, using the same set of caching and replacement algorithms may not be most efficient. In addition, this chapter concentrates on protocol selection and dynamic binding, based on the QoS requirements carried by SOAP messages on networks to support multimedia QoS requirements. To guarantee multimedia QoS requests, efficient routing algorithms are inevitable. Many challenging issues remain in the realm of multimedia Web service. The framework proposed in this chapter is based on a much simplified problem domain.

Despite these limitations that could be improved or resolved by further work, our model extends research on multimedia Web services in several ways. First, the SOAP enhancements provide a simple way to improve the ability and flexibility of the ad hoc standard SOAP protocol to serve for multimedia Web services, by supporting batch facilities and QoS requirements. Second, the CC/PP enhancements increase the flexibility of the system for users to manage multi-devices and ensure device independency. Third, three types of intelligent agents are synergistically integrated to form a framework to support efficient service-oriented multimedia Web services. This model also facilitates caching and streaming of multimedia transport. In addition, our model seamlessly incorporates cutting-edge technologies relating to Web services: SOAP, XML/XSL, and the CC/PP. The result of this research can be applied to the software industry and serves as an architectural design to construct multimedia Web service applications.

We intend to continue our research work in the following directions. First, we will explore efficient caching, replacement, and pre-fetching algorithms so as to improve QoS performance. Second, we will attempt to bind SOAP to other more multimedia-oriented transportation protocols, such as Real Time Streaming Protocol (RTSP). Third, we will investigate QoS routing algorithms on routers to support SOAP QoS requirements. Fourth, we will pursue a formal description language to facilitate protocols to be published on the Web and dynamically registered to networks. Finally, we intend to implement a mechanism to monitor multimedia QoS performances over different networks.

References

Axis. (2004). Apache AXIS project, SOAP protocol implementation. Retrieved from http://ws.apache.org/axis

Banchs, A., Effelsberg, W., Tschudin, C., & Turau, V. (1998, October 11-14). Multicasting multimedia streams with active networks. *Proceedings of the 23rd Annual Conference on Local Computer Networks* (pp. 150-154). Boston.

Benatallah, B., Sheng, Q.Z., & Ngu, A.H.H. (2002, February 26-March 1). Declarative composition and peer-to-peer provisioning of dynamic Web services. *Proceedings of the 18th International Conference on Data Engineering (ICDE'02)* (pp. 297-308), San Jose, CA.

CC/PP. (2001, March 15). *Composite Capability/Preference Profile*. Working Draft, W3C.

Fagrell, H., Forsberg, K., & Sanneblad, J. (2000). FieldWise: A mobile knowledge management architecture. *Proceedings of the ACM Conference on Computer Supported Cooperative Work (CSCW'00)* (pp. 211-220), Philadelphia.

Ferris, C., & Farrell, J. (2003). What are Web services? *Communications of the ACM, 46*(6), 31.

Floyd, S., Jacobson, V., Liu, C.G., McCanne, S., & Zhang, L. (1997). A reliable multicast framework for light-weight sessions and application level framing. *IEEE/ACM Transactions on Networking, 5*(6), 784-803.

Han, R., Perret, V., & Naghshineh, M. (2000). WebSplitter: A unified XML framework for multi-device collaborative Web browsing. *Proceedings of the ACM 2000 Conference on Computer Supported Cooperative Work (CSCW'00)* (pp. 221-230), Philadelphia.

HotMedia. (2004). Retrieved from http://www-306.ibm.com/software/awdtools/hotmedia

JPEG. (2004). Retrieved from http://www.jpeg.org

JRun. (2004). Retrieved from http://www.macromedia.com/software/jrun

Khan, M.F., Ghafoor, H., & Paul. R. (2002, December 11-13). QoS-based synchronization of multimedia document streams. *Proceedings of the IEEE 4th International Symposium on Multimedia Software Engineering (MSE '02)* (pp. 320-327), Newport Beach, CA.

Kirda, E. (2001). Web engineering device independent Web services. *Proceedings of the 23rd International Conference on Software Engineering (ICSE '01)* (pp. 795-796), Toronto, Canada.

MPEG-21. (2004). Retrieved from http://xml.coverpages.org/ni2002-08-26-b.html

NORTEL. (2004). Retrieved from http://www.nortelnetworks.com/products/01/mcs52/collateral/nn105360-091103.pdf

Paknikar, S., Kankanhalli, M.S., Ramakrishnan, K.R., Srinivasan, S.H., & Ngoh, L.H. (2000). A caching and streaming framework for multimedia. *Proceedings of the 8th ACM International Conference on Multimedia (pp. 13-20),* Marina del Rey, CA.

Pham, T., Schneider, G., & Goose, S. (2000). A situated computing framework for mobile and ubiquitous multimedia access using small screen and composite devices. *Proceedings of the 8th ACM International Conference on Multimedia (pp. 323-331),* Marina del Rey, CA.

Roy, J., & Ramanujan, A. (2001). Understanding Web services. *IEEE IT Professional,* (November), 69-73.

SMIL. (2004). *W3C synchronized multimedia activity statement.* Retrieved from http://www.w3c.org/AudioVideo/Activity.html

SOAP. (2004). Simple Object Access Protocol (SOAP) 1.1.

UDDI. (2004). Retrieved from http://www.uddi.org

Werner, C., Buschmann, C., & Fischer, S. (2004, July 6-9). Compressing SOAP messages by using differential encoding. *Proceedings of the IEEE International Conference on Web Services (ICWS '04)* (pp. 540-547), San Diego, CA.

WSDL. (2004). Retrieved from http://www.w3.org/TR/wsdl

Chapter VI

Adaptive Search-
and Learning-Based
Approaches for
Automatic Web Service
Composition

Nikola Milanovic, Technical University Berlin, Germany

Miroslaw Malek, Humboldt University Berlin, Germany

Abstract

We investigate architectural properties required for supporting automatic service composition. First, composable service architecture will be described, based on modeling Web services as abstract machines supported by formally defined composition operators. Based on the proposed infrastructure, we introduce and analyze several options for achieving automatic service composition by treating it as a search problem. Namely, basic heuristic search, probabilistic, learning-based, decomposition, and bidirectional automatic composition mechanisms will be presented and compared. Finally, we discuss the impact and outlook for automatic composition.

Introduction

Service-oriented architectures (SOAs) and Web services (WS) are present in the mainstream scientific and industrial focus for many years. SOA promised advances in enterprise integration, B2B interactions, and novel ways to process business workflows. However, industry is still using SOA mainly *inside* an enterprise as a helper for integration of different systems. Native WS capabilities are standardized: communication (SOAP), description (WSDL), and discovery (UDDI) (Papazoglu, 2003). Apart from that, the WS architecture stack is mainly empty, meaning not standardized.

There are many additional WS frameworks and specifications aspiring to become standards (e.g., WS-Addressing, WS-Transactions, and WS-Coordination). What is not clear, however, is how they can or will cooperate with one another. Each solution targets a specific problem, not taking into account other requirements. What is currently missing is a unification effort towards WS architecture (Vinoski, 2004). Our goal is to identify key SOA elements and constraints required to support service composition, and to verify composition correctness and automatic composition. In this chapter, we briefly present our previous work on architectural concepts and requirements, and focus on the problem of automatic service composition. Although the remaining part of the chapter is based on Web services as the most prominent SOA available today, proposed methods are not limited to solving WS-specific issues only, since they offer an architectural approach for designing SOA to support automatic service composition property.

The need for automatic service composition is justified by the ubiquity of the Internet which is forcing enterprises to abandon their heritage business models and legacy systems and organize themselves into virtual enterprises (Heuvel & Maamar, 2003). On-demand creation of virtual enterprises can shorten delivery times, increase product quality, deliver personalized services, decrease transaction costs, and accommodate short-term cooperating relationships, which can be as brief as a single business transaction. This paradigm requires a shift from tightly coupled business components to more flexible and loosely coupled ones (Webber & Parastatidis, 2003) that now dynamically interact with each other through automatic composition in ways that were not predefined and/or predicted at deployment time. The two major attributes required for such an environment are *extensibility* and *adaptivity*. It is clear that in open environment like this, where services dynamically interact with each other on demand, being able to ensure correctness (dependability, security, timeliness), plays a crucial role. Web service architecture is considered a solution that can support extensibility and adaptivity required for dynamic composition (Yang & Papazoglou, 2000).

The rest of the chapter is organized as follows: First, our previous work in the area of the composable service architecture and modeling services as abstract machines will be described; that will serve as an environment in which automatic composition will be performed. Then, automatic service composition will be defined as a search problem, and relevant properties of the problem will be examined. The state space and equality of abstract machines will be defined, before proceeding with the following automatic composition mechanisms: basic heuristic search, probabilistic, learning-based, backwards (decomposition), and bidirectional (hybrid). Finally, comparison with related approaches will be given, followed by conclusion and future work.

Composable Service Architecture

Web service composition, as well as component composition in general, can be observed at two levels: component (service) and architectural. Our survey of the composition proposals at the component level can be found in Milanovic and Malek (2004a). At this level, it is discussed how to orchestrate or choreograph services in different execution patterns using solutions like BPEL (Curbera, Khalaf, Mukhi, Tai, & Weerawarana, 2003; Andrews et al., 2004) and BPELJ (Blow et al., 2004), Web component (Yang & Papazoglou, 2002; Yang, 2003), Semantic Web and OWL-S (Ankolekar et al., 2002; McIlraith & Son, 2002; Narayanan & McIlraith, 2002), Petri nets (Hamadi & Benatallah, 2003; Zhang, Chang, Chung, & Kim, 2004), and finite state machines (Berardi, Calvanese, Giuseppe, Lenzerini, & Mecella, 2003; Fu, Bultan, & Su, 2002; Bultan, Fu, Hull, & Su, 2003). The general problem of "industrial" approaches is lack of formal verification mechanisms, while more "academic" approaches are not easily applied in real-word production and enterprise frameworks, and some face scalability problems. The issue that has been rarely addressed at all is modeling of non-functional properties, although it has received some attention lately (Zhang, 2005).

Modeling service composability at the architectural level is in its embryonic stage and has some roots in architecture description languages (ADLs) (Medvidovic & Taylor, 2000), which are used to specify a high-level compositional view of a software application. ADL focuses on software generation out of deployed components and offers state-transition semantics for analysis and verification of application speci-fication. However, it has been noted (Schmidt, Poernomo, & Reussner, 2001) that new mission-critical and service-oriented applications require additional properties, namely *trust* and *dependability* analysis.

Most of the composition approaches are concerned with application level—how to facilitate construction of complex applications from available Web services. We form an architectural foundation that enables not only creation of new applications by means of traditional programming techniques, but also adds methods for verification of composition correctness and automatic composition. The basic elements of *composable service architecture* are:

- Extended functional and non-functional (QoS) service description,
- Enhanced search capabilities compared to UDDI,
- Formal methods for composition and verification of composition correctness,
- Distributed transaction management,
- Distributed exception handling, and
- State management.

Detailed description of our previous work on one possible architectural solution supporting these requirements is described in Milanovic (2005) and Milanovic and Malek (2004, 2005). In this section we will present only the basic idea. The architectural concept is shown in Figure 1.

Extending service description is based on the Design by Contract paradigm (Meyer, 1992). We introduce an XML-based Contract Definition Language that enables specification of relevant functional and non-functional properties. Contract does not describe service implementation (how a service operates), but only the semantics of its execution (what and under which conditions it provides). The main contract elements are pre-conditions, post-conditions, and invariants. Pre-conditions are

Figure 1. Composable service architecture

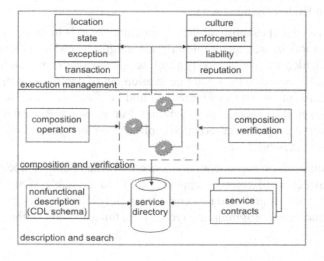

associated with Web methods and describe what a service expects from its clients. Post-conditions describe what a service will deliver in case pre-conditions are met. Invariants describe static service properties. Contract addresses issues other than connectivity (solved by Web Service Description Language, or WSDL), such as service non-functional properties like dependability, security, real-time, location, and price.

Searching is closely coupled with extended service description. UDDI directories limit searching for services belonging to organizations. Organizations can be searched by name, description (keywords), and classification. Only when an organization has been found can its services be further searched. It is also possible to search using WSDL document names. These limiting search possibilities present an obstacle for industrial exploitation of Web services. Introducing extended service description enables richer search options; for example, a possible query would be to find all services in the 1 km radius of the user's current location that accept postscript documents and print them in color with 1,200 dpi resolution, free of charge if a user can supply a security credential of a certain type. Besides being a clear advantage compared to UDDI when searching for single services, the ability to perform such complex queries is very important when searching for adequate composition partners.

Based on the contract description, a formal composition framework is provided. One possibility is to model service contracts as abstract machines (Abrial, 1996). An abstract machine is characterized by statics (state variables) and dynamics (state functions). Web methods are represented as functions that change the service state. All functions are equipped with formally defined pre-conditions, post-conditions, and invariants. An algorithm was developed that transfers XML contract representation into abstract machine notation. The abstract machine structure is:

```
MACHINE M(X,x)
CONSTRAINTS C
CONSTANTS c
SETS S; T={a,b}
PROPERTIES P
VARIABLES v
INVARIANT I
ASSERTIONS J
INITIALIZATION U
OPERATIONS
  u₁ <- O₁(w₁) = PRE Q₁ THEN V₁ END
  ...
  uₙ <- Oₙ(wₙ) = PRE Qₙ THEN Vₙ END
END
```

This is a parameterized abstract machine having free dimensions X (set) and x (scalar). CONSTRAINTS describes conditions on machine parameters. SETS contains finite or named sets that the machine can use, while CONSTANTS describes constants that the machine understands. PROPERTIES takes form of conjoined predicates specifying invariants involving constants and sets. VARI-ABLES lists state variables, and INVARIANT describes static properties of the machine that must be preserved before and after each operation. ASSERTIONS is deducible from PROPERTIES and INVARIANT, and exists purely to ease the proving of machine correctness. INITIALIZATION initializes state variables. OPERATIONS lists operations of an abstract machine, with pre-conditions PRE and post-conditions THEN.

Operation body of an abstract machine modifies a machine state. For expressing formally how such modification takes place, logical predicates relating the values of state variables just before the operation is invoked to the values just after the operation completes are used. This method is called substitution.

Therefore, service has dual representation: XML contract (transport over a network) and abstract machine (formal reasoning). Service composition is then performed by merging abstract machines using five basic composition patterns (operators):

- *Sequence* (∇) executes two or more services in a sequential order.
- *Choice* ($\blacklozenge$) executes two or more services in parallel, and then non-deterministically chooses output of one and only one of them.
- *Selection* ($\otimes$) selects one of the candidate services and executes it.
- *Parallel with communication* ($\|_p$) executes two or more services concurrently, then performs a logical operation on their outputs, and based on the operation result chooses one of the outputs.
- *Parallel without communication* ($\|$) executes two or more services concurrently without any communication and synchronization between them.
- *Loop* ($\propto_p$) executes a service iteratively until an exit condition is met.

New services are constructed by applying composition patterns to existing services. After a new composed service has been constructed, its correctness must be checked. The process of correctness verification takes the following steps:

- *Type checking* ensures that all types are correctly defined and that there is no infinite set inclusion in the resulting abstract machine.
- *Invariant preservation* ensures that composed invariant is preserved by all operations if pre-conditions hold.

Figure 2. Loan composition example

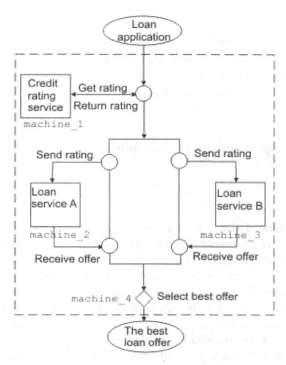

- *Correct termination* ensures that all operations will terminate correctly (establish their post-conditions or abort), and that all operations are feasible (will establish exactly one or none, but not any post-conditions).

A composition example is shown in Figure 2. Three services are composed, one that accepts a credit application from a client and returns its credit rating, and two banking services that accept credit rating and offer a loan. Banking services are executed asynchronously and the better offer is then chosen.

```
MACHINE loanExample
VARIABLES application:IN, rating ,offer1, offer2, result:OUT, pro-
cess_application, offer_loan, wcet
SETS App, Rating, Off, Time
INVARIANT process_application ∈ App → rating ∧ application ∈ App ∧ of-
fer_loan ∈ Rating → Off ∧ rating ∈ Rating ∧ result ∈ Off ∧ offer1 ∈ Off ∧
offer2 ∈ Off ∧ wcet ∈ Off → Time
OPERATION result <- ask_loan(application)
```

```
PRE rating>0∧offer1>0∧offer2>0∧wcet(offer1)<86400∧wcet(offer2)
<86400
THEN
rating := process_application(application);
[ ( offer1 := offer_loan(rating) ‖ offer2:=offer_loan(rating) );
( (offer1 > offer2) ⇒ result := offer2 } ♦
¬(offer1 > offer2) ⇒ result := offer1 ) ]
END
```

One possibility to express this composition formally is:

```
machine_1 ∇ (machine_2 ‖offer1>offer2 machine_3)
```

The elements introduced allow us to define a composable service architecture. It is defined as tuple $A(E,O)$ where E is a set of initial (atomic) services, and O is a set of composition operators. An operator $o \in O$ is a function that maps two (or more) services to a new service: $o: E \times E \times ... \times C \to C$, where C is the set of all possible compositions. Not all composed services are, however, valid members of the architecture. Therefore we introduce a function $correct$: $E \times E \times ... C \times O \to \{true, false\}$. Function $correct(e_1, e_2,... e_n, c_1,...,c_m, o)$, where $e_1...e_n \in E$, $c_1,..,c_m \in C$ and $o \in O$, is $true$ if the composition of elements $e_1...e_n c_1...c_m$ using composition operator o is correct, and returns $false$ otherwise. The function $correct$ is calculated for the composite element $e(e_1...e_n c_1...c_m,o)$ in the following way ($check(e)$ is type checking, $proof(e)$ is invariant preservation, $trm(e)$ is correct termination, and $fis(e)$ is feasibility):

$$correct(e) \Leftrightarrow check(e) \wedge proof(e) \wedge trm(e) \wedge fis(e)$$

In order to further support deployment of composed services, issues related to cooperative execution of components in different containers must be solved, namely transaction, exception, and state management. We implemented a distributed transaction management scheme known as *split* or *open nested* transaction model (Gray & Reuter, 1993; Mikalsen, Sai, & Rouvellou, 2002; Tartanoglu, Issarny, Romanovsky, & Levy, 2003). In this model, one transaction can be split into a number of subtransactions, that can commit independently. However, if one subtransaction aborts, others that have already committed must compensate (undo). Therefore, for each Web method that can be involved in a transaction, a service must provide a compensate method. This model is well suited for service architectures where it is expensive to lock resources for the duration of the whole transaction, and where transactions can take very long time to finish.

BPEL has an excellent solution for exception handling which is essentially distributed try…catch implemented within *scopes*. We augment it with generic exception wrappers enabling heterogeneous components (throwing platform-specific exceptions) to be included in exception handling chains.

Although Web services are inherently stateless, many of them allow for the manipulation of the state, such as persisting data into databases, file systems, or coordinating dependent messages. There is ongoing debate in the community whether Web services should or should not support state management. One view is that Web services are not another Object Request Broker architecture, and therefore should have no notion of state (Vogels, 2003), while the other view is that state management plays the critical role in distributed computing and as such must be addressed at the architectural level (Foster et al., 2004). The former point may be true at the fundamental level of Web services (discovery, description, invocation), but our position is that for the purpose of complex service interactions the latter view is correct. A solution for state management that we adopt is WS-Resource initiative (Czajkowski et al., 2004).

Equality of Abstract Machines

The problem of automatic service composition can be defined as follows: given the sets of available services E and composition operators O, and target (goal) service $t \notin E$, find the composition $e(e_1,...,e_n,o_1,...,o_m)$ where $e_1,...,e_n \in E$ and $o_1,...,o_m \in O$, such that *correct*(e) = *true*, and $e \equiv t$, where $t \notin E$. In other words, the task of automatic composition for a given target (goal) service t is to find adequate composition based on available services and operators that will produce a correct service e *equivalent* to t. We treat machine equivalency as syntax equivalence only. Therefore two machines are equivalent if and only if after renaming machine clauses (state variables and operation names) we obtain two identical machines.

However, information whether two machines are equivalent is not particularly useful on its own. In the process of automatic composition, it is more important to know how two machines differ and to be able to quantify their difference. Therefore we introduce metrics for calculating distance between two abstract machines. Distance is a number of dimensions and substitutions they differ in. Lexical differences are not taken into account, that is, it is allowed to rename clauses of one machine. The difference between machines m_1 and m_2 is thus given by:

$$\delta(m_1, m_2) = \frac{1}{2\alpha} \sum_{i=1}^{\alpha} \delta_d(d_{1i}, d_{2i}) + \frac{1}{2\beta} \sum_{j=1}^{\beta} \delta_s(s_{1j}, s_{2j})$$

where $|m|_d$ is the number of machine dimensions (state variables, machine formal parameters, and constants), $|m|_s$ is the number of substitutions that make operation body (post-conditions), $\alpha = max(|m|_{1d}, |m|_{2d})$, $\beta = max(|m|_{1s}, |m|_{2s})$, and δ_d and δ_s calculate number of differing dimensions and substitutions:

$$\delta_d(d_1, d_2) = \begin{cases} 0, d_1 = d_2 \\ 1, d_1 \neq d_2 \end{cases}$$

$$\delta_s(s_1, s_2) = \begin{cases} 0, s_1 = s_2 \\ 1, s_1 \neq s_2 \end{cases}$$

Two dimensions are equivalent if and only if their types and directions (in case of state variables) are equal. Dimensions are therefore compared using their types and directions, not their names. In that respect, variables `input` and `in` are equivalent:

```
MACHINE A
SETS InputSet = {x,y}
VARIABLES input:IN
OPERATION doSomething PRE input ∈ InputSet
...
END

MACHINE B
SETS InputSet = {x,y}
VARIABLES in:IN
OPERATION doElse PRE in ∈ InputSet
...
END
```

Although they have different names, these variables have the same direction (`IN`) and their type-checking evaluates to the same set: *type*(`input`)=`InputSet` and *type*(`IN`)=`InputSet`. Constants and machine formal parameters also constitute dimensions, and their properties and constraints are implicitly taken into account in the process of type checking the same way that invariants and pre-conditions are used to type state variables.

Two substitutions are equivalent if and only if they perform the same substitution on equivalent state variables in the equivalent order. Consequently, two operations are equivalent if and only if all their substitutions are equivalent. The following two machines have equivalent operations:

```
MACHINE A
SETS InputSet, OutputSet
VARIABLES input:IN, output:OUT
INVARIANT output ∈ OutputSet
OPERATION output <- doSomething(input)
PRE input ∈ InputSet THEN
input := input + 1 ♦ input := input -1;
output := input END
END
```

```
MACHINE B
SETS InputSet, OutputSet
VARIABLES int:IN, out:OUT
INVARIANT out ∈ OutputSet
OPERATION out <- doSomethingElse(in)
PRE in ∈ InputSet THEN
in := in - 1 ♦ in := in +1;
out := in END
END
```

For multiple generalized substitutions and choice substitution, the order is irrelevant. That is the reason why operations of machines A and B are equivalent, even if the order of substitutions under choice clearly differ. On the other hand, if operation of machine B is defined as:

```
OPERATION out <- doSomethingElse(in)
PRE in ∈ InputSet THEN
output := in; in := in -1 ♦ in := in + 1 END
END
```

operations are not equivalent anymore since they differ in the order of two substitutions. Generally speaking, judging difference of substitutions is far more difficult when compared to difference of dimensions. It is possible to develop a more precise measure of substitution difference by taking into account the actual substitution type and creating a function that is not purely binary, but offers a finer measurement of substitution equality. Therefore, function δ_s is modified as follows:

Table 1. Weight of substitutions

	S;T	S‖T	PRE	CHOICE	IF	ELSE	ANY	WHILE
S;T S? T	0							
S‖T	0.6	ι						
PRE	1	1	κ					
CHOICE	1	1	1	ι				
IF	1	1	0.5 1		κ			
ELSE	1	1	0.75 1		0.5	κ		
ANY	1	1	0.95	0.9	0.9	0.95	κ	
WHILE	0.9	0.95	0.9 1		0.9	0.95	0.95	κ

$$\delta_s(s_1,s_2) = \frac{1}{2} weight(s_1,s_2) + \frac{1}{2\gamma}\sum_{k=1}^{\gamma}\delta_d(d_{1k},d_{2k})$$

The second part of this function simply calculates the number of dimensions that two substitutions s_1 and s_2 differ in, where $\gamma = max(|s|_{1d},|s|_{2d})$ and $|s|_d$ is the number of dimensions of substitution s. The first part is the weighted function that describes a semantic difference between substitution types. The function *weight* is given in Table 1.

Value κ is used to compare two exact substitutions that may differ in their predicates. It makes sense to give two exact preconditions score 0 (equality), and score 0.5 otherwise, since two preconditions differ less than pre-condition and while substitution. The remaining difference in predicates will be calculated by the second part of the function δ_d. Therefore, κ is defined:

$$\kappa = \begin{cases} 0, & \text{predicates equal} \\ 0.5, & \text{otherwise} \end{cases}$$

Similarly, when comparing two multiple or choice substitutions, the value of 1 could be assigned if they differ, but again additional measure is introduced to soften this criteria by comparing number of operators (‖ or ♦) in which they differ. Therefore, ι is introduced:

$$\iota = 1 - \frac{min(|s_1|_{op},|s_2|_{op})}{max(|s_1|_{op},|s_2|_{op})}$$

where $|s|_{op}$ is the number of operations in a substitution s. Values in the weight table are not fixed, nor do they have any constraints imposed upon them. Each value is inductively developed by observing behavior of different substitutions.

Modeling State Space

The problem of automatic service composition is essentially a search problem. To be able to formulate strategies for automatic composition of abstract machines, certain elements need to be defined for designing adequate search methods:

- *State space* containing all possible configurations of the objects upon which a search is performed. State space comprises atomic services and all correct composition thereof.
- *Starting state* is one or more states from state space that describe possible situations (configurations) from which a search can start. These states are also called initial states. Starting/initial states are atomic services.
- *Goal state* is one or more states that can be accepted as a solution of a search. End state is a target service.
- Finally, a set of *rules* describes the actions that are available for transforming initial state towards goal state. In our case rules are obviously composition patterns.

We examine some properties of this problem, based on which we decide on search strategies (Rich, 1983). The problem of automatic service composition is decomposable, under the assumption that target service (machine) is correct. A problem is decomposable if it can be transformed into a set of independent smaller or easier subproblems. A typical example of decomposable problem is symbolic integration. In that sense service composition can be treated as decomposable, but the practical applicability of decomposability is somewhat limited. For example, a request for a service that makes flight and hotel room reservations can be decomposed into two subproblems: hotel reservation and flight reservation. Such decomposition, however, is not always obvious and/or easy to identify. Decomposition, as a divide-and-conquer methodology, will be investigated in more detail in the section about decomposition of abstract machines.

The problem universe is predictable since application of rules has a certain outcome. Indeed, predictability of composition properties was one of the main reasons for introducing abstract machines and composition patterns. It is always known what will be the exact result of applying a certain rule (operator) to the current state (composition). In other words, every time we make a move in the state space, we know precisely the following, resulting state. That means that we can plan an entire sequence of moves in advance. However, this is true only if trust is assumed. As already discussed, we compose service contracts trusting them to be correct and accurate representations of relevant properties of underlying implementation.

The rules application is recoverable. That means that we can go back if a certain search path is misleading, but we will need to backtrack to a certain point since rule application cannot just be ignored: a part of a solution will have to be "undone" or "uncomposed." For example, if we compose one hotel reservation service with one flight reservation service and then find out that flight reservation service does not support transactions causing the entire solution to not be able to execute in one transaction, we may decide to drop the particular flight reservation service and try to locate another one. However, once another candidate has been located, we cannot just compose it on top of a previous solution. We must first backtrack to the point in state space where the previous flight reservation has been composed. That means that adequate control structure must be introduced to enable backtracking. The simplest way to do this is to use a stack to record rule (composition patterns) applications.

Goal solution is absolute, assuming equality of machines is defined. Once a satisfactory solution has been found, the search can be stopped. That means that we do not need to search further and compare multiple solutions, since only an equivalent solution can be found. This is only true, however, if an absolute solution can be found. Otherwise, suboptimal solution can be negotiated. For example, if a travel reservation system cannot locate both hotel and flight for a given price, it can offer the next best (although more expensive) solution to the user.

Rules are consistent, assuming that composition patterns are defined and proved. It means that it is allowed to use only the patterns that were previously defined (sequence, choice, parallel, selection, and loop composition) to move through the state space. Under this assumption, problem is consistent. This is only true if no

Figure 3. Syntax tree

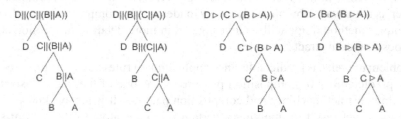

additional knowledge is being used for reaching the goal. Otherwise, as the following sections will show, special attention must be paid that additional knowledge is also consistent.

We aim for a solution where no intermediate interaction with the end (human) user will be required. In a case where two machine entities are communicating and trying to compose new service, such interaction is also not necessary. Human interaction can be required for two reasons: to provide additional input during the search process, or to provide additional reassurance and justification of the solution to the user. If a solution cannot be found, a solitary way of solving the automatic composition problem can be transformed into a conversational one, where the end user is offered a sub-optimal solution on one or more criteria, and must accept this solution explicitly via some sort of interface. This should not, however, be the basic mode of operation.

Finally, since the objective of automatic composition is to find a path through a state space connecting starting state and goal state, there are two directions in which the search can proceed: moving from starting state towards goal state (forward search) or moving from goal state towards starting state (backward search). When deciding which strategy to use, number of start and goal states is usually taken into account. We would like to move from the smaller set of states to the larger (thus easier to find) set of states and in the direction of the lower branching factor. The branching factor is the average number of states that can be reached directly from a single state. In both respects, backward search seems to be more appropriate, since branching factor

Figure 4. Composition graph

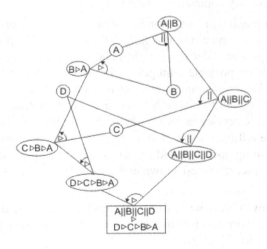

can be only equal or less when compared with forward search, and number of goal states is certainly smaller. However, applying composition patterns in the *reverse* order to decompose an abstract machine is not trivial. Therefore we first investigate and develop forward search mechanisms, then introduce a way to decompose abstract state machines, and finally propose a hybrid bidirectional solution.

Before proceeding to search methodologies, we must define how state space elements and traversals will be modeled. Basically, there are two choices: to model state space as a tree or as a graph (with option to switch between the two).

One form of a tree that can be used to represent state space transitions is a syntax tree (Aho, Sethi, & Ullman, 1987). In a syntax tree, inner nodes represent composition patterns and leaf nodes represent services (abstract machines). Examples of some syntax trees for services A, B, and C and composition patterns ∇ (sequence) and $\|$ (parallel) are given in Figure 3.

The benefit of using syntax tree to model state space is that a syntax tree can be converted to deterministic/nondeterministic finite automaton. Such an automaton can be queried whether a given composition can be found in a syntax tree. The problem is, however, that this would require that the entire (or at least a significant part of) state space is already expanded in a syntax tree. Syntax trees are not well balanced, and the addition of new nodes and elimination of duplicate ones are not trivial or cheap operations. An alternative to tree is to represent a state space as a graph.

The graph form we use is similar to AND-OR graphs which consist of OR edges and AND arcs, where one AND arc can point to any number of successor nodes. It is used primarily to represent problems that can be decomposed into smaller problems connected by AND arcs that must all be solved in order for the original problem to be satisfied. We use a similar idea to allow multiple arced edges to connect nodes that are being composed using given composition pattern. Instead of AND operation, arc can represent any composition pattern (Figure 4).

The benefit of using graph representation is that new nodes are added easily, as can be seen with composition resulting in $(A\|B\|C\|D) \nabla (D \nabla C \nabla B \nabla A)$. It is also possible to define operand order using right-hand rule. Naturally, right-hand rule serves only to eliminate possible ambiguities in graphic representation and does not carry any other deeper meaning, since this is not a geometric graph. Naturally, there is an option to switch to a search forest. For every atomic service a tree is created with the atomic service as its root by taking all graph nodes in which that atomic service is the leftmost operand, removing all nodes representing rightmost operands, and containing operators and rightmost operands implicitly in the graph arcs, thus producing a search forest shown in Figure 5. We will use both representations interchangeably.

The issue remains how to construct and move through such composition graph/forest in order to find desired composition. In the next sections we present a few strategies, starting with basic heuristic search.

Figure 5. Part of a search forest

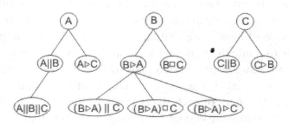

Basic Heuristic Search

It should be obvious that brute force search, where all possible combinations of services and composition operators are explored until a composition matching the target is found, is unrealistic because combinatorial explosion renders it non-practical. It is not so much a problem of number of services, as of number of composition operators. The fact that operators can be n-ary and that same service can appear in a composition more than once further complicates any kind of non-heuristic search.

We first investigate two well-known "weak" methods that require no additional heuristics, depth-first search and breadth-first search (West, 1996), in which we systematically generate correct compositions starting from available services and operators. Both algorithms deteriorate rapidly with the expansion of state space, the former with an increasing number of services and the latter with an increasing number of composition operators. Therefore, some additional knowledge of the problem domain is necessary. Here, we introduce a simple heuristic for abandoning a certain branch:

- If more states are generated than the target machine has, abandon the branch since further application of composition operators can only increase the number of states.
- If composition operator is commutative and equivalent branch has been explored, abandon the branch.
- If composition operator is associative, and one association has been explored, ignore the branch with other association.
- If composition operator is distributive, and either distributed or condensed formula has already been applied, ignore the branch with the other one.

This heuristic improves the performance, but has problems if many composition operators are introduced, especially if they are not commutative, associative, or distributive. Therefore we try to develop appropriate heuristic function. A heuristic function maps from problem state description to measure of desirability (usually quantified as a number). That means that for each element of state space, it gives a quantitative measure of how close that state is to a solution. The purpose of a heuristic function is to guide the search process in the most promising (profitable) direction. It does so by suggesting which path to follow through the state space when more than one is available. The more accurate heuristic function is (the more accurately it evaluates the merit of each state), the faster and more direct will be the whole search process. Two well-known heuristic approaches that fit our problem description are A* (Hart, Nilsson, & Raphael, 1968, 1972) and AO* (Martelli & Montanari, 1973, 1978; Nilsson 1980} search algorithms. We use them as the basis for developing a range of heuristic search approaches for automatic composition of abstract machines.

Before proceeding to the description of the search algorithm, several elements will be introduced. Since state space is infinite, a measure of *futility* is introduced in order to cut search paths that will never lead to the result. A value F will be a measure for the futility of a given search path. Different measures for futility can be accepted: it can be a value of heuristic function that shows that a distance to the goal is too big to be realistically reached, or a number of current solution's dimension which can be too large to fit into the goal machine. In any case, F must be such that it can guarantee that abandoning any search path will not result in a solution being missed, that is, that subsequent composition will not change the value of F so it becomes favorable again.

During the execution of the algorithm, three lists are maintained:

1. OPEN contains nodes that have been generated and heuristic function has been applied to them, but they have not yet been expanded (their successors have not yet been generated).

2. CLOSED contains nodes that have already been examined and expanded, and have not crossed futility value.

3. LIMIT contains expanded nodes that have crossed futility value.

For every CURRENT node that is being expanded, a heuristic function f' is given with:

$$f'(\text{CURRENT}) = \delta (\text{CURRENT, GOAL})$$

where GOAL is the node representing composition target (search goal), and δ is the distance function given in the section, "Equality of Abstract Machines." It will be used to pick the nodes that are closest to the goal node (with the smallest value of δ) to be expanded first.

Apart from using futility F and heuristic function δ to guide heuristic search, it is also important to detect and cut off equivalent search paths as early as possible. For example, it is obvious that compositions $A\|B$ and $B\|A$ are equivalent, yet they can appear more than once in a search forest. All subsequent compositions based on these two nodes would be also equivalent, therefore one of the nodes can be safely removed. In order to deal with this issue, several rules are introduced that enable detection and handling of such cases:

1. Every abstract machine is a term.

2. If A and B are terms, than $A \triangledown B$, $A \parallel B$, $A \blacklozenge B$, $A \parallel_p B$, $A \propto_p B$ are also terms.

3. Every abstract machine is equivalent to itself.

4. Two terms $A_1 \bullet B_1$ and $B_2 \bullet A_2$ are equivalent if:

    - operator $\bullet$ is commutative, and
    - A_1 is equivalent to A_2 and B_1 is equivalent to B_2, or
    - A_1 is equivalent to B_2 and B_1 is equivalent to A_2.

5. Two terms $A_1 \bullet (B_1 * C_1)$ and $(A_2 \bullet B_2) * C_2$ are equivalent if:

    - operators $\bullet$ and $*$ are associative, and
    - A_1 is equivalent to A_2, B_1 is equivalent to B_2, and C_1 is equivalent to C_2.

6. Two terms $A_1 \bullet (B_1 * C_1)$ and $(A_2 \bullet B_2) * (A_2 \bullet C_2)$ are equivalent if:

    - operator $\bullet$ is distributive with respect to $*$, and
    - A_1 is equivalent to A_2, B_1 is equivalent to B_2, and C_1 is equivalent to C_2

Finally, for every node, function g is defined that is used for algorithm termination, if the value of g exceeds the threshold value F. Function g is accumulated during the forest traversal, and for every NEW node is given by:

```
g(NEW) = g(CURRENT) + δ(NEW,GOAL)
```

The algorithm executes in the following steps:

1. OPEN contains the atomic services only. CLOSED and LIMIT are empty. Value of function g for every atomic service is 0. F is given an initial value.

2. Until the goal is reached or OPEN and CLOSED are empty, the following steps are repeated:

    •   The node with the smallest value of δ is chosen from OPEN, assigned identifier CURRENT, and removed from OPEN.

    •   If CURRENT is equivalent to GOAL, CURRENT is returned and search is ended.

    •   Otherwise, successors of CURRENT are generated. For each NODE in OPEN, CLOSED, and {CURRENT}, the following is performed:

        a. Node NEW is generated from CURRENT, operator, and NODE.

        b. If NEW is a solution, return NEW and exit.

        c. $g(\text{NEW}) = g(\text{CURRENT}) + \delta(\text{NEW}, \text{GOAL})$ is calculated.

        d. If there is no equivalent node to NEW in OPEN, CLOSED, or LIMIT, $g(\text{NEW})$ is compared to F. If $g(\text{NEW}) > F$, NEW is put to LIMIT, otherwise to OPEN.

    •   If no new nodes are added to OPEN, that is, all successors of CURRENT have g value larger than F, CURRENT is put to LIMIT, otherwise to CLOSED.

    •   If OPEN is empty, exchange OPEN and CLOSED.

At the start of the algorithm, list OPEN contains all atomic services, and all other lists are empty. F is assigned an initial value. The search will go on until a goal abstract machine is reached or all subsequent expansions cross the limit F. For each node in *OPEN*, function δ is calculated and stored. The node with the smallest value of δ—that is, the node that is closest to the goal machine—is chosen for composition. If more nodes have the same value of δ, choice is performed randomly. The chosen node is then composed with all nodes from OPEN and CLOSED using all operators. This is the expansion phase, where node successors are generated. The current node that is being expanded is always the leftmost operand. If any of the generated nodes is equivalent to the goal machine, search is ended. For each new node, function g is calculated and compared to futility value F. In case $g > F$ the node is too far away from the goal to be considered further and the cutoff is performed by storing the node in LIMIT. Each new node is also compared to all generated nodes

Figure 6. Cooperation graph

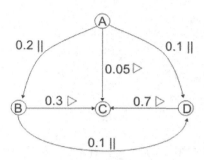

that are stored in OPEN, CLOSED, or LIMIT using equality rules. This step ensures that equivalent paths are detected and cut off. Finally, if OPEN is empty and no solution has been found yet, nodes that have not been considered (CLOSED) are moved to OPEN and expanded. A complete step-by-step example of the algorithm execution can be found in Lenk (2005).

The best way to guarantee an efficient and fast heuristic algorithm is to have quality heuristic function that will guide the search in the most promising direction. Various additions to the heuristic function presented here will try to improve this result by using more efficient heuristic functions. They will always have more favorable average execution complexity than this approach, as they will fall back to the basic heuristic search in case the solution has not been found using advanced heuristics.

Probabilistic Automatic Composition

Heuristic function from the previous section uses distance between abstract machines as a measurement which branch is most promising to follow. In this section we augment that heuristic with the idea of probabilistic search. The additional heuristic is represented as weighted directed graph with vertices representing services and edges representing composition patterns, as shown on Figure 6. Each edge is assigned a probability that a service from which an edge is originating will cooperate with a service in which the edge is ending. The sum of all outgoing weights for any node must be less or equal to one. If equal to one, all possible interactions for a given service are known (which is very unlikely). Otherwise, there is a possibility that unknown services can cooperate with a given one, with probability of $1 - \sum_{i=1}^{k} w_i$, where w_i is the weight of an outgoing edge and k is the number of outgoing edges.

The probability of a branch of length k is calculated by multiplying probabilities of constituent edges:

Figure 7. Causal cooperation graph

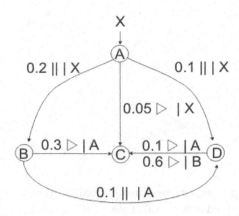

$$P(B_k) = \prod_{i-1}^{k} w_i$$

For example, if we are looking for sequential compositions ending with service C from Figure 6, there are four possible branches: $A \triangledown C, A \parallel B \triangledown C, A \parallel B \parallel D \triangledown C$, and $A \parallel D \triangledown C$, where $\parallel$ and $\triangledown$ denote parallel and sequential composition respectively. Probabilities of identified branches are 0.05, 0.06, 0.014, and 0.07, therefore the path $A \parallel D \triangledown C$ is chosen.

This assumes, however, that events of choosing next cooperating service are independent. In our example there is no difference whether we arrived at node D from A or B: node C will be subsequently picked with 0.7 probability. Therefore we introduce causality by adding conditional probabilities. Assume A and B are two events, then:

$$P(AB) = P(A \mid B)P(B)$$

where $P(A|B)$ denotes probability of event A under the assumption that event B took place, while $P(AB)$ is the probability that both events occurred. Furthermore, if $A_1,...,A_n$ are events, the following holds:

$$P(A_1 A_2 ... A_n) = P(A_1)P(A_2 \mid A_1)P(A_3 \mid A_1 A_2)...P(A_n \mid A_1 A_2 ... A_{n-1})$$

Using these results we create additional conditional probabilities in the cooperation graph that describes causality effect of choosing previous nodes (Figure 7). Let us assume that $P(D \nabla C \mid A)$=0.1 and $P(D \nabla C \mid B)$=0.6—that is, we now distinguish between cases $D \nabla C$ when we arrive to D from A and from B. Now $P(A \parallel D \nabla C)$ = $P(A \parallel D)P(D \nabla C \mid A) = 0.01$ and $P(A \parallel B \parallel D \nabla C) = P(A \parallel B)P(B \parallel D)P(D \nabla C|B)$ = 0.012. The most favorable path now changes to $A \parallel B \nabla C$. Using the formula for n-conditional events, we could go deeper into the cooperation graph. However, adding even this one level of causality provides a significant improvement compared to the graph with independent probabilities.

By creating cooperation (probability) graphs, we exploit implicit human knowledge of state space properties by assigning higher probabilities to combinations that are more likely to work out together. For example, a stock ticker service is more likely to cooperate with a stock trading or a printing service than with a book searching service, although all combinations are functionally possible. Fixed probabilities however are not very realistic. Therefore we try to make the approach more flexible by allowing probabilities to change over time. In an adaptive process, probabilities of branches (compositions) that are used more frequently are increased and vice versa. This change is made for all edges in a branch, while assuring that the sum of all edges originating from any node in a branch does not exceed 1. For all composition patterns two tables are maintained: *compositions* and *probabilities*. In *compositions* rows and columns represent services and entries number of successful compositions. Table *probabilities* has the same structure and at the beginning is populated with initial probabilities. After assigning initial probabilities $P_{init}(N_i,N_j,op)$, *compositions* table entry (N_i,N_j,op) is incremented when N_i and N_j are composed using pattern op. Total number of compositions for each pair (n) is also maintained. After each composition, current probability is calculated $P_{current}(N_i,N_j,op) = k(N_i,N_j,op)/n$, where k is

Figure 8. Service classification and initial probabilities

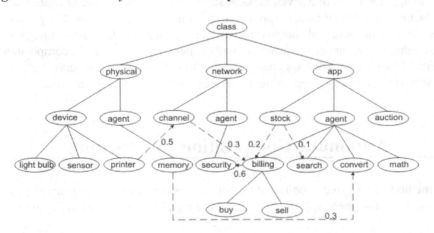

compositions table entry for (N_i,N_j,op). This probability is not automatically stored in the table *probabilities*. If any value in row N_i becomes such that $|P_{init}(N_i,N_j,op)$ - $P_{current}(N_i,N_j,op)| > \varepsilon$, probabilities of entire row are recalculated and stored in *probabilities*: $P_{new}(N_i,N_j,op) = P_{current}(N_i,N_j,op)$. To prevent fast (and non-realistic) oscillations, comparison of $P_{current}$ and values from *probabilities* can be done periodically and not every time *compositions* is updated. Also, table *compositions* can be reset, with current probabilities accepted as new initial probabilities. The value of ε can also change if necessary.

The usability of this approach depends almost entirely on the way initial probabilities are assigned. Initial probabilities are important for two reasons: they determine starting conditions under which services compete, and can also be used when resetting *compositions* table, if for some reason one does not want to use current probabilities. If initial probabilities are not realistic, convergence to optimal balance can take a lot of time and render the whole approach unusable. Therefore a method for assigning initial probabilities is proposed, using service classification.

Figure 8 shows layered service classification, similar to the OSI layered network model, comprising physical, network, and application service classes. Classes can talk to neighboring classes only, for example, service of the physical class can talk to network class only, network can talk to both physical and application, while application can interact with network class. This does not mean that actual interaction among physical class and application class is not possible, but only that in the process of distributing initial probabilities, such interactions are not taken into account. There is a special subclass of all three classes called agent. Agents represent generic properties of each class and can interact with each other across any class. For example, memory agent of the physical class interacts with convert agent of the application class with probability 0.3 (Figure 8).

Initial probabilities can be assigned directly in the classification or as a set of rules. Rules have the syntax (*source_class*, *destination_class*, *probability*). Rule is applicable to all subclasses of a given class. A subclass can redefine one or more rules, and the new rule is then further applicable to itself and its subclasses. Cooperation graphs define fine-grained interaction between services as they determine probabilities that particular service instances will cooperate using particular composition patterns. Classification defines coarse-grained interaction between service classes (not services) that can be applied to all services belonging to a given class.

Automatic Composition by Learning

The method of adaptive conditional probabilities works good when starting probabilities have favorable approximation and the weighted graph quickly converges towards optimal. When neither of these conditions are met—for example, when the nature of the requests changes frequently—the basic heuristic approach achieves better results. Another possible approach for relatively stable environments (one where requests can be at least typed) is learning-based composition.

Let T be a set of target abstract machines and S a set of all possible solutions (compositions). In a learning-based automatic composition, a system is presented a target abstract machine $t \in T$ and then demonstrated a solution $s \in S$ (possible composition), which is afterwards persisted in a directory. A system is then presented with a set of all possible target machines $\{t_1,...,t_n\} \subseteq T$ such that $\forall\ m \in \{t_1,...,t_n\} \mid \delta(t,m) = 1$ and demonstrated a set of solutions $\{s_1,...,s_n\} \subseteq S$. This completes a 1-distance training. If a system is then presented with a 2-distance target machine d ($\delta\ (t,d) = 2$), the solution is obtained as follows:

1. Create all combinations of 1-distance solutions $\{s_1,...,s_n\}$ x $\{s_1,...,s_n\}$ and see if they match d.

2. If any matches d exit, else start substitution.

    a. For each element of newly generated solution set, consult service hierarchy and substitute one service at a time in each composition.

    b. Revalidate solution.

    c. If new solution matches d exit, else continue with substitution until all elements in all solutions have been substituted.

3. No solution is found, use basic heuristic search, not considering branches already visited.

The key premise is that by combining 1-distance solutions, 2-distance targets can be reached quickly. Obviously this cannot be proved, therefore a process of additional substitution is introduced. It is based on service hierarchy introduced in the previous section that is developed from classification information provided in a service contract. Classification is hierarchical and determines what services are taken into consideration for substitution. If 1-distance solutions themselves cannot provide solution, substitution will try to locate services of similar capabilities and replace some of them. An element can be substituted with either an element or the same class or element from any of its subclasses. For example, member of network agent class can be replaced by another member of network agent class or by a member of security class.

A simple scenario of this idea would work like this: suppose we have a printer that can print only postscript. A system is taught to solve all printing requests by sending them to the printer. This works only if the document being printed is in the appropriate format. Therefore, a system is taught how to convert other formats: there is a class of converter services that supply different types of conversions. Suppose further that a system is taught how to convert jpg file to ps by invoking appropriate converter service. If a system now receives a request to print a pdf file, it will look into all 1-distance compositions offering printing and find how to print jpg files. Then it will try to substitute a converter service with another service from the same class, or to substitute a printer service. Either way it will end up with (a) a printer that can print pdf or (b) a converter service that can turn pdf into ps. This approach gives best results in more controlled environments (e.g., inside an enterprise) since precise classification and ability to determine whether two services can be substituted is required.

Decomposition of Abstract Machines

Decomposition of abstract machines is backwards search methodology. We begin from the goal state (target abstract machine) and iteratively try to decompose it into simpler machines connected with composition patterns until we reach a starting state consisting of atomic (available) machines. The inverse path taken from goal state to starting states is the required composition.

Decomposition should clearly be the preferred way of doing automatic composition, since we are moving from the known goal state (match of user's requirements) to the smaller (compared to all possible compositions) and thus easier to find set of starting states (atomic abstract machines). The approach to decomposition is based on transforming target machine substitutions to postfix form. The decomposition algorithm has three main phases:

1.   Convert operation body to postfix representation.

Table 2. Composition operator priority

priority o	perator
3	$\propto_P$
2	∇
1	$\mid\mid, \mid\mid_P$
0	$\blacklozenge, \otimes$

a. Generate relevant clauses for all variables copied to the output thus creating corresponding abstract machine.

b. Verify correctness of every variable (machine) copied to the output.

c. If a copied machine exists in directory, mark it as finished and put in finished list.

2. Scan finished postfix string and determine possible compositions.

3. Check composition to determine whether all elements are in the finished list.

We now describe the first phase in more detail. Postfix conversion is performed on the target machine operation body. During conversion, operator priorities are evaluated using Table 2. The result of conversion are variables and operators. Variables are machine state variables; operators are either composition patterns or generalized substitutions. In the process of postfix conversion, we gradually decompose abstract machine operation body by extracting its sub-elements (state variables) and composition patterns that build the goal abstract machine. The process of postfix conversion consists of the following steps:

1. Let the final END of the target abstract machine be a terminating symbol.

2. Terminating symbol is pushed onto the stack.

3. Variables are always copied to the output.

4. Left parenthesis is always pushed onto the stack.

5. When a right parenthesis is encountered, the symbol at the top of the stack is popped off the stack and copied to the output. This is repeated until top of the stack is left parenthesis. Then both parenthesis are discarded.

6. If an operator has a higher priority than the operator at the top of the stack, it is pushed onto the stack and stack pointer is incremented.

7. If the priority of the operator is lower or equal to the operator on top of the stack, one element of the stack is popped to output. The stack pointer is not decremented. Instead the current operator is compared with the new top of the stack.

8. When the end symbol is reached, the stack is popped to the output until terminating symbol is also reached. Then the conversion terminates.

Since we operate on operation body only, we need to generate other abstract machine clauses when a variable is copied to the output. For each state variable, target machine clauses are scanned. If a state variable appears in a given target machine

Figure 9. Postfix string scan

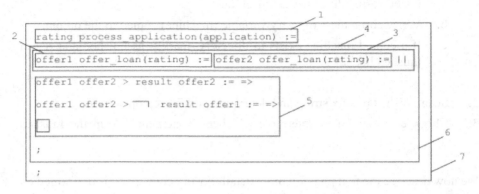

clause, that clause is copied to the output and joined to the corresponding variable. Therefore, if the current variable being scanned is `ticketPrice` and there exists a pre-condition `PRE ticketPrice > 0` in the target machine, then this pre-condition is associated with the variable at the output.

Finally, based on a postfix string and the content of the finished list, adequate composition is created. This step is best explained using an example. Suppose that we want to build a composite service that takes a loan application from the client, determines its credit rating, applies for a loan with two banks, and then chooses the better (higher) loan offer. We start by specifying target abstract machine (service), which we already used in the section Composable Service Architecture:

```
MACHINE loanExample
VARIABLES application:IN, rating ,offer1, offer2, result:OUT, pro-
cess_application, offer_loan, wcet
SETS App, Rating, Off, Time
INVARIANT process_application ∈ App → rating ∧ application ∈ App ∧ of-
fer_loan ∈ Rating → Off ∧ rating ∈ Rating ∧ result ∈ Off ∧ offer1 ∈ Off ∧
offer2 ∈ Off ∧ wcet ∈ Off → Time
OPERATION result <- ask_loan(application)
PRE rating > 0∧offer1>0∧offer2>0∧wcet(offer1)<86400∧wcet(offer2)<
86400
THEN rating := process_application(application);
[ ( offer1 := offer_loan(rating) ‖ offer2:=offer_loan(rating) );
( (offer1 > offer2) ⇒ result := offer2 ◆
¬ (offer1 > offer2) ⇒ result := offer1 ) ]
END
```

The machine accepts variable application representing loan application. The application is processed and as a result variable rating is produced representing applicant credit rating. Two loan offers, offer1 and offer2, are then generated in parallel by sending credit rating to two banks. After both loan offers are ready (the service will wait up to 24 hours, which is specified in the pre-condition), they are compared and the better (higher) one is chosen. The process of postfix conversion produces the following string (line breaks are added for clarification only):

```
rating process_appplication(application) :=
offer1 offer_loan(rating) := offer2 offer\_loan(rating) := ||
offer1 offer2 > result offer2 := ⇒
offer1 offer2 > ¬ result offer1 ⇒ ♦ ; ;
```

The postfix string is then iteratively scanned from left to right, in an attempt to extract possible constituent abstract machines and composition patterns connecting them. Variables are scanned until a first operator is reached, which is then applied to the variables. All variables scanned in a single pass are assigned to a single abstract machine. If the obtained abstract machine exists in the finished list, the machine construction is finished and the scan continues with the new machine. Otherwise new variables/operators are being added to the same machine. The process continues until the end of the postfix string is reached (Figure 9).

In step one, variables rating and process_application(application) are connected with assignment operator. Suppose that the following abstract machine is in the finished list—that is, it exists in a directory:

```
MACHINE machine_1
VARIABLES application:IN, rating:OUT, process_application
SETS App, Rating
INVARIANT process_application ∈ App → Rating ∧ application ∈ App ∧
rating ∈ Rating
OPERATION rating <- op_1 (application)
PRE THEN rating := process_application(application)
END
```

Note that clause PRE rating > 0 from the original machine is not included, since rating is the output parameter for which pre-conditions cannot be defined. Since the previous part of the string exists in a directory, in steps two and three, variables offer and offer_loan (rating), as well as offer2 and offer_loan(rating), are connected using assignment operator. Suppose that the following two machines are also in the finished list:

```
MACHINE machine_2
VARIABLES rating:IN, offer1: OUT, offer_loan
SETS Rating, Off
INVARIANT rating > 0 ∧ offer1 ∈ Off ∧ offer_loan ∈ Rating → Off
OPERATION offer1 <- op_2(rating)
PRE rating > 0
THEN offer1 := offer_loan(rating)
END


MACHINE machine_3
VARIABLES rating:IN, offer2: OUT, offer_loan
SETS Rating, Off
INVARIANT rating > 0 ∧ offer2 ∈ Off ∧ offer_loan ∈ Rating → Off
OPERATION offer1 <- op_3(rating)
PRE rating > 0
THEN offer2 := offer_loan(rating)
END
```

The postfix string is scanned further. The next symbol in step four is parallel composition operator that is applied to machine_2 and machine_3. In step five, the first scanned expression yields the following machine:

```
MACHINE machine_4
VARIABLES offer1:IN, offer2:IN, result:OUT, wcet
SETS Off, Time
INVARIANT offer1 ∈ Off ∧ offer2 ∈ Off ∧ result ∈ Off ∧ wcet ∈ Off
→ Time
OPERATION result <- op_4(offer1, offer2)
PRE offer1 > 0 ∧ offer2 > 0 ∧ wcet(offer1) > 86400 ∧ wcet(offer2)
> 86400
THEN (offer1 > offer2) ⇒ result := offer2
END
```

Suppose, however, that this machine does not exist in the finished list. This is the key point in the decomposition algorithm where a decision must be made whether to proceed further with postfix string or go back. If a decision to go back is taken, the previous compositions must be decomposed in a backtracking process. We would effectively try to incorporate machine_4 in machine_3 or machine_2. The other solution is to proceed forward and try to incorporate the next part of the postfix string in machine_4. The approach we adopt is that we move one time in each direction until a service that exists is reached. Therefore, in the continuation of step five, we modify machine_4 by scanning postfix string until we reach the next operator:

```
MACHINE machine_4
VARIABLES offer1:IN, offer2:IN, result:OUT, wcet
SETS Off, Time
INVARIANT offer1 ∈ Off ∧ offer2 ∈ Off ∧ result ∈ Off ∧ wcet ∈ Off
→ Time
OPERATION result <- op_4(offer1, offer2)
PRE offer1 > 0 ∧ offer2 > 0 ∧ wcet(offer1) > 86400 ∧ wcet(offer2)
> 86400
THEN (offer1 > offer2) ⇒ result := offer2 ♦
¬ (offer1 > offer2) ⇒ result := offer1
END
```

Supposing that this machine exists, we move to step six in which machine_4 is connected to parallel composition of machine_3 and machine_2 using sequence operator. Finally, in step seven, machine_1 is sequentially composed to the already built composition. The result is:

machine_1 ∇ (machine_2 ∥ machine_3) ∇ machine_4

In case machine_4 did not exist in a directory, the decomposition algorithm would try to backtrack and incorporate all scanned but unassigned variables into the last valid construction, that is, into parallel composition of machine_2 and machine_3. The result of this step is:

```
MACHINE machine_5
variables rating:IN, offer1, offer2, result:OUT, offer_loan, wcet
SETS Rating, Off, Time
INVARIANT offer_loan ∈ Rating → Off ∧ rating ∈ Rating ∧ offer1 ∈ Off∧
offer2 ∈ Off ∧ result ∈ Off
OPERATION result <- op_5(rating)
PRE rating > 0 ∧ offer1 >0 ∧ wcet(offer1) < 86400 ∧ offer2 > 0 ∧
wcet(offer2) < 86400
```

```
THEN [ ( offer1 := offer_loan(rating) || offer2:=offer_loan(rating)
);
( (offer1 > offer2) ⇒ result := offer2 ♦
¬ (offer1 > offer2) ⇒ result := offer1 ) ]
END
```

Now, if this machine exists in a directory, the decomposition result would be:

```
machine_1 ∇ machine_5
```

If not, a process of postfix conversion is applied again, this time to machine_5, which finally yields that:

```
machine_5 ≡ machine_2 ||  offer1>offer2  machine_3
```

and therefore final decomposition is:

```
machine_1 ∇ (machine_2 ||  offer1>offer2  machine_3)
```

Let us give the complete algorithm. Let $M(O,C,S)$ be the target service with operation body O, clauses C, and state variables S:

Figure 10. Bidirectional search problem

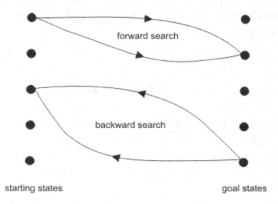

Figure 11. Bidirectional search example

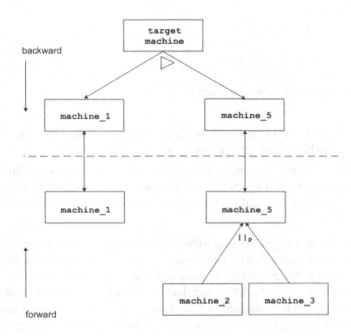

```
PF=∅
FINISHED=∅
elem=∅
CL=∅
PF=convert(O)
foreach s in S
 foreach c in C
 if s in c CL = CL ∪ {s,c}
while (elem != END)
 elem = scan (PF)
 switch(elem)
 case(variable): elem = elem ∪ scan (PF)
 case(operator)
 if(correct(elem,CL))
 if(exists(elem,CL))
 FINISHED=elem
 elem=∅
 elem=scan(PS)
```

```
if!(exists(elem,CL)
 elem=scan(FINISHED)
if elem = ∅ exit
else fail
```

Two major problems of decomposition are:

- *Incorrect Abstract Machines:* What is the behavior of the algorithm when the abstract machine scanned in a postfix string is not correct?
- *Algorithm Missing Decomposition Path:* What happens when the abstract machine scanned in a postfix string does not exist in the finished (list) directory, and moving forward/backward does not produce an existing machine?

In both cases, the decomposition algorithm cannot guarantee that a solution will be found. This is the consequence of a very simple control strategy that we adopted for both cases. When either a machine is incorrect or does not exist in a directory, first a forward scan is performed, and in case that also does not result in a valid/existing machine, a solution is backtracked in a backward scan. Instead of providing more complex control strategies that could achieve higher hit probability, we develop a hybrid bidirectional search mechanism.

Hybrid Bidirectional Automatic Composition

The last automatic composition mechanism that will be described is hybrid bidirectional search. The basic idea is to use advantages of both forward and backward search in order to eliminate two problems: long execution time of heuristic search and missing solution path in decomposition. Bidirectional search simultaneously performs forward and backward search thus creating two search paths. The search is over when (if) the two paths meet, and the solution is constructed by merging them. Forward search can be performed using any of the methodologies presented so far: basic heuristic search, probabilistic search, or search by learning. Backward search is performed by decomposing target abstract machines. There are three ways to perform bidirectional search: no special control strategy, depth specification, and means-ends analysis.

When no special control strategy is employed to steer direct bidirectional search, steps in both directions are made sequentially. After each step, current states are compared. If the current state of backward search is a subset of the current state of forward search, the algorithm terminates. This approach is simple to implement, as it does not require any additional control protocol. However it suffers from one problem: search paths may miss each other, completely or partially (Figure 10).

In the worst case of successful execution, this kind of search will perform complete forward search, and also spend additional overhead for unsuccessful backward search. That means that it will last longer than forward search only. Therefore, in the second approach, depth of both directions can be specified as an input parameter. For example, backward search can be allowed to progress for only one level, thus making it easier to satisfy several "smaller" target machines with a subsequent forward search. Similarly, forward search can be allowed to progress to a certain level, thus decreasing the number of goal states for subsequent decomposition. In this case, bidirectional search is not performed concurrently in both directions. Rather, first one direction is explored to a certain level, in order to make the search in the opposite direction easier and/or more effective. Bidirectional search (without special control strategy and with both depths set to one) for the loan application example from the previous section is shown in Figure 11.

There are still two open issues: which direction to favor (forward or backward) and up to which depth to limit the auxiliary search? We answer both questions by using means-ends analysis (Ernst & Newell, 1969). It detects differences between current and goal state, and tries to make a move in a state space that will reduce this difference. We modify this method to allow for a decision in which direction to move and for how many steps. The algorithm proceeds like this:

- Until the current state of backward search is not a subset of the current state of the forward search, or difference table offers no more options, do the following:

    1. Calculate the difference between two current states.
    2. Use a distance function and a difference table to determine whether to execute a forward or a backward move

Table 3. Difference table

	word2pdf	pdf2ps	fonts2pdf	printps
print				X
convert	X	X	X	
embed			X	

3.   Update current states accordingly

- If goal is achieved, the algorithm terminates successfully, otherwise it fails.

During search process, pre-conditions and post-conditions are evaluated in order to determine whether forward of backward search should be performed. In forward search, post-conditions of available services are matched against pre-conditions of target services. In backward search, pre-conditions of target services are matched to post-conditions of available services. Matching is performed using a difference table that describes which operation (direction) is appropriate to reduce the difference between the current and the goal state. Suppose we want to print a Word document and have only a printer that can print Postscript with embedded fonts. Available are also the following services: converter from Word to PDF, converter from PDF to Postscript, and service that can embed fonts to PDF. Abstract machines describing these services are:

```
MACHINE PrintPS
SETS Type={Word,PDF,PS}, Paper, Document
VARIABLES doc, print, fonts, type, result
INVARIANT print ∈ Document→Paper ∧ fonts ∈ Document→{Embedded,NotEmbedded} ∧
type ∈ Document → Type
OPERATION result <- printPS(doc)
```

Figure 12. Means-ends bidirectional search

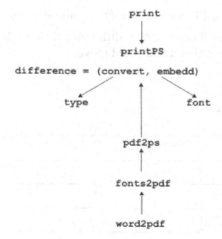

```
PRE type(doc) = PS ∧ fonts(doc)=Embedded ∧ doc ∈ Document
THEN result:= print(doc) ∧ result ∈ Paper
END


MACHINE Fonts2PDF
SETS Type={Word,PDF,PS}, Document
VARIABLES type, doc, fonts
INVARIANT type ∈ Document → Type ∧ fonts ∈ Document →
{Embedded,NotEmbedded}
OPERATION doc <- fonts2PDF(doc)
PRE type(doc) = PDF ∧ doc ∈ Document
THEN type(doc) = PDF ∧ fonts(doc) = Embedded
END


MACHINE PDF2PS
SETS Type={Word,PDF,PS}, Document
VARIABLES doc, type
INVARIANT type ∈ Document → Type
OPERATION doc <- pdf2PS(doc)
PRE type(doc) = PDF ∧ doc ∈ Document
THEN type(doc) = PS
END


MACHINE Word2PDF
SETS Type={Word,PDF,PS}, Document
VARIABLES doc, type
INVARIANT type ∈ Document → Type
OPERATION doc <- word2PDF(doc)
PRE type(doc) = Word ∧ doc ∈ Document
THEN type(doc) = PDF
END
```

A difference table is shown in Table 3. Sometimes there may be more than one operator that can reduce a given difference, but also one operator may be able to reduce more than one difference.

Assuming that the target machine is given below, the search proceeds as in Figure 12:

```
MACHINE print
SETS Type={Word,PDF,PS}, Paper, Document
VARIABLES doc, type, print, result
INVARIANT type  ∈ Document → Type ∧ print ∈ Document → Paper
PRE type(doc) = Word ∧ doc ∈ Document
THEN result := print(doc) ∧ result ∈ Paper
END
```

In the first step, backward search is performed and from difference table operation printPS is selected. However, service PrintPS is not equivalent to the goal state, since it accepts only Postscript documents with embedded fonts. Further decomposition yields no result, because there is no way to either transfer a Word file directly to Postscript or to embed fonts into a Postscript document. Therefore, at this point a difference is determined and forward search is attempted. The difference is the type of input parameters and whether fonts are embedded within the document. The difference table suggests using operation fonts2pdf to reduce font difference. By examining pre-conditions we see that this operation can be performed for PDF documents only. That means that this difference cannot be reduced at this point. The difference table suggests three operations for reducing type differences: word2pdf, pdf2ps, and again fonts2pdf. Pre-conditions determine that only word2pdf operation can reduce the difference. At this point we have a PDF document without embedded fonts. Now operation fonts2pdf can be applied, thus eliminating one difference (font embedding). After that pdf2ps is applied to reduce the last remaining difference (document type). The two searches meet and the algorithm terminates.

Finally, the algorithm for the means-ends control analysis is given. Let $G(PRE,POST)$ be the target service with pre-condition, post-conditions and $S(S_1(PRE_1,POST_1),\ldots,$ $S_m(PRE_m,POST_m))$ be the set of available (atomic) services:

```
BACKWARD = G
FORWARD = ∅
while(!(BACKWARD ⊂ FORWARD))
  distance = δ(BACKWARD,FORWARD)
  operation=lookup(difference_table,distance)
  switch(operation)
  case(forward): FORWARD=FORWARD ∪ compose(operation)
  case(backward):BACKWARD=BACKWARD ∪ decompose(operation)
```

Table 4. Performance comparison of automatic search algorithms

	average execution time [s]	number of compositions [expanded nodes]
heuristic	2.59	412
fixed probabilities	3.24	350
adaptive probabilities	2.16	297
learning	4.03	308
decomposition	1.57	284
bidirectional (depth spec.)	1.07	302
bidirectional (means-ends)	1.69	202

It is implicitly assumed that function *lookup* performs matching of pre- and post-conditions when doing difference table lookup, as well as that pre- and post-conditions are updated in *FORWARD* and *BACKWARD*.

Analysis and Comparison

Since automatic service composition was modeled as a search problem, the analysis of developed algorithms will be performed according to this fact. There are two fundamental approaches for judging the quality of a search algorithm: determining how fast it executes (time and space complexity) or how good the answers (solutions) are that it produces. In this case, the latter metric is not relevant, since absolute solution is either achieved or not: at the moment human interaction with suboptimal solution is not taken into account. Therefore, we will concentrate on the complexity and execution speed.

Let us first examine the basic heuristic search algorithm. The complexity of one algorithm cycle (search for candidate nodes with the smallest δ and their expansion) will be observed as a function of the number of nodes n in the OPEN list. The complexity is proportional to:

$$n \cdot (n + n \cdot n) = n^3 + n^2$$

Figure 13. Automatic composition average execution time

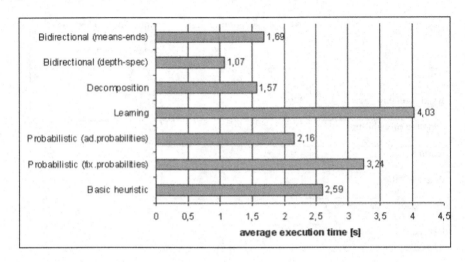

Figure 14. Automatic composition average number of compositions

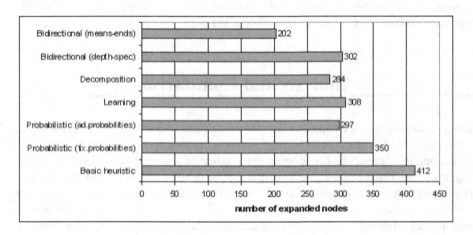

Therefore, complexity of one algorithm cycle is $O(n^3)$, where n is the current number of the nodes in the OPEN list. This number, however, changes with every algorithm cycle, therefore a more important question is how this number changes in every algorithm cycle and how many cycles the algorithm requires in order to find a solution. Let m be the number of atomic services, o the number of composition operators, and s the number of algorithm cycles. The number of generated nodes in each algorithm cycle is then given by:

$$m \cdot (o+1)^s$$

Clearly, it follows that the algorithm has an exponential complexity. However, s is the function of F, meaning that exponential growth of generated nodes is the upper complexity bound, or the worst case complexity, when all generated nodes fall below the futility value. Analytical dependency between s and F is very difficult to express in the general case as shown in Gasching (1979) for the A* algorithm. Instead, we will discuss the possible ways to build value F in order to reduce the complexity.

There are two ways to determine F: to define the maximum value of the distance function δ for which it is still feasible to examine the current path or to use some other metric. If distance function is used as futility metric, futility can be either chosen as the distance function value of nodes without successors, or the value can be determined empirically (application specific). Another metric applicable for F is to calculate the number of generated state variables for each node. If this number is greater than the number of state variables for the goal, the current node is moved to the LIMIT list, as subsequent compositions can only increase the number of state variables. This means that machines with more states than the goal machine are not accepted as solutions, which is compliant with the definition of distance function. This is somewhat problematic as subsets are not taken into account: services that can satisfy search criteria and offer extra functionality will not be accepted as solutions. The problem in such cases is, however, easily mitigated by comparing operations of abstract machines that offer extra functionalities (more Web methods) separately. Apart from determining futility value, other methods can be used to improve search performance, such as introducing execution time to limit the search temporally. This clearly makes sense in some applications where time limit can be naturally determined (e.g., bank transaction involving currency conversion, credit card verification, and payment should not take longer than 1 minute). The number of generated nodes can also terminate the search, as storage capacity is not infinite, and all generated nodes must be stored, even those that have crossed the futility value (LIMIT) or have already been expanded (CLOSED). This is required because of the equivalence comparison when new nodes are generated in order to detect equivalent and redundant paths.

In the worst case, the other two forward search strategies fall back to the basic heuristic search, thus having the same upper bound complexity. On the other hand, worst case complexity of backwards search is $O(n^2)$, assuming a very simple conflict control strategy that has been described. Finally, the complexity of the bidirectional search is very difficult to determine analytically, as it depends on the direction depth. It can vary from $O(n^3)$ to $O(n^8)$. Clearly, the analytical analysis shows that the preferred method for automatic composition should be decomposition (backwards search), at least judging by the worst-case complexity. However, in many heuristic approaches, average-case complexity is much more important. Since we expect that these heuristics will hopefully never execute in their upper complexity bounds, it is both worth and relevant to examine their average performance through experiments.

The experiment was performed using 20 basic operations from the well-known holiday booking scenario exposed through Web services (e.g., reserve a flight, reserve hotel room, rent a car, charge credit card, etc.), and the task was to solve 10 different composite requests. The results are, therefore, averaged over 10 algorithm runs for different goals. Non-functional properties that were modeled included security (access right to different services), dependability (some services could run inside a single transaction, others not), and timeliness (execution time was defined for several operations). The results given in Table 4 relate to physical execution speed (the absolute time in seconds required to find a solution) and to the number of compositions (expanded nodes) in each case. Note that values reflect only the search for the adequate composition and not the execution of the composition itself once it has been found.

On the average, the fastest algorithm is bidirectional search with depth specification, followed by decomposition and bidirectional search using the difference table which execute with almost identical speed (Figure 13). The reason that depth specification is clearly superior to means-ends analysis in terms of speed is that means-ends analysis requires costly operations of difference table lookup in every step. The probabilistic approach with adaptive probabilities leads the second group, closely followed by surprisingly fast basic heuristic search. The reason why basic heuristic search outperforms probabilistic and learning-based search lies in the simplicity of calculating heuristic function and the fact that it does not require maintenance of complex structures (cooperation graph, classification). The slowest approach is the learning-based approach, which is almost four times slower compared to the fastest solution, because of the complex data structures that it maintains.

Figure 15. Constraint satisfaction-based automatic composition

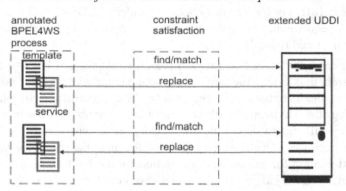

The other metrics, however, present a somewhat different picture (Figure 14). The best algorithm in terms of number of compositions performed (number of expanded nodes) is bidirectional search using means-ends analysis (difference table). The fastest algorithm, bidirectional search with depth specification, is only the third here, since even decomposition offers a slightly better path through the state space. Probabilistic search with adaptive probabilities and learning follow closely, while by far the worst performance is offered by basic heuristic search which executes with over $O(n^2)$ average complexity in this case.

It can be concluded that there is no single metric that can be used for comparison of developed methods. It has been shown, on the example of best performing algorithms in both categories, that fast movement through the state space requires significant computing overhead in maintaining helper data structures. It is also visible that relatively simple basic heuristic search executes very quickly (easy calculation of heuristic function) despite the worst average execution complexity. The two design criteria (execution time and minimizing number of expanded nodes) are clearly conflicting. Based on the presented results, it would be wrong to conclude that execution time is the only relevant metrics, since in this experiment all services were executing on the same machine and node expansion cost may not have been realistic enough (e.g., network latency penalty was not included). However, the results clearly show that bidirectional search and decomposition offer the best compromise. An even more important result is that the average execution complexity of all presented heuristics is below $O(n^2)$ in this example, which is a favorable feasibility indication. All the experiments were performed when the solution was existing—that is, when the given trip plan (goal service) could be satisfied using available operations (atomic services). When the solution does not exist, all algorithms execute in their upper complexity bound before reporting that a solution does not exist, except when they are time limited (e.g., timeout). In this case the superior solution is decomposition ($O(n^2)$), but as already shown, the penalty is that it does not guarantee a solution. Apart from decomposition, all other algorithms will execute with exponential upper complexity bound, with high probability that a bidirectional search will report a non-existing solution in polynomial time, if the difference table or depth specification favor backward (polynomial) instead of forward (exponential) direction.

Related Approaches

In this section a discussion of the existing related approaches to automatic service composition is presented. Two generic strategies will be described, namely constraint satisfaction/planning and ontology-based logic reasoning (deductive databases), together with a comparison with the methods we have proposed.

Aggarwal et al. (2004) presented a method that reduces service composition to a constraint satisfaction problem. The main entity is an abstract process which contains abstract services. An abstract service is a placeholder for a set of physical (real) services that match the abstract service template, effectively competing for its place. Competition is based on the idea of automated service discovery (Cardoso & Seth, 2003; Paolucci, Kawamura, Payne, & Sycara, 2002a). Automated discovery is performed using user defined requirements, and it produces a set of candidate services, after discovery candidate services are selected on the basis of process and business constraints.

The main stages of creating dynamic process are development, annotation, discovery, composition, and execution. Different semantics can be used: data, functionality, and quality of service. The part that is most relevant for automatic composition deals with design of abstract processes. It involves the following steps (Figure 15): creation of desired flow using control flow constructs provided by BPEL4WS, annotation of BPEL flow using templates that express service properties, and specification of constraints that will be used for optimization.

BPEL annotation is performed using different ontologies. Partner services are represented as annotated abstract services. A search on extended UDDI is performed, and for each template a set of matching services is identified. In the process of optimization, constraints are evaluated and candidates are eliminated. Constraint satisfaction can be performed on service dependencies, querying and cost estimation, or process constraints. After candidate services have been filtered and identified, BPEL process is translated into executable form by adding physical addresses of selected partner services to BPEL deployment descriptor and sent to BPEL server for execution.

Ghandeharizadeh et al. (2003) presented a system called Proteus that uses planning techniques for dynamic composition and execution of Web services. The main feature of Proteus is dynamic composition of plans that integrate Web service. Besides planning, Proteus offers plan execution and monitoring. The system behavior is very similar to constraint satisfaction. Service description is annotated with additional expressions using WS-Inspection (Ballinger et al., 2001). The annotated plan is submitted to a search engine that tries to find adequate services at run-time and substitute them in the plan. An integration plan is generated that binds identified services into the requested plan, and this plan is then executed.

Zeng et al. (2004) presented another method similar to constraint satisfaction. Composition is modeled using statecharts over which execution paths are constructed. Statecharts comprise generic elements called tasks. An execution path is any complete path of tasks from a starting state to an ending state. Any subset of a set of all possible execution paths for which quality of service properties are evaluated is a potential execution plan. The problem is how to identify the execution plan that corresponds to the user-expressed requirements. If there are n tasks (states) and m

candidate Web services that are identified for each task, the number of all execution plans is m^n, which makes this method of automatic composition impractical. Therefore, integer programming (Karloff, 1991) is used for selecting an optimal execution plan without the need to generate all possible plans.

Inputs to planning are a set of variables, objective function, and a set of constraints. A set of variables describes the quality of service properties of each task that is being considered. Constraints are user-defined limitation on price, execution duration, execution price, reputation, success rate, and availability. Objective function compares the current execution plan to the constraints. Both objective function and constraints are linear. In the process of composition, the value of objective function is maximized or minimized by adjusting the values of variables while enforcing the constraints. The output is the maximum (or minimum) value of the objective function from which the values of the variables can be extracted for this maximum (minimum). The set of variables determines which candidate service instances actually populate tasks during physical execution.

Finally, Sirin, Hendler, and Parsia (2003) presented an approach to automatic composition based on the semantic Web and on OWL-S ontologies. More specifically, the OWL-S process model is used to develop a desired composition by creating a composite process comprising choreographed atomic processes. After composite OWL-S process is created, a search is performed to find the best matching services that can replace atomic processes (abstract service placeholders).

Automatic composition has two main components: composer and inference engine. The inference engine is essentially a directory that has the capability to find matching services that best fit specified abstract processes. It is designed as a knowledge base using Prolog. The composer is the interactive part of the system. It enables the user to create a workflow of services, and it also presents all available choices to the user at every step. That means that despite knowledge base, composition must be performed (partly) manually. At every step, functional and non-functional properties of participating services are matched, and some candidates are rejected. This process can also be assisted by a human operator. After a desired composition has been found—that is, after all abstract processes from the OWL-S process model have been substituted by real services from a directory—the entire composite process is stored in a directory from which it can be invoked.

The second group of approaches for automatic service composition is based on reasoning performed upon deductive databases. Rules describing the system (onotolgies) and descriptions of available services are stored in a database. The system is presented with a query describing current (starting) state and the goals. It is expected that the reasoning engine will be able to compute a state transition from the current to the goal state using rules and available services. Reasoning mechanisms are dependant on the formalism used for rule and service description, and several relevant solutions will be described.

The MyGrid project (Sabou, Wroe Goble, & Mishne, 2005) uses federated UDDI directories annotated with RDF to provide semantic description. The language used for ontology description is OWL-S. Based on the given goal and available semantically enriched service advertisements, this approach uses description logic (Baader, Calvanese, McGuiness, Nardi, & Patel-Schneider, 2003) to perform reasoning in order to match the request with available resources (services). Reasoning operations that can be performed are instance checking, subsumption reasoning, and so forth.

InfoSleuth (Bayardo et al., 1997) is an agent-based system that uses Open Knowledge Base Connectivity (OKBC) to represent and store ontologies. Several agents are available in the system that are used to match the user's goal: user agent, ontology agent, broker agent, resource agent, data analysis agent, task execution agent, and monitor agent. Agents communicate using Knowledge Query and Manipulation Language (KQML). When the user submits goal task, the deductive database storing semantic description of available services and rules is queried using deductive database language (DDL++), thus semantically checking if the query matches available advertisements.

Language for Advertisement and Request for Knowledge Sharing (Sycara, Widoff, Klusch, & Lu, 2002) is an agent-based approach for agent (service) matching. There are three agent categories: service providers, service requesters, and middle agents. The middle agent matches the query against the advertised providers' capabilities. In this process the middle agent uses advertisement database and partial global ontology. A frame-based language is used to describe queries (goals) and advertisements. Ontologies are used to describe the meanings used in queries and advertisements. The language used for ontology description is ITL. The reasoner offers the following matchings: subsumption reasoning (context and profile matching), subtype inference rules (signature matching), and subsumption reasoning for Horn clauses (constraint matching).

The Web Service Modeling Ontology (WSMO) (Roman et al., 2005; ESSI, 2006) is a framework for automated Web service discovery, selection, composition, execution, and monitoring. Ontologies in WSMO are described using one of the Web Service Modeling Language variants (WSML, 2006): WSML-Core, WSML-DL, WSML-Flight, WSML-Rule, and WSML-Full. They are based on description logic, first-order logic, logic programming, and description logic programming. Several reasoners (e.g., WSML-Rule and WSML-DL) have already been developed, while other native WSML reasoners are works in progress. Based on descriptions of user requirements and service advertisements, reasoners perform matching with the help of information found in ontologies.

Finally, there are numerous approaches to use reasoning upon OWL-S ontologies to perform automatic composition (Li & Horrocks, 2003; Paolucci et al., 2002b). They all use description logic formalism and are able to compute the following degrees of matching: exact matching, subsumes matching, intersection matching, and disjoint matching (failed matching). Naturally, OWL-S specifications are used to describe both user requests (goals) and available service descriptions. Methods like subsumption reasoning and instance checking are then performed for submitted goals in order to identify services (capabilities) that can fulfill them.

From the solution we proposed and from the related solutions presented in this section, it can be seen that there are two fundamentally different ways to handle automatic service composition:

1. Start with the pre-defined composition described in a generic manner (empty service placeholders connected using execution logic) and perform 1-1 search in a directory to replace every generic element of a composition with a real service.

2. Describe a set of goals and try to achieve them by building the whole composite process from scratch, without prejudicing either the number of services or the logic that is used to connect them.

Clearly, constraint satisfaction, planning, and integer programming belong to the first approach. They all provide methodology to describe pre-designed service choreography (empty composition skeleton) with placeholders that are to be filled with actual (real) services. They thus reduce the problem of automatic composition to the problem of finding adequate replacement for every abstract element of the pre-defined composition. It is not possible, for example, to replace two abstract activities with one concrete service that matches the sum of two constraints instead of each of these constraints alone. We feel the service-oriented application designer should not think in terms of pre-defined compositions, but in terms of the problem that is to be solved. Our approach therefore does not require the composition to be pre-defined. Target abstract machine specifies properties of the problem (goal) itself, and not the way to achieve it. It does not prejudice the composition process by requiring that certain services be composed in the given manner. Identification of composition patterns and candidate services is left to the automatic composition algorithm based on the target abstract machine.

Let us consider a decomposition example of modeling loan flow composite service. For constraint satisfaction and planning solutions presented in this section, an expert human knowledge would have to be used not only to describe problem properties, but also to make an initial composite process layout in terms of services and their compositions. In this case, it would mean that input to the system would be pre-defined BPEL composition without deployment descriptor, that is, without binding to existing services. This would require that assumptions should be made about the number of services required to solve the problem, their properties, and ways to connect them. The designer would have to specify abstract credit rating service, abstract bank services, and logic that controls their execution. In the subsequent process of directory search, each partnerLink element from the above will be instantiated with a real service, admittedly with checking whether it preserves overall composition properties. On the other side, our approach does not require human knowledge in the area of service placeholder selection and their connection. It is enough that composite process is described using either abstract machine notation or CDL, and both the number of services and their connections (composition logic) will be discovered during automatic composition. That way, many solutions can be covered, contrary to the approaches that try to fit existing services in a single, predefined composite logic. Automated planning methodologies other than constraint satisfaction (e.g., deductive planning, resource scheduling, task decomposition, propositional satisfiability, or model checking) could eliminate the downside of constraint satisfaction approaches, as they allow for the goal-based automatic plan generation (Ghallab, Nau, & Traverso 2004). However, there are no current proposals to use these techniques for automatic Web service composition.

The problem specification domain is in this way decoupled from the solution specification domain. By specifying target abstract machine, we do not think about how to solve a problem, but what and under which conditions we need to achieve. We see this as a clear advantage compared to other automatic composition concepts that require that the entire solution be premeditated in advance.

Reasoning-based approaches admittedly belong to the second group, as they all allow specification of goals and compute the solution out of available services, without requiring the user either to know properties of existing services or predefine an abstract composition skeleton. However, the following problems can be identified in reasoning-based approaches, which are eliminated by our approach of treating automatic composition as a search problem:

- *Speed:* Search algorithms are simpler, offer lower complexity, and execute faster when compared to the logic reasoners.

- *Manual Composition:* The proposed approaches are not well suited for manual composition, which limits their usage in the application development scenarios, where the user (designer) requires greater, manual control over composition partners, but still needs powerful verification mechanisms.

- *Deductive Databases Limitations:* The existing deductive databases are limited technologically, as they do not support transaction handling, load balancing, and similar properties that are required in a highly dynamic and stressed environment.

- *Ontology Dependence:* All reasoners depend on the ontology quality. If an ontology is partial, ambiguous, or in some other way incomplete, the reasoner cannot guarantee a solution, even if it exists. Furthermore, current reasoners cannot load ontologies on demand, meaning that all necessary ontologies must be known in advance and preloaded.

For the reasons explained, it is our belief that the novel approach of treating automatic service composition as a search problem presents a research direction that should be further investigated

Conclusion and Future Work

Development of a unified WS-Architecture is an enormous task, and as such cannot be carried out by a single person or institution. Our intended contribution is to offer an architectural approach that can be used for achieving a certain degree of automatization of service composition. We presented foundations of such architecture and then considered several mechanisms for automatic composition: from basic heuristic search that guarantees solution but can take a long time to find one, to probabilistic composition and learning, which in some cases converge to a solution very quickly. In non-favorable conditions however, they degrade to slower methods, claiming additional overhead.

Probabilistic composition and learning are more suited to limited use in a controlled environment where nature and frequency of service requests are known or can be predicted, while the basic heuristic search approach is universally applicable, but faces some performance issues. We expect that by combining proposed methods, a viable architectural solution for automatic service composition will be devised. We also presented additional hybrid mechanisms, such as backwards search, where state space is traversed from the goal (target service) to the starting state (available services) by means of algebraic decomposition of abstract machines, or a bidirectional search which performs forward and backward search simultaneously. We are currently investigating use cases in which average performance of presented algorithms can be determined, using implementation of the composition and verification server presented in Milanovic (2005).

Introduction of composable service architecture can impact both business and infrastructure (application development) layers. Business advantages and impact of moving towards an economy where services are associated on demand in short running transactions have been discussed to some extent. At the application development layer, profiling of three roles can be expected: architecture deployer, application developed, and user. Architecture deployer defines composability rules, sets up service directory, and deploys atomic services. Application developer acts upon deployed infrastructure in an attempt to build value-added functionalities on demand using composition patterns. Finally, users invoke atomic or composite services from a directory. This profiling can make a dramatic change in the ways applications are developed and consumed. Potential impact lies in increased code dependability (through verification of predeployed services), easier application management, and automated end user support.

Acknowledgment

The authors would like to acknowledge Maren Lenk, who helped in developing basic heuristic search as part of her master's thesis.

References

Abrial, J.R. (1996). *The B book.* Cambridge: Cambridge University Press.

Aggarwal, R., Verma, K., Miller, J., & Milnor, W. (2004). Constraint driven Web service composition in METEOR-S. *Proceedings of the IEEE Service Computing Conference* (pp. 23-30), Shangai, China.

Aho, A.V., Sethi, R., & Ullman, J.D. (1987). *Compilers, principles and tools.* Boston: Addison-Wesley.

Andrews, T. et al. (2004). *Business process execution language for Web services.* Retrieved April 2005 from *http://www.ibm.com/developerworks/library/ws-bpel*

Ankolekar A. et al. (2002). DAML-S: Web service description for the Semantic Web. *Proceedings of the International Semantic Web Conference* (pp. 348-363), Sardinia, Italy.

Baader, F., Calvanese, D., McGuiness, D., Nardi, D., & Patel-Schneider, P. (2003). *The description logic handbook.* Cambridge: Cambridge University Press.

Ballinger, K. et al. (2001). *Web services inspection language (WS-Inspection).* Retrieved June 2005 from *http://www-106.ibm.com/developerworks/webservices/library/ws-wsilspec.html*

Bayardo, R.J. et al. (1997). InfoSleuth: Agent-based semantic integration of information in open and dynamic environments. *Proceedings of the ACM SIGMOD International Conference on Management of Data* (pp. 195-206), New York.

Berardi, D., Calvanese, D., Giuseppe, D.G., Lenzerini, M., & Mecella, M. (2003). Automatic composition of e-services that export their behavior. *Proceedings of the 1st International Conference on Service Oriented Computing* (pp. 43-58), Trento, Italy.

Blow, M. et al. (2004). *BPELJ: BPEL for Java.* Retrieved May 2005 from *http://www-106.ibm.com/developerworks/webservices/library/ws-bpelj/*

Bultan, T., Fu, X., Hull, R., & Su, J. (2003). A new approach to design and analysis of e-service composition. *Proceedings of the 12th International World Wide Web Conference* (pp. 403-410), Budapest, Hungary.

Cardoso, J., & Seth, A.P. (2003). Semantic e-workflow composition. *Journal of Intelligent Information Systems, 21*(3), 191-225.

Curbera, F., Khalaf, R., Mukhi, N., Tai, S., & Weerawarana, S. (2003). The next step in Web services. *Communications of the ACM, 46*(10), 29-34.

Czajkowski, K. et al. (2004). *The WS-Resource framework.* Retrieved May 2005 from *http://www.globus.org/wsrf/specs/ws-wsrf.pdf*

ESSI WMO Working Group. (2006). *Web services modeling ontology.* Retrieved March 2006 from *http://wsmo.org*

Ernst, G.W., & Newell, A. (1969). *GPS: A case study in generality and problem solving.* New York: Academic Press.

Foster, I. et al. (2004). *Modeling stateful resources with Web services.* Retrieved June 2005 from *http://www.ibm.com/developerworks/library/ws-resource/ws-modelingresources.pdf*

Fu, X., Bultan, T., & Su, J. (2002). Formal verification of e-services and workflows. *Proceedings of the Workshop on Web Services, E-Business and the Semantic Web: Foundations, Models, Architecture, Engineering and Applications* (pp. 188-202), Toronto, Canada.

Gasching, J. (1979). *Performance measurement and analysis of certain search algorithms.* PhD Dissertation, Carnegie-Mellon University, USA.

Ghallab, M., Nau, D., & Traverso, P. (2004). *Automated planning.* San Francisco: Morgan Kauffman.

Ghandeharizadeh, S. et al. (2003). Proteus: A system for dynamically composing and intelligently executing Web services. *Proceedings of the 2003 International Conference on Web Services* (pp. 17-21), Las Vegas, NV.

Gray, J., & Reuter, A. (1993). *Transaction processing: Concepts and techniques.* San Francisco: Morgan Kaufmann.

Hamadi, R., & Benatallah, B. (2003). A Petri Net-based model for Web service composition. *Proceedings of the 14th Australasian Conference on Database Technologies* (pp. 191-200), Adelaide, Australia.

Hart, P.E., Nilsson, N.J., & Raphael, B. (1968). A formal basis for the heuristic determination of minimum cost paths. *IEEE Transactions on SSC, 4*(2), 100-107.

Hart, P.E., Nilsson, N.J., & Raphael, B. (1972). Correction to 'a formal basis for the heuristic determination of minimum cost paths'. *SIGART Newsletter, 37.*

Heuvel, W.J., & Maamar, Z. (2003). Moving toward a framework to compose intelligent Web services. *Communications of the ACM, 46*(10), 103-109.

Karloff, H. (1991). *Linear Programming.* Birkhauser.

Lenk, M. (2005). *Heuristic composition of abstract machines.* Master's Thesis, Humboldt University Berlin, Germany.

Li, L., & Horrocks, I. (2003). A software framework for matchmaking based on Semantic Web technology. *Proceedings of the 12th International Conference on the World Wide Web* (pp. 331-339), Budapest, Hungary.

Martelli, A., & Montanari, U. (1973). Additive and/or graphs. *Proceedings of the 3rd International Joint Conference on Artificial Intelligence* (pp. 1-11), Stanford, CA.

Martelli, A., & Montanari, U. (1978). Optimization decision trees through heuristically guided search. *Communications of the ACM, 21*(12), 1025-1039.

McIlraith, S., & Son, T.C. (2002). Adapting Golog for composition of Semantic Web services. *Proceedings of the International Conference on the Principles of Knowledge Representation and Reasoning* (pp. 482-496), Toulouse, France.

Medvidovic, N., & Taylor, R.N. (2000). A classification and comparison framework for software architecture description languages. *IEEE Transactions on Software Engineering, 26*(1), 70-93.

Meyer, B. (1992). Applying design by contract. *IEEE Computer, 25*(10), 40-51.

Mikalsen, T., Sai, S., & Rouvellou, I. (2002). Transactional attitudes: Reliable composition of autonomous Web services. *Proceedings of the Workshop of Dependable Middleware-Based Systems* (pp. 44-53), Washington DC.

Milanovic, N. (2005). Contract-based Web service composition framework with correctness guarantees. *Proceedings of the 2nd International Service Availability Symposium* (pp. 46-59), Berlin, Germany.

Milanovic, N., & Malek, M. (2004a). Current solutions for Web service composition. *IEEE Internet Computing, 8*(6), 51-59.

Milanovic, N., & Malek, M. (2004b). Extracting functional and non-functional contracts from Java classes and enterprise Java beans. *Proceedings of the Workshop on Architecting Dependable Systems* (pp. 282-286), Florence, Italy.

Milanovic, N., & Malek, M. (2005). Architectural support for automatic service composition. *Proceedings of the International Service Computing Conference* (pp. 133-140), Orlando, FL.

Narayanan, S., & McIlraith, S. (2002). Simulation, verification and automated composition of Web services. *Proceedings of the 11th International World Wide Web Conference* (pp. 77-88), Honolulu, HI.

Nilsson, N.J. (1980). *Principles of artificial intelligence.* Palo Alto, CA: Tioga.

Paolucci, M., Kawamura, T., Payne, T.R., & Sycara, K. (2002a). Importing the Semantic Web in UDDI. *Proceedings of Web Services, E-Business and Semantic Web Workshops* (pp. 225-236), Toronto, Canada.

Paolucci, M., Kawamura, T., Payne, T.R., & Sycara, K. (2002b). Semantic matching of Web services capabilities. *Proceedings of the 1st International Semantic Web Conference* (pp. 333-347), Sardinia, Italy.

Papazoglou, M.P., & Georgakopoulos, D. (2003). Service oriented computing. *Communications of the ACM, 46*(10), 25-28.

Rich, E. (1983). *Artificial intelligence.* New York: McGraw-Hill.

Roman, D., Keller, U., Lausen, H., de Bruijn, J., Lara, R., Stollberg, M., Polleres, A., Feier, C., Bussler, C., & Fensel, D. (2005). Web services modeling ontology. *Applied Ontology, 1*(1), 77-106.

Sabou, M., Wroe C., Goble, C., & Mishne, G. (2005). Learning domain ontologies for Web service description: An experiment in bioinformatics. *Proceedings of the International Conference on the World Wide Web* (WWW2005) (pp. 190-198), Chiba, Japan.

Schmidt, H., Poernomo, I., & Reussner, R. (2001). Trust-by-contract: Modelling, analysing and predicting behavior of software architectures. *Journal of Integrated Design and Process Science, 5*(3), 25-51.

Sirin, E., Hendler, J., & Parsia, B. (2003). Semi-automatic composition of Web services using semantic descriptions. *Proceedings of the Web Services: Modeling, Architecture and Infrastructure Workshop at ICEIS* (pp. 17-24), Angers, France.

Sycara, K., Widoff, S., Klusch, M., & Lu, J. (2002). Larks: Dynamic matchmaking among heterogeneous software agents in cyberspace. In *Autonomous agents and multi-agent systems* (pp. 173-203). Boston: Kluwer Academic.

Tartanoglu, F., Issarny, V., Romanovsky, A., & Levy, N. (2003). Coordinated forward error recovery for composite Web services. *Proceedings of the 22nd International Symposium on Reliable Dependable Systems* (pp. 167-176), Florence, Italy.

Verma, K., Sivashanmugam, K., Sheth, A., Patil, A., Oundhakar, S., & Miller, J. (2004). METEOR-S WSDI: A scalable infrastructure of registries for semantic publication and discovery of Web services. *Journal of Information Technology and Management,* 17-39.

Vinoski S. (2004). WS-nonexistent standards. *IEEE Internet Computing,* 8(6), 25-28.

Vogels, W. (2003). Web services are not distributed objects: Common misconceptions about the fundamentals of Web service technology. *IEEE Internet Computing,* (November/December), 59-66.

Webber, J., & Parastatidis, S. (2003). Demystifying service-oriented architectures. *Web Services Journal, 3*(11). Retrieved May 2005 from *http://webservices. sys-con.com/read/39908.htm*

West, D.B. (1996). *Introduction to graph theory.* Englewood Cliffs, NJ: Prentice Hall.

WSML Working Group. (2006). *The Web services modeling language.* Retrieved March 2006 from *http://www. wsmo.org/wsml/wsml-syntax/*

Yang, J. (2003). Web service componentization. *Communications of the ACM, 46*(10), 35-40.

Yang, J., & Papazoglou, M.P. (2000). Interoperation support for electronic business. *Communications of the ACM, 43*(6), 39-47.

Yang, J., & Papazoglou, M.P. (2002). Web component: A substrate for Web service reuse and composition. *Proceedings of the 14th Conference on Advanced Information Systems and Engineering* (pp. 21-36), Toronto, Canada.

Zeng, L., Benatallah, B., Ngu, A.H.H., Dumas, M., Kalaganam, J., & Chang, H. (2004). QoS-aware middleware for Web services composition. *IEEE Transactions on Software Engineering, 30*(5), 311-327.

Zhang, J. (2005). Trustworthy Web services: Actions for now. *IEEE IT Professional, 7*(1), 32-36.

Zhang, J., Chang, C.K., Chung, J.Y., & Kim, S.W. (2004). S-Net: A Petri Net-based specification model for Web services. *Proceedings of the IEEE International Conference on Web Services* (pp. 420-427), San Diego, CA.

Chapter VII

XWRAPComposer:
A Multi-Page
Data Extraction Service

Ling Liu, Georgia Institute of Technology, USA

Jianjun Zhang, Georgia Institute of Technology, USA

Wei Han, IBM Research, Almaden Research Center, USA

Calton Pu, Georgia Institute of Technology, USA

James Caverlee, Georgia Institute of Technology, USA

Sungkeun Park, Georgia Institute of Technology, USA

Terence Critchlow, Lawrence Livermore National Laboratory, USA

David Buttler, Lawrence Livermore National Laboratory, USA

Matthew Coleman, Lawrence Livermore National Laboratory, USA

Abstract

We present a service-oriented architecture and a set of techniques for developing wrapper code generators, including the methodology of designing an effective wrapper program construction facility and a concrete implementation, called XWRAP-Composer. Our wrapper generation framework has two unique design goals. First, we explicitly separate tasks of building wrappers that are specific to a Web service from the tasks that are repetitive for any service, thus the code can be generated as a wrapper library component and reused automatically by the wrapper generator system. Second, we use inductive learning algorithms that derive information flow and data extraction patterns by reasoning about sample pages or sample specifications. More importantly, we design a declarative rule-based script language for multi-page information extraction, encouraging a clean separation of the information extraction semantics from the information flow control and execution logic of wrapper programs. We implement these design principles with the development of the XWRAPComposer toolkit, which can semi-automatically generate WSDL-enabled wrapper programs. We illustrate the problems and challenges of multi-page data extraction in the context of bioinformatics applications and evaluate the design and development of XWRAPComposer through our experiences of integrating various BLAST services.

Introduction

With the wide deployment of Web service technology, the Internet and the World Wide Web (Web) have become the most popular means for disseminating both business and scientific data from a variety of disciplines. For example, vast and growing amount of life sciences data reside in specialized Bioinformatics data sources, and many of them are accessible online with specialized query processing capabilities. Concretely, the Molecular Biology Database Collection currently holds over 500 data sources (DBCAT, 1999), not even including many tools that analyze the information contained therein. Bioinformatics data sources over the Internet have a wide range of query processing capabilities. Typically, many Web-based sources allow only limited types of selection queries. To compound the problem, data from one source often must be combined with data from other sources to provide scientists with the information they need.

Motivating Scenario

In the Bioinformatics and Bioengineering domain, many biologists currently use a variety of tools, such as DNA microarrays, to discover how DNA and the proteins they encode may allow an organism to respond to various stress conditions such as exposure to environmental mutagens (Quandt, Frech, Karas, Wingender, & Werner, 1995; Altschul et al., 1997; DBCAT, 1999). One way to accomplish this task is for genomics researchers to identify genes that react in the desired way, and then develop models to capture the common elements. This model will be used to identify previously unidentified genes that may also respond in similar fashion based on the common elements. Figure 1 illustrates a workflow that a genomics researcher has created to gather the data required for this analysis. This type of workflow significantly differs from traditional workflows, as it is iteratively generated to discover the correct process with a small set of data as the initial input. At each step the researcher selects and extracts the part of the output data that is useful for his genomic analysis in the next step, and determines which services should be used in the next step in his data collection process. Once the workflow is constructed, the genomic researcher will use the workflow as the data collection pattern to collect large quantities of data and perform large scale genomic analysis. Concretely, Figure 1 shows a pattern of a promoter model where the data collection is performed in eight steps using possibly eight or more Bioinformatics data sources through service oriented computing interfaces.

In Step (1), microarrays containing the genes of interest are produced and exposed to different levels of a specific mutagen in the wet-lab, usually in a time dependent manner.

In Step (2) gene expression changes are measured and clustered using some computational tools (e.g., *Clusfavor* (Peterson, 2002)), such that genes that changed significantly in a micro-array analysis experiment are identified and clustered. The representative genes from Clusfavor analysis will be used as the input for the next data collection step. Typically the researcher must choose from a wide variety of tools available for this task either manually based on his past experience or using a Web service selection facility. Each tool offers specific advantages in terms of their ability to analyze the microarray data, and each requires a different method of execution.

In Step (3), the full sequence from each of the representative genes chosen in the second step is retrieved from gene-banks.

Figure 1. An example workflow for developing a promoter model

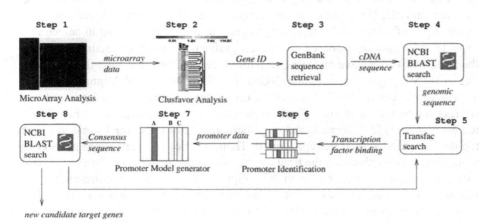

In Step (4), each gene sequence retrieved in Step (3) will be submitted to a gene matching service, such as NCBI Blast Web service, that will return homologs (other genes with similar sequences). The returned sequences will be further examined to find promoter sequences. Again, there are several services that provide gene similarity matching, many of which specialize in a particular species, such as ACEdb (Stein & Thierry-Mieg, 1999).

Once related sequences are discovered, approximately 1000-5000 bases of the DNA sequence around the alignment are extracted to capture the promoter regulatory elements — the region of a gene where RNA polymerase can bind and begin transcription to create the proteins that regulate cell function. In Step (5), these promoter sequences are identified and analyzed using specific tools, such as Mat-Inspector (Peterson, 2002), TRANSFAC, TRRD, or COMPEL (Quandt et al., 1995) to find the common transcription binding factors. To extract specific data, such as portions of a DNA sequence, returned by the sources, the data needs to be converted into a well-known format, such as XML, and post-processed in order to extract just the portions that are relevant for the next step.

In Step (6), regulatory profiles are then compared across each gene in the cluster to delineate common response elements that can be fed into the promoter model generator to create a promoter model in Step (7). Once the model is created, it can be used to search gene databases to find other candidate genes relevant to the study in Step (8), which starts a new iteration where these genes are fed back into this general workflow to refine and expand the promoter model until the genomic researcher is satisfied with the result. The collection of genes found in this iterative process will be presented as the final results of this complex data analysis task.

It is important to point out that each of these steps requires service selection, automated data extraction, service composition and integration. Choosing the appropriate source depends on the content, capabilities and load of the source, as well as the trustworthiness of the source. Some sites have much stricter standards on the quality of the data that they admit, while others publish information as soon as it is available. Depending on the current needs of a particular researcher, different types of sites may be more appropriate to query. In addition to selecting a capable and trustworthy source, there are significant issues in extracting data from the sites. Most sites have custom query interfaces and return results through a series of HTML pages. For example, NCBI BLAST (Basic Local Alignment Search Tool) (Altschul et al., 1997) requires the user to take three or four steps in order to retrieve the matching sequence homologs. First, a gene sequence must be submitted through an HTML form. Users may then optionally select the format in which the data returned should be represented. Then, a series of delay pages are shown while the service calculates the final answer. Once the answer is computed, a page listing the related sequence ids and their alignment information are presented. The full homolog sequence is available by following a link from each alignment. Just to retrieve one set of similar sequences from this tool requires a significant amount of human effort in following each link, extracting the 1000-5000 bases of the DNA sequence around the alignment and integrating the data from each extraction to form the final result of one BLAST search.

Challenges of Data Extraction and Data Integration

The extraordinary growth of service oriented computing has been fueled by the enhanced ability to make a growing amount of information available through the Web. This brings good news and bad news.

The good news is that Web services provide the standard invocation interface for remote service calls and the bulk of useful and valuable information is designed and published in a human browsing format (HTML or XML). The bad news is that these "human-oriented" Web pages returned by Web services are difficult for programs to capture and extract information of interests automatically, and to fuse and integrate data from multiple autonomous and yet heterogeneous data producer services. Also different Web services use different and evolving custom data formats.

A popular approach to handle this problem is to write data wrappers to encapsulate the access to Web sources and to automate the information extraction tasks on behalf of human. A wrapper is a software program specialized to a single data source or single Web service (e.g., a Web site), which converts the source documents and queries from the source data model to another, usually a more structured, data model (Liu, Pu, & Han, 1999).

Several projects have implemented hand-coded wrappers for a variety of sources (Haas, Kossmann, Wimmers, & Yan, 1997; Bayardo, Jr. et al., 1997; Li et al., 1997; Knoblock et al., 1998). However, manually writing such a wrapper and making it robust is costly due to the irregularity, heterogeneity, and frequent updates of the Web site and the data presentation formats they use. Hand-coding wrappers can become a major pain in situations where the data integration applications are more interested in integrating new data sources or frequently changing Web sources. We observe that, with a good design methodology, only a relatively small part of the wrapper code deals with the source-specific details, and the rest of the code is either common among wrappers or can be expressed at a higher level, more structured fashion. There are a number of challenging issues in automation of the wrapper code generation process.

First, most Web pages are HTML or XML documents, which are semi-structured textiles, annotated with various HTML presentation tags. Due to the frequent changes in presentation style of the HTML documents, the lack of semantic description of their information content, and the difficulty in making all applications in one domain use the same XML schema, it is hard to identify the content of interest using common pattern recognition technology such as string regular expression specification used in LEX and YACC.

Second, wrappers for Web sources should be more robust and adaptive in the presence of changes in both presentation style and information content of the Web pages.

It is expected that the wrappers generated by the wrapper generation systems will have lower maintenance overhead than handcrafted wrappers for unexpected changes.

Third, wrappers often serve as interface programs and pass the Web data extracted to application-specific information broker agents or information integration mediators for more sophisticated data analysis and data manipulation. Thus it is desirable to provide a wrapper interface language that is simple, self-describing, and yet powerful enough for extracting and capturing information from most of the Web pages. In scientific computing domains such as bioinformatics and bioengineering, information extraction over multiple different pages imposes additional challenges for wrapper code generation systems due to the varying correlation of the pages involved. The correlation can be either horizontal when grouping data from homogeneous documents (such as multiple result pages from a single search) or vertical when joining data from heterogeneous but related documents (a series of pages containing information about a specific topic). Furthermore, the correlation can be extended into a graph of workflows as describe in Figure 1.

Therefore, there is an increasing demand for automated wrapper code generation systems to incorporate a multi-page information extraction service. A multi-page wrapper not only enriches the capability of wrappers to extract information of interests but also increases the sophistication of wrapper code generation.

Surprisingly, almost all existing wrappers generated by application code generators (DISL Group, Georgia Institute of Technology, 2000; Sahuguet & Azavant, 1999; Baumgartner, Flesca, & Gottlob, 2001) are single-page wrappers in the sense that the wrapper program responds to a keyword query by analyzing only the page immediately returned.

Most wrappers cannot follow the links within this page to continue the information extraction from other linked pages, unless separate queries are issued to locate other linked pages.

Bearing all these issues in mind, we develop a code generation framework for building a semi-automated wrapper code generation system that can generate wrappers capable of extracting information from multiple inter-linked Web documents, and we implement this framework with XWRAPComposer, a toolkit for semi-automatically generating Java wrapper programs that can collect and extract data from multiple inter-linked pages automatically. XWRAPComposer has three unique features with regard to supporting multi-page data extraction.

First, we introduce interface, outerface, and composer script for each wrapper program we generate. By encoding wrapper developers' knowledge in Interface Specification, Outerface Specification, and Composer Script, XWRAPComposer integrates single-page wrapper programs into a composite wrapper capable of extracting information across multiple inter-linked pages from one service provider.

Second, XWRAPComposer transforms the multi-page information extraction problem into an integration problem of multiple single-page data extraction results, and utilizes the composer script to interconnect a sequence of single-page data extraction results, offering flexible execution choices to address diverse needs of different users. It generates platform-independent Java code that can be executed locally on users' machine. It also provides a WSDL-plugin module to allow users to produce WSDL enabled wrappers as Web Services (W3C, 2003).

Third but not the least, XWRAPComposer supports micro-workflow management, such as intermediate information flow or result auditing. We demonstrate this capability by integrating XWRAPComposer and its generated wrappers with some process modeling tools such as Ptolemy (Berkeley, 2003), allowing users to interactively manage different components of a wrapper and the interaction between them. In the following sections, we first give an overview of the XWRAPComposer system architecture, and then describe some important design and development efforts, using our motivating scenario described in this section as our application environment. Finally, we describe the status of the XWRAPComposer system development and discuss the future work.

The Design Framework

A multi-page wrapper code generation is a complex process and it is not reasonable, either from a logical point of view or from an implementation point of view, to consider the construction process as occurring in one single step. For this reason, we partition the wrapper construction process into a series of subprocesses called *phases*, as shown in Figure 2. A phase is a logically cohesive operation that takes as input one representation of the source document and produces as output another representation. XWRAPComposer wrapper generation goes through six phases to construct and release a Java wrapper. Tasks within a phase run concurrently using a synchronized queue; each runs its own thread. For example, we decide to run the task of fetching a remote document and the task of repairing the bad formatting of the fetched document using two concurrently synchronous threads in a single pass of the source document. The task of generating a syntactic-token parse tree from an HTML document requires as input the entire document; thus, it cannot be done in the same pass as the remote document fetching and the syntax reparation. Similar analysis applies to the other tasks such as code generation, testing, and packaging.

The interaction and information exchange between any two of the phases is performed through communication with the bookkeeping and the error handling routines. The *book keeping* routine of the wrapper generator collects information about all the data objects that appear in the retrieved source document, keeps track of the names used by the program, and records essential information about each. For example, a wrapper needs to know how many arguments a tag expects, whether an element

Figure 2. XWRAPComposer system architecture

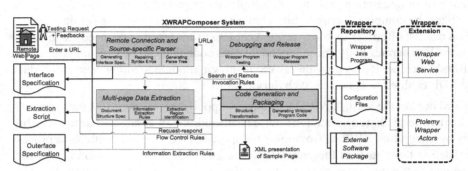

represents a string or an integer. The data structure used to record this information is called a symbol table. The *error handler* is designed for the detection and
reporting errors in the fetched source document. The error messages should allow
a wrapper developer to determine exactly where the errors have occurred. Errors
can be encountered at virtually all the phases of a wrapper. Whenever a phase of
the wrapper discovers an error, it must report the error to the error handler, which
issues an appropriate diagnostic message. Once the error has been noted, the wrapper must modify the input to the phase detecting the error, so that the latter can
continue processing its input, looking for subsequent errors. Good error handling
is difficult because certain errors can mask subsequent errors. Other errors, if not
properly handled, can spawn an avalanche of spurious errors. Techniques for error
recovery are beyond the scope of this paper.

Figure 2 presents an architecture sketch of the XWRAPComposer system. The
system architecture of XWRAPComposer consists of four major components: (1)
Remote Connection and Source-specific Parser; (2) Multi-page Data Extraction; (3)
Code Generation and Packaging; and (4) Debugging and Release. Other components
include GUI interface, bookkeeping and error handling. The GUI interface allows
wrapper developers to specify workflow of the multi-page data extraction, the request-
respond flow control rules and cross-page data extraction rules interactively.

Remote Connection and Source-specific Parser is the first component which
prepares and sets up the environment for information extraction process by performing the following three tasks. First, it accepts an URL selected and entered by
the XWRAPComposer user, issues an HTTP request to the remote service provider
identified by the given URL, and fetches the corresponding Web document (or so
called page object). During this process, the XWRAPComposer will learn the search
interface and the remote service invocation procedure in the background and generate a set of rules that describe the list of interface functions and parameters as well

as how they are used to fetch a remote document from a given Web source. The list of interface functions include the declaration to the standard library routines for establishing the network connection, issuing an HTTP request to the remote Web server through a HTTP Get or HTTP Post method, and fetching the corresponding Web page. Other desirable functions include building the correct URL to access the given service and pass the correct parameters, and handling redirection, failures, or authorization if necessary. Second, it cleans up bad HTML tags and syntactical errors using an XWRAPComposer plugin such as HTML TIDY (Raggett, 1999; W3C, 1999). Third, it transforms the retrieved page object into a parse tree or so-called syntactic token tree. This page object will be used as a sample for XWRAP-Composer to interact with the user to learn and derive the important information extraction rules, and the list of linked pages the user is interested in extracting information in conjunction with this page. In addition, all wrappers generated by XWRAPComposer use the streaming mode instead of the blocking mode. Namely, the wrapper will read the Web page block[1] one at a time. An interface specification will be created in this phase.

Multi-page Data Extraction is the second component which is responsible for deriving information flow control logic and multi-page extraction logic. Both are represented in form of rules. The former describes the flow control logic of the targeted service in responding to a service request and the latter describes how to extract information content of interest from the answer page and the linked pages of interest. XWRAPComposer performs the multi-page information extraction task in four steps: (1) specify the structure of the retrieved document (page object) in a declarative extraction rule language. (2) identify the interesting regions of the main page object and generating information extraction rules for this page; (3) identify the list of URLs referenced in the extracted regions in the main page; and (4) generating information extraction rules for each of the pages linked from the interesting regions of the main page object. We perform single page data extraction process using the XWRAPElite (DISL Group, Georgia Institute of Technology, 2000) toolkit, a single page data extraction service developed by the XWRAP team at Georgia Tech. At the end of this phase, XWRAPComposer produces two specifications: an outerface specification that describes the output format of the extraction result will be produced, and a composer script that describes both the information flow control patterns and the multi-page data extraction patterns.

Code Generation and Packaging is the third component, which generates the wrapper program code by applying three sets of rules about the target service produced in the first two steps: (1) the search and remote invocation rules; and (2) the request-respond flow control rules, and the information extraction rules. A key technique in our implementation is the smart encoding of these three types of semantic knowledge in the form of active XML-template format. The code generator interprets the XML-template rules by linking each executable component with the corresponding rule sets.

The code generator also produces the XML representation for the retrieved sample page object as a by-product.

Debugging and Release is the fourth component and the final phase of the multi-page wrapping process. It allows the user to enter a set of alternative service requests to the same service provider to debug the wrapper program generated by running the XWRAPComposer's code debugging module. For each page object obtained, the debugging module will automatically go through the syntactic structure normalization to rule out syntactic errors, the flow control and information extraction steps to check if new or updated flow control rules or data extraction rules should be included. In addition, the debug-monitoring window will pop up to allow the user to browse the debug report. Whenever an update to any of the three sets of rules occurs, the debugging module will run the code generator to create a new version of the wrapper program. Once the user is satisfied with the test results, he or she may invoke the release to obtain the release version of the wrapper program, including assigning the version release number, packaging the wrapper program with application plug-ins and user manual into a compressed tar file.

The XWRAPComposer wrapper generator takes the following three inputs: interface specification, outerface specification, and composer script, and compiles them into a Java wrapper program, which can be further extended into either a multi-page data extraction Web service (with WSDL specification) or a Ptolemy wrapper actor, which can be used for large scale data integration.

In the next section, we focus our discussion primarily on multi-page data extraction component of the XWrapComposer, and provide a walkthrough example to illustrate the multi-page extraction process, including a brief description of the wrapping interface and remote invocation component as the necessary preprocessing step for information extraction, a short summary of code generation as the postprocessing for the multi-page extraction.

Example Walkthrough

Before describing the detailed techniques used in designing multi-page data extraction services, we first present a walkthrough of XWRAPComposer using the motivating example introduced earlier.

Recall the workflow presented in Figure 1, where a biologist first uses a program called *Clusfavor* to cluster genes that have changed significantly in a micro-array analysis experiment. After extracting all gene IDs from the Clusfavor result, he feeds them into the NCBI Blast service, which searches all related sequences over a variety of data sources. The returned sequences will be further examined to find promoter sequences. Let us focus on the NCBI BLAST service. Figure 3 shows the

Figure 3. A scientific data integration example scenario

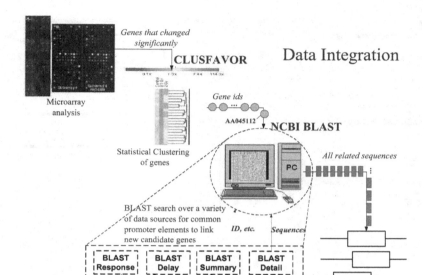

workflow of how a BLAST service request to NCBI will be served. It consists of four steps: (1) BLAST response step presents the user with a request ID. (2) BLAST delay step presents the user with the time delay for the result. (3) BLAST Summary presents the user with an overview of all gene IDs that match well with the given gene sequence id. And finally, (4) BLAST Detail shows for each gene id listed in the summary page, the full sequence detail and the goal is to extract approximately 1000-5000 bases of the DNA sequence around the alignment to capture the promoter regulatory elements, the region of a gene where RNA polymerase can bind and begin transcription to create the proteins that can regulate cell function.

Figure 4 illustrates a typical BLAST query using the NCBI service (NCBI, 2003). A BLAST query involves five steps. The first step is to feed a gene sequence into the text entry of the query interface. Due to the time complexity of a BLAST search, the NCBI service provider typically returns a response page with a request ID and the first estimate of the waiting time for each BLAST search. The biologist may later ask NCBI for the BLAST results using the request ID (Step 2), the NCBI service will presents a delay page if the BLAST search is not completed and results are not yet ready to display (Step 3). Once the BLAST results are delivered, they are displayed in a BLAST summary page, which contains a summary of all genes matching the search query condition. Each of the matching genes will provide a link to the NCBI

Figure 4. Multipage query with an NCBI Web site

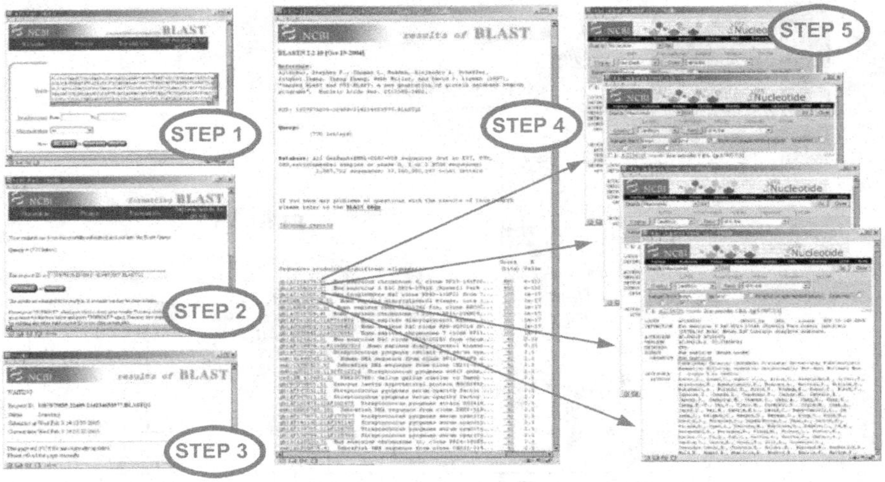

BLAST Detail page (Step 4). If the gene ID used for the BLAST query is incorrect gene ID or NCBI does not provide BLAST service for the given gene ID, an error page will be displayed. If the summary page does not include detailed information that the biologist is interested in, he has to visit each detail page (Step 5) through the URLs embedded in the summary page.

A critical challenge for providing system-level support for scientists to achieve such complex data integration tasks is the problem of locating, accessing, and fusing information from a rapidly growing, heterogeneous, and distributed collection of data sources available on the Web. This is a complex search problem for two reasons. First, as the example in Figure 3 shows, scientists today have much more complex data collection requirements than ordinary surfers on the Web. They often want to collect a set of data from a sequence of searches over a large selection of heterogeneous data sources, and the data selected from one search step often forms the falter condition for the next search step, turning a keyword-based query into a sophisticated search and information extraction workflow. Second, such complex workflows are manually performed daily by scientists or data collection lab researchers (computer science specialists). Automating such complex search and data collection workflows presents three major challenges.

- Different service providers use different request-respond flow control logics to present the answer pages to search queries.

- Cross-page data extraction has more complex extraction logic than the single page extraction system. In addition, different applications require different sets of data to be extracted by the cross-page data extraction engine. Typically, only portions of one page and the links that lead the extraction to the next page need to be extracted.

- Data items extracted from multiple inter-linked pages require being associated with semantically meaningful naming convention. Thus, mechanisms that can incorporate the knowledge of the domain scientists who issued such cross-page extraction job are critical.

There are several ways to design an NCBI BLAST wrapper. First, we can develop two wrappers, one for NSBI BLAST summary and one for NCBI BLAST Detail. The NCBI BLAST summer wrapper can be integrated with the NCBI BLAST Detail wrapper by service composition. In this approach, we need to capture the request-respond flow control through a flowcontrol logic in the composer script of NCBI Summary wrapper.

The outerface specification of the NCBI summary wrapper consists of the general overview of the given gene id and the list of gene IDs that are relevant to the given gene ID. The NCBI BLAST Detail wrapper needs to extract approximately 1000-5000 bases of the DNA sequence around the alignment. The composite wrapper NCBI BLAST will be composed of the NCBI summary wrapper and a list of executions of the NCBI BLAST Detail wrapper. In the next section we describe the XWRAPComposer design using this example.

Multi-Page Data Extraction Service

We have developed a methodology and a framework for extraction of information from multiple pages connected via Web page links. The main idea is to separate what to extract from how to extract, and distinguish information extraction logic from request-respond flow control logic. The control logic describes the different ways in which a service request (query) could be answered from a given service provider. The data extraction logic describes the cross-page extraction steps, including what information is important to extract at each page and how such information is used as a complex falter in the next search and extraction step.

We use interface description to specify the necessary input objects for wrapping the target service and the outerface description to describe what should be extracted and presented as the final result by the wrapper program. We design and develop an XWRAPCom-poser Script language (a set of functional constructs) to describe the request-respond flow control logic and multi-page data extraction logic. It is also to implement the output alignment and tagging of data items extracted based on the outerface specification.

The compilation process of the XWRAPComposer includes generating code based on three sets of rules: (1) Remote connection and interface rules, (2) the request-respond flow control logic and multi-page extraction logic outlined in the composer script, (3) the correct output alignment and semantically meaningful tagging based on the outerface specification.

Interface and Outerface Specification

Interface specification describes the schema of the data that the wrapper takes as input. It defines the source location and the service request (query) interface for the wrapper to be generated. Outerface specification describes the schema of the result that the wrapper outputs. It defines the type and structure of objects extracted. The composer script consists of two sets of rule-based scripts. The request-respond flow control script describes the alternative ways that the target service will respond to a remote service request, including result not found, multiple results found or single result found, or server errors. The multi-page data extraction script which describes (1) the extraction rules for the main page, (2) the extraction rules for each of the interesting pages linked from the main page, and (3) the rules on how to glue single page data extraction components. XWRAPComposer's scripting language has domain-specific plugins to facilitate the incorporation of domain-dependent correlations between the fragments of information extracted and the domain-specific tagging scheme. Each wrapper generated by XWRAPComposer will be associated with an interface specification, an outerface description, and a composer script.

The design of the XWRAPComposer Interface and Outerface Specification serves two important objectives. First, it will ease the use of XWRAPComposer wrappers as external services to any data integration applications. Second, it will facilitate the XWRAPComposer wrapper code generation system to generate Java code. Therefore, some components of the specification may not be directly useful for the users of these wrappers. In the first release of the XWRAPComposer implementation, we describe the input and output schema of a multi-page (composite) wrapper in XML Schema and use the two XML schemas as the interface and outerface specification. Concretely, the interface specification describes the wrapper name and which data provider's service needs to be wrapped by giving the source URL and other related information. The outerface specification describes what data items should be extracted and produced by the wrapper and the semantically meaningful names to be used to tag those data items. Figure 5 shows a fragment of the interface and outerface description of an example NCBI BLAST summary wrapper (LDRD Team, 2004).

Multi-Page Data Extraction Script

The XWRAPComposer multi-page data extraction service will generate a composer script for each wrapper it creates. Each composer script usually contains three types of root commands, document retrieval, data extraction and post processing. The document retrieval commands construct a file request or an HTTP request and fetch the document.

The data extraction commands specify the detailed instructions on how to extract information from the fetched document. The post processing commands allow adding semantic falters to make the extracted results conform to the outerface specification.

The general usage of commands is as shown in Figure 5.

Where <object id> is the id of the output object from the command, <input id> is the id of the input object. Both input and output objects are XML nodes. For example, FetchDocument returns the content of a Web page, which is a text node in XML. Each command specifies a set of built-in properties. <value> can be a string value, enclosed by a pair of quotes, such as *"this is a string value"*, or an XPath expression, enclosed by a pair of brackets, such as *[detailLink/text()]@<xpathroot>*. The value of "xpathroot" should be either <input id> or <object id> generated from previous commands.

If the command is used for data extraction, such as extractLink and extractContent Extraction code, the detail extraction logic needs to be specified. The main command type for the extraction script is grab functions. XWRAPComposer also provides miscellaneous commands for request-respond flow control, process management and Boolean comparison.

In order to output XML data more flexibly, an XSL style sheet may be applied to any XML object using the ApplyStyleSheet command. Table 1 shows a list of commands that are currently supported in the first release of the XWRAPComposer toolkit (DISL Group, Georgia Institute of Technology, 2003).

Figure 6 gives an extraction script example for the NCBI Summary wrapper. Given a full sequence as the input, we first construct an NCBI Blast search URL based on the NCBI Blast interface description. The script fragment *Set variable { [text()]}* indicates the sequence is in the input with the XPath, *"text()"*. The first script command *FetchDocument* retrieves the NCBI Blast response page that contains a request ID. We extract the ID and construct the URL of the search results from the main page object. The control-flow command *while...do...* periodically invokes the second *FetchDocument* to retrieve the result page until the results are delivered. Finally we use *GrabXWRAPEliteData* to extract useful data from the main result page. We use the command *ExtractLink* to locate each of the linked pages of interest from the main page object and use the command *ExtractContent* to invoke the

Figure 5. An example of interface and outerface specification: NCBi summary

```
<XCwrapper name="XC BlastN Summary" sourceURL=
"http://www.ncbi.nlm.nih.gov/blast/Blast.cgi?PAGE=Nucleotides">
<interface><!-- input schema in XML Schema -->
<xsd:element name="input" type="xsd:string">
<xsd:complexType>
<xsd:sequence>
<xsd:element name="select db" type="string"/>
<xsd:element name="query sequence" type="string"/>
</xsd:sequence>
</xsd:complexType>
</xsd:element>
</interface>
<outerface><!-- output schema in XML Schema -->
<xsd:element name="resultDoc">
<xsd:complexType>
<xsd:element name="output">
<xsd:complexType>
<xsd:choice minOccurs="0" maxOccurs="unbounded">
<xsd:element name="homolog">
<xsd:complexType>
<xsd:sequence>
<xsd:element name="geneid" type="string"/>
<xsd:element name="description" type="string"/>
<xsd:element name="length" type="int"/>
<xsd:element name="score" type="string"/>
<xsd:element name="expect" type="string"/>
<xsd:element name="identities" type="string"/>
<xsd:element name="strand" type="string"/>
<xsd:element name="link" type="string"/>
<xsd:element name="beginMatch" type="int"/>
<xsd:element name="endMatch" type="int"/>
<xsd:element name="alignment" type="string"/>
<xsd:element name="beginMatch" type="string"/>
</xsd:sequence>
</xsd:complexType>
</xsd:element>
</xsd:choice>
</xsd:complexType>
</xsd:element>
<xsd:attribute name="docLocation" type="string"/>
<xsd:attribute name="docType" type="string"/>
<xsd:attribute name="createdBy" type="string"/>
<xsd:attribute name="creationDate" type="string"/>
</xsd:complexType>
</xsd:element>
</outerface>
</XCwrapper>
```

Generate <object id> :: <command name> (<input id>) *f* Set <property1 name> *f* <value> *g* [more value]
Set <property2 name> *f* <value> *g* /* if the command is data extraction. */
[extraction code]
g

Table 1. Supported XWRAPComposer extraction root commands

Command	Category
ConstructHttpQuery	Document Retrieval
ReadFile	Document Retrieval
FetchDocument	Document Retrieval
ExtractLink	Data Extraction
ExtractContent	Data Extraction
GrabSubstring	Grab Function
GrabXWrapEliteData	Grab Function
GrabConsecutiveLines	Grab Function
GrabCommaDelimitedText	Grab Function
ContainSubstring	Boolean Comparison
While...Do...	Control Flow
If...Then...	Control Flow
ApplyStyleSheet	Post Processing
Sleep	Process Management

XWRAPElite single page data extraction service to extract useful data from each linked page. Due to the space restriction, we omit the concrete techniques used in XWRAPComposer for single page data extraction and refer readers to Buttler, Liu, and Pu (2001) and Wei (2003) for further detail.

Code Generation

XWRAPComposer generate its wrapper programs in two steps. First, it reads the user specified interface, outerface and composer script, and generates an XWRAPComposer wrapper, which contains the Java source code, an executable Java program, and a set of configuration files. The configuration files include the input and output schemas obtained from interface and outerface specification of the wrapper, and the resource files used in the data extraction phase such as XSLT files. Concretely, the code generation phase consists of three main functions, as shown in Figure 2. The code generation process starts with reading the interface specification and generating the code for search interface construction, followed by generating the remote invocation method to establish the remote connection.

Then, the code generator will generate the Java code that implements the request-respond flow control logic described in the composer script. For each possible request-respond state, the code for parsing the corresponding respond page will be generated. Furthermore, based on the extraction logic specified for each of the

Figure 6. Extraction Script Example For NCBi Summary

```
/* Start constructing wrapper ncbisummary.  */
WrapperName "ncbisummary";

/* Contruct the URL for NCBi Blast search */
Generate blastSummaryPage ::  ConstructHttpQuery (input){
  Set inputSource {
    Set url {"http://www.ncbi.nlm.nih.gov/blast/Blast.cgi?QUERY=$$&..."};
    Set queryString { };
    Set method {"get"};
    Set variable { [text()] } ;
  }
}
Generate blastSummaryData ::  FetchDocument (blastSummaryPage) {}
Generate recordid ::  ExtractContent (blastSummaryData) {
  GrabSubstring {
    Set BeginMatch {"The request ID is <input name=\"RID\" size=\"50\"
type=\"text\" value=\"};
    Set EndMatch {"\" >" };
  }
}
Generate answerurl ::  ConstructHttpQuery (recordid){
  Set inputSource {
    Set url {"http://www.ncbi.nlm.nih.gov/blast/Blast.cgi?FORMAT_PAGE
_TARGET=Format_page_31680&RESULTS_PAGE_TARGET=Blast_Results_for_31680
&RID=$$&SHOW_OVERVIEW=on...&AUTO_FORMAT=Semiauto"};
    Set queryString { };
    Set method { "get" };
    /* The first recordid is the input id.*/
    Set variable { [text()] };
  }
}
Generate answerPage ::  FetchDocument(answerurl) {}
While {
  ContainSubstring(answerPage) {
    Set compSubstring {"This page will be automatically updated in"};
  }
} Do {
  Generate answerPage ::  FetchDocument(answerurl) {}
  /* Pause for 10 seconds.  */
  Sleep {
    set inverval {"10000"};
  }
}
Generate output ::  ExtractContent (answerPage) {
  GrabXWRAPEliteData {
  /* The following properties should be generated from a XWRAPELite tool.  */
  ...
  }
}
```

possible respond pages, we can generate the data extraction code fragment for each respond page and generate the glue code to compose the list of single page data extraction code into a multi-page data extraction routine.

The third functional component is to generate debugging and release code to support an iterative process of testing, fixing bugs, re-packaging, and release. An XWRAPComposer user may feed a series of input pages to the debugging and release module to debug the wrapper program generated by XWRAPComposer. For each input page, the debugging module will automatically go through the search interface construction, remote connection establishment, document parsing, and multi-page data extraction to check if the expected output (specified in the outer-face description) is returned. Once the user is satisfied with the test results, he or she may choose to release the generated wrapper program, which contains the Java source code, configuration files, the release version number, the required jar files (Java executables), and the user manual.

Execution Model of an XWRAPComposer Wrapper

A typical XWRAPComposer wrapper consists of the following five basic functional modules.

The **Search Interface** module accepts the user input through the protocols defined by the user, such as the SOAP request in the Web service scenario. It constructs the service request (query command) and parameter list that will be forwarded to the wrapped target service. Consider the NCBI BLAST wrapper, its search interface accepts the gene sequence and the other parameters such as alignment precision from the input specification file or GUI interface. It composes the HTTP POST command, which will be used to execute the query.

The **Remote Invocation** module accepts the service request (query command) and parameters generated by the search interface and converted them into the query acceptable by the wrapped target service. The query can be an HTTP POST command, an FTP GET command, or an RPC call. The remote invocation module interacts with the wrapped target service following the remote connection protocol defined by the wrapped target service and the communication procedure defined by the configuration file. The query result page will be forwarded to the parser for preprocessing before entering the multi-page data extraction module.

The **Page Parser** translates the result page received from the remote invocation module into a token tree structure, filters out the uninteresting information such as advertisements from Web pages, and converts the received document into a standard format such as HTML or XML. In addition to building a token based parse tree, the page parser should incorporate the domain specific knowledge about the page encoded in the composer script to facilitate the data extraction process. For multi-page wrappers, the page parser will parse the main respond page based on its extraction rules and locate the list of linked pages of interest. For each of the linked pages of interest, the parser triggers the remote invocation module to fetch the actual page and parses the page based on its corresponding extraction rules.

The **Information Extraction** module processes each of the parsed documents passed from the parser and extracts the objects of interest defined by the outerface specification. It uses the domain specific knowledge about the pages of interest, encoded in the composer extraction script, to guide the concrete multi-page data extraction process. For each extracted data object, the XML tagging procedure is applied to assign a tag name to the object based on the tagging rules encoded in the composer script.

The **Output Packaging** and Delivery module merges the output from the information extraction module and packages it into the final result format defined by the outerface specification. Then it delivers the data package to the user who initiates the execution of the wrapper program.

The first prototype of XWRAPComposer system is written in Java. Wrappers generated by XWRAPComposer are also coded in Java. In our first prototype implementation, the five components execute sequentially ; a component starts execution only after the previous component finishes. The next extension of XWRAPComposer code generation system is to introduce parallel extraction among these five components. Parallel execution improves the performance, but it also incurs higher complexity in implementation.

Figure 7 and Figure 8 demonstrate two XWRAPComposer wrappers and their mini-workflow structure. The GUI interface is developed using Ptolemy (Berkeley, 2003) (a process modeling tool). Each wrapper can be used as a Ptolemy actor (see the left menu on the screen shot) and is composed of four steps: **StartWrapping** initiates all the environment parameters, and triggers **ReadInputFile** to read a gene ID from a specified input file. The gene ID will then be sent to **NCBiSummary** Wrapper actor which performs the wrapping function upon receiving a BLAST service request with the given gene ID, and returns the set of ids of related genes as results. The

Figure 7. NCBI blast summary wrapper

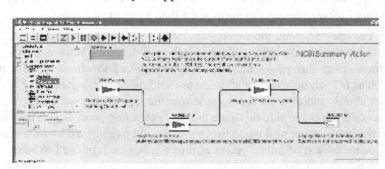

Figure 8. NCBI blast detail wrapper

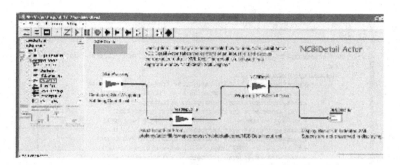

Figure 9. Ptolemy wrapper actor result example NCBi BLAST summary

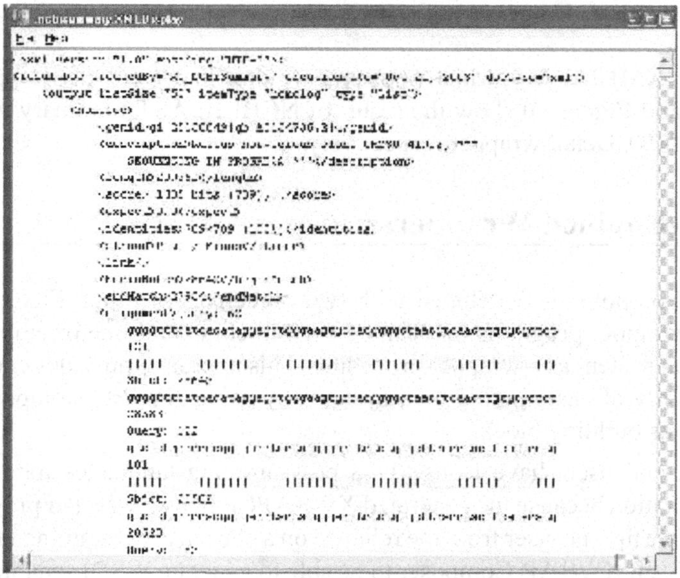

Figure 10. Ptolemy wrapper actor result example NCBi Blast Detail

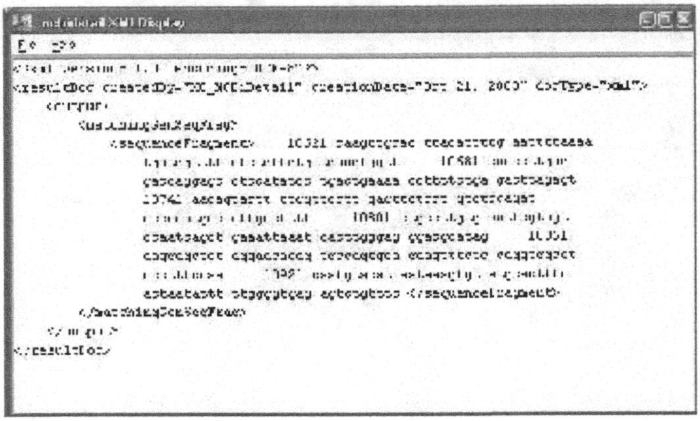

last step is **XMLDisplay**, which pops up a window to present the wrapping results. Figure 9 and Figure 10 show the result of NCBI BLAST Summary wrapper and NCBI BLAST Detail wrapper respectively.

WSDL-Enabled Wrappers

XWRAPComposer is developed with two objectives in mind. First, we want to generate wrapper programs that can be used in command line or embedded in an application system as a wrapper procedure. This approach provides end users with the flexibility of customizing their systems by using XWRAPComposer wrapper programs as building block.

However, end users have to use Java programming languages for their system implementation because the generated XWRAPComposer wrapper programs are in Java. To free the end-user from the reliance on a chosen programming language like Java, we want XWRAP-Composer to be able to generate WSDL-enabled wrappers to allow each wrapper program to be used as a Web service (W3C, 2002), which is our second objective. We chose Web services because it was proposed and has been successfully adopted by many systems for providing platform-independent and programming language-independent service access. End users can implement their client applications with full flexibility as long as their systems can access our server using SOAP protocol. Our discussion so far has been focused on the first objective. In this section we briefly describe how to generate WSDL enabled wrappers.

In order to enable XWRAPComposer to generate WSDL-enabled wrapper services, we add two extensions to the XWRAPComposer wrapper generation system. First, we encapsulate an XWRAPComposer wrapper into a general Web service servlet. The servlet automatically extracts the input from a SOAP request, feeds it into the wrapper, and inserts the wrapping results in a SOAP envelope before sending back to the user. In this sense, XWRAPComposer wrappers are working as service providers to end users. When they interact with wrapped data sources, those XWRAPComposer wrappers act as the clients of those services. Second, to ease the implementation and deployment of XWRAPComposer wrappers as Web services, we incorporate a WSDL generator to automatically generate Web service description by binding the wrapper's interface and outerface with the servlet configuration. Figure 11 shows the extensions added to the XWRAPComposer to produce wrappers as WSDL Web services.

Wrapper Program Repository

As a part of the XWRAPComposer effort, we design and develop an online wrapper generation and registration system to assist the usage of XWRAPComposer wrappers and simplify the wrapper generation and management overhead. All wrappers generated by XWRAPComposer can be registered directly into our online wrapper repository. A snapshot of this repository is shown in Figure 12.

Figure 11. Web-service enabled wrappers

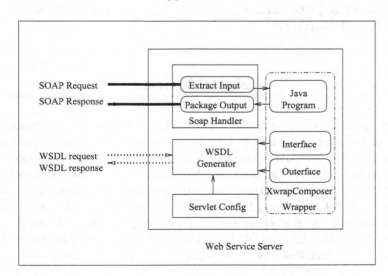

Figure 12. XWRAPComposer online wrapper repository

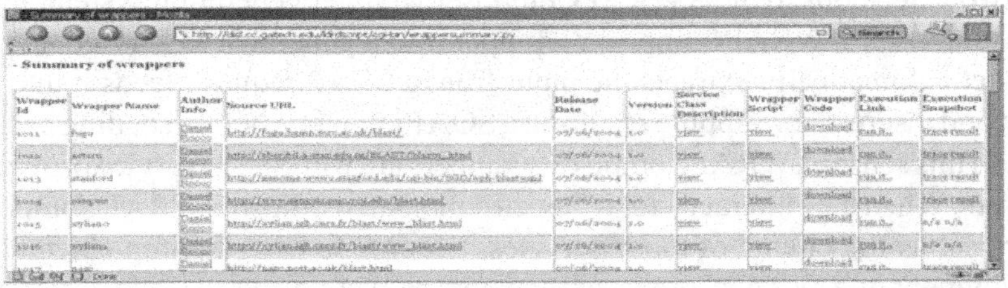

Consider the first wrapper shown in Figure 12. The target service provider is http://fugu.hgmp.mrc.ac.uk/blast/. It provides a standard BLAST interface. After obtaining the XWRAPComposer wrapper source code and jar file, the user can upload this wrapper through an online registration interface, available at http://disl.cc.gatech.edu/ldrdscript/html/registerwrapper.htm. One can download the generated wrapper source code directly by clicking on wrapper code column of the corresponding target service provider. Using the XWRAPComposer library and the composer scripts that we released, this wrapper source code can be compiled on the user's local machine and executed as command line Java application. A user can also use our online wrapper execution interface to execute each registered wrapper either as a servlet or a Web service. An example of online execution result is given in Figure 13. All XWRAPComposer wrappers for BLASTN services are presenting a uniform interface to the end users, which facilitates the large scale integration of multiple BLASTN services.

Related Work

The very nature of scientific research and discovery leads to the continuous creation of information that is new in content or representation or both. Despite the efforts to fit molecular biology information into standard formats and repositories such as the PDB (Protein Data Bank) and NCBI, the number of databases and their content have been growing, pushing the envelope of standardization efforts such as mmCIF (Westbrook & Bourne, 2000). Providing integrated and uniform access to these databases has been a serious research challenge. Several efforts (Critchlow, Fidelis, Ganesh, Musick, & Slezak, 2000; Davidson et al., 1999; Goble et al., 2001; Haas et al., 2001; McGinnis, 1998; Siepel et al., 2001) have sought to alleviate the

Figure 13. XWRAPComposer wrapper execution result: An example

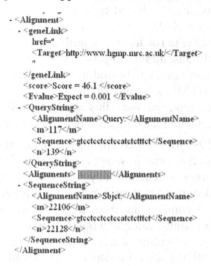

interoperability issue, by translating queries from a uniform query language into the native query capabilities supported by the individual data sources. Typically, these previous efforts address the interoperability problem from a digital library point of view, i.e., they treat individual databases as well-known sources of existing information. While they provide a valuable service, due to the growing rate of scientific discovery, an increasing amount of new information (the kind of hot-off-the-bench information that scientists would be most interested in) falls outside the capability of these previous interoperability systems or services.

Wrappers have been developed either manually or with software assistance, and used as a component of agent-based systems, sophisticated query tools and general mediator-based information integration systems (Wiederhold, 1992; Liu & Pu, 1997; Liu, Pu, & Lee, 1996). For instance, the most documented information mediator systems (e.g., Ariadne (Knoblock et al., 1998), CQ (Liu, Pu, & Tang, 1999; Liu et al., 1998), Internet Softbots (Kushmerick, Weld, & Doorenbos, 1997), TSIMMIS (Garcia-Molina et al., 1997; Hammer et al., 1997), Araneus (Atzeni, Mecca, & Merialdo, 1997)) all assume a pre-wrapped set of Web sources. However, developing and maintaining wrappers by hand is labor intensive and error-prone, due to technical difficulties such as undocumented HTML/XML tags and subtle variations in the content (small to the human perception, but difficult for programs).

Tova Milo and Sagit Zohar (Milo & Zohar, 1998) use schema matching to simplify the wrapper generation, when both the source schema and the result schema are available. They observe that in many cases the schema of the data in the source system is very similar to the result schema. In such cases, much of the translation work can be done automatically based on the schema similarity. They define a middleware schema, and each data source to be used in their system needs a mapping of its data and schema to (or from) the middleware format. They develop an algorithm to match and translate the objects in the source with the objects in the result comparing the two instances of the middleware schema. Since most Web pages are still in schema-less HTML, schema matching does not work. However, if more XML information appears on the Web, this approach will speed up the wrapper generation, since XML documents contain schema information.

SoftBot (Kushmerick, 1997) developed a wrapper generation system using inductive learning techniques. Several generic wrapper classes with adjustable parameters are predefined in the wrapper generation system. Each wrapper class can extract information from one document pattern. Wrapper developers highlight interesting sections in many sample documents, and then a machine learning algorithm will adjust those parameters to find a combination of wrapper classes to extract the highlighted sections correctly. If such a combination is not available, the algorithm will return the best combination with the fewest mistakes. The developers can either correct the best combination manually or add more wrapper classes fitting new patterns to find a complete correct combination.

NoDoSE also adopts the inductive learning technique. Using a GUI, the user hierarchically decomposes a plain text file, outlining its regions of interest and then describing their semantics. The task is expedited by a mining component that attempts to infer the grammar of the file from the information the user has identified so far.

XWRAPComposer is different from those systems in three aspects. First, we explicitly separate tasks of building wrappers that are specific to a Web service from the tasks that are repetitive for any service, thus the code can be generated as a wrapper library component and reused automatically by the wrapper generator system. Second, we use inductive learning algorithms that derive information flow and data extraction patterns by reasoning about sample pages or sample specifications. Most importantly, we design a declarative rule-based script language for multi-page information extraction, encouraging a clean separation of the information extraction semantics from the information flow control and execution logic of wrapper programs.

Conclusion

Both enterprise systems and science and engineering integration applications require gathering information from multiple, heterogeneous information services. Although Web service technology such as WSDL, SOAP, and UDDI, has provided a standardized remote invocation interface, there exist other types of heterogeneity in terms of query capability, content structure, and content delivery logics due to inherent diversity of different services.

A popular approach to handling such heterogeneity is to use wrappers to serve as mediators to facilitate the automation of collecting and extracting data from multiple diverse data providers.

We have described a service-oriented framework for development of wrapper code generators and a concrete implementation, called XWRAPComposer, to evaluate our framework in the context of bioinformatics applications. Three unique features distinguish XWRAPComposer from existing wrapper development approaches. First, XWRAPComposer is designed to enable multi-stage and multi-page data extraction. Second, XWRAP-Composer is the only wrapper generation system that promotes the distinction of information extraction logic from request-respond flow control logic, allowing higher level of robustness against changes in the service provider's Web site design or infrastructure. Third, XWRAPComposer provides a user-friendly plug-and-play interface, allowing seamless incorporation of external services and continuous changing service interfaces and data format.

The XWRAPComposer project continues along three dimensions. First, we are interested in extending XWRAPComposer code generation capability to allow wrappers to be generated for a wide variety of complex data sources. Second, we are interested in exploring data provenance techniques for large scale data integration. In particular, we are interested in extracting data provenance information from the vast amount of data contents provided in many scientific data service providers. We believe that the data provenance information is critical for facilitating the scientific data integration process, and improving scientific data integration quality. Third but not the least, we are working on providing user-friendly GUI to support for interactive specification of interface, outerface and composer script.

Acknowledgment

This work is a joint effort between the Georgia Institute of Technology Team led by Ling Liu and the LLNL team led by Terence Critchlow. The work performed by the authors from Georgia Tech was partially sponsored by DoE SciDAC, LLNL LDRD, NSF CSR, an IBM faculty award, and an IBM SUR grant. The work by the authors from LLNL was performed under the auspices of the U.S. Department of Energy by University of California Lawrence Livermore National Laboratory under contract No. W-7405-ENG-48, UCRL-JRNL-218270. Any opinions, findings, and conclusions or recommendations expressed in the project material are those of the authors and do not necessarily reflect the views of the sponsors.

References

Altschul, S., Madden, T., Schaffer, A., Zhang, J., Zhang, Z., Miller, W., et al. (1997). Gapped BLAST and PSI-BLAST: A new generation of protein database search programs. *Nucleic Acids Research, 25,* 3389-3402.

Atzeni, P., Mecca, G., & Merialdo, P.(1997). Semi-structured and structured data in the Web: Going back and forth. *Proceedings of ACM SIGMOD Workshop on Management of Semi-Structured Data,* Tucson, Arizona.

Baumgartner, R., Flesca, S., & Gottlob, G. (2001). Visual Web information extraction with Lixto. *Proceedings of the 27th International Conference on Very Large Data Bases (VLDB),* Rome, Italy.

Bayardo, R. J., Jr., Bohrer, W., Brice, R., Cichocki, A., Fowler, J., Helal, A., et al. (1997). Semantic integration of information in open and dynamic environments. *Proceedings of ACM SIGMOD Conference,* Tucson, Arizona.

Berkeley. (2003). Ptolemy group in EECS. Retrieved from http://ptolemy.eecs. berkeley.edu/

Buttler, D., Liu, L., & Pu, C. (2001). A fully automated object extraction system for the World Wide Web. *Proceedings of the 2001 International Conference on Distributed Computing Systems ICDCS,* Phoenix, Arizona.

Critchlow, T., Fidelis, K., Ganesh, M., Musick, R., & Slezak, T. (2000). Datafoundry: Information management for scientific data. *IEEE Transactions on Information Technology in Biomedicine, 4*(1), 52-57.

Davidson, S., Buneman, O., Crabtree, J., Tannen, V., Overton, G., & Wong, L. (1999). Biokleisli: Integrating biomedical data and analysis packages. In S. Letovsky (Eds.), *Bioinformatics: Databases and systems* (pp. 201-211). Norwell, MA: Kluwer Academic.

DBCAT. (1999). *The public catalog of databases.* Retrieved from http://www. infobiogen.fr/services/dbcat

DISL Group, Georgia Institute of Technology. (2000). XWRAP Elite Project. Retrieved from http://www.cc.gatech.edu/projects/disl/XWRAPElite

DISL Group, Georgia Institute of Technology. (2003). XWRAP Composer. Retrieved from http://www.cc.gatech.edu/projects/disl/XWRAPComposer/

Garcia-Molina, H., Papakonstantinou, Y., Quass, D., Rajaraman, A., Sagiv, Y., Ullman, J. D., et al. (1997). The TSIMMIS approach to mediation: Data models and languages. *Journal of Intelligent Information Systems, 8*(2), 117-132.

Goble, C. A., Stevens, R., Ng, G., Bechhofer, S., Paton, N., Baker, P. G., et al. (2001). Transparent access to multiple bioinformatics information sources. *IBM Systems Journal, 40*(2), 532-551.

Haas, L., Kossmann, D., Wimmers, E., & Yan, J. (1997). Optimizing queries across diverse data sources. *Proceedings of the 23rd International Conference on Very Large Databases (VLDB),* Athens, Greece.

Haas, L., Schwarz, P., Kodali, P., Kotlar, E., Rice, J., & Swope, W. (2001). Discoverylink: A system for integrated access to life sciences data sources. *IBM Systems Journal, 40*(2), 489-511.

Hammer, J., Brennig, M., Garcia-Molina, H., Nesterov, S., Vassalos, V., & Yerneni, R. (1997). Template-based wrappers in the tsimmis system. *Proceedings of ACM SIGMOD Workshop on Management of Semi-structured Data,* Tucson, Arizona.

Knoblock, C. A., Minton, S., Ambite, J. L., Ashish, P. J. M. N., Muslea, I., Philpot, A. G., et al. (1998). Modeling Web sources for information integration. *Proceedings of the Fifteenth National Conference on Artificial Intelligence.* Madison, WI.

Kushmerick, N., Weld, D. S., & Doorenbos, R. (1997). Wrapper induction for information extraction. *Proceedings of Int. Joint Conference on Artificial Intelligence (IJCAI),* Nagoya, Japan.

Kushrnerick, N. (1997). *Wrapper induction for information extraction.* Unpublished doctoral dissertation, University of Washington.

LDRD Team. (2004). LDRD Project. Retrieved from http://www.cc.gatech.edu/projects/disl/LDRD

Li, C., Yerneni, R., Vassalos, V., Garcia-Molina, H., Papakonstantinou, Y., Ullman, J., et al. (1997). Capability based mediation in tsimiss. *Proceedings of ACM SIGMOD Conference.* Tucson, Arizona.

Liu, L., & Pu, C. (1997). An adaptive object-oriented approach to integration and access of heterogeneous information sources. *Distributed and Parallel Databases: An International Journal, 5*(2), 167-205.

Liu, L., Pu, C., & Han, W. (1999). XWrap: An ExtensibleWrapper construction system for Internet information sources. In *Technical report.*

Liu, L., Pu, C., & Lee, Y. (1996). An adaptive approach to query mediation across heterogeneous databases. *Proceedings of the International Conference on Cooperative Information Systems,* Brussels, Belgium.

Liu, L., Pu, C., & Tang, W. (1999). Continual queries for Internet-scale event-driven information delivery. *IEEE Knowledge and Data Engineering, 11*(4), 610-628.

Liu, L., Pu, C., Tang, W., Biggs, J., Buttler, D., Han, W., et al. (1998). CQ: A personalized update monitoring toolkit. *Proceedings of ACM SIGMOD Conference,* Seattle, Washington.

McGinnis, S. (1998). Genbank user services, National Center for Biotechnology Information (NCBI), National Library of Medicine, US National Institute of Health. Personal Communication.

Milo, T., & Zohar, S. (1998). Using schema matching to simplify heterogeneous data translation. *Proceedings of the 24th International Conference on Very Large Data Bases (VLDB),* New York.

NCBI. (2003). National Center for Biotechnology Information. Retrieved from http://www.ncbi.nlm.nih.gov/BLAST/

Peterson, L. (2002). *CLUSFAVOR.* Baylor College of Medicine. Retrieved from http://mbcr.bcm.tmc.edu/genepi/

Quandt, K., Frech, K., Karas, H., Wingender, E., & Werner, T. (1995). MatInd and MatInspector: New fast and versatile tools for detection of consensus matches in nucleotide sequence data. *Nucleic Acids Research, 23,* 4878-4884.

Raggett, D. (1999). *Clean up your Web pages with HTML TIDY.* Retrieved from http://www.w3.org/People/Raggett/tidy/

Sahuguet, A., & Azavant, F. (1999). WysiWyg Web Wrapper Factory (W4F). *Proceedings of World Wide Web (WWW) Conference,* Orlando, Florida.

Siepel, A. C., Tolopko, A. N., Farmer, A. D., Steadman, P. A., Schilkey, F. D., Perry, B., et al. (2001). An integration platform for heterogeneous bioinformatics software components. *IBM Systems Journal, 40*(2), 570-591.

Stein, L. D., & Thierry-Mieg, J. (1999). Scriptable access to the Caenorhabditis elegans genome sequence and other ACEDB databases. *Genome Res., 8,* 1308-1315.

W3C. (1999). *Reformulating HTML in XML.* Retrieved from http://www.w3.org/TR/WD-html-in-xml/

W3C. (2002). *Web services.* Retrieved from http://www.w3c.org/2002/ws/

W3C. (2003). *Web Services Description Language (WSDL) version 1.2 part 1: Core language.* Retrieved from http://www.w3c.org/TR/wsdl12/

Wei, H. (2003). *Wrapper application generation for Semantic Web: An XWRAP approach.* Unpublished doctoral dissertation, Georgia Institute of Technology.

Westbrook, J., & Bourne, P. (2000). Star/mmcif: An extensive ontology for macromolecular structure and beyond. *Bioinformatics, 16*(2), 159-168.

Wiederhold, G. (1992). Mediators in the architecture of future information systems. *IEEE Computer, 25*(3), 38-49.

Endnote

[1]   A block here refers to a line of 256 characters or a transfer unit defined implicitly by the HTTP protocol.

Appendix

XWRAPComposer Extraction Script Command

The first release of the XWRAPComposer supports seven categories of command. They are listed as follows.

(1) Document Retrieval Command

We support the following Document Retrieval Commands in the first release of the XWRAPComposer toolkit.

ConstructHTTPQuery

This command constructs an HTTP query that contains three components: URL, queryString, and HTTP method. It has four properties: URL, queryString, httpMethod, and vars. The first three properties are actually templates with placeholders, "$$". The last property is a list of strings to replace the placeholders.

Example:

```
Generate genbankSummaryPage ::  ConstructHttpQuery {
  Set inputSource {
    Set url { "http://www.amazon.com/book-search.cgi" }
    Set queryString { "keyword=$$&author=$$&start=1" }
    Set httpMethod { "post" }
    Set vars {
    /* the sub property names are only for reading.  */
    /* We replace the placeholders by the order of the vars.  */
      Set keyword { "java" }
      Set author { "john" }
      }
    }
  }
}
```

The result will be:

```
<inputSource>
    <URL>http://www.amazon.com/book-search.cgi</URL>
    <queryString>keyword=java&author=john&start=1</queryString>
    <httpMethod>get</httpMethod>
<inputSource>
```

ConstructFileQuery

This command constructs a file request, which contains only one property, file name.

FetchDocument

This command takes a file request or an HTTP request as input and returns the content of the file or the Web page. It does not have any properties.

(2) Data Extraction

Currently we support two types of data extraction commands. They are used for extracting links or extracting content.

ExtractLink

This command indicates to extract an HTTP request from the input. It usually needs to extract URL, queryString, and httpMethod. If queryString and httpMethod are not extracted, the default values will be used. The default httpMethod is "get" and queryString is "".

ExtractContent

This command indicates to extract content from the input, which contains all kinds of data. The extraction method needs to be specified with GrabFunctions and XML construction commands as well as other commands.

(3) Grab Function

The Grab function is designed to facilitate the text parsing and sting analysis during the extraction process. We support the following four grab functions.

GrabSubstring

Assuming the input is a text node, this command extracts a substring by two properties, beginMatch and endMatch. It will return the string between beginMatch and endMatch. If there are multiple result strings, we only choose the first one.

GrabXWrapEliteData

This command applies an XWRAPElite wrapper to the input. The input should be a text node that represents the content of a Web page. The properties are generated by the XWRAPElite toolkit. It allows modification for fine-tuning.

GrabCommaDelimitedText

This command extracts comma-delimited data into XML. It has the following properties.

- *LineDelimiters:* The delimiters to separate data into rows. The default is the system line separators.
- *Delimiters:* The delimiters to separate data in a row to a list of cells. The default is comma.
- StopStrings: String that will be ignored.
- *Filters:* It contains two subproperties, minColCount and maxColCount. We will filter out all the rows whose column numbers are not in the range of [minColCount, maxColCount] inclusively.
- *RowOutput:* It specifies how to output the tabular data for each row in XML.

GrabConsecutiveLines.

This command is to extract consecutive text lines from the input. It has three properties, beginMatch, endMatch, and matchingMethod. The default matching method is to match the first string of the beginning line and the ending line with beginMatch and endMatch properties. However, we might need some domain-specific matching method in some cases. Then we can use external functions as shown in NCBiDetail example.

(4) Boolean Comparisons

ContainSubstring

This command returns a Boolean value, which indicates if the input contains a substring. It has one property, compSubstring.

Example:

```
ContainSubstring (answerPage) {
    Set compSubstring { "This page will be automatically updated in"}
}
```

The example demonstrates a command that checks if the text value of answerPage contains a string of "This page will automatically updated in".

(5) Control Flow

While ... Do ...

This command checks the conditions in the while clause, while the conditions are true, repeat the do clause. The while clause contains Boolean commands and the do clause contains other extraction-related commands.

(6) Post Processing

ApplyStylesheet

This command applies a style sheet to the input XML. It has a property, StyleSheet-File.

(7) Process Management

Sleep

This command pauses the process for a certain amount of time.

Usage: Sleep "<number of milliseconds>"

This work was previously published in International Journal of Web Services Research, edited by Zhang, pp. 33-60, 3(2), copyright 2005 by IGI Publishing, formerly known as Idea Group Publishing (an imprint of IGI Global).

Chapter VIII

An SLA-Based Auction Pricing Method Supporting Web Services Provisioning

Jia Zhang, Northern Illinois University, USA

Ning Zhang, Cornell University, USA

Liang-Jie Zhang, IBM T.J. Watson Research, USA

Abstract

Applying auctions to Web services selection and invocation calls for examination due to the unique features of Web services, such as interoperable machine-to-machine interactions and re-enterable bargaining services. In this chapter we propose a formal model for Web services-based auctions. Examining the one-sided sealed auction type, we prove mathematically that service requestors' risk preferences could lead to different pricing strategies for service providers towards higher profit. We argue that Service Level Agreement (SLA) documents can be used to analyze service requestors' preferences. On top of WS-Agreement, we propose a basic service requestor risk preference elicitation algorithm, as well as a historical data-based service requestor risk preference prediction model. Guidelines are provided to iteratively approach the learning rate of the proposed risk preference prediction model. The methods and techniques presented in this chapter can be reused to investigate and examine more facades of services-oriented auctions, towards establishing a new research realm on comprehensive services-oriented auctions.

Introduction

The paradigm of Web services has opened a new era for business service providers. This new model not only allows easier management and maintenance for provider-hosting services, but also creates a lot more potential business opportunities for service providers. Gartner Group, a leading industry analyst firm, predicted that by 2008 more than 60% of businesses would adopt Web services and transform into new types of enterprises (Gartner, 2003).

As for traditional server providers, how to establish appropriate pricing models to pursue the highest profits is an essential concern for Web service providers. To date there are two major pricing models in the field of Web services that are derived from traditional business: periodic pricing and fluctuant pricing. Periodic pricing means that a service provider predefines a fixed price for a period of time, when every service requestor subjects to the same price value. In recent years, in order to attract more customers, many service providers offer a variant of the periodic pricing model, called staging price model. As shown in Figure 1, Comcast, a cable company, offers a $0 first-month trial benefit for new customers and a fixed $40/month service fee afterwards. Fluctuant pricing means that the price of a service is ever changing based on marketing situations. Stock pricing is a typical example of the fluctuant pricing model. The price of a stock symbol constantly changes depending on the number of transactions at the moment. Figure 1 shows the stock price curve of Yahoo (NASDAQ: YHOO) from November 15, 2005, to February 15, 2006, according to published data from E*TRADE (2006) financial.

As shown in Figure 1, the fluctuant pricing model automatically adjusts the service price subject to market demand, activity capacity, and changing environment. It obvi-

Figure 1. Illustration of fixed/interactive pricing model

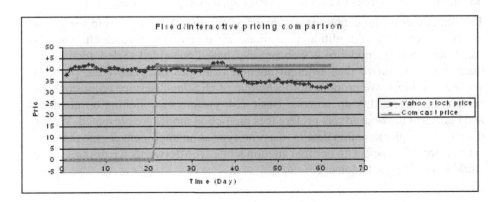

ously promises higher flexibility and larger optimization space for service providers. However, to date most service providers merely adopt traditional fluctuant pricing models without adaptation. There is rarely research focusing on justification and verification of traditional pricing models in the context of Web services paradigm. We argue that because of the unique features of Web services, such as dynamic service discovery and invocation and heterogeneous interactions, traditional pricing models deserve re-examination.

Auction, as one of the fundamental business operation approaches, can be used as one fluctuant pricing model. However, both traditional physical auctions and recently emerged electronic auctions (e-auctions) are basically conducted by human beings, although computer technology is adopted in e-auctions to facilitate auction processes. Conducting auctions in the context of Web services poses significant challenges, because the unique features of Web services implies machine-to-machine interactions, re-enterable bargaining services, and a more ideally independent bidding.

To our best knowledge, to date there is no published research formally modeling Web services-oriented auctions. Some reported works adopted the basic format of auction as a negotiation method between Web service providers and requestors (Esmaeilsabzali & Larson, 2005; Huang, Chen, & Zhang, 2005). Some other researchers adopted the Web services technology to implement e-auctions, such as eBay (*www.ebay.com*). Contrast with their work, our research aims at establishing a fundamental model for adopting an auction mechanism to facilitate Web services negotiation and interactions.

The ultimate goal of our research is to examine the feasibility of applying the traditional auction theories to the field of Web services and establish corresponding Web services-specific auction models. In detail, we first examine the specific features of Web services towards applying auctions. Then we establish a Web services-oriented auction model. We focus on investigating and mathematically proving how service providers can decide different service auction strategies to obtain higher profit. Furthermore, we propose to utilize the technique of Service Level Agreement (SLA) documents as resources to deduce service requestors' preferences.

The remainder of the chapter is organized as follows. After preparing readers for the basic concepts of traditional auctions, we motivate our research. Then we construct a formal model of a Web services-based one-sided sealed auction, and mathematically prove that different auction strategies bring different profits to service providers. We propose our technique of eliciting a service requestor's risk preferences from SLA documents. Basic risk preferences eliciting an algorithm and historical data-based risk preferences prediction model are presented. We then discuss the implementation details of a prototype as an intelligent engine that helps service providers select an optimal auction strategy. Afterwards we discuss related work and offer conclusions.

Basic Auction Concepts

In this section, we will briefly introduce the basic auction concepts to prepare readers for the rest of the chapter. McAfee and McMillan (1987) formally defined an auction as "a market institution with an explicit set of rules determining resource allocation and prices on the basis of bids from the market participants." Auction has been used extensively as one of the fundamental bargaining forms in human society since antiquity for the sale of objects as early as 500 B.C. (Krishna, 2002). An auction event may involve independent auction activities on multiple auction items. A specific auction activity typically includes one or more identical auction items, one or more sellers, and one ore more bidders. Bidders compete for the auction item(s), and the bidders biding for the highest prices will be granted the auction items.

Electronic auctions, or so-called e-auctions, refer to the virtual auctions conducted via the Internet. E-auctions differ from spot auctions in several significant ways. First, the average time limit is longer than spot auctions. Second, electronic bidders may participate in a common auction via the Internet at different times and different places. Third, e-auctions need to serve a scalable and growing Internet population. Fourth, bidders may obtain more information during the bid as they can surf online or do some research on the object at the same time as they bid. However, both physical auctions and e-auctions are conducted by human beings. E-auctions have been typically applying traditional auction theories and methodologies in practices and have been successful. During the past two decades, a variety of popular Web sites were established to support electronic auction activities, such as eBay, onSale (www.onsale.com), AuctionNet (http://www.auction.net), and NETIS auction Web (http://www.auctionweb.com/online).

Research Motivation

The rapidly emerging Web services paradigm has been catching significant momentum from both academia and industry in recent years. Simply put, a Web service is a programmable Web application that is universally accessible through standard Internet protocols (Ferris & Farrell, 2003). Web services typically adopt an Service Oriented Architecture (SOA)-based operational model (Roy & Ramanujan, 2001). Three types of components (i.e., roles) are identified: service provider, service requestor, and service broker. Service providers develop, deploy, and host Web services on their own sites. Then the service providers register with public or private service brokers (or so-called service registries) the Web services of their metadata descriptions, for example, their service types, capabilities, and network addresses. The services brokers subsequently publish registered Web services to the world. Service requestors describe to public service brokers the demand for specific kinds of services; then the service brokers search the registered service metadata and deliver back the results that match the requests. Using the network addresses retrieved from the service brokers, the service requestors bind to the located service providers. After negotiating with the service providers as appropriate, the service requestors access the required Web services and execute the services from the sites of the service providers.

In this negotiation process, theoretically any traditional business negotiation approaches could be used for Web services bargaining. Auction, one of the fundamental business negotiation methods, can be considered as a good candidate in such a context. Here we informally define a Web services-based auction. A service provider, or auctioneer, acts as a seller who hosts a Web service; multiple service requestors bid for the service. The service requestor, or bidder, who bids the highest wins the service. Without losing generality, we follow the way of traditional auction research to consider only one type of bidding object in such an auction. If the service provider can support multiple service requestors simultaneously, multiple service requestors can be chosen. As shown in this definition, the form of auction fits well in the Web services negotiation context; thus, it obviously could be applied to the field of Web services. For the rest of this chapter, we interchangeably use the terms "Web services-based auction," "Web services-oriented auction," "Web services auction," and "service auction."

However, the unique features of Web services decide that a Web services-oriented auction bear several significant differences compared with the traditional auctions. First, bidders in a traditional auction bid for goods, while service requestors in a service auction bid for Web services. In a traditional auction, the winner wins the bidding goods and owns the goods. In a service auction, the winner wins the service in the sense that the service provider needs to provide the service to the winner only once (or multiple times if it is defined so). Therefore, in a traditional auction, the ownership of the bidding object belongs to the winner, whereas in a service auction, the ownership of the bidding service is still possessed by the service auctioneer such that the same service can be put for another bid after the winner finishes using it. In one word, a service auction is a re-enterable auction type.

Second, Web services interactions imply machine-based interactions, instead of human-based interactions. In the traditional auction research, one typical mechanism is to investigate optional bidders' strategies based on all participants' preferences. These preferences are normally formed from auction participants' personal background information, for example, household income, personal taste, education levels, reputation, and other generic characteristics. In a machine-to-machine service auction, a participant's preference can only be deduced from published machine-readable documents available. These documents include the Web Services Description Language (WSDL) specifications from service providers and the Service Level Agreement documents from both service providers and service requestors. These two kinds of documents are *ad hoc* industry standard languages specifically coined for Web services communications. A WSDL document allows a service provider to define the functionality of a Web service and how to invoke the service. An SLA document defines a formal contract between a service requestor and a service provider, aiming at specifying quantifiable issues under varying contexts based on mutual understandings and expectations (WS-Agreement, 2005). In other words, an SLA document defines the agreements to govern service provision and receipt.

Third, the essential aspect of an SOA model is the concept of dynamic discovery and invocation. Service requestors dynamically search and locate services from service brokers, and invoke the Web services from the service providers over the Internet on an on-demand basis. Therefore, it is unlikely that the service requestors in one Web service auction would ally to bargain a better price. As a matter of fact, under most circumstances the only reason for the bidders (i.e., service requestors) to come to the same service auction is that they happen to discover the same service from the same service provider. Hence compared to the human-based auction, it is more reliable to believe that bidders are independent in information collecting, price bidding, and private value of the service. We will come to this point in later sections.

Due to these apparent differences, the mature research results on traditional auctions deserve to be re-examined in the context of service auctions. Meanwhile, computing technologies should be utilized to facilitate service auctions. Note that the term *Web services-based auction* marries the Web services technology and the auction model. It can refer to two directions: on one side, it refers to conducting auctions utilizing the Web services technology as vehicles and tools; on the other hand, it refers to conducting inter-Web services communication utilizing the auction as approach. In this research, we refer to the latter meaning. Throughout the rest of this chapter, we use the term "traditional auctions" to refer to human-based auctions including the traditional physical auctions and e-auctions, as opposed to "Web services-based auctions" that are machine-based auctions.

Web Services Auction Model

In this section, we will present our Web services auction model. First we formally define a generic service auction problem; second we mathematically prove that different auction strategies may bring different profits to service providers based on service requestors' risk preferences.

Definition 1. A Web services auction problem can be defined as a six-element tuple $SA = (ws, WS, AM, SR, R_c, R_s)$ where:

- $ws = (ws_{wsdl}, ws_{impl}, ws_{sla}, sp)$ is a four-element tuple that represents the Web service to be bid on, where:
  - ○ ws_{wsdl} is the interface description of the Web service in WSDL;
  - ○ ws_{impl} is the executable implementation of the Web service;
  - ○ ws_{sla} is the SLA document associated with the Web service;
  - ○ sp is the service provider who acts as the *seller* in the action.
- $WS = \{ws_1, ws_2, ..., ws_m\}$ is the set of identical Web services that the service requestors face. In other words, the service provider may be able to simultaneously support multiple service requestors.
- $AM = \{am_1, am_2, ..., am_n\}$ is a set of alternative auction methods (i.e., pricing strategies) that can be either statically or dynamically applied over the auction.
- $SR = \{sr_1, sr_2, ..., sr_p\}$ is a set of service requestors acting as *bidders* that bid for the Web services. $p =|SR|$ is the total number of bidders, which is an unpredictable finite natural number. This means that a Web service provider cannot set up the number of bidders, and both service provider and requestors do not know how many requestors altogether participate in the auction before the auction is completed. Each service requestor is a tuple $sr_k = (sr_{k,contact}, sr_{k,sla})$, where:
  - ○ $sr_{k,\inf o}$ is the unique information of the *kth* service requestor (to be discussed in detail in Definition 6);
  - ○ $sr_{k,sla}$ is the SLA document associated with the *kth* service requestor.
- $R_c = \{r_{c1}, r_{c2}, r_{cc}\}$ is the innate common set of rules that governs the service auction.
- $R_s = \{r_{s1}, r_{s2}, ..., r_{ss}\}$ is a set of rules that is defined for the specific service auction and governs the auction.

Definition 2. The unique concept of Web services implies the following three fundamental rules to a Web service auction:

- r_1 **(Private Value):** The private information of a Web service requestor is her own value for the service, and it does not depend on what other requestors know.

- r_2 **(Independent Service Requestor):** All Web service requestors are independent in terms of what they need, when and where they find the service site, whether to participate in the auction, and what to bid for the service. In addition, there is no communication between them.

- r_3 **(Symmetry):** Requestor's private value comes from the same distribution function that is commonly known by all service requestors and the corresponding service seller.

Rationale: In order to enable auction research, a set of definitions or pre-defined assumptions are commonly established to simplify auction environments (Fudenberg & Tirole, 1991). Examining the common auction assumptions in the context of Web services, the above three rules are established as the fundamental rules to delimit a quantifiable Web services-based auction environment. In Rule r_1, the private value that a requestor bids is the maximum amount of money she is willing to pay for the service. Rule r_2 states that the requestor's value is known only to herself, regardless of what others think. Rule r_2 also implies that the requestor would not change his value even if she learns others' private information.

Web services are executable and programmable Web applications published on the Internet; they can be discovered from common public registries (here we omit the private service registry) and retrieved using standard Internet protocols. Thus, it is reasonable to consider that service requestors are independent from each other and that there is no coalition among them. They come to the same service auction just because they happen to discover the same Web service from public registries and they are guided by those service registries to the same service provider. In addition, this rule can be further supported by the targeted scenario of Web services: service requestors dynamically discover the Web service and request for service in an on-demand manner. Therefore, it is reasonable to expect no assembly among service requestors. Since service requestors do not form any assembly, they only know of their own expected value for the bid service—that is, price range that they are willing to pay for the bid service (as specified in the second common Rule c_2).

Definition 3. Without losing generality, we predefine a set of rules that governs all service auctions to simplify the Web services auction. In a Web service auction:

- r_4: No entry fee is needed for service requestors.
- r_4: The service provider bears no operation cost in selling services.
- r_6: Only the service provider knows the true value of the bidding service.
- r_7: Only the winner requestor needs to pay for the bid service; other bidders who lose the auction pay nothing.
- r_8: All service requestors in the same service auction adopt the same strategy.
- r_9: Service requestors always adopt a symmetric Nash equilibrium strategy in auctions.

- r_{10}: The service provider is aware of the service requestors' strategy (i.e., Nash equilibrium).

Rationale: Rules $r_4 \sim r_{10}$, along with the Rules $r_1 \sim r_3$, are acceptable for service auctions. Rules $r_4 \sim r_7$ are widely adopted in the traditional auctions and present online e-auctions; therefore, it is reasonable to introduce them as pre-defined rules into generic Web services auctions without enforcing unrealistic limitations. Rule r_8 aims to simplify Web services auction by assuming that all participants bear the same strategy, as adopted by the game theory. It can also be stated, for example in a two-bidder auction, as "I know that you know what I know; you know that I know what you know; both of us know that what we adopt a strategy."

Rules r_9 and r_{10} intend to simplify Web services auction by applying widely adopted auction assumptions. These two rules state that we focus on equilibrium state in the Web service auction. The Nash equilibrium is the set of strategies that no player can benefit by changing the strategy while the other players keep their strategies unchanged. For the sake of completeness, here we provide the definition of the Nash equilibrium. For detailed information, refer to Fudenberg and Tirole (1991). A strategy profile $\hat{a} = (\hat{a}_1, \hat{a}_2, ..., \hat{a}_p)$ is a Nash equilibrium if for each player i and $\hat{a}_i \in A_i$, $u_i(a) \geq u_i(\hat{a}_1, \hat{a}_2, ..., \hat{a}_p)$ where $\hat{a}_i$ is the strategy that person i takes, A_i is alternative strategy sets. For $a = (a_1, a_2, ..., a_p) \in \prod_{j=1}^{i} A_i$, $u_i(a)$ is i's payoff if the strategy profile a is played. In one word, a Nash equilibrium strategy is a strategy profile in which each agent is as good a response to what others do as any other strategy alternatives.

Furthermore, since our main purpose in this research is to prove that service providers can adopt different auction strategies to obtain different profits under different auction scenarios, we introduce these reasonable assumptions to narrow down to some auction scenarios to facilitate our discussions, instead of exhausting all auction scenarios.

Auction Strategies

As we specified in Definition 1: $AM = \{am_1, am_2, ..., am_n\}$ refers to a set of alternative auction methods (i.e., pricing strategies) that can be either statically or dynamically applied over a service auction. In this section, we will discuss the available auction strategies that can be applied to Web services auctions.

Looking inside the traditional auctions and e-auctions, several types of taxonomy (Klemperer, 1999; McAfee & McMillan, 1987; Wurman, Wellman, & Walsh, 1998) were identified regarding auction seller strategies. Four major taxonomies are summarized in Table 1.

Table 1. Auction categories

Price trend	Seller request		Bidder price		Marketable
English	One-sided	First-price	Sealed	Single-item	Marketable
		Second-price		Discriminatory	
Dutch	Two-sided		Outcry	One price	Non-marketable
				All prices	

The first categorization is based on the trend of the auction prices: whether the bidder prices increase or decrease in the process of an auction. Two categories are identified, namely, English and Dutch. In an English auction, auctioneers start at a low price and incrementally increase the price; in a Dutch auction, auctioneers start at a high price and incrementally decrease the price.

The second categorization is based on a seller's request: whether only bids are permitted. Two categories are identified, namely, one-sided and two-sided. In a one-sided auction, only bids are permitted; sellers are not allowed to "ask." In a two-sided auction, not only bids are permitted, sellers can "ask" prices at the same time. As shown in Table 1, a one-sided auction can in turn be divided into two sub-categories, based on the "winner payment" method. In both types, the bidder with the highest price will win the auction. However, in a first-price auction, the winner pays the highest bidding price; in a second-price auction, the winner pays the second highest bidding price.

The third categorization is based on how bidders submit bidding prices: whether the bids are published or kept secret. Two categories are identified, namely, sealed and outcry. In a sealed auction, all bidding prices are kept secret to other bidders; in an outcry auction, some bidding price can be viewed by other bidders. As shown in Table 1, a sealed auction can in turn be divided into two sub-categories, based on the number of bidding items. In a discriminatory auction, more than one bidding item exists. An outcry auction can in turn be divided into two sub-categories, based on whether part or all of the bidding prices are available to other bidders. In a one-price auction, only the upper-bound or lower-bound bidding price at the checking moment will be visible, based on whether the auction is an English or Dutch one. In an all-price auction, all bidding prices are available to all bidders.

The fourth categorization is based on whether a seller must sell a bidding item—in other words, whether a seller can cancel a bidding item in the process of an auction. In a marketable auction, as long as a bidding item is published, a final winner will be granted and the seller must give the bidding item to the winner. In an unmarketable auction, a seller can decide to cancel an auction if she believes that the prices the bidders are willing to pay are lower than her predefined lowest price.

Auction Strategies Under Investigation

After carefully examining the possible auction strategies identified from the traditional auctions and e-auctions, we found that some auction strategies are symmetric to others, such as English auctions and Dutch auctions; and some auction strategies are extensions to others, such as one-price outcry auctions and all-price outcry auctions. Therefore, we needed to investigate only one auction type; the results can be applied to the other ones.

In our research, we decided to focus on English auctions, because the English auction type is more popular in traditional auctions. In addition, how single-item sealed auction type and discriminatory sealed auction type lead to different seller strategies is rather a generic economics research topic, instead of one limited to Web services auctions. Therefore, we only consider single-item auctions. In other words, using the notations in the Definition 1, the set of Web services to be bid on contains only one Web service instance: $WS = \{ws\}$. Sealed auctions and outcry auctions are both possibly applicable to Web services auctions. However, outcry auctions require a standard way for service providers to publish bidding prices and to communicate with service requestors automatically. Although the requirement is possible to be implemented in the future, the solution may require extra standardization efforts. Therefore, we only consider sealed auction type. Finally, whether a service provider allows herself to cancel an auction in the process is rather related to her advertisement profile than a scientific decision. It is more likely to depend on her own business requirements predefined. Therefore, we do not consider the marketable/non-marketable auctions.

As a result, the auction categories under investigation in this research are summarized in Table 2, with excluded categories in grey.

Using our notations in Definition 1: $SA = (ws, WS, MM, SR, R_c, R_s)$, each auction category above predefines some rules into $R_s = \{r_{s1}, r_{s2}, ..., r_{sq}\}$.

Table 2. Auction categories under investigation

Price trend	Seller request		Bidder price		Marketable
English	Single-sided	First-price	Sealed	Single-item	Marketable
		Second-price		Discriminatory	
Dutch	Double-sided		Outcry	One price	Non-marketable
				All prices	

Decision on Auction Strategies

Economists have been carefully examining the auctioners' behaviors and auctioneer's decision-making process. Their research results, summarized in the well-known framework game theory (Fudenberg & Tirole, 1991; Mas-Colell, Whinston, & Green, 1995), provide a guideline and starting point for Web services auction practices. According to the game theory, buyers' strategy is different from auction rules set by sellers; thus, it is critical for sellers to choose an optimal auction type to stimulate bidders. In order to decide the best auction type, sellers need to predict the behaviors of bidders and their expected profits thereafter. Hence, our goal is embodied into two directions from the service providers' perspective: how to predict the behaviors of service requestors, and how to decide on auction strategies (types). Our approach starts from the latter direction and is two-fold: first, we examine the seller's process of deciding auction types, thus we extract the criteria of predicting service requestor behaviors; second, we propose how to extract and predict service requestor behaviors, which will be discussed in detail in the section of SLA-based service requestor preference deduction.

Service Requestor Information

According to the game theory, auction sellers or auctioneers need to understand and examine bidder behaviors based on bidder types, goals, and preferences. Applying this theory, we introduce the following formal definition of service provider preferences:

Definition 4. In a Web service auction, a utility function u is a numerical value to a service provider or service requestor when she chooses a strategy: $WS = \{ws\}$, and $sr \in SR = \{sr_1, sr_2, ..., sr_p\}$. The function value represents her preference: $u(x) \geq u(y)$, if and only if the party prefers strategy x to strategy y. A von Neumann-Morgenstern (vNM) utility function is that a function has the expected utility property: the service provider or service requestor is indifferent between receiving a given bundle or a gamble with the same expected value.

Definition 5. Consider that in a Web service auction, a service provider/requestor (called an agent) chooses a strategy x. It bears a vNM utility function U over x as $U(x)$ and a mathematical mean function E over x as $E[x]$. The agent x is risk averse if $E[U(x)] < U(E[x])$. The agent is risk neutral if $E[U(x)] = U(E[x])$. The agent is risk proclivity (or risk loving or risk seeking) if $E[U(x)] > U(E[x])$.

Figure 2. Categorization of service requestors in a service auction

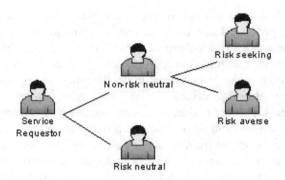

As shown in Figure 1, a service requestor's preference towards a service auction is defined in two categories: risk neutral and non-risk neutral. A service requestor is considered as risk neutral to a service auction if she is indifferent to bidding for it. Otherwise, the service requestor is considered as non-risk neutral. A non-risk neutral service requestor can be further defined as risk averse if she refuses the bidding service, or risk seeking if she happily accepts the bidding service.

Definition 6. The unique information of the *ith* service requestor sr_i in a service auction is represented by a tuple $sr_{i,\text{info}} = (t_i, u_i)$ where:

- $t_i = (t_{i,1}, t_{i,2}, ..., t_{i,o}), t_{i,a} \in R, o \in I$ represents the type of service requestor sr_i, which contains a list of attributes specific to the auction and the service requestor; t_i is the *type* of bidder i, or we can call requestor i a *type t requestor.*
- By rules $r_1 \sim r_3$, t_i is uniformly distributed—that is, $t_i \propto \bigcup [0, V]$.
- $u_i : AM \times t_i \to R$ is the real value of the utility function applied on the service requestor sr_i based on her type. (Recall that AM represents the alternate auction strategies that can be applied onto the service auction.)
- Every service requestor sr_i is an expected utility maximizer—that is, $u_i = \underset{u_i}{MAX}\, Eu_i(t_i)$

In a traditional auction, what a seller cares most about is the bidders' risk preferences: the bidders' strategies are different under the conditions whether the bidders really want to win the auction or not. If a seller in some way knows, or assumes, the bidders' risk preferences, she could adjust the auction strategy accordingly so as to gain the most profit. Let us examine in a Web service auction how a service provider should adjust auction strategy based upon service requestors' various types of preferences.

Definition 7. In the process of a service auction, each service requestor sr_i specifies five values $(e_i, l_i, h_i, b_i, B_i)$ to a service on bid:

- $e_i \in R$ represents the private value that the requestor holds for the service;
- $l_i \in R$ represents the lowest value that the service requestor would pay for the service;
- $h_i \in R$ represents the highest value that the service requestor would pay for the service;
- $b_i \in R$ represents the requestor's bidding price during a service auction; and
- $B_i \in R$ represents the value that the service requestor finally pays for the service. This paying price, or requestor's payment, depends on the auction type.

If the service requestor wins the bid, she will pay B_i; otherwise, she will pay nothing.

Definition 8. A service requestor sr_i's utility function u_i is defined as a function over her risk preference rp_i: $u_i = f(rp_i)$. u_i can exhibit in one of the two forms, either as a linear function yielded by risk neutral preference or a non-linear function yielded by non-risk neutral preference:

$$u_i = \begin{cases} e_i - B_i, & \text{if } p_i \text{ is risk neutral;} \\ (e_i - B_i)^\theta, \theta \in (0,1) \cup (1,\infty), & \text{if } p_i \text{ is non-risk neutral;} \end{cases} \begin{cases} \theta \in (0,1), & \text{if } sr_i \text{ is risk averse;} \\ \theta \in (1,\infty), & \text{if } sr_i \text{ is risk seeking} \end{cases}$$

where e_i is the private value service requestor sr_i assigns to the service, and B_i is the final payment of sr_i.

In other words, if the service requestor sr_i wins the bid, she will obtain the value of $e_i - B_i$, and 0 otherwise.

Since a service requestor's utility function can exhibit in two forms due to different preference types, we now examine the service provider's expected profits with respect to the two forms.

Service Provider Strategy Decision Deduction

With the previous notations and preparation, in this section we prove mathematically how a service provider should select optimal auction strategy towards higher profit. We utilize the categorization information in Table 2 to guide our discussions.

As shown in Table 2, we will consider in a one-sided sealed auction how a service provider will decide whether a first-price or a second-price strategy should be used. The decision should be made based on different utility functions adopted by the corresponding service requestors. As we discussed in the last section, there are two types of utility functions: linear or non-linear. We will discuss each type in detail as follows.

Risk-Neutral Bidders

When service requestors are risk neutral, their utility functions exhibit as linear functions. As specified in Rule r_8 in Definition 2, all service requestors in the same auction always adopt the symmetric Nash equilibrium strategy (e.g., Mas-Colell et al., 1995):

$$b_i = b_i(e_i) = \frac{p-1}{p} e_i$$

where p represents the total number of service requestors in the bid at the moment, and $e_i \in R$ represents the private value the service requestor sr_i assigns to the service.

Now let us compare the service provider's profit under first-price and second-price strategy. First, we calculate the service provider's expected profit (revenue) under first-price strategy. Recall that under uniform distribution on (0,1), for which:

$$F(u) = u, \text{ and } f(u) = 1, \text{ for every } u \sim (0,1)$$

The expected profit for the service provider is the mean of what she gets from the winner, that is:

$$r_{\pi 1} = E[\text{winner's payment}] = E[b_i \mid i \text{ wins the bid}]$$

$$= \frac{p-1}{p} E \max \{e_1, e_2, \ldots e_p\}$$

$$= \frac{p-1}{p} \int_0^1 u p f(u) [F(u)]^{p-1} du$$

$$= \frac{p-1}{p} \int_0^1 u p u^{p-1} du$$

$$= \frac{p-1}{p+1} \tag{1}$$

Then let us consider the service provider's profit under the second-price auction:

$r_{\pi 2} = E[\text{winner's payment}] = E[b_j | i \text{ wins}, b_j < b_i, \text{ for } i \neq j, \text{ and } b_j > b_k, \text{ for all } j \neq k$ and $k \ k \neq i]$

$$= E[2^{nd} \, highest\{e_1, e_2, ..., e_p\}]$$
$$= \int_0^1 u p (p-1) f(u) [1 - F(u)] (F(u))^{p-2} du$$
$$= p(p-1) \int_0^1 u(1-u) u^{p-2} du$$
$$= p(p-1) \int_0^1 (u^{p-1} - u^{p-2}) du$$
$$= p(p-1)(\frac{1}{p} - \frac{1}{p+1})$$
$$= \frac{p-1}{p+1} \tag{2}$$

Comparing (1) and (2), $r_{\pi 1} = r_{\pi 2}$. This means that if service requestors are risk neutral, the service provider can choose either the first-price or second-price strategy, without affecting their profit.

Non-Risk Neutral Bidders

In most cases, however, service requestors do have preferences over bidding service. In other words, service providers need to consider non-linear utility functions for participating service requestors. Taking the functional form as defined in Definition 8, we will come to the symmetric Nash equilibrium strategy that a service requestor has for bidding (Mas-Colell et al., 1995):

$$b_i(e_i) = \frac{p-1}{p-1+\theta} e_i$$

The service provider's expected revenue can be deduced as:

$r_{\pi 3} = E[\text{winner's payment}] = E[b_i \mid i \text{ wins the bid}]$

$$= \frac{p-1}{p-1+\theta} P(i \text{ wins}) E[b_i \mid b_i \geq b_j, \forall i \neq j]$$

$$= \frac{p-1}{p-1+\theta} P(t_i \geq t_j) E[b_i \mid b_i \geq b_j, \forall i \neq j]$$

$$= \frac{p-1}{p-1+\theta} \int_0^1 [F(u)]^{p-1} uf(u) p\,du$$

$$= \frac{(p-1)p}{(p+1)(p-1+\theta)} \tag{3}$$

Under the second-price auction setup, the bidder's dominant Nash equilibrium strategy is the same as if she were risk neutral—that is, $b_i(t_i) = t_i$. Therefore, the service provider's expected profit will not change:

$$r_{\pi 4} = \frac{p-1}{p+1} \tag{4}$$

Comparing (3) and (4), we can see that $r_{\pi 3} \neq r_{\pi 4}$. If $\theta \in (0,1)$, $r_{\pi 3} > r_{\pi 4}$; if $\theta \in (1, \infty)$, $r_{\pi 3} < r_{\pi 4}$. Either way, the service provider expects different profits under different auction strategies. Intuitively, if the service seller believes that bidders are risk averse ($\theta \in (0,1)$), she prefers to conduct the first-price auction to the second-price auction. On the other hand, if the service seller believes that bidders are risk seekers ($\theta \in (1, \infty)$), she prefers the second-price auction.

In summary, we have proved that a service provider should adopt different auction strategies to obtain high profit if she knows corresponding service requestors' risk preferences. Thus, our research challenge has turned into how to discover and predict service requestors' risk preferences. In traditional auctions, bidders' risk preferences are typically predicted based upon bidders' background information such as personal taste and household wealth, as well as bidding object's perspectives, such as its price range, durability, functions, and personality (McAfee & McMillan, 1987). This information is normally obtained from survey investigation and bidding objects' selling experience (Zhang, Zhang, & Chung, 2004). However, a Web service auction is dynamically formed with unpredictable service requestors; this normally used information cannot be easily found. Therefore, a service provider needs a new method to predict service requestors' risk preferences. Our approach is to utilize service requestors' Service Level Agreement documents in addition to the service provider's SLA document.

SLA-Based Service Requestor Preference Deducation

Introduction of SLA

The term Service Level Agreement was coined to define a formal contract between a Web service requestor and service provider, aiming at specifying quantifiable issues under various contexts on the grounds of mutual understandings and expectations (WS-Agreement, 2005). In other words, an SLA intends to produce an agreement regarding the guarantees of a Web service. It should be noted that SLA can be used as an approach to formally define any service-related issue, not limited to the final mutual agreement. An SLA can facilitate Web services adoption and distribution by benefiting both service providers and requestors. A published SLA from a service provider will not only assure potential service requestors that they will get the service they pay for, but also obligate herself to achieve the service promises as well. Meanwhile a service requestor can use an SLA to express her requirements regarding a service, so that a service provider can adjust service quality and quantity accordingly. For example, consider a service provider is facing two service requestors, one requiring service delivery within 10 seconds while the other requires 30 seconds. Based on the different SLAs, the service provider can assign more resources to the service requestor requiring faster service than the other one, thus to satisfy both requestors.

In theory, the quantifiable issues could cover whatever each or both sides are interested in, including Quality of Service (QoS), prices, constraints, and any other requirements or preferences. An interested issue is described as a single or multiple SLA parameters, which are normally based on domain-specific vocabularies. A Web service provider may define one or more SLAs for one Web service in order to serve different service requestors. For example, United Airlines may offer different SLAs with different qualities to serve different categories of clients (e.g., business organizations, frequent flyers, and casual customers).

To date, several SLA specifications and proposals have emerged. The two attracting the most attention are Web Services Agreement Specification (WS-Agreement, 2005) from Global Grid Forum and Web Service Level Agreement (WSLA) from IBM (2003). Their goals are to standardize the terminology, concepts, agreement structure, agreement terms, agreement templates, as well as WSDL for defining state and message exchanges.

WS-Agreement defines a language and a protocol for service providers to advertise Web services. It allows business parties to use extensible XML language to specify the nature of the agreement and agreement templates, so as to facilitate business match and discovery, and emphasize flexibility, extensibility, and compatibility. A

WS-Agreement-based specification generally contains three parts: (1) the schema of the agreement, (2) the schema of the agreement template, and (3) agreement-specific lifecycle management port types and operations. Such an agreement defines one to many service level state-dependent requirements as expressions of resource availabilities (e.g., memory, CPU, disk space) and service qualities (e.g., response time).

WSLA also defines a language primarily for service providers based on XML. As a matter of fact, it is defined as an XML schema. WSLA provides a technique to define service parameters and algorithms that specify how to measure and decide the deviation and failure of a promised service guarantee, and a technique that monitors and governs services. In addition, WSLA provides an extensible mechanism to allow users to specify domain-specific vocabularies, which largely increases the extensibility of WSLA to be applied in different domains.

SLA-Based Preference Elicitation

In our research, we decide to deduce service requestor's risk preferences from service requestor SLA documents in the WS-Agreement format. The main reason of our selection of WS-Agreement is its popularity. WS-Agreement is proposed by Global Grid Forum (GGF; www.ggf.org), whose community consists of thousands of individuals in both research and industry, and represents over 400 organizations in more than 50 countries. WS-Agreement has been gaining significant attention from both the Web services field and the Grid computing field. It is a pure XML-based approach to formally describe service level requirements as well as service provider or requestor's information. It should be noted that our approach of SLA-oriented preference elicitation is not limited to WS-Agreement. Instead, it can be easily applied to any XML-based SLA standards, such as WSLA, with limited changes.

It should be noted that the term *risk preference* in traditional economics is an abstract concept representing a buyer's tendency of participating in a lottery and of paying the price. As described above, it is one characteristic that an agent processes by disclosing features of utility function. The comparison of risk preference is mainly on who is more risk averse, using the risk averse ratio (Arrow, 1963, 1965). In other words, risk reference, *per se,* is not numerically representable. However, we believe that certain types of risk preference lead to some certain behaviors, which gives us the idea that "risk preference" can be deduced, or revealed, from observed behaviors. The rest of this chapter discusses how we conduct an analysis to reveal a service requestor's risk preference from some of its behaviors. For example, SLA documents define some agreement that is related to risky behaviors, such as delivery time, penalty care if failing to fulfill the agreement, urgency of the service, confidentiality of participants, and so forth. A service requestor ranks each of the criteria, which by combination exposes her risk preference. We provide a formal definition of this "revealed" risk preference idea later in this chapter (see Definition 10). On all accounts, in the machine-to-machine only, re-enterable, dynamic services auctions, abstract concepts must be translated into quantifiable concepts that are numerical representative, before they can be used in the process. This chapter is the first attempt to extend and digitize the traditional risk preference concept into calculable and comparable numbers on top of Web services specific and available machine-understandable SLA documents.

Recall that in the last section, we concluded that a service provider can adopt different auction strategies to gain higher (expected) profit by analyzing and predicting service requestors' risk preferences. In an SLA document, both service providers and requestors can decide to specify their background information and specific requirements on the bidding service. These specifications can assist each part to understand the other part's basic information and requirements related to the service requesting or provision. On one hand, as we state above, an SLA from a service provider can document the service description, features, and delivery parameters. On the other hand, an SLA document from a service requestor can reveal how urgently she needs a service, how serious she is, how much she plans to pay for the service, and what her risk preference type is regarding the service. The serious requestor, or those who need the service urgently, or both, will more likely specify detailed and specific quality requirements on a bidding service, and are more likely to compete for the bidding service if possible. If a requestor is risk loving for one type of service, she may be highly willing to pay more to obtain a service, regardless of other market environments. Furthermore, it has been extensively accepted that SLA is an indispensable element in Web services paradigm; thus, it is reasonable to assume that service providers and requestors will provide more or less SLA documents. Consequently, we believe that SLA documents are appropriate resources for service providers to elicit bidding service requestors' risk preferences. Our research challenge has turned into how to uncover and predict service requestors' preferences from published SLA documents written in WS-Agreement standard.

Basic Risk Preference Deduction Model

Our fundamental idea is that the definitions in an SLA document of a service requestor can be used to compare with the corresponding definitions in the SLA document of the corresponding service provider, to deduce the service requestor's risk preference. An SLA document from a service provider describes the basic information of a Web service, which is a guideline for service requestors to prepare their SLA documents related to that service. Note that we only consider interested service requestors as (potential) service bidders. If a service requestor provides completely unrelated or unmatched SLA documents compared with the service provider's SLA document, she can be considered as not serious about the bidding service; thus, she can be ignored by the corresponding service auction. This means that the relatedness of a requestor's SLA to a provider's produces the service bidder base. We thus delimit the temporal relationship between the SLA documents in a Web service auction as follows: a service provider (i.e., seller) publishes her SLA document to be associated with her published Web service; interested service requestors (i.e., bidders) submit their own SLA documents defining their specific requirements based upon the service provider's SLA document. These specific requirements may strengthen or emphasize some quality requirements, or release some.

A WS-Agreement-based SLA document is a pure XML-based document, which defines a set of service-related attributes as XML tags. For example, a service provider may declare in her SLA document that the service is guaranteed to be delivered in 10 seconds, by specifying a user-defined tag <DeliveryTime = 10 Unit = s>. The composer of an SLA document owner defines any number of attributes based upon specific service logic. Some of the defined attributes are more important than others if they are shared and used by both the service provider and corresponding requestors. We call these attributes *primary attributes,* such as delivery time, response time, reliability, and all other attributes (except service provider personal information such as contact address) defined by the service provider by default. Other attributes are defined by some service requestor alone. For example, a service requestor may independently set a requirement on a QoS attribute "fault tolerance." The corresponding service provider may not have a mutual agreement on the attribute. These service requestor-specific attributes are called *secondary attributes.* We formally define an SLA document in Definition 9.

Definition 9. An SLA document ws_{sla} associated with a Web service in a service auction *SA* is defined as a tuple:

$$ws_{sla} = (PATT, SATT, ATTV), \text{ where:}$$

- $PATT = \{att_1, att_2, ...att_{N_p}\}$ is a list of primary attributes that are used by both the service provider (sp) and service requestors (SR), $N_p \in I$ is the number of primary attributes defined;
- $SATT = \{att_1, att_2, ...att_{N_{SA}}\}$ is a list of secondary attributes that are defined by either the service provider sp or a service requestor $sr_j \in SR$, N_{SA} is the number of secondary attributed defined;
- $ATTV = \{<att_1, v_1>, <att_2, v_2>, ... <att_{N_p+N_{sA}}, v_{N_p+N_{sA}}>\}$ is a list of name/value pairs containing the attribute (both primary attributes and secondary attributes) names and corresponding values specified.

We now define the risk preference of an interested service requestor on a specific primary service attribute. We propose to compare the corresponding specifications on the same attribute from both the service provider and a requestor. For example, a service provider may declare in her SLA document that the service is guaranteed to be delivered in 10 seconds, while one service requestor may ask for 5 seconds as the upper bound, and yet another service requestor allows a 20-second response timeframe. For a specific service QoS attribute, if a service requestor sets higher or tighter requirements than set by the service provider, the service requestor is considered as risk loving on the attribute; if a service requestor sets lower require-ments, she is considered as risk averse on the attribute; if a service requestor sets the same value or does not set a value for the attribute, she is considered to accept the default value and thus can be viewed as risk neutral on the attribute. Using the example we discussed before, since the first service requestor sets more stringent requirements (5 seconds) on the response time, it is more likely that it is willing to bid a higher price for the service than the latter requestor. In other words, the first service requestor is more risk seeking, while the second one is more risk averse.

It is possible that a service requestor sets acceptance ranges on some attributes more than others. Consider the previous example when the service provider sets the default values of response time as 10 seconds and a service requestor asks for 5 seconds. According to our previous definition, the service requestor should be considered as risk seeking on the attribute. However, if the service requestor declares that it does not matter if the timeframe is met, then its risk preference should be adjusted to risk neutral. Therefore, we introduce a concept of *acceptance range* parameter to represent this constraint. The formal definition of the risk preference of a service requestor is summarized in Definition 10.

Definition 10. The revealed risk preference of a related service requestor $sr_j \in SR$ on a specific service attribute $att_i \in MATT = \{att_1, att_2, ...att_{N_A}\}$ is defined as follows:

$$rp_{j,i} = \alpha_{j,i} p_{j,i} = \begin{cases} = 1 \ \text{if it is risk seeking;} \\ = 0 \ \text{if it is risk neutral;} \\ = -1 \ \text{if it is risk averse;} \end{cases} \quad (5)$$

Table 3. Risk preference decision table

	Tighter requirements	Same requirements	Looser requirements
Urgent	Risk seeking	Risk neutral	Risk averse
Non-Urgent	Risk neutral	Risk neutral	Risk averse

where $\alpha_{j,i}$ is the acceptance range of sr_j on attribute att_i, $p_{j,i}$ is the risk preference of sr_j on attribute att_i.

In order to further illustrate our consideration and facilitate our discussion, let us consider binary acceptance range parameter. In more detail, there are two acceptance settings associated with each service attribute, *urgent* and *non-urgent*. The crossover of isolated requirements levels (tighter requirements, looser requirements, same requirements) and the acceptance range parameters leads to 3 x 2 = 6 combinations as shown in Table 3.

As shown in Table 3, if a service requestor specifies that the request on the service attribute is urgent, and defined values are tighter, the same, or looser requirements than the defined values of the service provider, its risk preference is risk seeking, risk neutral, or risk averse, respectively. If she specifies that the request is not urgent, and her defined values are tighter, the same, or looser requirements, her risk preference becomes risk neutral, risk neutral, or risk averse, respectively. Note that it may sound like a trivial situation when a service requestor specifies a highly tighter requirement on a service attribute but declares that she can accept any service not meeting its requirement; for completeness reason, we still list the possibility.

As shown in Table 3, binary acceptance rate situations can be resolved using a matrix sufficiently. It is possible that a service requestor specifies more than two levels of acceptance rate (e.g., a vector of acceptance rates). We will consider the more complicated cases in our future research.

Risk preference of a service requestor is not easy to be observed directly. It is also unreliable by being revealed from only one SLA document because even for requestors with the same type of risk preferences, they may have different satisfaction levels with one requirement. For example, one risk averse service requestor may consider response time more important than fault tolerance, while another risk averse requestor may consider in the opposite way. In other words, the importance level of a certain service attribute is arbitrary and may differ across service requestors. Therefore, any information on an isolated attribute of a service is not sufficient for the service provider to induce a requestor's risk preference. Rather, a better way is that risk preference is statistically induced from the requirements of a variety of attributes. We use a simple example to explain this idea. Suppose there is a person-based, self-reported survey. We do not know a person's actual risk preference, and are unable to get the reliable and true information even if we ask them. We then set up a series of hypothetical questions related to risk preferences that people can easily answer. For example: Are you going to buy a new product that no one else whom you know ever heard of? How do you rank a new product in a wish list from a recent shopping trip? Would you consider being the volunteer user of a new product? In the end, we can come up with the likelihood of a risk preference type that a person can be, based on all the answers to the questions. Similarly a service provider can only analyze a service requestor's risk preference through all requests that include a different valuation of various service attributes. The conclusion that the provider draws is the form of possibility in percentage point that a service requestor is any of the type of preferences.

The formal definition of the risk preference of a service requestor is listed in Definition 11 as follows.

Definition 11. The risk preference of a related service requestor $sr_j \in SR$ is defined as:

$$rp_j = \sum_{i=1}^{N_A} \omega_i q_i + \gamma = \begin{cases} > \varepsilon \Rightarrow rp_j = 1 \text{ is risk seeking;} \\ \in [-\varepsilon, \varepsilon] \Rightarrow rp_j = 0 \text{ is risk neutral;} \\ < -\varepsilon \Rightarrow rp_j = -1 \text{ is risk averse;} \end{cases} \quad (6)$$

where $\sum_{i=1}^{N_A} \omega_i = 1$, N_A is the number of attributes specified, ε and γ are two predefined configurable small real numbers.

ω_i is decided based on each specific service requestor. Various algorithms can be adopted. We will discuss one algorithm in the section on implementation details.

As shown in Definition 11, we introduce a small number ε to add precision. Because a service may include a number of attributes, combined with the corresponding weights, it is difficult to lead to an exact value 0. By introducing this small number ε, if the result is close enough to 0, we consider that the service requestor is risk neutral. Similar conclusions can be made to risk seeking and risk averse.

Furthermore, as shown in Definition 11, we introduce another small number γ to represent the impact from secondary attributes. It is up to the service provider to decide whether to consider secondary attributes and associated values from service requestors. Their influences are absolutely smaller than the primary attributes. For example, it is possible that a service requestor asks for a slightly higher quality of a Web service. Consider again the example we used before, a service provider promises 10 seconds of response time, and a service requestor asks for 8 seconds. If the service provider considers that it can satisfy the requirement, it could notify the service requestor and considers that the service requestor is risk seeking. On the other hand, if the requirement cannot be fulfilled, it could notify the service requestor and removes the requestor from further consideration. Since this exception can be handled accordingly, in this chapter we do not consider this complicity for simplicity.

Finally, we define the risk preference of the whole body of service requestors that a service provider is facing.

Definition 12. The risk preference of a body of related service requestors *SR* is defined as:

$$
rp = \sum_{j=1}^{N_R} rp_j / N_R = \begin{cases} > \varphi \Rightarrow rp = 1 \text{ is risk seeking;} \\[2mm] \in [-\varphi, \varphi] \Rightarrow rp = 0 \text{ is risk neutral;} \\[2mm] < -\varphi \Rightarrow rp = -1 \text{ is risk averse;} \end{cases} \quad (7)
$$

where $N_R \leq | SR |$ is the number of related service requestors, and φ is a predefined configurable small real number.

As shown in Definition 12, another small number φ is introduced to decide when the result is not equal to value 0 but very close to it. If the result is close enough to 0, we consider that the base of service requestors is risk neutral. Similar conclusions can be made to risk seeking and risk averse.

As we have prepared all algorithms for calculating risk preferences, our basic risk preference deduction algorithm is summarized as follows:

Basic Risk Preference Deduction Algorithm

1.   Obtain the SLA document of the service provider
2.   Analyze the document {
     2.1. Parse the document
     2.2. Extract a list of analysis attributes and default values
     2.3. Normalize the SLA attributes
}
3.   Obtain the SLA documents of all participating service requestors
4.   Iterate through the SLA documents from all participating service requestors
     {
     4.1. Parse the document
     4.2. Use normalized primary attributes from Step 2.3 to extract corresponding values required
     4.3. Iterate through each attribute from Step 2.3 {
 If the specified value is semantically more stringent than the default value and is urgent {

The service requestor is set to be risk seeking on the attribute

} else if the specified value is semantically looser than the default value {

The service requestor is set to be risk averse on the attribute

} else {

The service requestor is set to be risk neutral on the attribute

}

    4.4. Calculate the risk preference of the service requestor with weighted attributes

    4.5. Obtain secondary attributes and required values

    4.6. Normalize the secondary SLA attributes

    4.7. Use predefined secondary SLA attributes weight to adjust risk preference from Step 4.4

}

5.   Predict the risk preference of the base of service requestors

In Step 1, the service provider obtains her own SLA document. By analyzing the document in Step 2, she first parses the XML document and extracts a list of primary attributes and secondary attributes associated with their values defined. These attributes need to be normalized using the word normalizing technique, which will be discussed in detail in the section on implementation details.

In Step 3, the service provider fetches the SLA documents of all participating service requestors. How to fetch the SLA document of a service requestor is out of the domain of this chapter. Then in Step 4, the service provider iterates through all SLA documents. First, she parses the document and uses the normalized primary attributes from her own SLA document to extract corresponding attribute values specified by the service requestor. For each primary attribute, Formula 1 is used to decide whether the service requestor is risk seeking, risk neutral, or risk averse on the attribute. After the risk preference value on each primary attribute is obtained, the risk preference of the service requestor on the bidding Web services is calculated using Formula 2.

Then the service provider analyzes secondary attributes and values defined. Specific algorithms can be applied to adjust the risk preference value obtained above based on the secondary attributes, based on the service provider's strategy. After getting the adjusted risk preference values of each service requestor, finally in Step 5, Formula 3 can be used to predict the risk preference of the whole base of related service requestors.

Historical Data-Based Risk Preference Prediction Model

In the last section, we propose a basic risk preference deduction model based on SLA documents. When the service is published for a Web service auction for the first time, it is impossible for the service provider to predict the risk preference of the body of service requestors she is facing. Then the basic deduction model is the only way for the service provider to analyze and set up her pricing strategy after all service requestors report in the service auction. After the first time, the service provider can predict the risk preference of the service requestors in the next coming auction, since she has some historical data from the SLA documents of the services requestors from the previous service auctions. Therefore, she can establish and publish a proper pricing strategy before she opens a new auction cycle of the same service (recall that a Web service includes re-enterable auctions). Thus, we propose a historical data-based polynomial risk preference prediction model as follows:

$$rp^p(t+1) = \sum_{i=1}^{t} \frac{(1-\eta^i)rp^p(i) + \eta^i rp^r(i)}{e^{t-i}} \qquad (8)$$

where $rp^p(t+1)$ denotes the predicted auction requestors' risk preference at the $(t+1)$th auction cycle, $rp^p(i)$ is the predicted risk preference at the ith auction cycle, $rp^r(i)$ is the actual risk preference at the ith auction cycle, and η is the learning rate.

Rationale: The time point when we try to predict is right before the $(t+1)$th auction cycle, while no service requestors' SLA documents are available. Formula 8 predicts the risk preference in a coming auction cycle using the historical data from all of the previous auction cycles. As shown in Formula 8, more recent auction cycles weigh more than earlier ones due to the setting of the denominator. Our model utilizes both the previous prediction data and actual data, so as to gradually approach an appropriate learning rate. The learning rate is obtained from every auction cycle iteration between predicted risk preference and actual risk preference as follows:

$$rp^p(t) = (1-\eta^t)rp^p(t) + \eta^t rp^r(t) \qquad (9)$$

The initial learning rate can start from a randomly assigned number such as 0.1. According to statistics theorem, when $t \to \infty, \eta^t \to 0$. Thus, $rp^p(t) \to rp^r(t)$ after a large number of iterations (i.e., auction cycles).

The actual risk preference of a service requestor is calculated as follows: Based upon all the actual bid prices, we calculate a mean value. If a service requestor's bidding price is higher than the mean value, its actual risk preference is recorded as risk seeking; if its bidding price is lower than the mean value, its actual risk preference is recorded as risk averse; and if its bidding price is close to the mean value by a predefined small number, its actual risk preference is recorded as risk neutral.

SLA Document Parser

We constructed an SLA document parser to automate the process of SLA document analysis and risk preference elicitation. An SLA parser in our research takes an SLA document as an input and generates a structured file as an output. The output document contains three parts: (1) SLA document goal, (2) SLA owner information, and (3) SLA requirements. Each part is a list of (name, value) pairs, with the name extracted from SLA document tags. The first part describes the intention of the SLA document. The second part describes who writes the SLA document, as well as some owner's background information (e.g., owner address). The last part lists a set of quality requirements over the targeted Web service, such as its availability, response time, quality, and so forth. Here we will focus on discussing how to obtain SLA requirements.

SLA documents following WS-Agreement use XML tags to define service level requirements. The same terms with different associated tags may generate different affections to the semantics of the documents. Since we are interested in SLA definitions regarding service quality requirements, we focus on the following two tag types: <wsag:Serviceproperties> and <wsag:GuaranteeTerm>. In detail, we do a global search over an SLA document for the starting points of the two tags. If found, the total tree of the nodes in the SLA document with one of the two tags above will be fetched as a whole for further investigation.

The tag *ServiceProperties* is used to define service-oriented quantifiable properties, such as response time and throughout. It normally includes a sub-tag <wsag:VariableSet> to define a list of customized attributes and corresponding values. In the following very simplified example, the <wsag:ServiceProperties> tag defines one service level requirement *ResponseTime* delimited by the tag <wsag:Variable>.

<wsag:ServiceProperties wsag:Name="*xs:AName*" wsag:ServiceName="xs:*My-Service*">

 <wsag:Variable> name="ResponseTime" metric="job:ResponseTimeCount">

 <wasg:Location>

//TaskDescription/Resources/IndividualResponseTime/Exact

 </wsag:Location>

 </wsag:Variable>

</wsag:WerviceProperties>

The tag *GuaranteeTerm* is constructed to define quantifiable assurance of service level quality, associated with the service described by the service level bounds, or Service Level Objectives (SLOs). An SLA document may contain zero or more guarantee terms. We need to find all of these guarantee terms delimited by the tag <wsag:GuaranteeTerm>. In the following very simplified example, the <wsag: GuaranteeTerm> tag defines a requirement from a service requestor. The service requestor requests that the requirement be assured on any operations of the Web service *MyService*. A precondition (a date) is also defined as delimited by the tag <wsag:QualifyingCondition".

```
<wsag:GuaranteeTerm Obligated="wsag:ServiceConsumer">
 <wsag:ServiceScope ServiceName="xsd:MyService">
 xsd:any
 <wasg:QualifyingCondition>"01302006"</wasg:QualifyingCondition>
</wsag:GuaranteeTerm>
```

Our SLA document parser fetches the segments, parses the content, and generates a tree-like structure with SLA requirements as internal nodes with associated values. In general, any XML parser-based tool can be used to fulfill the task. Our previous research yields a Web application code generator WebGen (Zhang & Chung, 2003), which we used in this work as a document parser, so that we can easily add features and custom interface code to facilitate the SLA document analysis.

The SLA document developers may use different variants of a keyword to define the same meaning. Plurals, gerund forms, and past tense suffixes are examples of syntactical variants that may lead to divergences of one semantic concept. For instance, an SLA document may define a requirement on a service availability using different forms, for example, "availability," "available," "availabilities," and so forth. This problem can be partially resolved by substituting words with their respective stems. A stem is the portion of a word that is left after the removal of its affixes—prefixes and suffixes. For example, "availability" is the stem of "availabilities." Comparatively, suffix removal is more important because most variants of a word are generated by the introduction of suffixes. There have been many algorithms in the literature regarding affixes removal. We decided to adopt the Porter (1980) stemming algorithm in our research due to its popularity, simplicity, and efficiency. The Porter algorithm, or so-called 'Porter stemmer," removes common morphological and in-flexional endings from English words for the purpose of term normalization. After the word stemming process, the tags of an SLA document are changed into a normalized form, all variants of a word are represented by its root. Thus, it is easier to capture the semantics of service specification from an SLA document. Note that the word

Figure 3. Intelligent auction registry

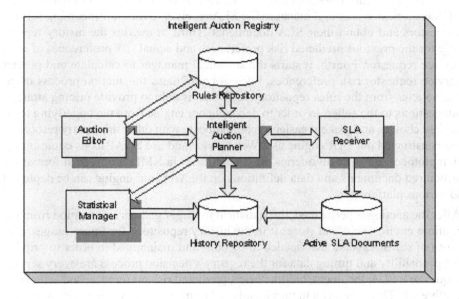

stemming process should be applied to both service provider SLA documents and service requestor SLA documents, for consistency and precision.

Prototype Implementation

We constructed an Intelligent Auction Registry (IAR) engine that is a prototype to help service auction providers make proper pricing decisions. Figure 2 illustrates the architecture and the components of our IAR engine. Four components are set up in the IAR engine, namely, auction editor, intelligent auction planner, statistical manager, and SLA document receiver. Three repositories are included in the engine: rules repository, active SLA repository, and history repository. In order to help service providers better describe the bidding services they want to register, the auction editor provides a user interface to prompt service providers to input the WSDL document and the SLA document. The rule repository stores both the auction selling price selection algorithm and corresponding information, such as the parameters needed. Service providers can also define specific rules for a service auction and store them into the rule repository.

The intelligent auction planner component has five functionalities. First, it coordinates with the auction editor to get bidding service and the associated service provider-side SLA document. Second, it manages the SLA receiver to monitor incoming service requestors and obtain their SLA documents. Third, it queries the history repository for the previous predicted risk preferences and actual risk preferences of each service requestor. Fourth, it starts the statistical manager to calculate and predict service requestor risk preferences. Fifth, it coordinates the auction process using the policies from the rules repository. IAR thus is able to provide pricing strategy suggestions to the seller. In order to decouple our engine from the underlying technology choices and make it easier to communicate with other third-party resources, we constructed our IAR engine as a Web service and use SOAP as its communication protocol. Because all queries are transmitted via XML, a universal format for structured documents and data definitions on the Web, our engine can be deployed to various platforms.

After the auction is performed, the statistical manager gathers information from the runtime environment and stores it in the history repository for future usages. The types of statistical data that needed to be built and maintained in order to provide the probability and timing data for the registry's decision process are every service requestor's SLA document, bidding price, predicted risk preference, and actual risk preference. These data can in turn be utilized to further verify the pricing selection algorithm.

The system has been under development. The agent, including the data-collecting capability described in this chapter, is in place. The principle elements of the Intelligent Auction Registry agent are complete, including a highly adaptable search engine designed to support bid evaluation in this environment.

Related Work

A comprehensive set of theories and techniques has been established in the traditional auction field. In recent years, an enormous amount of research has been conducted in the field of electronic auction. Bajari and Hortacsu (2003) conducted a comprehensive survey on e-auction. A rich body of literature focuses on establishing efficient negotiation protocols in order to automate electronic auctions by customers and merchants (Byde, 2003). Kikuchi (2001) proposed a new protocol for multiple distributed auctioneers to find the highest price and the set of winners; Hirakiuchi and Sakurai (2001) proposed a group of signatures and the identity escrow-based, anonymous sealed-bid auction protocol. Subramanian (1998) proposed a secure electronic auction protocol to favor security, privacy, anonymity, atomicity, and low overhead. Some researchers constructed electronic auction systems to explore various online auction frameworks. Among them, AuctionBot (Wurman et al., 1998) is an experimental Internet auction server established at the University of Michigan. AuctionBot provides a list of predefined auction types for sellers to choose from. Sellers can also customize related parameters. After an auction is set up, the system will enforce the multilateral distributive negotiation protocols. Panzieri and Shrivastava (1999) replicate auction servers to achieve data integrity, responsiveness, and scalability. These specific protocols significantly extend the traditional physical auction model into online electronic auctions that provide more flexibility, dynamicity, and friendly auction environments. These protocols enrich the traditional ones and can be used as starting points of Web services-oriented auctions.

There exist popular Web sites to support electronic auction activities, such as eBay, onSale, and AuctionNet. In recent years, many known e-auction Web sites have started to adopt the Web services technology to extend and broaden their services. The most typical example is eBay. Its site offers a rich body of eBay APIs to allow user applications to directly communicate the eBay databases in XML format. In other words, the eBay APIs permit an easy construction of custom applications with eBay as the backend. Since 1999, more than 100 eBay APIs have been published to expose eBay Web services, such as pricing information, buy-it-now features, and payment options through its PayPal subsidiary.

Esmaeilsabzali and Larson (2005) use the game theory to model Web services allocation. In their work, they map service providers to auction sellers, and service requestors to auction buyers, but do not consider any Web services-specific features as auction constraints. In other words, they directly apply the existing auction models to Web services negotiation without any adjustments. Defining Web services auction as single-round auctions, they do not consider the re-enterable feature of Web services. Unlike traditional bidding objects that will transfer their ownership from sellers to winners after auctions end, bidding services will never change ownerships away from service providers. Therefore, we argue that Web services auctions should not be simply considered the same as traditional auctions.

Zeng et al. (2004) propose a linear programming approach to maximize a service requestor's quality requirements based on a vector of quality concerns. They present a global planning selection approach that not only takes into account multiple criteria (e.g., price, duration, reliability), but also global constraints and preferences set by service requestors (e.g., budget constraints). A predetermined quality and price are assumed for a service requestor to select among a group of service providers. Their work is completely from the computer science's perspective, without taking into consideration essential economic dynamics of the services negotiation and selection.

Li, Chao, Younas, Huang, and Lu (2005) constructed a testing auction system using multi-agents-based Web services. Templates are defined as generic processes to enable seamless integration and collaboration among services within and across auction places. Zhu and Shan (2005) use agent-oriented modeling language and abstract specification to guide an online auction system construction using Web services.

Researchers have been exploring applying the auction mechanism in Web service resource allocation. Vohra (2001) proves that if users' preferences are incorporated in the centralized resource allocation, searching optimal allocation in terms of economic efficiency is an NP complete problem. Huang et al. (2005) propose a progressive auction mechanism for resource allocation that allows user differentiation of the service value with least resource acquisition latency. Their market-based service bidding model contains four types of components: auctioneer, user agent, market update server, and secured bank. The four roles map to service providers, service requestors, and service registry. Comparing with their work focusing on building a market-oriented resource allocation and pricing rules using progressive auction technique, our research focuses on establishing a fundamental auction model in the context of Web services and explores how to obtain machine-understandable information to predict auctioneers' risk preferences through their risky behaviors.

In summary, a significant amount of research has been conducted on affiliating the Web services technology and auction model. Some reported works adopt the basic format of auction as a negotiation method between Web service providers and requestors. However, since the Web services-specific auction is not the focus of their research, they intuitively utilize the basic concept of auctions to realize price bargaining. These researchers do not consider the specific features of Web services-based auctions, nor do they intend to build a formal model specific for Web services-based auctions. Some other researchers adopt the Web services technology to implement electronic auctions, such as eBay. Essentially they focus on utilizing SOAP messages as communication channels among auction participants. However, the electronic auction models are unchanged from typical electronic auction models. Contrast with either type of their work, our research aims at establishing a fundamental model for adopting an auction model to facilitate Web services negotiation and interactions.

Our earlier research (Zhang et al., 2004) explored the seller-side pricing strategy on e-auctions. We examined the possible pricing strategies based upon how they can differentiate a seller's profits. The work was conducted in the context of the online electronic human-oriented auction. Compared to our previous work, this chapter reports our continuous research on applying the auction model to the interoperable machine-oriented Web services field. We formally define and build a Web services-based auction model. Possible pricing strategies are examined in the context of Web services subject to specific constraints and requirements in the field. In addition, instead of using human background to predict buyers' risk preferences, we propose to analyze WS-Agreement-based SLA documents to automatically elicit service requestors' risk preferences, and propose a dynamic model to adjust predictions based on historical data.

Conclusion

Conducting auctions in the context of Web services introduces unprecedented requirements into the traditional auction model, such as interoperable machine-to-machine interactions, re-enterable bargaining, independent bidding, and so forth. This deeply explored field thus needs reexamination, and new auction models tailored in the field of Web services are in demand. In this chapter we proposed a formal model of Web services-based auctions. We examined the one-sided sealed auction type, a popular auction model that could be applied to Web services-based auctions. We proved mathematically that service providers need to adopt different pricing strategies to pursue higher profit based on service requestors' risk preferences. We argue that Service Level Agreement documents can be used to analyze, quantify, and predict service requestors' preferences. On top of WS-Agreement, we proposed a basic service requestor risk preference elicitation algorithm and a historical data-based service requestor risk preference prediction model. We reported our construction of a prototype of an intelligent engine that helps service providers to select optimal auction strategy for higher profit, which provides a proof-of-concept of our services-oriented auction model.

In order to simplify the discussions of our auction model, we focus on the one-sided sealed auction type. Further work will widen the understanding of the Web services-oriented auction model. Furthermore, at the current stage, we do not consider the overhead and efficiency of the risk preference prediction model and algorithms. This topic will be pursued in future work. However, the work reported in this chapter is an important starting point. To the best of our knowledge, our work is one pioneer work in the topic of applying the auction model into the Web services field. A formal services-oriented model is established, and its usages and applicability are shown. A history data-based risk preference prediction model is presented. In addition, we extend and digitize the traditional abstract concept of risk preference into an interoperable, machine-understandable and processable, quantifiable format based on industry standard-based SLA specifications. The methods and techniques presented in this chapter can be reused to investigate and examine more facades of services-oriented auctions, towards establishing a new research realm on comprehensive services-oriented auctions.

We plan to continue our research along the following directions. We will examine how a service provider's risk preference type influences its auction pricing set up. We will also investigate what kinds of marketing promotions a service provider should take to attract a larger range of potential service requestors. We will enhance the GUI of the intelligent auction registry, and explore how to increase its intelligence on auction strategy prediction and decision. Finally we will closely examine WS-Agreement and formally define extensions for better facilitating service level requirements specifications oriented to Web services auctions.

References

Arrow, K. J. (1963). Comment. *Review of Economics and Statistics, XLV,* 24-27.

Arrow, K. J. (1965). *Aspects of the theory of risk-bearing.* Helsinki.

Byde, A. (2003, June). Applying evolutionary game theory to auction mechanism design. *Proceedings of the IEEE International Conference on E-Commerce* (pp. 347-354).

Esmaeilsabzali, S., & Larson, K. (2005, July 10). Service allocation for composite Web services based on quality attributes. *Proceedings of the 2005 Seventh IEEE International Conference on E-Commerce Technology Workshops* (CECW) (pp. 71-79), Munich, Germany.

E*TRADE. (2006). *Homepage.* Retrieved from *https://us.etrade.com*

Ferris, C., & Farrell, J. (2003). What are Web services? *Communications of the ACM, 46*(6), 31.

Fudenberg, D., & Tirole, J. (1991). *Game theory.* Cambridge, MA: MIT Press.

Gartner. (2003, October 16). *Composite applications head toward the mainstream.* Retrieved from http://www.gartner.com

Hirakiuchi, D., & Sakurai, K. (2001, June). English vs. sealed bid in anonymous electronic auction protocols. *Proceedings of the 10th IEEE International Workshops on Enabling Technologies: Infrastructure for Collaborative Enterprises* (pp. 171-176).

Huang, S., Chen, H., & Zhang, L.-J. (2005, July 11-15). Progressive auction based resource allocation in service-oriented architecture. *Proceedings of the 2005 IEEE International Conference on Services Computing* (SCC) (pp. 85-92), Orlando, FL.

IBM. (2003, January 28). *Web Service Level Agreement (WSLA) language specification, version 1.0.* Retrieved from http://www.research.ibm.com/wsla/WS-LASpecV1-20030128.pdf

Kikuchi, H. (2001, January). Power auction protocol without revealing winning bids. *Proceedings of the 15th International Conference on Information Networking* (ICOIN'01) (pp. 61-64).

Klemperer, P. (1999). Auction theory: A guide to the literature. *Journal of Economic Surveys, 13*(3), 227-286.

Krishna, V. (2002). *Auction theory.* London: Academic Press.

Li, Y., Chao, K.-M., Younas, M., Huang, Y., & Lu, X. (2005, July 20-22). Modeling e-marketplaces with multi-agents Web services. *Proceedings of the 2005 11th International Conference on Parallel and Distributed Systems* (ICPADS) (pp. 175-181), Fukuoka, Japan.

Mas-Colell, A., Whinston, M., & Green, J. (1995). *Microeconomic theory.* Oxford: Oxford University Press.

McAfee, R.P., & McMillan, J. (1987). Auctions and bidding. *Journal of Economic Literature, 25,* 699-738.

Panzieri, F., & Shrivastava, S.K. (1999, October). On the provision of replicated Internet auction services. *Proceedings of the 18th IEEE Symposium on Reliable Distributed Systems* (pp. 390-395).

Porter, M. (1980). An algorithm for suffix stripping program. *Automated Library and Information Systems, 14*(3), 130-137.

Roy, J., & Ramanujan, A. (2001). Understanding Web services. *IEEE IT Professional,* (November), 69-73.

Subramanian, S. (1998, October). Design and verification of a secure electronic auction protocol. *Proceedings of the 17th IEEE Symposium on Reliable Distributed Systems* (pp. 204-210).

Vohra, R.V. (2001, November). Research problems in combinatorial auctions. *Proceedings of the DIMACS Workshop on Computational Issues in Game Theory and Mechanism Design,* Piscataway, NJ.

WS-Agreement. (2005, September 20). *Web Services Agreement Specification (WS-Agreement).* Retrieved from http://www.ggf.org/Public_Comment_Docs/Documents/Oct-2005/WS-AgreementSpecificationDraft050920.pdf

Wurman, P.R., Wellman, M.P., & Walsh, W.E. (1998, May). The Michigan Internet AuctionBot: A configurable auction server for human and software agents. *Proceedings of the 2nd International Conference on Autonomous Agents* (Agent-98) (pp. 301-308), Minneapolis, MN.

Zeng, L., Benatallah, B., Ngu, A.H.H., Dumas, M., Kalagnanam, J., & Chang, H. (2004). QoS-aware middleware for Web services composition. *IEEE Transactions on Software Engineering, 30*(5), 311-327.

Zhang, J., & Chung, J.-Y. (2003). Mockup-driven fast-prototyping methodology for Web application development. *Software Practice & Experience Journal, 33*(13), 1251-1272.

Zhang, J., Zhang, N., & Chung, J.-Y. (2004, July 7-9). Assisting seller pricing strategy selection for electronic auction. *Proceedings of the IEEE Conference on Electronic Commerce* (CEC 2004) (pp. 27-33), San Diego, CA.

Zhu, H., & Shan, L. (2005, February 2-4). Agent-oriented modeling and specification of Web services. *Proceedings of the 10th IEEE International Workshop on Object-Oriented Real-Time Dependable Systems* (WORDS) (pp. 152-159), Sedona, AZ.

Chapter IX

Dynamic, Flow Control-Based Information Management for Web Services

Zahir Tari, RMIT University, Australia

Peter Bertok, RMIT University, Australia

Dusan Simic, RMIT University, Australia

Abstract

Information Flow Control (IFC) is a method of enforcing confidentiality by using labels, data structures for specifying security classifications. IFC is used in programming languages to monitor procedures in an attempt to detect and prevent information leakage. While it ensures greater security, IFC excessively restricts flow of information. This chapter presents a model of information flow control using semi-discretionary label structures. We propose a set of rules that not only increase the flexibility of IFC, but also define labels as a practical component of a security system. We propose a dynamic approach using a centralized model for dynamic label checking, and verify the proposed model using theoretical proofs.

Introduction

Web services have greatly improved the way businesses deal with transactions over the Internet. One of their attractive features is that they operate in a loosely coupled way that facilitates their cooperation and makes them flexible. This advantage, however, comes with some drawbacks—for example, restrictions on access to data are difficult to enforce. Information leak, also called declassification, is a growing concern, as Web services handle customer data that include highly sensitive information. The possibility of unauthorized access to data can affect several aspects of Web service security. Confidentiality of data can be compromised—for example customer credit card data can be accessed by criminals. Privacy breaches also become possible, when data is used for purposes other than those the data was provided for, such as leaking health records of a person.

Several standards have been developed to enhance Web service security. XML Encryption (W3C, 2002a) and XML Signature (W3C, 2002b) are for securing communication. SAML (OASIS, 2005) is designed to facilitate authentication and authorization via exchanging security assertions. In a typical example an SAML message describes that a particular subject has been authenticated by a certain method at a given point in time, or if a subject is allowed to access a particular resource. While SAML provides a mechanism to exchange such security assertions, it is not concerned with establishing or enforcing them; it is the responsibility of the communicating partners to define the security features and implement the relevant mechanisms.

Proposed Approach

In this chapter we propose information flow control as the means to prevent information leakage and declassification. Access to information is controlled by the system, whose modules are distributed, and each participant carries the access control logic that must be applied when handling data. Security labels attached to objects carry information about the sensitivity of the data and describe accessibility. The only way to retrieve or update data is through special modules or plug-ins that are part of the communication infrastructure. The modules check flow legality and administer access rights in a distributed manner.

The approach is suitable to any message-exchange-based system. Our solution uses XML description that suits the XML-SOAP environment of Web services well.

Outline of the Solution

The solution aims at setting up a framework, such as Web services, for subjects who wish to access a set of objects. We define two basic relationships between subjects and objects: ownership and readership. Each object has a set of owners, and each owner can nominate a set of subjects for read access. An object's importance is reflected in the list of subjects who can access it, but the owners' identities have no effect on how valuable an object is. A set of rules that control owners' and readers' rights is strictly enforced. The rules ensure flow legality, so that only subjects with appropriate rights can access an object. The information flow control system is implemented as a set of functions that are linked to the communication modules, for example to SOAP messaging services, and every access to data is performed via these functions.

The rest of this chapter is organized as follows. First, we provide background to the problem of declassification of information. This is followed by a detailed description of the problem. We then detail the core model, and define the label structure and rules that govern system policy. The checking of security labels follows, and an implementation of the model is proposed. Before concluding the chapter, we summarize existing work in the context of databases, programming languages, and Web services, as well as the main elements of the proposed model.

Background

Information Declassification

Web services are based on insecure technology, such as the *Extensible Markup Language* (XML) (W3C, 2000). A number of research publications focused on regulating access to XML documents over the Web (e.g., Damiani, di Vimercati, Paraboschi, & Samarati, 2002a; Gabillon & Bruno, 2001). Due to its flexibility, *Discretionary Access Control* (DAC, commonly referred to as simply "Access Control") (di Vimercati, Paraboschi, & Samarati, 2003) is an obvious choice for enforcing confidentiality throughout a system; it allows policies to be specified at varying granularity levels: from coarsely grained (whole documents and collections) to finely grained (elements and attributes of XML).

Access control, however, operates from the database perspective, preserving security policies only within the scope of a database. Since no security policies are known once information has been retrieved from a resource, it is possible to declassify information (expand access permissions to other users) from within the system itself

(Lampson, 1973). A subject (user or process) attempting declassification must have read permissions on a classified object (resource on the system) and write permissions on another object of lower classification. While systems in general are built of trusted software, in Web services, systems may embrace software they know little about (Deitel, Deitel, DuWaldt, & Trees, 2003).

Declassification occurs when information of a highly classified object flows to an object of lower classification. This may be part of a legal operation, but it also has the potential of information leakage. Direct modification of security policies is easily detected with access control. However, declassification can occur using procedures within the system, and sensitive information can flow to less trusted resources. Flow of information may be explicit (through direct assignment) or implicit (by deriving information through *if* statements and loops) (Denning, 1976). Detection of implicit flow is a delicate operation and requires static analysis (Denning & Denning, 1977).

Access Control vs. Information Flow Control

Information flow control is a method of enforcing confidentiality through a procedural approach. *Labels* (informational capsules containing security classifications) are attached to objects upon access from a resource. Label checking ensures that declassification is detected and prevented. Information flow control models provide robust security grounds in enforcing confidentiality. Bell and LaPadula (1973) applied flow control to programming languages by introducing a simple classification hierarchy and a set of strict rules. However, the lack of flexibility imposes excessive restrictions on information flow. Classification in Radical innovations in flow control was proposed by Denning (1976), presenting a unique dynamic classification hierarchy in the form of a lattice. The work by Denning motivated later research in this area resulting in the development of more flexible flow control models (Myers & Liskov, 1997; Bertino, di Vimercati, Ferrari, & Samarati, 1998).

Applying security involves delicate decision making as we often trade between different characteristics in a security system. Existing work produces a large gap between flexibility and security, which is often the tradeoff in enforcing confidentiality. Access control provides great flexibility for databases in various environments, including Web services. However, since individual users are given the discretion over their own security specifications, mandatory policies are difficult to implement. Information flow control imposes a security structure built on mandatory rules, which, however, lacks in flexibility.

This chapter proposes a model to reduce the tradeoff between security and flexibility. Motivated by Myers and Liskov (1997), our approach looks into both procedural and database perspectives of defining information flow control. We introduce a label structure that allows users to specify semi-discretionary policies, enabling collective declassification and policy change. The proposed model preserves inter-owner trust. This trust can then be used to define rules of permissions given over resources on the system. A complete set of label joining algorithms is also given to assist computational and derivational procedures—rules that define not only permissions, but also object creation and deletion, and modification of label structures, as well as rules that govern the flow of information throughout the system. Furthermore, we define our label structure for specifying policies to objects at varying granularity.

Problem Statement

Every security system defines two primitive entities: *subjects* (active entities representing users and processes) and *objects* (representing resources on the system). Declassification occurs when information of a classified object becomes available to a wider audience. In reality, the number of subjects with read permission for that objects increases. This can be a legal procedure; the owner of the object may declassify it whichever way he or she wants. However, the owner will not be able to control what the users (that have been given access) do with the information they retrieve from that object. In other words, the owner of the object has no control over the dissemination of the object's contents. This problem is common in Access Control, as it applies no control over the flow of information.

Scenario 1

A travel agent prepares programs for travelers, which can include air travel, hotel accommodation, car hire, local programs, and other services. To make reservations with these services, the agent must collect and forward various data about the traveler, such as credit card number, passport number, driver's license number, and so forth. Not all participants are equipped to store sensitive data, in particular if the data is not relevant to the main business activity. For example, the local program organizer does not need drivers' license numbers and should not have access to them. In a simple environment, however, nothing prevents, for example, the car rental agency from forwarding this information to the local program organizer. A subject having access to unnecessary information can misuse it, and at the same time it becomes an attractive target for malicious attacks.

Scenario 2

An online bookshop accepts orders from customers. Each order includes data about the book as well as about the customer. Some data, such as book title and author, must be passed on to the warehouse; other data, such as customer's name and address, must go to the mailing department; and payment data, including credit card numbers, must go to the billing department. While forwarding book data to the billing department is a minor issue, allowing access to customer data by the warehouse may lead to more serious problems, such as access to credit card numbers by unauthorized personnel.

In the following we look at the problem in a more formal way.

Example 1.

Assume existence of a set of subjects, such as that including travel agent (s_a), car rental agency (s_c), local programs organizer (s_l), and a set of objects, such as traveler's personal data (q_c and q_a). Both have a classification hierarchy, which is given in Table 1. The classification of a subject or an object represents its sensitivity.

Assume that object q_c is owned by subject s_c and object q_a is owned by s_a. Data access permissions are given in Table 2 in the form of a DAC access matrix.

From Tables 1 and 2, we can see that subject s_c, who owns q_c, has allowed subject s_a to read the contents of that object, while subject s_l has no access to object q_c. However, since subject s_a has read permission on q_c and read/write permission on q_a, it can flow (copy or derive) information from q_c to q_a (usually denoted as $q_c \rightarrow q_a$). This way, subject s_l gains access to the content of object q_c through object q_a, that is, information is leaked to s_l and object q_c is declassified. Revoking the read access right of s_a on q_c may eliminate the potential of information leakage, but also prevents legal access of s_a to q_c. This example illustrates that looking at access rights in isolation cannot prevent information declassification.

Monitoring the flow of information from object q_c and disallowing any flow to objects of lower classification, such as to object q_a, would be a better solution in the above case. Information flow control works with labels that denote security classifications, instead of relying on capability lists that describe access control policy. Labels can contain conditional requirements for execution, and label checking can be done statically (at compile time) or dynamically (at run time), as will be discussed later in this chapter.

Declassification can occur in two ways: explicitly or implicitly. Explicit flow can arise by assignment or input/output statements via procedures that return values.

Table 1. Simple classification hierarchy

Classification	Objects	Subjects
Top secret	q_c	s_a, s_c
Unclassified	q_a	s_l

Table 2. Simple access matrix

Subject/Object	q_c	q_a
s_a	Read	Read/write
s_l	None	Read
s_c	Read/Write	None

All these are easy to monitor, and disallowing information flow that could lead to declassification is fairly simple in this case. Implicit flow is more difficult to handle, as it can occur in programs using decision-based statements—such as *if* statements, loops, and exceptions—to manipulate objects. Take for example the following code:

```
qa = false;
if(qc == true) {
  qa = true;
}
```

Let us assume that the two variables represent objects q_a and q_c from the previous example. If this code runs on behalf of subject s_a, a flow will be permitted but declassification will occur as q_a effectively contains the value of q_c, so subject s_l now has access to the contents of q_c.

The Model

The proposed model introduces a label structure to assist in defining rules of information flow. It enforces the concept of collective classification change by defining objects with multiple owners through our label structure. To share information, each owner of an object has the ability to nominate other subjects for potential read and write permissions.

Critical modifications of labels, such as owner change, object deletion, permission changes, and legal declassification, are governed by strict rules that preserve inter-owner trust. Effective owners (owners trusted by all co-owners of an object) are entrusted to perform these modifications.

The rules determine permissions, object creation and deletion, legal and collective declassification, modification of label contents, and legality of information flow. As a result, we define a flexible model of information flow control.

A Web-based system can include diverse participants, and the trust relationship between them can vary; some participants may not even know each other. Our model includes a description of trust relationships between participants.

Subjects and Objects

Every information system can be divided into two primitive sets: *subjects* and *objects*. A subject represents an active entity; from the surface it can symbolize a user, underneath it may be a process, operation, or service. An object is a resource on the system; it may be a physical device, such as a printer, or a logical component, a file.

Our focus of Internet-based Web services brings us to a definition of specific subsets. We therefore introduce the following concepts.

Definition 1.
(Subject) A subject is a Web service running on behalf of a user.

Definition 2.
(Object) An object represents data in the form of an XML document. It may be an element of a document, a document itself, or a collection of documents.

We will use the following notation:

- $Q = \{ q_i \mid i = 1,...,n \}$, where n is the number of objects on the system.
- $S = \{ s_g \mid g = 1,...,u \}$, where u is the number of subjects on the system.

Q will be used to define the set of all objects on a system and S will represent the set of all subjects on the same system. A system is a collection of Web services and its resources that comply with the rules of this model.

Labels

Labels contain flow-control-specific information vital for detecting illegal flow. They are attached to and carried along with objects. Their purpose is to map relationships between subjects and objects (such as access control and capability lists), and they reflect user trust in a distinctive way.

We introduce Owners and Readers of objects. A Reader is a subject nominated by an Owner of an object to have read access to the object. Each owner of an object has a set of Readers, that is, a set of subjects who can potentially read that object. Different owners of the same object may have different Reader sets, and the intersection of all Reader sets on an object is called the Effective Reader set of the object. A necessary but not sufficient condition for read access is to be a Reader of an object, as anyone nominated by an Owner is a Reader. A subject can read an object only if all Owners of the object agree to it, that is, the subject has to be a member of the Effective Reader set. Owners of an object also have read access to it. We define the Joint Reader set as one that includes all subjects having read access to the object, that is, it includes Effective Readers and Owners of an object. An Owner of an object may not trust all co-Owners of the same object; those trusted are members of the Owner's Trusted Owners set. The intersection of all Trusted Owner sets is the set of Effective Owners—they are Owners trusted by all co-Owners.

Definition 3.

(Label)

- *A label l_i associated with an object q_i consists of an Owner set O_i, $O_i = \{ o_j \mid j = 1,...,m \}$, where m is the number of owners in O_i.*
- *Every owner o_j has a Reader set R_i, $R_j = \{ r_k \mid k = 1,...,p \}$, where p is the number of readers in R_j.*
- *Every owner o_j also has a Trusted Owner set TO_i, $TO_j = \{ o_h \mid h = 1,...,v \}$, where v is the number of owners in TO_j.*

From that, we can make the following assumptions:

- $O_i \subseteq S$, where S is a set of all subjects on the system, $i = 1,...,n$, and n is the number of objects. Thus, an Owner set is a set of subjects on the system.

- $R_i \subseteq S$, such that $R_i \cup O_i = 0$, where $j = 1,...,m$, and m is the number of owners in O_i. Thus, a Reader set is a set of subjects on the system that are not part of the Owner set for that object.

- $TO_i \subseteq S$, such that $TO_i \subseteq O$. Thus, a Trusted Owner set is a set of subjects on the system that are also part of the Owner set for that object.

For each owner, Reader and Trusted Owner sets provide a nomination-based mechanism. All owners have to come to an agreement in order to modify the classification of an object. Read and write permissions are allocated to subjects elected through this mechanism using an absolute nomination method (requiring nomination of all owners). In accordance to that, we introduce the following sets:

Definition 4.

(Effective Reader set) Let l_i be a label for some object q_p, $\forall o_j$ $(o_j \in O)$, $\exists R_j$ such that $ER_i = \cap_{j=1}^{m} R_j$, where $i = 1,...,n$, and n is the number of objects, m is the number of owners in O_p, defining ER_i as an Effective Reader set of label l_i.

According to the above, Effective Reader set (ER_i) is an intersection between Reader sets of all owners. This implies that all subjects that belong to ER_i have been nominated by all owners to read the object's information. ER_i is also a subset of every R_j in O_i (Reader set of all owners).

Definition 5.

(Effective Owner set) Let l_i be a label for some object q_p, $\forall o_j$ $(o_j \in O)$, $\exists TO_j$ such that $EO_i = \cap_{j=1}^{m} TO_j$ where $i = 1,...,n$, n is the number of objects, m is the number of owners in O_p, defining EO_i as an Effective Owner set of label l_i.

According to Definition 5, Effective Owner set (EO_i) is an intersection between Trusted Owner sets of all owners. This implies that all subjects that belong to EO_i are trusted by all owners. They inherit the ability to perform delicate operations on both the object and its label. EO_i is also a subset of every TO_j in O_i (Trusted Owner set of all owners).

As we will see later in the chapter, permissions are allocated in a hierarchical structure. The following definition forms the basis for defining read permission over objects:

Definition 6.

(Joint Reader set) Let l_i be a label for some object q_p, $JR_q = ER_i \cup O_p$ where i = 1,...,n, and n is the number of labels. JR_q represents the set of all subjects to whom read permission is granted.

Example 2.

Figure 1 shows a simple label defined using XML. Using this structure for Scenario 1 above, we can derive the label sets as defined in this section. This derivation is shown in Table 3. According to this, we can see how our label definition can be applied to Web services using XML. We can also see how different sets within labels are derived.

Label Sets and Permission Rules

In this section, we define and explain rules that are necessary for applying security on a system. While some may be restrictive and convey less flexibility, in handling declassification related problems it is essential to incorporate them. We also present mathematical proofs to verify their existence and importance. We present three sets of rules, one for data access, one for access right modification, and one for creating/deleting objects.

Data Access Rules

We introduce the operator $\triangleright$ to denote permission allowed over an object or its label as follows:

- $\triangleright^r$ denotes *read* permission.
- $\triangleright^>$ denotes *append* permission.
- $\triangleright^w$ denotes *full write* permission.

Reading is the most basic of all access rights and requires the least privileges. Appending to existing data allows dissemination of new information, and hence it needs a more trusted subject. Full write access includes the right to modify/over-

Figure 1. XML representation of the label structure

```
<Label>
    <LabelID>Hotel-booking</LabelID>
    <Owner>
     <OwnerID>Travel-agent</OwnerID>
     <ReaderSet>
        <Read>Local-program-organiser</Read>
        <Read>Car-rental</Read>
     </ReaderSet>
     <TrustedSet>
        <Trust>Hotel</Trust>
        <Trust>Travel-agent </Trust>
     </TrustedSet>
    </Owner>
    <Owner>
     <OwnerID>Hotel</OwnerID>
     <ReaderSet>
        <Read>Local-program-organiser </Read>
     </ReaderSet>
     <TrustedSet>
        <Trust>Hotel</Trust>
     </TrustedSet>
    </Owner>
</Label>
```

write existing data, which is always a delicate operation, as some information may disappear as a result.

Rule 1.

(Read permission) A subject s can read object q if and only if $s \in JR_q$, where $JR_q = ER_q \cup O_q$. Therefore $s \vartriangleright^r q$ iff $s \in JR_q$.

Taking into account Definition 4 (Effective Reader set), we can observe that the rule gives read permission only to subjects that are either owners or effective readers of that object. Since we know that a subject must be trusted by all owners to be an effective reader, read permission is easily justified with comparison to discretionary access control.

Table 3. Derived sets (Abbreviations: TA–Travel agent, H–Hotel, LPO–Local program organizer, CR–Car rental agency)

Set name	Members (Elements of the set)
O	{TA, H}
R_{TA}	{LPO, CR}
R_{H}	{LPO}
TO_{TA}	{TA, H}
TO_{H}	{H}
$ER(R_{TA} \cap R_{H})$	{LPO, CR} ∩ {LPO} = {LPO}
$EO\ (TO_{TA} \cap TO_{H})$	{TA, H} ∩ {H} = {H}
$JR\ (ER \cup O)$	{LPO} ∪ {TA, H} = {LPO, TA, H}

Rule 2.

(Append permission) A subject s can append to object q iff s $\in O_q$. Hence we have: s $\triangleright^>$ q iff s $\in O_q$.

Owner rules are harder to conform and moderate than reader rules, since flexibility is the main tradeoff in defining security. Note that no overwrite (modification) permission is given to owners at this point. Although the above rule appears to offer less flexibility, population of regular owners is easily controlled and conformed. While it prevents regular owners from modification, it does allow them to append to the object's information.

One of the main contributions to the proposed model is the usage of owner trust. We use this concept to form an Effective Owner set.

Rule 3.

(Modification permission) A subject s can update information of object q if and only if s $\in EO_q$. Thus we have: s $\triangleright^w$ q iff s $\in EO_q$.

Let us consider Definition 5 (Effective Owner set) with respect to this rule. We can notice that the restriction of modification operations slightly decreases in the previous three rules. According to the definition of an Effective Owner set, we can comprehend that only subjects who are trusted by all owners may gain the object modification permission.

Modifying Access Rights

Rule 4.

(Reader set) Every subject s (where $s \in O_q$, and owner of some object q) may manipulate its own Reader set such that $s \vartriangleright^w R_{sq}$.

This rule gives a certain amount of discretion to owners by allowing them to manipulate their Reader sets. In using this concept, owners have the right of expression of trust towards other subjects in the system.

A subject s will not be able to exclusively declassify information from an object q, where $s \in O_q$, $O_q \neq \{s\}$ and $s \notin EO_q$, despite $s \vartriangleright^w R_{sq}$. If s is one of the owners of q, where s is not effective (not trusted by other owners), despite being able to both expand and contract its Reader set, s will be unable to declassify information of q.

From the above, we can easily state that Rule 4 has the ability to collectively declassify information. This type of declassification however, taking into account Definition 4 (Effective Reader set), is acceptable as it represents an absolute nomination method, requiring agreement of all owners in order to expand the Effective Reader set.

Rule 5.

(Trusted Owner set) Every subject s, where $s \in O_q$ for some object q, may only expand their Trusted Owner set. Therefore we have $s \vartriangleright^> TO_{sq}$.

The above rule prevents effective owner restriction. For example, when an effective owner adds a new owner to the set, in insuring that he or she will remain effective, the new owner x is assigned a replica of the Effective Owner set, where $TO_x = EO$ by default. Rule 5 prevents the new owner from diminishing effective owners by distrust.

Rule 6.

(Owner change) A subject s can add owners to object q if and only if $s \in EO_q$, but s cannot remove subject p if $p \in EO_q$. Therefore, let $s \in O_q$ and $p \in O_q$, $s \vartriangleright^w O_q$ and s.RemoveOwner(p)$_q$ iff $s \in EO_q$ and $p \notin EO_q$.

Adding new owners to an object can be performed by any effective owner. Effective owners can also remove other owners that do not belong to the Effective Owner set. The function *RemoveOwner(s)$_q$* is used to remove subject s from O_q, the Owner set of some object q, if s does not belong to the Effective Owner set.

Rule 7.

(Declassification) A subject s can add readers to the Effective Reader set ER_q of object q directly by expanding every owners' Reader set, and thus declassify information if and only if $s \in EO_q$. Therefore $s \triangleright^> ER_q$ iff $s \in EO_q$.

Declassification may not be an illegal operation; an owner should have the discretion of declassifying the information of some object if it is trusted by other owners of that object.

Creating and Deleting Objects

Rule 8.

(Object creation) A subject s can create an object q_2 as a child of object q_1 if and only if $s \in O_1$.

Objects on the system form a tree structure. This becomes clear when we examine XML documents, where any element or attribute may be an object. Every element is a child of another object; root elements are children of the document object. We can base our rules on this tree structure and accommodate child labels according to their parents.

Rule 9.

(Object deletion) Subject s can delete an object q if and only if $s \in EO_q$ and $EO_q = \{s\}$.

Deletion of objects is a delicate operation, particularly in security systems; it may disadvantage co-owners of that object. This rule ensures that only a sole effective owner can delete the object. Rule 9 is dependent on Rule 6. Since object deletion requires removal of all owners first, and according to Rule 6, if another owner belongs to the Effective Owner set, it cannot be removed, and thus the object cannot be deleted.

From the above rules we derive the following lemma.

Lemma 1.

Each subject to whom a read permission is allowed for an object is an outcome of agreement of all owners for that object, if that subject is not an owner.

Proof

Let us consider Rule 1 (read permission) in relation to Definition 4 (Effective Reader set), a subject s may read information from an object q only if $s \in ER_q$ or $s \in O_q$, that is, if it belongs to the Effective Reader set or Owner set of that object.

Let us assume that the subject is not an owner ($s \notin O_q$). Since the Effective Reader set is an intersection or all owners' Reader sets, a subject may belong to the Effective Reader set only if it belongs to every owner's Reader set. Thus, if $s \in ER_q$, then $s \in R_1, \dots, s \in R_m$, where m is the number of owners in O_q. Therefore, all owners must come to agreement to allow read permission to a subject.

Permission Hierarchy

The proposed model looks at primitive permissions that form a hierarchy and are determined by the type of access a subject has to an object. The hierarchy consists of the sets listed below with members' access rights listed in brackets.

* *Reader set* (potential to obtain read permission by becoming an Effective Reader).
* *Effective Reader set* (permission to read information of an object).
* *Owner set* (permission to read from and append information to an object).
* *Effective Owner set* (permission to read and write information of an object).

According to the rules of the system, these sets of subjects have additional functionality that follows:

* *Effective Reader set* (copies information according to declassification prevention rules).
* *Owner set* (inherits Effective Reader set functionality, reduces the reader set, collectively declassifies information).
* *Effective Owner set* (inherits Owner set functionality, declassifies information, expands Effective Reader set, deletes an object collectively, removes owners).

Example 3.

Let us consider Example 2 with respect to the above permission hierarchy. We can easily detect all types of subjects:

- *Readers: Car-rental, no permission.*
- *Effective Readers: Local-program-organizer, reader permission.*
- *Regular Owners: Travel-agent, owner rights.*
- *Effective owners: Hotel, full permission.*

Flow Legality

Flow of information may occur explicitly (by direct assignment of value) or implicitly (by deriving a value using loops and conditional statements). We can now define rules to monitor and govern transactions of a system and to prevent explicit information flow. We introduce a new operator, denoted as →, which will help us express the direction of information flow. Note that in any form of information flow, label properties are carried from source to destination.

When information flows from one object to another, access legality must be maintained and no declassification should occur. This is enforced by directly copying Owner sets from source to destination. Original label properties from the destination object are then joined with the properties of the source label by following the rules defined in this chapter.

In maintaining consistent security on the system, we must define rules to conform with the following:

1. *A flow of information must never expand the Joint Reader set.* This means that no new object can gain read access to an object indirectly by flowing information from another subject. By increasing the Joint Reader set, information becomes subject to declassification. Since every object has a number of Reader sets, and an Effective Reader set (ER) is derived from Definition 4, by taking into account Rule 1 (read permission), such a concept is easily established.

2. *Adding owners through information flow may be acceptable only if the new owners already have read access to the source object.* Any owner of an object has the right to read its information and simultaneously append to its given storage space. Since information flow involves passing one object's information on to another, granting append access to a new subject does not leak information, provided that the subject already has read access to the original

object. Furthermore, since declassification depends on owner trust and collective agreement on change of policy, such operations can be allowed.

Rule 10.

(Legal Flow) Information can flow from object q_1 to object q_2 if and only if the Joint Reader set of object q_2, JR_2 is a subset of JR_1 (Joint Reader set of object q_1), where $JR_i = ER_i \cup O_i, i = 1, \ldots , n$, and n is the number of objects on the system. Therefore $q_1 \rightarrow q_2$ iff $JR_2 \subseteq JR_1$.

The above rule ensures that the new object (to which information flows) maintains the same Joint Reader set.

Derived Labels

Rule 10 relies on joining both source and destination labels, and assigning a new label to the destination. We now introduce a new operator $\sqcup$ to indicate label join. Also, every computational procedure on the system (such as *expressional operation, string concatenation, etc.*) requires the inclusion of properties from all objects used in the derivation. In accordance with that, the joining process is expressed as:

$$l_x = l_1 \sqcup l_2$$

where l_1 and l_2 are labels of objects used in deriving l_x. For example, assume two strings (textual objects) "Hello" and "World". The product of concatenating these two strings ("Hello World") must include properties of both objects. By joining labels, we must ensure that $JR_x \subseteq JR_1 \cap JR_2$ always holds. Therefore, the derived label must not give read permission to subjects outside the scope of an intersection between Joint Reader sets of the two objects.

We define the joining function in three different forms: *assigning join* ($\sqcup^a$), *restrictive join* ($\sqcup^r$), and *fusing join* ($\sqcup^f$).

Definition 7.

(Assigning Join - $\sqcup^a$) $l_x = l_1 \sqcup^a l_2$, where $O_x = O_1 \cup (O_2 \cap JR_1)$, such that $\forall o_j (o_j \in O_2), R_{jx} = ER_1 \cup R_j$ and $TO_{jx} = EO_1 \cup TO_j$, where $i = 1, \ldots , m$, and m is the number of owners in O_2.

Figure 2 describes the algorithm for Assigning Join based on Definition 7. The owner set size is represented as m_i where i corresponds to the identity of an object q_i. The product of Assigning Join firstly consumes properties of the source label. Afterward, every owner from the destination object that intersects the Effective Reader set (ER_1) of the source is added to the product, modifying its Reader (R_j) and Trusted Owner (TO_j) sets by union with the Effective Reader (ER_1) and Effective Owner (EO_1) sets of the source, respectively.

Definition 8.

(Restrictive Join - $\sqcup^r$) $l_x = l_1 \sqcup^r l_2$, where $O_x = O_1 \cap O_2$, such that $\forall\ o_j (o_j \in O_x)$, $R_j = R_{j1} \cap R_{j2}$ and $TO_j = TO_{j1} \cap TO_{j2}$, where $j = 1, \dots , m$, and m is the number of owners in O_x.

The algorithm for Restrictive Join is given in Figure 3 based on Definition 8. Firstly, the product of Restrictive Join consumes properties of label l_1. Following that, every owner from l_1 that does not own l_2 is removed from the derived label. In the case where no common owners exist, read permissions are preserved through a new owner μ representing the system itself, after which the object cannot be deleted.

Definition 9.

(Fusing Join - $\sqcup^f$) $l_x = l_1 \sqcup^f l_2$, where $O_x = (O_1 \cup O_2) \cap (JR_1 \cap JR_2)$, such that $\forall\ o_j$, where $o_j \in O_1$ and $o_j \in O_2$, $R_j = R_{j1} \cap R_{j2}$ and $TO_j = TO_{j1} \cap TO_{j2}$, where $j = 1, \dots , m$, and m is the number of owners in O_x.

Figure 4 describes the algorithm for Fusing Join (Definition 9). The product of the Fusing Join is firstly assigned the properties of l_1. All subjects of l_1 that do not belong in the intersection of Joint Reader sets $(JR_1 \cap JR_2)$ of the two objects are removed. Following that, every subject in l_2 that lies in the intersection of JR_1 and JR_2 is added to the derived label. Furthermore, for each subject that owns both objects, the Reader and Trusted Owner sets are intersected by those defined in both labels.

According to Definition 7, the joining procedure combines owners of both objects. In addition to that, every owner in O_2 combines its Trusted Owner set with the Effective Owner set of l_1 $(TO_j \cup EO_1)$. Assigning join will only add owners to the derived label if they belong to the Joint Reader set of the source object (JR_1). This definition is ideal for object assignment. Instead of maintaining the full label of the source, it is combined with the label of destination, embracing the properties of object storage.

Definition 8 is a restrictive joining function. It intersects the Owner sets of both labels, such that every owner in the derived label contains an intersection of both

Figure 2. Assigning Join algorithm

function $AssigningJoin(l_1, l_2)$
$\quad l_x \Leftarrow l_1$
$\quad$ **for all** j such that $0 \leq j \leq m_2$ **do**
$\quad\quad$ **if** $o_j \in ER_1$ **then**
$\quad\quad\quad R_j \Leftarrow R_j \cap ER_1$
$\quad\quad\quad TO_j \Leftarrow TO_j \cup EO_1$
$\quad\quad\quad O_x \Leftarrow O_x \cup \{o_{jj}\}$
$\quad\quad$ **end if**
$\quad$ **end for**
$\quad$ **return** l_x

Figure 3. Restrictive Join algorithm

function $RestrictingJoin(l_1, l_2)$
$\quad l_x \Leftarrow l_1$
$\quad$ **for all** j such that $0 \leq j \leq m_2$ **do**
$\quad\quad$ **if** $o_j \in O_2$ **then**
$\quad\quad\quad R_j \Leftarrow R_{j1} \cap R_{j2}$
$\quad\quad\quad TO_j \Leftarrow TO_{j1} \cap TO_{j2}$
$\quad\quad$ **else** $\{o_j \notin O_2\}$
$\quad\quad\quad O_x \Leftarrow O_x \{o_j\}$
$\quad\quad$ **end if**
$\quad$ **end for**
$\quad$ **if** $O_x = 0$ **then**
$\quad\quad O_\mu \Leftarrow System$
$\quad\quad R_\mu \Leftarrow JR_1 \cap JR_2$
$\quad\quad O_x \Leftarrow \{o_\mu\}$
$\quad$ **end if**
$\quad\quad$ **return** l_x

Reader sets (R_j) and Trusted Owner sets (TO_j) of itself from both labels. This definition is ideal for delicate computational procedures.

We can notice that Definition 9 is more flexible than other joining definitions. This is a result of a union between owners, allowing a discretionary joining procedure and focusing on label specification depending on trust among users.

Figure 4. Fusing Join algorithm

function *FusingJoin(l_1, l_2)*
  $l_x \Leftarrow l_1$
  for all j such that $0 \leq j \leq m_x$ **do**
    if $o_j \notin (JR_1 \cap JR_2)$ **then**
      $O_x \Leftarrow O_x\{o_j\}$
    end if
  end for
  for all j such that $0 \leq j \leq m_2$ **do**
    if $o_j \in O_x \wedge o_j \in (JR_1 \cap JR_2)$ **then**
      $R_{jx} \Leftarrow R_{j1} \cap R_{j2}$
      $TO_{jx} \Leftarrow TO_{j1} \cap TO_{j2}$
    else $o_j \notin O_x \wedge o_j \in (JR_1 \cap JR_2)$
      $O_x \Leftarrow O_x \cup \{o_j\}$
    end if
  end for
  return l_x

The joining of labels occurs when an object is derived from another. Assume that q_1 and q_2 are to be joined. It is obvious that the final product should be available to only those subjects that lie in the intersection between the Joint Reader sets of the two objects. Thus, JR_x (Joint Reader Set of the derived label) would be a subset or equal to $JR_1 \cap JR_2$ (intersection between Joint Reader sets of q_1 and q_2). The following prove that Definitions 7, 8, and 9 do not declassify.

Example 4.

Applying the operations for Scenario 1 above, we can derive the resultant sets for the operations defined in this section. We use the first object (O_1) as shown in Table 3. We also define a second object, and the results are shown in Table 4.

Lemma 2.

In assignment of labels, objects using Assigning Join (Definition 7) will at most retain the Joint Reader set of the source object. Thus, $JR_x \in JR_1$.

Table 4. Derived sets (Abbreviations: TA-Travel agent, H-Hotel, LPO-Local program organizer, CR-Car rental agency)

		Owners	Readers and Trusted Owners	Effective and Joint sets
Object 1	O_1	$O = \{TA, H\}$	$R_{TA} = \{LPO, CR\}$ $R_H = \{LPO\}$ $TO_{TA} = \{TA, H\}$ $TO_H = \{H\}$	$ER_{O1} = \{LPO\}$ $EO_{O1} = \{H\}$ $JR_{O1} =$ $\{TA, H, LPO\}$
Object 2	O_2	$O = \{H, LPO\}$	$R_H = \{H, LPO\}$ $R_{LPO} = \{LPO\}$ $TO_H = \{H, LPO\}$ $TO_{LPO} = \{LPO\}$	$ER_{O2} = \{LPO\}$ $EO_{O2} = \{LPO\}$ $JR_{O2} = \{H, LPO\}$
Assigning Join	O_x	$O = \{H, LPO, TA\}$	$R_{HX} = \{H, LPO\}$ $R_{LPOX} = \{LPO\}$ $TO_{HX} = \{H, LPO\}$ $TO_{LPOX} = \{H, LPO\}$	$ER_{OX} = \{LPO\}$ $EO_{OX} = \{H, LPO\}$ $JR_{OX} =$ $\{H, LPO, TA\}$
Restrictive Join	O_x	$O = \{H\}$	$R_{HX} = \{LPO\}$ $TO_{HX} = \{H\}$	$ER_{OX} = \{LPO\}$ $EO_{OX} = \{H\}$ $JR_{OX} = \{H, LPO\}$
Fusing Join	O_x	$O = \{H, LPO\}$	$R_{HX} = \{LPO\}$ $R_{LPOX} = \{empty\}$ $TO_{HX} = \{H\}$ $TO_{LPOX} = \{empty\}$	$ER_{OX} = \{empty\}$ $EO_{OX} = \{empty\}$ $JR_{OX} = \{H, LPO\}$

Proof

Let us assume l_1 and l_2 are labels for two objects on the system q_1 and q_2 respectively, where information flows from q_1 to q_2 by assignment. Following Definition 7 (Assigning Join), $O_x = O_1 \cup (O_2 \cap JR_1)$, implying that the owners of the source object q_1 are preserved. Additionally, owners of the destination object are kept only if they belong to the Joint Reader set of the source object. Therefore, since $O_1 \subseteq JR_1$, $O_1 \cup (O_2 \cap JR_1) \subseteq JR_1$. According to that, we have: $O_x \subseteq JR_1$. In preserving the properties of the source object, effective readers and owners are appended to every new owner's Reader set and Trusted Owner set respectively. Since $R_{jx} = ER_1 \cup R_j$ for every owner accepted from O_2, $ER_x = ER_1$ (from Definition 4), $ER_x \subseteq JR_1$.

According to Definition 6 (Joint Reader set), $JR_i = O_i \cup ER_i$ for some object q_i. Thus, since $O_x \cup ER_x \subseteq JR_1$, $JR_x \subseteq JR_1$. Rule 1 (read permission), states that a read permission on an object O_i may be allowed to a subject s if and only if $s \subseteq JR_i$. Therefore, Definition 7 (Assigning Join) does not declassify.

Lemma 3.

In derivation of labels, objects using Restrictive Join (Definition 8) will at most retain their Joint Reader sets. Thus, $JR_x \subseteq JR_1 \cap JR_2$.

Proof

Let us assume l_1 and l_2 are labels for two objects on the system q_1 and q_2 respectively. By following Definition 8 (Restrictive Join), $O_x = O_1 \cap O_2$, implying that the derived Owner set (O_x) will be an intersection between Owner sets of q_1 and q_2. Since $O_1 \subseteq JR_1$ and $O_2 \subseteq JR_2$, $O_1 \cap O_2 \subseteq JR_1 \cap JR_2$. Therefore, we have: $O_x \subseteq JR_1 \cap JR_2$. By taking into account Definition 4 (Effective Reader set), $ER_x = \cap_{j=1}^{m} JR_j$ where $j = 1, \ldots, m$, and m is the number of owners in O_x, $O_1 \cap O_2$ implies $ER_1 \cap ER_2$. Then we have: $ER_x \subseteq JR_1 \cap JR_2$. According to Definition 6 (Joint Reader set), $JR_i = O_i \cup ER_i$ for some object q_i. Thus, since $O_x \cup ER_x \subseteq JR_1 \cap JR_2$, $JR_x \subseteq JR_1 \cap JR_2$. Rule 1 (read permission) states that a read permission on an object O_i may be allowed to a subject s if and only if $s \in JR_i$. Therefore, Definition 8 (Restrictive Join) does not declassify.

Lemma 4.

In derivation of labels, objects using Fusing Join (Definition 9) will at most retain their Joint Reader sets. Thus, $JR_x \subseteq JR_1 \cap JR_2$.

Proof

Let us assume l_1 and l_2 are labels for two objects on the system q_1 and q_2 respectively. By following Definition 9 (Fusing Join), $O_x = (O_1 \cup O_2) \cap (JR_1 \cap JR_2)$, implying that the derived Owner set (O_x) will be a union between Owner sets of q_1 and q_2 that belong to the intersection of Joint Reader sets of the two objects $(JR_1 \cap JR_2)$. According to this, we have $O_x \subseteq JR_1 \cap JR_2$. This implies that every owner of the derived label must previously have read access—that is, belong to either the Owner set or Effective Reader set of both objects. Also, by taking into account Definition 4 (Effective Reader set), $ER_x = \cap_{j=1}^{m} JR_j$ where $j = 1, \ldots, m$, and m is the number of owners in O_x, $O_1 \cup O_2$ implies $ER_1 \cap ER_2$. Therefore, we have: $ER_x \subseteq JR_1 \cap JR_2$. According to Definition 6 (Joint Reader set), $JR_i = O_i \cup ER_i$ for some object q_i. Thus, since $O_x \cup ER_x \subseteq JR_i \cap JR_2$, $JR_x \subseteq JR_i \cap JR_2$. Rule 1 (read permission), states that a read permission on an object O_i may be allowed to a subject s if and only if $s \in JR_i$. Therefore, Definition 9 (Fusing Join) does not declassify.

Lemma 5.

The definitions 7-9 are reflexive—that is, $l_i \sqcup l_i = l_i$.

Proof

Assigning Join (Definition 7) will reflexively perform its joining by $O_x = O_i \cup (O_i \cap JR_i)$. Since $O_i \subseteq JR_i$, $(O_i \cap JR_i) = O_i$. Also, $O_i \cup O_i = O_i$, and therefore $O_x = O_i$. Furthermore, $\forall o_j$, where $o_j \in O_i$, $R_{jx} = ER_i \cup R_j$ and $TO_{jx} = EO_i \cup TO_j$. Since $ER_i \subseteq R_j$ and $EO_i \subseteq TO_j$ (according to Definitions 4 and 5 respectively), $ER_i \cup R_j = R_j$ and $EO_i \cup TO_j = TO_j$, so $R_{jx} = R_j$ and $TO_{jx} = TO_j$. According to that, nothing changes in the label structure, and therefore we have: $l_i \sqcup^a l_i = l_i$.

Restrictive Join (Definition 8) will reflexively perform its joining by $O_x = O_i \cap O_i$. Since $O_i \cap O_i = O_i$, $O_x = O_i$. Then, $\forall o_j$, where $o_j \in O_x$, $R_j = R_{ji} \cap R_{ji}$ and $TO_j = TO_{ji} \cap TO_{ji}$. As $O_x = O_i$, $R_j = R_{ji}$ and $TO_j = TO_{ji}$. No changes are made to the label, thus $l_i \sqcup^r l_i = l_i$.

Fusing Join (Definition 9) will reflexively perform its joining by $O_x = (O_i \cup O_i) \cap (JR_i \cap JR_i) = O_i \cap JR_i$. Since $O_i \subseteq JR_i$, $O_x = O_i$. Also, $\forall o_j$, where $o_j \in O_i$, $R_j = R_{ji} \cap R_{ji}$ and $TO_j = TO_{ji} \cap TO_{ji}$, implying that $R_j = R_{ji}$ and $TO_j = TO_{ji}$. Since no changes occur in the label structure $l_i \sqcup^f l_i = l_i$.

Example 5.

Assume existence of two objects q_1 and q_2 in a scenario where information is to flow in the form of $q_1 \rightarrow q_2$ by assignment. Assume two labels l_1 and l_2, which are respectively mapped to the objects, described in Table 5.

From Table 5, we can conclude the following sets: $ER_1 = \{s_6, s_7\}$, $EO_1 = \{s_1\}$, $JR_1 = \{s_1, s_2, s_3, s_6, s_7\}$, $ER_2 = \{s_{10}\}$, $EO_2 = \{s_7\}$, and $JR_2 = \{s_6, s_7, s_{10}\}$.

Both owners and readers belong to S (set of all subjects on the system). In performing an assigning join of the two labels, we can trace the following steps.

1. *Manipulate every owner's Reader set and Trusted Owner set in l'_2 by uniting it with ER_1 (Effective Reader set of l_1) and EO_1 (Effective Owner set of l_1) respectively. $TO(s_6)' \cup EO_1 = \{s_1, s_7\}$, $TO(s_7)' \cup EO_1 = \{s_1\}$*

2. *Owner sets are joined with the standard union operator $\cup$. We have: $O'_2 = \{s_1, s_2, s_3, s_6, s_7\}$.*

Table 5. Label structure example

Label	Owner	Reader set	Trusted Owner set
l_1	s_1	s_4, s_6, s_7	s_1
	s_2	s_6, s_7	s_1, s_2, s_3
	s_3	s_4, s_5, s_6, s_7	s_1, s_2, s_3
l_2	s_6	s_9, s_{10}	s_6, s_7
	s_7	s_8, s_{10}	s_7

3.   Compilation of a new label following elimination of new owners from Reader sets, as seen in Table 6.

From these simple computational steps, we can conclude that the new label has the following properties: $ER'_2 = 0$, $EO'_2 = \{s_1\}$, and $JR'_2 = \{s_1, s_2, s_3, s_6, s_7\}$.

Through subject conversion, we can clearly see that no read permission is allowed outside the scope of original object's label. Also, the new object's Effective Reader set and Effective Owner set are kept strict to ensure no additional owners can declassify this information. This procedure must also follow the modification rules of the destination object. According to Rule 3 only an effective owner can modify the object's information, while full label modification rights depend on the individuality of that effective owner. From Example 5 we may notice that s_7 can perform this type of information flow, while s_6 cannot since it is not trusted by s_7 in the original label.

Lemma 6.

By taking into account the joining Definitions 7, 8, and 9, we can state that Rule 10 will not leak information to unauthorized subjects in the event of information flow.

Proof

In accordance with Rule 3 (modification permission), a subject s initiating information flow must belong to EO_d ($s \in EO_d$, the Effective Owner set of q_d). Also, according to Rule 1 (read permission), s must be either an effective reader ($s \in ER_s$) or an owner ($s \in O_s$) of the source object. Therefore, s should be given read permission on the new object. Our proposal states that in such a situation, s can become a new owner.

Table 6. Derived label structure example

Label	Owner	Reader set	Trusted Owner set
l'_2	s_1	s_4	s_1
	s_2		s_1, s_2, s_3
	s_3	s_4, s_5	s_1, s_2, s_3
	s_6	s_9, s_{10}	s_1, s_6, s_7
	s_7	s_8, s_{10}	s_1, s_7

In relation to Rule 5 (Trusted Owner set) and Definition 7 (Assigning Join), when flow of information occurs, the Effective Owner set of the source object joins each new owner's Trusted Owner set. Also, taking into perspective Rule 4 (Reader set) and Lemma 1 on read permission, each new owner can expand their Reader sets without illegal declassification. Thus, as long as every owner of q_d belongs to either the Effective Reader set (ER_s) or Owner set (O_s) of the source object, or as we have simply defined JR_s, no information can leak. Also, Definitions 8 and 9 at most retain the intersection of Joint Reader sets between the objects used in the derivation (as proven by Lemmas 3 and 4 respectively). According to this, information can only flow upward in the lattice, preventing information leakage.

Label Checking

In the previous section we described a model that provides the level of flexibility as required for developing XML-based Web services. In this section we describe how declassification can be prevented and security enforced by checking labels in both static and dynamic fashion, for implementing our model.

Combined Label Checking

Imposing access control at varying granularity and enforcing control over information flow heavily relies on two primitive methods of label checking:

- *Dynamic* (run time) checking monitors information flow, including computational inputs and outputs. It conforms to the rules of the model and inherits the power to prevent information from flowing into suspect objects that may cause information leakage.

- *Static* (compile time) checking obtains a snapshot of subjects and objects, their respective rights and security classes, and captures computational flow at a specific point in time.

Information flow can occur both *explicitly* (by direct influence of one object to another) and *implicitly* (by logical influence, including loops and if statements). Explicit flow can easily be detected using both static and dynamic label checking, by observing inputs and outputs, and simple computation throughout a transaction.

Implicit flow, however, cannot easily be detected using dynamic checking, and in accordance, usually relies on static analysis (Denning, 1977). On the other hand, in such an immensely distributed environment such as the Web, dynamic label checking is vital for providing flexibility to systems that frequently change shape.

Static Label Checking

Static checking involves taking a snapshot of the system structure at a given time and analyzing its information flow. In a Web service architecture, static checking is divided into two components:

- **Build time static analysis:** This configures compilers and service builders to analyze information flow (for example, analyzing a service at ant build time for Java Web services, or at javac Java compiler).
- **Dynamic certificate manager:** This examines application certificates, subject permissions (effective in accordance to object labels), and object classifications and structures. Certified code may be allowed to perform computations on its own.

Build time static analysis requires reconfiguration of compilers and build tools in order to let applications become aware of objects' labels. While its implementation may be difficult to accomplish, its existence is vital for providing a guarantee of security compliance. Dynamic checking may fail; upon its failure, statically analyzed code will not leak information (Myers & Liskov, 1997).

Dynamic certificate manager is a method of adopting a semi-centralized model. While dynamic checking relies on a centralized architecture, moderating all information flow throughout the scope of the system, statically analyzed code should be granted computational access over the system's objects locally.

As we have seen, flow of information can occur both explicitly (by direct assignment or derivation) and implicitly (through loops and decision statements). Static checking must monitor all information flow in order to fulfill its duty in preventing declassification. Explicit flow is easily detected using dynamic label checking, which can easily be incorporated into compilers and therefore can be used to keep track of information flow statically.

Implicit flow, however, requires a projection of possible inputs and outputs to and from services; in this case, a parser or a stack can be used to map a program's structure and observe its behavior. However, even in such a case, it can be complicated to know all combinations of information flow, particularly in large and complex software.

In our approach we consider the solution proposed in Myers and Liskov (1997) for static label checking using *basic block labels*. Every block of code is assigned a label that propagates throughout the code, specifying security classification levels at every stage.

Consider Table 7 where a simple segment of code is given. Unlabelled information is given the value $\perp$, effectively available to every subject on the system. While ordinary assignment into b from unlabelled information is legal, the *if* statement (lines 2-4) implicitly flows information from a into b. By checking labels at run time, it would be difficult to capture this type of information flow. Dynamic checking can still be implemented for this purpose, however the amount of information necessary for securing the transaction increases complexity and reduces efficiency. Furthermore, it may be impractical to perform this type of label checking at all.

Myers and Liskov (1997) discuss issues on handling this problem; we will extend their solution to comply to our proposal. Let us consider all blocks of code where assignment is used (such as lines 1 and 3). Now we can label each block according to the information that is assigned. We will also take into account loops and *if* statements, and extend the basic block label according to the information assessed within those statements. In the event of assigning unlabelled information to objects, we will use the $\perp$ operator. Every basic block label is denoted as l_B.

Now we can examine Table 7. Line 1 assigns a basic block of $\perp$ since 0 is unlabelled. Line 2 contains an *if* statement which assesses object a, and hence we extend the statement with l_a (label of a). Then b is assigned the value of 1 in line 3. Since the statement itself was extended, we assign the new basic block label with l_a.

The idea behind the basic block label is to understand the label properties required in the final outcome in order to insure that no information leaks. The process of assigning the new label follows code completion and union of all basic block labels consumed in the program's execution. Therefore:

$$\sqcup_z l_x = l_1 \sqcup l_2 \sqcup \ldots \sqcup l_x$$

where z is the number of blocks consumed, and x is the final label.

Table 7. Code with basic block labels

	Normal code	Basic block labels
1	$b \Leftarrow 0$	$l_B = \perp$
2	if $a = 1$ then	*extend l_a*
3	$b \Leftarrow 1$	$l_B = l_a$
4	endif	$l_B = \perp$

Dynamic Label Checking

Dynamic label checking follows the rules of the security system and ensures that all transactions are compliant with the model. While it is difficult to gain knowledge of computations within applications, static checking can improve its efficiency. Detailed procedures regarding dynamic checking are given in the following section.

Dynamic Checking Architecture

It is important to outline an architectural design before allocating resources in a distributed environment. A significant factor in securing Web services is trust. Once this is evident, we may build security systems accordingly. This chapter investigated implications of information flow control (IFC) in a distrusted environment.

Subjects and objects represent separate entities on the system, and therefore they can be mapped as separate bodies. However, the predicament lies in controlling the flow of information throughout the scope of the system. According to that, we propose an architecture as given in Figure 5.

Dynamic label checking requires detailed knowledge of individual calculations and derivations. In a simple case we will make an assumption that the code has not been checked using static analysis, and all transactions made by it require dynamic checking.

Using the architecture given in Figure 5, we can incorporate a system to evolve around the information flow control service. This can be done by hiding detailed information about services and objects from each other. A location of the IFC is given instead of the service location itself, along with an identification number. As a result, when a service requests another service, IFC is notified and the request is forwarded, leaving the reply-to location of IFC and the requester's identification number. An example sequence of this process is illustrated in Figure 6.

On the other hand, computations may be performed without notifying IFC causing modification of label properties, in which case we must ensure that all computations

Figure 5. Dynamic checking architecture

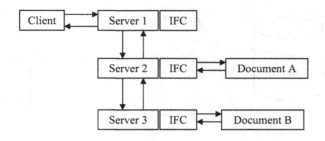

Figure 6. Dynamic checking sequence

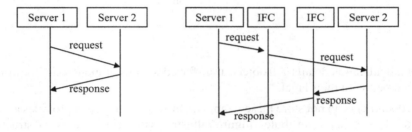

and derivations are performed in IFC. This can be achieved using static analysis, by introducing services to the system on the basis of certificates. However, this considerably decreases flexibility as we often incorporate distrusted services as part of the system. A better way of enforcing this architecture is by encrypting all transactions, compelling services to perform computations on IFC. Furthermore, by using encryption, we can eliminate the buffer between services on the system. According to that, IFC is used only as a buffer between subjects and objects.

Information Flow Control (IFC) Service

IFC service is the most important component of the system. Its purpose is to perform dynamic checking according to the rules of the model, carry out computations for services, and validate computational activity. Web services are classified only by

Figure 7. Label database

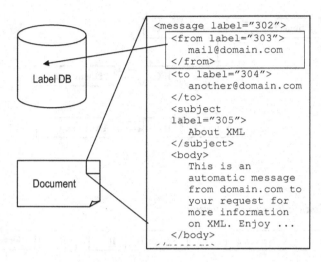

```
<message label="302">
    <from label="303">
        mail@domain.com
    </from>
    <to label="304">
        another@domain.com
    </to>
    <subject
    label="305">
        About XML
    </subject>
    <body>
        This is an
        automatic message
        from domain.com to
        your request for
        more information
        on XML. Enjoy ...
    </body>
```

their authentication details. All objects transferred within components of the system are wrapped with their label.

XML documents do not store these wrappers. Instead, each object provides a reference to a label by using attributes. Figure 7 illustrates this. Having a nested structure, the propagation of labels depends on the extensiveness of recursive depth, provided that elements included contain no label. This is illustrated in Figure 7. The <from> element contains a local label (label properties do not propagate), while properties of <message> propagate to <body>.

As the architecture suggests, documents are hidden behind the IFC. When a service requests for an object, IFC will check the authenticity of the subject on whose behalf it is running, wrap the object with its label, and respond. Object wrapping is encrypted with a key that only IFC knows. By using encryption, object contents are hidden from services, forcing them to make computations only through IFC. Services certified using static analysis may be given the key, allowing computations to be performed outside IFC.

Implementation

Developing Web services alone requires detailed design and deep understanding of distributed computing. While it has become an increasingly popular method of information exchange between businesses on the Internet, its design and maintenance comes at a high price. Having XML as a main communication language, which despite its popularity and wideness of use remains to this date insecure, substantially raises the level of complexity of Web services. This section discusses issues specific to implementation and provides solutions that form the basis for implementing our model.

IFC Functions

IFC provides functions to aid computational procedures. In this chapter, we will examine simple types such as String, int, float, and Boolean objects. We introduce a Wrap structure, containing an object and its relevant label, together encrypted with a key that is only known by IFC. From these types, we can produce computational functions. Note that each of the following functions return a Wrap object containing the derived object and a new label.

- **Wrap Assign(Wrap to, Wrap from):** Simple flow by assignment from one object to another that follows Rule 10 using Assigning Join (Definition 7).
- **Wrap StrictExpr(Wrap to, String expr, Wrap[]):** Flow information by deriving an expression with included wrapped objects using Restrictive Join (Definition 8).
- **Wrap FlexiExpr(Wrap to, String expr, Wrap[]):** Flow information by deriving an expression with included wrapped objects using Fusing Join (Definition 9).
- **Wrap Wrapper(Object source):** Wrap unlabelled information.

In addition to the above, IFC also provides functions to handle object requests and direct label modifications. In each of the following, Auth object is passed through methods, containing authentication details of the subject in process. OPath uses the XPath language (W3C , 2001) to reference the object in access. In addition to that, we also use Subject to represent a subject on the system for label modification functions.

- **Wrap Read(OPath object, Auth subject):** Request read access to an object (follows Rule 1, read permission).
- **boolean Append(OPath object, Auth subject, Wrap newobject):** Request append access to an object (follows Rule 2, append permission).
- **boolean Write(OPath object, Auth subject, Wrap newobject):** Request write access to an object (follows Rule 3, modification/write permission).

- **boolean AddReader(OPath object, Auth subject, Subject reader):** Add a reader to the label (follows Rule 4, reader set).

- **boolean RemoveReader(OPath object, Auth subject, Subject reader):** Remove a reader from the label (follows Rule 4, reader set).

- **boolean AddOwner(OPath object, Auth subject, Subject owner):** Add a new owner to the label (follows Rule 6, owner change).

- **boolean RemoveOwner(OPath object, Auth subject, Subject owner):** Remove an owner from the label (follows Rule 6, owner change).

- **boolean TrustOwner(OPath object, Auth subject, Subject owner):** Add an owner to the trusted set (follows Rule 5, trusted owner).

- **boolean Declassify(OPath object, Auth subject, Subject reader):** Add a reader to the Effective Reader set (follows Rule 7, declassification).

Implementation of the above functions takes into account the status of the invoking subject. They follow the rules of this model, and return either *null* or *false* when the rules are broken. The following functions are exclusive to IFC:

- **Label AssigningJoin(Label source, Label destination):** Assigning join of two labels in accordance to Definition 7.

- **Label RestrictiveJoin(Label l1, Label l2):** Restrictive join of two labels in accordance to Definition 8.

- **Label FusingJoin(Label l1, Label l2):** Fusing join of two labels in accordance to Definition 9.

- **Wrap WrapObject(Object obj, Label lab):** Encrypt an object and its label, and wrap them together for uncertified services.

- **Object UnwrapObject(Wrap object):** Decrypt an object from its wrap for use within IFC and certified services.

- **Label UnwrapLabel(Wrap object):** Decrypt an object's label from its wrap for use within IFC and certified services.

Testing

The proposed model was examined in a laboratory environment. The experiments tested the results of operations, in particular how the different read and owner sets were derived by the system in different scenarios. In this section we provide some of the results produced by the system. The examples show a comparison between Restrictive Join (Definition 8) and Fusing Join (Definition 9) algorithms using different label contents.

Table 8 presents results of joining two labels with intersecting Owner and Effective Reader sets. As we can see, subject s_3 is deliberately placed as an effective reader of l_1 for the purpose of testing Restrictive Join. In reality, both joining algorithms should produce a near intersection of Joint Reader sets (i.e., $JR_x \subseteq JR_1 \cap JR_2$). According to that, the resulting label should contain the following elements: $\{s_2, s_3, s_5\}$, where s_2 is an owner of both objects, and s_3 and s_5 exist in both l_1 and l_2 as either owners or effective readers.

The problem of Restrictive Join is evident. By intersecting Owner sets, only subjects that belong to a consistent class for both objects (i.e., either only owners or effective readers of both objects) are included in the derived label. Subject s_3 is an owner of one object, but an effective reader of the other. Since it does not lie in the intersection of Owner sets or Effective Reader sets, it has automatically restricted access.

In a different context, we have defined two labels of symmetric structure, as shown in Table 9. According to the Restrictive Join algorithm (Figure 3), a derived label

Table 8. Screenshot of intersecting label joining

Label l_1		Label l_2	
Owner s_1		Owner s_2	
Readers	$\{s_3, s_4, s_5\}$	Readers	$\{s_4, s_5\}$
Trusted Owners	$\{s_1, s_2\}$	Trusted Owners	$\{s_2, s_3\}$
Owner s_2		Owner s_3	
Readers	$\{s_3, s_5, s_6\}$	Readers	$\{s_4, s_5\}$
Trusted Owners	$\{s_2\}$	Trusted Owners	$\{s_2, s_3\}$
Effective Readers	$\{s_3, s_5\}$	Effective Readers	$\{s_4, s_5\}$
Effective Owners	$\{s_2\}$	Effective Owners	$\{s_2, s_3\}$
Joint Reader set	$\{s_1, s_2, s_3, s_5\}$	Joint Reader set	$\{s_2, s_3, s_4, s_5\}$
$l_1 \sqcup^r l_2$		$l_1 \sqcup^s l_2$	
Owner s_2		Owner s_2	
Readers	$\{s_5\}$	Readers	$\{s_5\}$
Trusted Owners	$\{s_2\}$	Trusted Owners	$\{s_2\}$
		Owner s_3	
		Readers	$\{s_4, s_5\}$
		Trusted Owners	$\{s_2, s_3\}$
Effective Readers	$\{s_5\}$	Effective Readers	$\{s_5\}$
Effective Owners	$\{s_2\}$	Effective Owners	$\{s_2\}$
Joint Reader set	$\{s_2, s_5\}$	Joint Reader set	$\{s_2, s_3, s_5\}$

Table 9. Screenshot of symmetric label joining

Label l_1		Label l_2	
Owner s_1		Owner s_3	
Readers	$\{s_3, s_4\}$	Readers	$\{s_1, s_2\}$
Trusted Owners	$\{s_1, s_2\}$	Trusted Owners	$\{s_3, s_4\}$
Owner s_2		Owner s_4	
Readers	$\{s_3, s_4\}$	Readers	$\{s_1, s_2\}$
Trusted Owners	$\{s_1, s_2\}$	Trusted Owners	$\{s_3, s_4\}$
Effective Readers	$\{s_3, s_4\}$	Effective Readers	$\{s_1, s_2\}$
Effective Owners	$\{s_1, s_2\}$	Effective Owners	$\{s_3, s_4\}$
Joint Reader set	$\{s_1, s_2, s_3, s_4\}$	Joint Reader set	$\{s_1, s_2, s_3, s_4\}$
$l_1 \sqcup l_2$		$l_1 \sqcup^r l_2$	
Owner s_μ		Owner s_1	$\ldots$
Readers	$\{s_1, s_2, s_3, s_4\}$	Owner s_2	$\ldots$
Trusted Owners	$\{s_\mu\}$	Owner s_3	$\ldots$
		Owner s_4	$\ldots$
Effective Readers	$\{s_1, s_2, s_3, s_4\}$	Effective Readers	0
Effective Owners	$\{s_\mu\}$	Effective Owners	0
Joint Reader set	$\{s_\mu, s_1, s_2, s_3, s_4\}$	Joint Reader set	$\{s_1, s_2, s_3, s_4\}$

must always preserve the intersection of Effective Reader sets in spite of the extents of its Owner set. According to this testing scenario, restrictive label joining leaves the label without an owner. Since effective readers must be specified through object owners, a new owner is created on behalf of the system, notated as s_μ.

According to these demonstrations, and in verification from Lemmas 3 and 4, we find that Fusing Join (Definition 9) provides greater flexibility in joining labels than Restrictive Join (Definition 8).

Related Work

A large amount of work has been done in the area of information flow control. Early work in this area was presented by Bell and LaPadula (1973) where a model of information flow control is proposed. This model provides a fixed classification hierarchy, however the proposed rules are rigid and excessively restrict the flow of information as they focus only on read and write permissions, overlooking modification of security classifications. Later, Denning (1976) focused on the definition of rules to characterize legal information flow and presented a lattice model of secure information flow in computer systems. The lattice properties allow the formulation of requirements to aid the enforcement of security. Further work by Denning and Denning (1977) described a certification mechanism for verifying secure information flow throughout programs using static analysis. This procedure provided the basis for implementing static analysis in the well-known compilers.

In what follows we will provide a summary of information flow control techniques in three main areas, namely programming languages, databases, and Web services.

Programming Languages

An early work in this area is from Jones and Liskov (1978) where an extended programming language is proposed to express constraints on data access. This extension provides controlled information sharing in programming languages. The constraints can be stated declaratively and enforced by static checking. This model can be applied to different types of languages, while its full potential is unveiled in languages that support abstract data types.

A sound type system for a secure flow analysis was proposed by Volpano, Smith, and Irvine (1996). The model contributes towards a secure information flow within programs in the context of multiple sensitivity levels. In relation to the semantics of programming languages, verification of soundness is confirmed showing that well-typed programs feature a non-interference property.

Probably the most recent and significant work in the area of information flow control for programming languages is by Myers and Liskov (1997). They proposed a label model with mutual trust and decentralized authority. The label structure preserves the sources of information (owners), allowing property manipulation of security classifications in a decentralized way. Furthermore, they showed how static label checking could be used to certify legality of information flow, while reducing the requirement for dynamic label checking. Further work by Myers and Liskov (1998) extended the decentralized label model by increasing flexibility and expressiveness. The solution addressed the limitations of their previous work, such as replacement of owners and expansion of readers. Later Myers and Liskov (2000) showed how the decentralized label model could be used for protecting privacy. Further, they introduced an extension to the Java language, providing a static checking mechanism using the proposed label model (Jif).

The work by Myers and Flow (1999) introduced a new language, called Jflow, for static information flow checking. This extends the Java language to add annotations for statically checked information. The proposed features include a decentralized label model (Myers & Liskov, 1997), label polymorphism, dynamic label checking, and automatic label inference.

Li (2002) analyzed information flow in Java programs and proposed a slicing technique. The usage of this technique allows computation of the amount, width, and correlation of information flow.

Bandhakavi, Zhang, and Winslett (2006) proposed a logic for controlling the reuse and release of information. They included constructs that gave the data owner a range of options to mark information, from freely available (immediate declassification) to permanently blocked, and allowed controlled declassification. Blocking was applicable to data items as well as to any conclusion derived from the data itself. They used sticky policies, in which the data carried the classification information wherever it went, and the content of the data was revealed only to those parties that proved that they were authorized to view it. To avoid unwanted declassification, users could not override policies of other parties. Re-classification, the opposite of declassification, was not supported by the system. The authors mentioned time constraints, for example policy expiry or time-based declassification, as future work.

Database Systems

A flexible approach for information flow control in object-oriented systems was described by Ferrari, Samarati, Bertino, and Jajodia (1997). Exceptions to restrictions in information flow are specified by means of waivers associated with methods. A set of formal conditions is defined to ensure consistency in safe information flow. Bertino and Ferrari (2002) presented a verification of applying waivers to invocation and reply of methods by providing experimental results in enforcing safe information flow.

Modification of subject permissions in access control requires change in all authorization policies for which the subject takes effect (di Vimercati et al., 2003). Park, Sandhu, and Ahn (2001) presented two architectures for *RBAC* (Role-Based Access Control) on the Web. These architectures are identified as User-pull and Server-pull. A dynamically authorized role-based access control model for a secure distributed computation is proposed by Kuo and Humenn (2002). By using role-based credentials to accommodate subject properties, modification of user permissions is simplified.

Lategan and Olivier (2001) presented a solution to the problem of granting limited access to private information. Classification of private information is based on the purpose it is acquired for. Private information is revealed at the very last stage. Park and Sandhu (2002) suggested a concept of Usage Control (UCON) that encompasses traditional access control, trust management, and digital rights management. Usage Control moderates access and usage of information on both the client side and server side.

An approach of information flow analysis for an RBAC system is proposed by Osborn (2002). A general mapping is given, which from an arbitrary role graph produces a graph of information flow that can result from the defined roles. In a similar way, Belokosztolszki, Eyers, and Moody (2003) presented an approach that examines the potential for unintentional leakage of information during RBAC policy enforcement.

Web Services

An important piece of work done in the area of Web services security is by Damiani et al. (2000). An access control model is proposed to protect information distribution, allowing the definition and enforcement of access restrictions directly on the XML structure and its content. Authorization policies provide a mapping of subjects and objects to include permission types, propagation through the XML structure, and definition of authorization depth at both document and schema level. Further work by Damiani et al. (2001) describes an access control for XML documents as a simple and effective way of protecting data at the same granularity level provided by the XML scheme. A general technique (to specify and enforce access control for Web services) is later presented by Damiani et al. (2002b). In relation to that, Damiani et al. (2002a) described a fine-grained access control system for XML documents, where the access control model takes the semi-structured organization of data and their semantics into consideration.

Other work on XML is pretty extensive. Here we summarize some of these techniques. Devanbu et al. (2001) presented an approach to signing XML documents to allow distrusted servers to answer certain types of path and selection queries over XML (without the need for trusted online signing keys). This approach increases both security and scalability of using XML as means of publishing information over the Internet.

A security model for regulating access to XML documents is proposed by Gabillon and Bruno (2001). This model recommends the smallest protection granularity on the level of a node, representing an element, attribute, text, or comment of an XML document. The proposed model allows authorization rules to be defined over single nodes, and to create authorization sheets. These sheets can then be translated into *XSLT* (Extensible Style-sheet Language Transformations) (W3C, 2002c), providing a compliant method of document filtering. However, according to Bartlett and Cook (2003), XML security using XSLT is still immature. As a result, encryption may become a better choice in providing security to XML documents.

Bertino and Ferrari (2002) described a number of solutions to the problem of a secure and selective dissemination of XML documents. One of the solutions encourages encryption on portions of documents using different encryption keys and selective key distribution. In addition to that, it proposes a practical method of information push using encryption in place of access control.

Preserving privacy in Web services was discussed by Rezgui, Ouzzani, Bouguettaya, and Medjahed (2002), and a mobile agent-based solution was proposed. The security of mobile agents, however, is still a major issue. Using anonymization was proposed by Bayardo and Agrawal (2005), but anonymity cannot be used in environments where subjects have to be accountable for their actions, as is the case in Web service transactions. In fact, privacy in Web services is still an open issue, as a recent overview revealed (Hung, Ferrari, & Carminati, 2004).

For dynamic compositions of Web services, Hutter and Volkamer (2006) proposed a type calculus to propagate security requirements, primarily confidentiality and integrity. The method is based on programming-language concepts; types are attached to all constructs, and typing rules describe the result of every statement execution. Each data type has a security classification, and type checks are performed both on input and on output data to see if an operation is allowed. An invoked Web service must have a clearance to work with the data type given to it as input, and the invoking Web service must be authorized to deal with the data type returned by the invoked service. Developing an appropriate language that has the required types to encode the security requirements of heterogeneous Web services, however, may not be an easy task and has not been reported yet.

Summary and Discussion

In this chapter we propose a system that maintains legal information flow and introduce label-joining definitions that, according to Lemmas 2, 3, and 4, do not declassify information. The concept in preventing declassification focuses on restricting the expansion of Joint Reader sets. In deriving labels, we may choose to either expand (Definition 9 on Fusing Join) or contract (Definition 8 on Restrictive Join) the owner sets of the joining objects.

A contracting method may appear to enforce greater strictness in preventing declassification, but in reality it has no advantage. Moreover, by contracting owner sets, rules relying on collectivity, such as Rule 7 (declassification), become more vulnerable to attack—for example, a product of label joining, which allows an individual owner to expose the object to declassification by allowing it to become effective, regardless of its effective state from the derived objects. This is shown in Table 8. The expanding method of label joining combines owner sets. However, the problem, while weakened, still poses a threat; Fusing Join will only accept owners that lie in the intersection of Joint Reader sets into the new label. This issue can be eliminated by disallowing rules that depend on the collectivity of ownership. As a result, such a model would present a great decrease in flexibility.

Midway through the chapter, we propose an architecture for dynamic label checking. In accordance with the distributed nature of Web services, a centralized model ensures consistency with the rules of the information flow control. In assuming that the system comprises distrusted services, computations must be performed on the controlling service-side (IFC). While this architecture enforces control of information flow and prevents information from leaking, the IFC must be constructed to withstand immense load. Furthermore, the usage of encryption in all transactions throughout the system comes at a high price.

Validating consistency in relation to the rules of IFC involves both static and dynamic label checking. A dynamic architecture based on Web services requires a centralized model. Fortunately, static analysis can assist in reshaping a dynamic architecture into a semi-centralized model. By certifying statically checked services, we can allow computations to be performed in their own domain, reducing the load of IFC. Furthermore, hiding of resources can be disregarded, removing the buffer caused by IFC and increasing the speed of transactions. In spite of that, IFC is required to at least monitor service certificates. Consequently, the architecture remains centralized.

Conclusion

In this chapter we proposed a model of information flow control using a flexible label structure. The proposed label model preserves owners of objects, allowing them the capability of voting on policy modification. This model extends the decentralized label model in several ways. Above all, it supports collective classification change using the absolute nomination method. Furthermore, we provide a model of preserving inter-owner trust in assisting the establishment of delicate object and label modification rules.

We have presented label-joining definitions to aid in the development of rules based on derived labels. In accordance, we have shown how our label model conforms to the lattice structure defined by Denning (1976). The defined rule on flow legality establishes the foundation of preventing information leakage.

The proposed model has the ability to adopt to a common static checking method as described in this chapter. Furthermore, we propose a centralized architecture for Web services using dynamic label checking. While static analysis can assist in the reduction of IFC load and influence the shape of the architectural design, it is only necessary for detecting implicit flow.

Information flow control remains an open research area. Although it poses immense potential for securing Web services, the practical component remains an issue. In particular, static checking is yet to be adopted to programming languages used in building Web services. Above all, a less centralized architecture would prove to be more practical in enforcing control of information flow. Finally, the rules presented in this chapter can be improved with the purpose of providing a more flexible and practical approach to information flow control.

Acknowledgment

This work is performed in the context of the project titled "Designing a Scalable and Robust Infrastructure for Highly Dynamic Web Services," which is funded by the Australian Research Council (ARC) under Linkage-Project scheme (no. LP0347217).

References

Bandhakavi, S., Zhang, C.C., & Winslett, M. (2006, October). Super-sticky and declassifiable release policies for flexible information dissemination control. *Proceedings of the Workshop on Privacy in the Electronic Society* (WPES'06) (pp. 51-57), Alexandria, VA.

Bayardo, R.J. Jr., & Agrawal, R. (2005, April). Data privacy through optimal K-anonymization. *Proceedings of the 21st International Conference on Data Engineering* (ICDE 2005) (pp. 217-228), Tokyo, Japan.

Bartlett, R.G., & Cook, M.W. (2003, January). XML security using XSLT. *Proceedings of the 36th Hawaii International Conference on System Sciences* (HICSS) (vol. 4, p. 122b), Big Island, HI.

Bell, D.E., & LaPadula, L.J. (1973). *Secure computer systems: Mathematical foundations and model.* Technical Report 2547, MITRE Corporation, USA.

Belokosztolszki, A., Eyers, D.M., & Moody, K. (2003, June). Policy contexts: Controlling information flow in parameterized RBAC. *Proceedings of the IEEE 4th International Workshop on Policies for Distributed Systems and Networks* (pp. 99-110), Como, Italy.

Bertino, E., di Vimercati, S.C., Ferrari, E., & Samarati, P. (1998). Exception-based information flow control in object-oriented systems. *ACM Transactions on Information and System Security, 1*(1), 26-65.

Bertino, E., & Ferrari, E. (2002). Secure and selective dissemination of XML documents. *ACM Transactions on Information and System Security, 5*(3), 290-331.

Damiani, E., di Vimercati, S.C., Paraboschi, S., & Samarati, P. (2000, March). Securing XML documents. *Proceedings of the 2000 International Conference on Extending Database Technology* (EDBT 2000) (pp. 121-135), Konstanz, Germany.

Damiani, E., di Vimercati, S.C., Paraboschi, S., & Samarati, P. (2001, May). Fine grained access control for SOAP e-services. *Proceedings of the 10th International World Wide Web Conference* (WWW10) (pp. 504-513), Hong Kong.

Damiani, E., di Vimercati, S.C., Paraboschi, S., & Samarati, P. (2002a). A fine-grained access control system for XML documents. *ACM Transactions of Information and System Security, 5*(2), 169-202.

Damiani, E., di Vimercati, S.C., Paraboschi, S., & Samarati, P. (2002b). Securing SOAP e-services. *International Journal of Information Security, 1*(2), 100-115.

Deitel, H.M., Deitel, P.J., DuWaldt, B., & Trees, L.K. (2003). *Web services, a technical introduction.* Upper Saddle River, NJ: Prentice Hall.

Denning, D.E. (1976). A lattice model of secure information flow. *Communications of the ACM, 19*(5), 236-243.

Denning, D.E., & Denning, P.J. (1977). Certification of programs for secure information flow. *Communications of the ACM, 20*(7), 504-513.

Devanbu, P., Gertz, M., Kwong, A., Martel, C., Nuckolls, G., & Stubblebine, S.G. (2001, November). Flexible authentication of XML documents. *Proceedings of the 8th ACM Conference on Computer and Communications Security* (pp. 136-145), Philadelphia, PA.

di Vimercati, S.C., Paraboschi, S., & Samarati, P. (2003). Access control: Principles and solutions. *Software—Practice and Experience, 33*(5), 397-421.

Ferrari, E., Samarati, P., Bertino, E., & Jajodia, S. (1997, May). Providing flexibility in information flow control for object-oriented systems. *Proceedings of the IEEE Symposium on Security and Privacy* (p. 130), Oakland, CA.

Gabillon, A., & Bruno, E. (2001, July). Regulating access to XML documents. *Proceedings of the 15th Annual IFIP WG 11.3 Working Conference on Database Security* (pp. 299-314), Niagara, Ontario, Canada.

Hung, P.C.K., Ferrari, E., & Carminati B. (2004, July). Towards standardized Web services privacy technologies. *Proceedings of the International Conference on Web Services* (ICWS'04) (p. 174), San Diego, CA.

Hutter, D., & Volkamer, M. (2006, April). Information flow control to secure dynamic Web service composition. *Proceedings of the 3rd International Conference on Security in Pervasive Computing (SPC-2006) (pp. 196-210)*, York, UK.

Jones, A.K., & Liskov, B.H. (1978). A language expression for expressing constraints on data. *Communications of the ACM, 21*(5), 358-367.

Kuo, C.J., & Humenn, P. (2002, November). Dynamically authorized role-based access control for secure distributed computation. *Proceedings of the 2002 ACM Workshop on XML Security* (pp. 97-103), Fairfax VA.

Lampson, B.W. (1973). A note on the confinement problem. *Communications of the ACM, 16*(10), 613-615.

Lategan, F.A., & Olivier, M.S. (2001, May). On granting limited access to private information. *Proceedings of the 10th International Conference on World Wide Web* (pp. 21-25), Hong Kong.

Li, B. (2002). Analyzing information-flow in Java program based on slicing technique. *ACM SIGSOFT Software Engineering Notes, 27*(5), 98-103.

Myers, A.C., & Liskov, B. (1997, October). A decentralized model for information flow control. *Proceedings of the 16th ACM Symposium on Operating Systems Principles* (pp. 129-142), Saint-Malo, France.

Myers, A.C., & Liskov, B. (1998, May). Complete safe information flow with decentralized labels. *Proceedings of the 1998 IEEE Symposium on Security and Privacy* (pp. 186-197), Oakland, CA.

Myers, A.C., & Flow, J. (1999, January). Practical mostly-static information flow control, *Proceedings of the 26th ACM SIGPLAN-SIGACT Symposium on Principles of Programming Languages* (pp. 228-241), San Antonio, TX.

Myers, A.C., & Liskov, B. (2000). Protecting privacy using the decentralized label model. *ACM Transactions on Software Engineering and Methodology, 9*(4), 410-442.

OASIS. (2005). *Security Assertion Markup Language (SAML) 2.0 technical overview.* Retrieved September 19, 2005, from *http://xml.coverpages.org/SAML-TechOverview20v03-11511.pdf*

Osborn, S.L. (2002, June). Information flow analysis of an RBAC system. *Proceedings of the 17th ACM Symposium on Access Control Models and Techniques* (pp. 163-168), Monterey, CA.

Park, J., & Sandhu, R. (2002, June). Towards usage control models: Beyond traditional access control. *Proceedings of the ACM Symposium on Access Control Models and Technologies* (pp. 57-64), Monterey, CA.

Park, J.S., Sandhu, R., & Ahn, G.J. (2001). Role-based access control on the Web. *ACM Transactions on Information and System Security, 4*(1), 37-71.

Rezgui, A., Ouzzani, M., Bouguettaya, A., & Medjahed, B. (2002, November). Preserving privacy in Web services. *Proceedings of the 4th International ACM Workshop on Web Information and Data Management* (WIDM'02) (pp. 56-62), McLean, VA.

Volpano, D., Smith, G., & Irvine, C. (1996). A sound type system for secure flow analysis. *Journal of Computer Security, 4*(3), 167-187.

W3C. (2000). *Extensible Markup Language (XML)*. Retrieved September 19, 2005, from *http://www.w3c.org/TR/REC-xml*

W3C. (2001). *XML Path Language (XPath) 2.0*. Retrieved September 19, 2005, from *http://www.w3.org/TR/xpath20*

W3C. (2002a). *XML encryption syntax and processing*. Retrieved September 19, 2005, from *http://www.w3.org/TR/xmlenc-core/*

W3C. (2002b). *XML signature syntax and processing*. Retrieved September 19, 2005, from *http://www.w3.org/TR/xmldsig-core/*

W3C. (2002c, April). *XSL Transformations (XSLT) version 2.0*. Retrieved September 19, 2005, from *http://www.w3.org/TR/2002/WD-xslt20-20020430*

Chapter X

Model-Driven Semantic Web Services

Gerald C. Gannod, Miami University (Ohio), USA

John T.E. Timm, Arizona State University–Tempe, USA

Raynette J. Brodie, Arizona State University–Tempe, USA

Abstract

The Semantic Web promises automated invocation, discovery, and composition of Web services by enhancing services with semantic descriptions. An upper ontology for Web services called OWL-S has been created to provide a mechanism for describing service semantics in a standard, well-defined manner. Unfortunately, the learning curve for semantically-rich description languages such as OWL-S can be steep, especially given the current state of tool support for the language. This chapter describes a suite of automated software tools that we have developed to facilitate the construction of OWL-S specifications. The tools operate in two stages. In the first stage, a Model Driven Architecture technique is used to generate an OWL-S description of a Web service from a UML model. This allows the developer to focus on creating a model of the Web service in a standard UML tool, leveraging existing knowledge. In the second stage, an interactive approach for generating groundings is used. This chapter describes both tools and demonstrates how the use of lightweight interactive tools facilitates creation of OWL-S specifications.

Introduction

A Web service is a loosely coupled component that exposes functionality to a client over the Internet (or an intranet) using Web standards such as HTTP, XML, SOAP, WSDL, and UDDI. Of the many challenges of using Web services are the problems of specification, search, discovery, selection, composition, and integration. The current state of practice in Web services is dominated by the use of the Web Service Description Language (WSDL) (Christensen, Curbera, Meredith, & Weerawarana, 2001) to specify access to services. This language lacks an ability to address the aforementioned challenges due to a lack of semantic constructs, although the proposal for WSDL-S addresses it in part (Akkiraju et al., 2005). A *Semantic Web service* extends the capabilities of a Web service by associating semantic concepts to the Web service in order to enable better search, discovery, selection, composition, and integration. Semantically rich languages such as OWL-S (Martin et al., 2005) have been created in order to provide a mechanism for describing domain concepts and the semantics of Web services as ontologies. Unfortunately, for the common developer, the learning curve for such languages can be steep, providing a barrier to widespread adoption.

Model Driven Architecture (MDA) (Miller & Mukerji, 2003) is an approach to software development that is centered on the creation of models rather than program code. The primary goals of MDA are portability, interoperability, and reusability through an architectural separation of concerns between the specification and implementation of software. In MDA-based approaches, the focus is on creation of software via the development of models specified using standard and widely adopted languages such as the Unified Modeling Language (UML) (OMG, 2005b).

We are developing an approach that allows a developer to focus on creation of Semantic Web services and associated OWL-S specifications via the development of a standard UML model. By using an MDA approach, the technique facilitates creation of descriptions of semantic concepts while hiding the syntactic details associated with creating OWL-S specifications. As such, difficulties caused by a steep learning curve for OWL-S can be mitigated with a language that has a wide user base, thus facilitating adoption of Semantic Web approaches.

One of the advantages of OWL-S is its flexibility in allowing the creation of many groundings or bindings for a single Semantic Web service. As part of our method, we have developed an interactive approach for generating OWL-S groundings. In this approach, the semantic and architectural concerns associated with specifying Semantic Web services can be performed by software and knowledge architects. The mapping of Web services described using WSDL to operations contained in the profile and process specifications are intended to be performed by developers of Web services as they are constructed or by architects as they identify existing services that meet the intended behaviors of the semantic services.

This chapter describes our combined approach for specifying OWL-S specifications through the use of Model Driven Architecture to describe OWL-S profiles and process models, and user interaction to describe OWL-S groundings. In addition, we describe an example that demonstrates the full approach including partial verification of correctness using Protégé (Gennari et al., 2002). The remainder of this chapter is organized as follows. First, the background section describes background information relevant to our research. Next, the specifics of our approach and the details of a conversion tool are presented. We then present an example demonstrating the approach, discuss related work, and finally draw conclusions.

Background

This section provides a brief description of Web services, ontologies, and the XML-based technologies that are referred to throughout the chapter.

Web Services

A Web service is a modular, well-defined software component that exposes its interface over a network. Applications use Web services by sending and receiving XML messages over HTTP as shown in Figure 1. Web services provide the foundation for loosely coupled, service-oriented software systems. They allow multiple organizations to interact in a uniform, well-defined manner. This is a major step towards interoperability between multiple heterogeneous distributed systems.

Web service interfaces are defined using the Web Service Description Language (WSDL) (Christensen et al., 2001). WSDL is an XML-based language for describing the interface of a Web service including message types and bindings. WSDL does not provide any sort of formal semantic description of the Web service. In order to provide semantics for Web services, they must be enhanced using ontologies.

Ontologies

An ontology is a set of concepts, their properties, and the relationships between them. Ontologies provide the building blocks for expressing semantics in a well-defined manner (Berners-Lee, Hendler, & Lassila, 2001). A shape simple ontology example is shown in Figure 2. The example shows many of the different aspects of ontologies, including concepts, relationships (including subclasses and properties). A concept describes some significant semantic element or instantiable object. In the

Figure 1. Web service interaction between requestor and provider

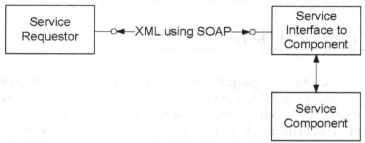

example, *shape* constitutes such an element or concept. *Concepts* can be subclassed in order to show specialization and generalization. *Properties* describe attributes of concepts in order to help partition a domain.

Efforts to define the ontology definition metamodel (OMG, 2005a) have been undertaken to bridge the gap between the knowledge engineering and software engineering communities by defining mappings from ontologies to the relevant visual metaphors in the UML. These goals meet our own in supporting the specification of OWL-S services using UML and Model Driven Architecture.

The Web Ontology Language (OWL) is an XML-based language for describing ontologies (Smith, Welty, & McGuinness, 2004). OWL was designed to allow for the specification of semantic descriptions for resources on the Web in order to support interpretation by autonomous software agents. These resources can be anything from simple Web pages to Web services. Because the syntax of OWL is XML, it is platform independent, can be easily transferred over a network, and manipulated with existing automated tools. OWL-S is an ontology for services created by the DAML group (Martin et al., 2005). The ontology is broken into three parts. The *service profile* describes the capabilities of the service. The *service model* describes how the service works internally. Finally, the *service grounding* describes how to

Figure 2. Simple example of an ontology

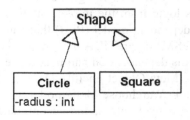

access the service. The OWL-S ontology is useful in that it provides a uniform mechanism for describing the semantics of a Web service.

SWRL, UML, and OCL

The Semantic Web Rule Language (SWRL) is a language for expressing rules that extend the axiomatic capabilities of OWL (Horrocks et al., 2003). These rules can be used to express conditions for OWL-S specifications including pre-conditions, post-conditions, and effects. SWRL rules can also be used to express conditions in control constructs of OWL-S composite processes.

The Unified Modeling Language (UML) is a general-purpose modeling language for software systems (OMG, 2005b). The language can be used to model all static and dynamic aspects of the system including both structure and behavior. The UML uses a graphical notation to illustrate various aspects of a software system and can also be serialized into an XML-based textual format for interoperability between modeling tools. The semantics of the UML can be extended using *profiles* to fit modeling into a particular domain such as Semantic Web services. UML profiles can contain stereotypes and tagged values. Stereotypes are names that, when attached to model elements, are used to convey the meaning of that element. Tagged values are name/value pairs that are attached to model elements and provide a mechanism for supplying additional information about the element. UML has widespread tool support and has been widely adopted in both industry and academia. The Object Constraint Language (OCL) is a language used for representing expressions for UML models (OMG, 2005c). Typically, OCL expressions are used to represent invariants that hold true over a UML model. One important aspect of OCL conditions is that they do not have side effects. Evaluating an OCL expression will not modify the state of a model. Evaluating an expression, however, may call an operation that does change the state of the model.

Model Driven Architecture, UML, XMI, and XSLT

Model Driven Architecture (Miller & Mukerji, 2003) is a standard produced by the Object Management Group (OMG). The goal of MDA is to separate the design of application or business logic from the implementation platform. Designs are specified in a platform-independent model (PIM) that can then be translated to a platform-specific model (PSM) by an MDA tool, which is then used to generate the implementation. MDA is dependent on and makes use of several other OMG standards including UML, Meta-Object Facility (MOF), XML Meta-Data Interchange (XMI), and Common Warehouse Meta-model (CWM). A UML profile is a collection of stereotypes, tagged values, and custom data types used to extend the capabilities of the UML modeling language. We use a UML profile to model various OWL-S constructs in conjunction with the UML static structure diagram. In terms of MDA, the stereotypes, tagged values, and data types serve to markup the platform-independent model, in order to facilitate transformation to an OWL-S specification. Stereotypes work well to distinguish different types of classes and create a meta-language on top of the standard UML class modeling constructs. XMI is an XML-based, platform-independent representation of a UML model (OMG, 2005). XMI was originally designed to allow modeling tools to exchange model data in a standardized format. Because of its XML format, XML-based tools can be used to manipulate and transform XMI documents into other formats. The eXtensible Stylesheet Language Transformations (XSLT) is an XML-based functional and declarative programming language for transforming XML documents of one type to another (Clark, 1999). XSLT is used in this project to convert an XML representation of a UML model into an OWL-S description. The transformation rules in the style sheet rely on the UML profile that we have created for OWL-S.

Approach

This section describes the approach that we are developing for synthesizing OWL-S specifications including the use of MDA tools to create OWL-S core specifications and interactive tools to specify OWL-S groundings.

Overview

In order for many new techniques and technologies to gain entry into a market, many factors must be considered. While standardization can often be a major reason why adoption of a new technology succeeds, another factor is ease of use. That is, if a technology adds little new overhead or requires little in the way of new training, then it is more likely to be adopted. For instance, the benefits of formal methods for software development have been described numerous times (Clarke & Wing, 1996). However, an adoption barrier to formal methods by much of the software development community remains in the form of a lack of education. From this standpoint, one of the overarching philosophies of the research described in this chapter is the following:

Development of applications that are based on the use of Semantic Web services should not require knowledge beyond the use of the UML modeling language.

Specifically, it is our belief that for techniques that are based on the use of the Semantic Web and Semantic Web services, a bridge should be created using UML

Figure 3. Structure of OWL-S specifications

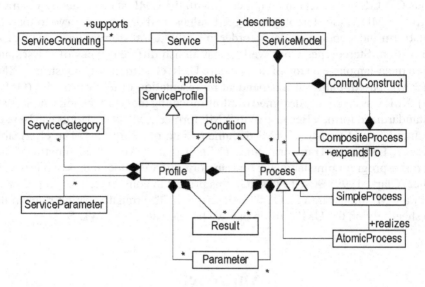

that facilitates adoption. In our work, this bridge is enabled via the use of Model Driven Architecture.

Web services have gained a great deal of attention as a way for organizations to use information as a commodity. While many Web services currently exist, very few have semantic descriptions associated with them. Furthermore, from the viewpoint of an "end user," a given Web service may or may not provide exactly the data that is needed for a given task. However, it may be the case that a group of Web services, when properly composed and integrated, will provide the desired outcomes. Based on the above, we have identified two primary requirements that are being used to drive our approach:

R1: The approach should be able to incorporate the use of both Web services (e.g., services with WSDL specifications only) and Semantic Web services (e.g., services with semantic descriptions).

R2: The approach should facilitate composition of services to form applications or federations.

The intent of requirement R1 is to leverage existing Web services regardless of the state of their specification. Specifically, the requirement is a recognition of the facts that adoption issues exist in the community and the expectation of widespread use of semantically rich languages such as OWL-S is unreasonable. However, we do assume that at the very least, a WSDL specification does exist, which is reasonable given that frameworks such as the .NET platform and Apache Axis provide facilities to automatically generate WSDL specifications.

Requirement R2 and the philosophy stated above embody the heart of our approach: a technique for integrating services into composite services by generating an OWL-S specification via the use of MDA.

As depicted in Figure 3, the OWL-S ontology (as represented by the Service class box) consists of three major parts. The ServiceProfile is a description of what the service does. In this sense, the service presents a particular process. The Servic-eModel is a description of how the service works (e.g., the semantics and operational composition of the service). Within this context, a service may use either a single process or several atomic processes in "implementing" the ServiceProfile. Finally, the ServiceGrounding is a description of how to access the Web service. The ground-ing maps processes to specific realizations of the processes as implemented by Web services. The classes shown on the right side of the diagram represent processes or operations of differing levels of granularity and are typically related to the Servic-eModel through the use of the ControlConstruct class and the CompositeProcess class. The lower part of the model depicts classes used to represent the inputs and outputs of processes.

From a WSDL description, an OWL-S description can be generated using XSLT (Paolucci, Srinivasan, Sycara, & Nishimura, 2003). However, for Semantic Web service compositions, other information is required to describe the operational behavior of a service (e.g., the ServiceModel). We have developed an approach for generating an OWL-S ServiceModel by taking an XML-based representation of a UML activity diagram and using XSLT to transform the diagram into an appropriate CompositeProcess specification. Specifically, the class structure of the composite shown in the class diagram must be unified with an activity diagram in order to fully specify the composition. As such, in our approach the software developer specifies the operation of a Web service as a composition of other services using UML. An automated design tool then takes the UML description of the service and converts it into the OWL-S Service Model description.

As part of our investigations, we are developing domain models for Web services and Web service composition as a way to facilitate translation via XSLT of WSDL specifications to OWL-S Grounding Models and UML Activity Diagrams to OWL-S Service Models, respectively. Furthermore, we are investigating the use of different service matchmaking techniques, including lightweight signature-based techniques (Gannod & Bhatia, 2004) and more computationally expensive semantic techniques (Sycara, Paolucci, Ankolekar, & Srinivasan, 2003).

Framework

Figure 4 shows the process workflow for our approach. The framework uses a model-driven development approach for specifying, mapping, and executing Semantic Web services. In this regard, the framework not only allows the specification of Semantic Web services, but facilitates the mapping of constructs in those semantic descriptions to concrete service realizations. These concrete service realizations are transformed into executable specifications for infrastructures such as a BPEL (Andrews et al., 2003) execution engine. In this framework, an architect is responsible for creating models using UML. The framework manages the transformation process to OWL-S with very little additional effort on behalf of the developer. This benefits the developer in two ways. First, the developer is able to focus on creating models instead of writing code or in the case of Semantic Web services creating a semantic specification. Secondly, the developer becomes more efficient because low-level details are abstracted away and the developer can focus more on the top-level structure and semantics. The developer can leverage existing skills in popular UML tools such as Poseidon (Gentleware, 2005).

The second stage of the framework involves a tool that we have developed to automate the process of mapping concepts in the OWL-S description to concepts in the WSDL file of a concrete service realization (Gannod, Brodie, & Timm, 2005). This tool uses the profile and process model portions of the OWL-S description and a set of WSDL files for corresponding services to automatically generate the OWL-S grounding portion of the OWL-S description.

Once the grounding is created, the final step in the model-driven development process involves execution of the OWL-S specification. In order to leverage existing technologies, a tool will be created as part of the general framework to automatically

Figure 4. Framework

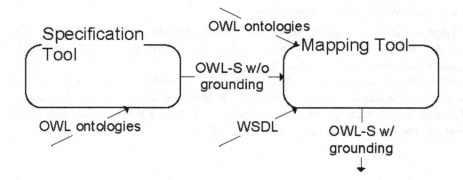

generate an executable BPEL specification. Using BPEL (Andrews et al., 2003) we can leverage existing execution engines. Semantic discovery and composition can take place utilizing the generated OWL-S specification. Once a service is composed, the BPEL specification can be used for execution.

Table 1. UML to OWL mapping (atomic processes)

UML Extension	Model Element	OWL-S Construct
<<presents>>	Association	Service instance presents
<<describedBy>>	Association	Service instance describedBy
<<supports>>	Association	Service instance supports
<<AtomicProcess>>	CallAction	AtomicProcess instance
<<Service>>	Class	Service instance
<<Profile>>	Class	Profile instance
<<AtomicProcess>>	Class	AtomicProcess instance
<<Grounding>>	Class	Grounding instance
<<owl:Class>>	Class	inline OWL class definition
serviceName tagged value	Class	Profile instance serviceName
textDescription tagged value	Class	Profile instance
actor:name tagged value	Class	Profile instance actor:name
actor:title tagged value	Class	Profile instance actor:phone
actor:phone tagged value	Class	Profile instance actor:fax
actor:fax tagged value	Class	Profile instance actor:email
actor:email tagged value	Class	Profile instance actor:email
actor:physicalAddress tagged value	Class	Profile instance actor:physicalAddress
actor:webURL tagged value	Class	Profile instance actor:webURL
xsd:decimal data type	DataType	XML Schema decimal data type
xsd:float data type	DataType	XML Schema float data type
xsd:gYearMonth data type	DataType	XML Schema gMonthYear data type
xsd:string data type	DataType	XML Schema string data type
<<AtomicProcess>>	Operation	AtomicProcess instance
hasResultVar tagged value	Operation	Process instance hasResultVar
hasResult tagged value	Operation	Process instance hasResult
hasLocal tagged value	Operation	Process instance hasLocal
hasPrecondition tagged value	Operation	Process instance hasPrecondition
inCondition tagged value	Operation	Process instance inCondition
hasEffect	Operation	Process instance hasEffect
<<owl:Ontology>>	Package	external ontology
uriRef tagged value	Package	external ontology URI reference

OWL-S Core

To facilitate the transformation process of the first stage of our approach, we extended the standard UML static structure diagram by creating a UML profile in order to accommodate some of the constructs in the OWL-S specification. The UML profile includes stereotypes, custom data types, and tagged values which each map to a particular construct in the OWL-S description as shown in Table 1. The table provides a subset of the profile for atomic processes. Composite processes are discussed in the next section. The leftmost column provides the abstract type represented by the constructs. The middle column in the table shows the UML constructs that are used to specify semantic services using class diagrams. Finally, the rightmost column names the corresponding target construct in an OWL-S specification. The table forms the basis for the transformations that we have developed to convert UML XMI specifications into OWL-S specifications.

Figure 5 demonstrates how stereotypes are used in a UML class diagram to represent specification elements of an OWL-S specification. In the diagram, a UML class combined with a *Service* stereotype is used to model a service instance in an OWL-S specification, a UML association with a *Presents* stereotype is used to identify a "presents" property in an OWL-S specification, and a UML class combined with a *ServiceProfile* stereotype is used to model a service profile instance. These UML extensions are used to facilitate the transformation process. The stereotypes help to identify which classes must be generated in the OWL-S description. Tagged values correspond primarily to property values in the output representation. The custom data types are necessary to represent the XML Schema data types. There are other ways that UML could have been utilized. For example, attributes with default values could have been used instead of tagged values (our current method); however, the latter method is conducive to the transformation process. In general the transformation rules to map from the UML model to the OWL-S specification are straightforward. The main classes marked with the Service, ServiceProfile, ServiceModel, and ServiceGrounding stereotypes each map into a separate output file. These constructs are linked semantically through the stereotyped associations in a diagram (e.g., *presents, describedBy,* and *supports*) and are used to generate the respective elements in output documents. Tagged values are used primarily to model properties in the OWL-S specification, especially in the ServiceProfile. Custom data types are used to model XML Schema data types that are used typically used in an OWL-S specification.

The general architecture of the specification tool is shown in Figure 6. First, a UML Class Diagram is created in Poseidon (Gentleware, 2005) with the UML profile for OWL-S. The class diagram is exported in XMI format. The conversion tool is invoked from the command line and runs multiple transformations on the input file to produce the corresponding Service, ServiceProfile, ServiceModel, and Service-Grounding OWL-S documents. The transformations come in the form of XSLT that

Figure 5. UML classes representing a service and its associated profile

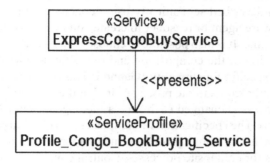

we have written to automatically convert XMI input into OWL-S specifications. From the standpoint of MDA terminology, the process of creating a UML diagram can be considered equivalent to creating a platform-independent model. The XSLT transformations correspond to "Other Information" necessary to generate a second-level PIM in the form of an OWL-S specification. The act of specifying groundings, which is part of the framework we are developing but outside the scope of the tool described here, corresponds to creating a platform-specific model in the sense that the mapping provides information specific to creating a specific executable implementation of a semantic service.

Composite Services

Individual Web services can be composed to create complex composite behaviors and workflows. A composition, in turn, can itself be exposed as a Web service.

Figure 6. Basic architecture

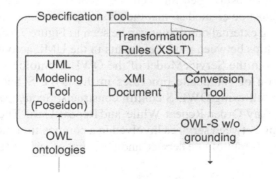

Services can be reused in multiple, different compositions. Compositions can be static (determined *before* runtime) or dynamic (determined *at* runtime). If a Web a service has been described semantically using concepts from an ontology, it is possible for a software agent or reasoner to create compositions using that service dynamically at runtime. It is also possible to choose which services to bind to using a semantic description of the composition and plugging in concrete services that are required for a specific functionality (Gannod, Timm, & Brodie, 2006). Composite processes differ from atomic processes in that they maintain state. The state of a composite process is changed each time a message is sent to it by the client (Martin et al., 2005). The specification of composite processes involves additional complexity beyond that of atomic processes. In our approach, atomic processes are the building blocks for composite processes. Control constructs are used to "glue" together atomic processes into compositions. These control constructs also require the specification of conditions. Additional complexity comes from the requirement to support data binding between processes in a composition. Certain processes may require complex compositions that involve many atomic processes and even other composite processes. In order to support these types of complex compositions, a hierarchical approach is required. Using the UML Activity Diagram patterns in Figures 9-11, the developer creates complex compositions by nesting these simpler patterns inside one another creating one activity diagram for each activity with the <<CompositeProcess>> stereotype.

Class diagrams used to model composite processes contain several features that facilitate the specification of service compositions. UML Operations in the class with the stereotype <<Composite- Process>> also contain stereotypes. An operation with the <<AtomicProcess>> stereotype is transformed directly into OWL-S AtomicProcess constructs. Operations with the <<CompositeProcess>> stereotype indicate that a corresponding UML Activity Diagram with the same name has been (or must be) specified. These stereotypes are used during the transformation process to determine which UML Operations must be expanded using a UML Activity Diagram. It is possible to reference classes in external ontologies using UML packages. The developer specifies a UML package with the stereotype <<owl:Ontology>> and the tagged value uriRef. Then for each class that will be used in the model, a placeholder class must be created so that the class can be referenced in the model. An example of using external ontologies can be seen in Figure 7. Mappings encapsulate the relationships between model elements in the UML activity diagram and concepts/properties in the ServiceModel of the OWL-S ontology. The mappings support specification of composite processes in the OWL-S ServiceModel and can use any of the following OWL-S control constructs: Sequence, If-Then-Else, Split-Join, Choice, Any-Order, Repeat-While, and Repeat-Until. The mappings also support data binding between services involved in a composition (i.e., the mapping of data between the output of one service and the input of another service).

Figure 7. UML class diagram with stereotypes and packages

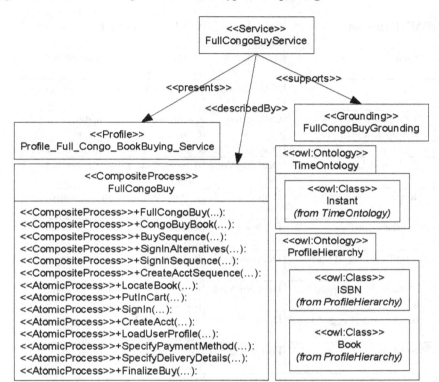

The additional UML profile extensions for composite processes are shown in Table 2. Specifically, semantic extensions for modeling elements in the UML activity diagram have been added to the profile, including stereotypes on call actions, decision nodes, merge nodes, fork nodes and join nodes, and tagged values. The stereotypes identify instances of control constructs in the Service model of the OWL-S ontology. An example of stereotypes identifying processes and control constructs can be seen in Figure 8a. This figure contains one atomic process named LocateBook and one composite process named CongoBuyBook. The If-Then-Else construct is also used as indicated by the <<If-Then-Else>> stereotype on the decision node. The decision node contains a condition named FullCongoBuyBookInStock, which is used to conditionally execute the CongoBuyBook process.

The tagged values in Table 2 are used for data binding between processes in the composition. The hasDataFrom tagged value is used to specify how a parameter for a particular process binds to a parameter in another process. The ifCondition tagged value represents the condition which must be true in order to execute the "then" path in the If-Then-Else construct. In a UML activity diagram, the "then" path is

Table 2. UML to OWL mapping (composite processes)

UML Extension	Model Element	OWL-S Construct
<<then>>	ActivityEdge	If-Then-Else control construct instance then
<<else>>	ActivityEdge	If-Then-Else control construct instance else
<<CompositeProcess>>	CallAction	CompositeProcess instance
<<CompositeProcess>>	Class	CompositeProcess instance
<<Choice>>	DecisionNode	Choice control construct instance
<<If-Then-Else>>	DecisionNode	If-Then-Else control construct instance
<<Repeat-While>>	DecisionNode	Repeat-While control construct instance
<<Repeat-Until>>	DecisionNode	Repeat-Until control construct instance
ifCondition tagged value	DecisionNode	If-Then-Else control construct instance
whileCondition tagged value	DecisionNode	Repeat-While control construct instance whileCondition
untilCondition tagged value	DecisionNode	Repeat-Until control construct instance untilCondition
<<Split-Join>>	ForkNode	Split-Join control construct instance
<<Any-Order>>	ForkNode	Any-Order control construct instance
<<CompositeProcess>>	Operation	CompositeProcess instance
<<Produce>>	Operation	Produce instance
hasDataFrom tagged value	Operation	Process instance hasDataFrom
producedBinding tagged value	Operation	Produce instance producedBinding
withOutput tagged value	Operation	Process instance withOutput

identified with the <<then>> stereotype. Similarly, the "else" path is marked, in the diagram, with the <<else>> stereotype.

Figures 9-11 contain patterns of UML activity diagrams that are used to model equivalent OWL-S composition constructs. Activity diagrams use a graphical notation similar to flowcharts, where activities are represented using boxes with rounded corners and decision structures are represented using diamonds. In the diagrams, the activities marked with the <<AtomicProcess>> stereotypes can be alternatively stereotyped with <<CompositeProcess>>. This allows for more complex compositions to be specified. The Sequence construct uses a straightforward representation.

Figure 8. UML activity diagram with stereotypes

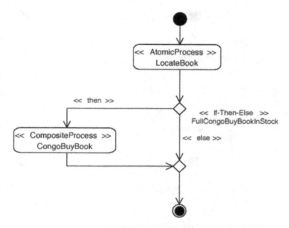

(a) Full CongoBuy Example

```
<process:If-Then-Else>
<xsl:choose>
<xsl:when test="contains($condition, ':')">
<process:ifCondition>
<expr:SWRL-Condition rdf:ID="...">
<expr:expressionBody rdf:parseType="Literal">
<xsl:call-template name="ocl2swrl">
<xsl:with-param name="expression" select="..."/>
<xsl:with-param name="operationName" select="..."/>
</xsl:call-template>
</expr:expressionBody>
</expr:SWRL-Condition>
</process:ifCondition>
</xsl:when>
<xsl:otherwise>
<process:ifCondition rdf:resource="#{$condition}"/>
</xsl:otherwise>
</xsl:choose>
<process:then>
<xsl:call-template name="handleNode">
<xsl:with-param name="node" select="$thenNode"/>
</xsl:call-template>
</process:then>
<xsl:if test="name($elseNode)='UML2:CallAction'">
<process:else>
<xsl:call-template name="handleNode">
<xsl:with-param name="node" select="$elseNode"/>
</xsl:call-template>
</process:else>
</xsl:if>
</process:If-Then-Else>
```

(b) If-Then-Else Transformation Rule (Excerpt)

Figure 9. UML activity diagram patterns of OWL-S constructs

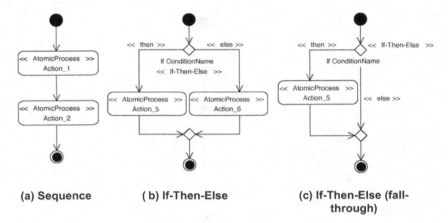

(a) Sequence   (b) If-Then-Else   (c) If-Then-Else (fall-
                                                        through)

Figure 10. UML activity diagram patterns of OWL-S constructs

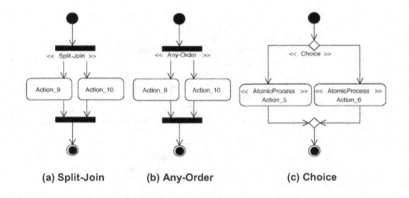

(a) Split-Join   (b) Any-Order   (c) Choice

Figure 11. UML activity diagram patterns of OWL-S constructs

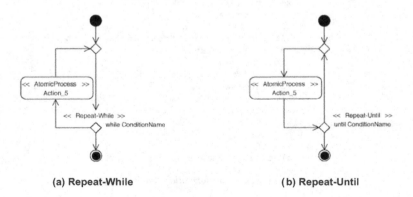

(a) Repeat-While   (b) Repeat-Until

A Sequence is a series of processes which execute one after another. The semantics of UML activity diagrams matches the OWL-S Sequence construct. An example of the Sequence construct in UML is seen in Figure 9a. The If-Then-Else construct comes in two versions. The first version has two paths of execution—a "then" path and an "else" path—and is seen in Figure 9b. The second version has no "else" path and translates to the conditional execution of one atomic or composite process; this is seen in Figure 9c.

The Split-Join construct represents concurrent execution of multiple processes. It closely follows the parallel activity construct in UML activity diagrams. The Split-Join construct was also straightforward to implement. An example of the Split-Join construct is seen in Figure 10a. The Any-Order construct is modeled similarly to a Split-Join. An Any-Order construct specifies that processes are executed in any order but not concurrently. The UML activity diagram for the Any-Order construct is shown in Figure 10b. In this respect, Split-Join and Any-Order are syntactically similar. However, the semantics are different and thus the stereotype provides the mechanism by which the two visual constructs are differentiated. The Choice construct is similar in structure to If-Then-Else in terms of UML implementation and is shown in Figure 10c. A Choice construct specifies that any path can be chosen and executed from a given set of paths. The two looping constructs Repeat-While and Repeat-Until are modeled using single-entry, single-exit design patterns. They are represented by using analogous UML activity merge and decision nodes. The primary difference between the two looping mechanisms is the control flow. This can be seen in Figures 11a and 11b. The Repeat-While construct evaluates the whileCondition before it conditionally executes the whileProcess. The Repeat-Until construct executes the untilProcess first and then checks the untilCondition before continuing. The semantics of these constructs are similar to the *while* statement and *do-while* statement in a general programming language.

In order to support composite service specifications, additional transformation rules are required above those we have developed for atomic processes (Gannod et al., 2006). These rules are based on the additions to the UML Profile for OWL-S. Because composite processes can contain other composite processes, a recursive approach was used in creating the rules for composite processes. An excerpt of the transformation rule for the If-Then-Else construct is seen in Figure 8b.

OCL to SWRL

To support complex activities such as automated reasoning and matchmaking, semantic information needs to be provided in the control specifications described above. Through the use of OCL and UML activity diagrams, the SWRL specifications generated by our approach capture a portion of the behavioral semantics of

Table 3. OCL tagged value syntax

Tag Definition	Tagged Value Syntax (pseudo-BNF)
hasPrecondition	\<precondition-name\>:\<ocl-expression\> | \<precondition-name\>
hasDataFrom	\<input-name\>,\<var-name\>,\<process-name\> | \<input-name\>,\<data-value\>
hasLocal	\<local-name\>,\<parameter-type\>
hasResult	\<result-name\>
inCondition	\<result-name\>,\<condition-name\>:\<ocl-expression\> | \<result-name\>,\<condition-name\>
hasResultVar	\<result-name\>,\<result-var-name\>,\<parameter-type\>
withOutput	\<result-name\>,\<output-name\>,\<var-name\>,\<process-name\> | \<output-name\>,\<data-value\>
producedOutput	\<output-name\>,\<var-name\>,\<process-name\> | \<output-name\>,\<data-value\>
hasEffect	\<result-name\>,\<effect-name\>:\<ocl-expression\> | \<result-name\>,\<effect-name\>

the Web service composition (e.g., preconditions, post-conditions, and conditions on control constructs).

In order to support all of the information required to make the transformation between UML/OCL and OWL-S/SWRL, a well-defined tagged value syntax was created. Table 3 summarizes the syntax. The syntax provides a standard mechanism for the developer to specify OCL expressions and data binding information in a UML model. The syntax consists of comma separated lists, with OCL expressions and their names being separated using a colon. The developer may omit the expression in which case the name refers to an expression that has been defined elsewhere in the model. This provides a convenient way for the developer to reuse expressions.

The hasPrecondition, inCondition, and hasEffect tag definitions are used to specify various conditions and expressions. The hasLocal and hasResultVar are used to declare variables that are used in these expressions. The hasDataFrom, withOutput, and producedOutput are tag definitions used to specify the input and output bindings used in data flows between processes. All of the tags are used as extensions to a UML operation which is part of the process class. The producedOutput tag definition is used in conjunction with the <<Produce>> stereotype.

The SWRL language specification (Horrocks et al., 2003) was used as a guideline to develop transformation rules (encoded in XSLT) that transform OCL expres-

Table 4. SWRL atoms and OCL syntax mappings

SWRL Atom Type	OCL Syntax	Example
Class	instance.oclIsType(class)	aCustomer.oclIsType(Person)
Individual Property	instance.property = instance	aPerson.hasFather = aFather
Datavalued Property	instance.property = 'string'	aPerson.hasPhoneNumber = '555-1234'
Builtin (lessThan)	var1 < var2	CP_BNPriceAmount < CP_AmazonPriceAmount

sions into SWRL. The SWRL language uses a conjunction of atoms to represent expressions. There are four primary types of atoms which are supported: class atoms, individual property atoms, data-valued property atoms, and built-in atoms. An individual property atom holds true if an OWL individual is related to another OWL individual via a property. A class atom holds true if an OWL individual is a member of the specified OWL class. A data-valued property atom holds true if the property of an individual has a particular data value. The data value can be one of the following: an OCL number, an OCL string, or the name of a variable. Built-in atoms are used to provide access to built-in functionality such as math functions, string functions, and comparison operators. Our transformation system provides support for the following comparison operators: equal, notEqual, greaterThan, lessThan, greaterThanOrEqual, and lessThanOrEqual. The OCL syntax for the various types of atoms used in a SWRL expression is shown in Table 4.

Multiple atoms can be conjuncted together to form an atom list. The atom list can be represented in OCL using the *and* keyword. For example, consider the expressions condition1 and condition2 and condition3, where condition1, condition2, and condition3 can be any of the atom types listed in Table 4. The transformation tokenizes the OCL expression using *and* as the delimiter and generates the corresponding SWRL in RDF/XML concrete syntax.

Groundings

Figure 12 shows an excerpt of a model for the Web Service Description Language. From the perspective of a user of a Web service, the structure showing the PortType and the contained Operation in the lower right-hand corner of the diagram is most relevant. Specifically, the PortType provides access to the service. With respect to groundings, the PortType represents the target of a mapping from an OWL-S process.

Figure 13 shows a UML diagram that captures the main idea behind groundings in an OWL-S specification. The diagram combines concepts from Figure 3 and Figure 12. Specifically, a Service-Grounding (shown on the top right) is made of up

Figure 12. Excerpt of a model of WSDL

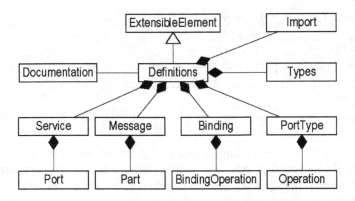

a number of AtomicProcessGroundings. These AtomicProcessGroundings contain mappings from Process types in an OWL-S specification to Port-Types in a WSDL specification. In the diagram, these mappings are represented with an association class called ProcOpMap. The AtomicProcessGrounding also contains mappings from parameters in an OWL-S specification to parameters in a WSDL specification and is captured with an association class (ParaMap) in a manner similar to that described above. In the case of parameters, the mappings can be realized by XSLT transformations as well as other complex translations from XML and XSD types to OWL types.

Figure 13. OWL-S to WSDL groundings

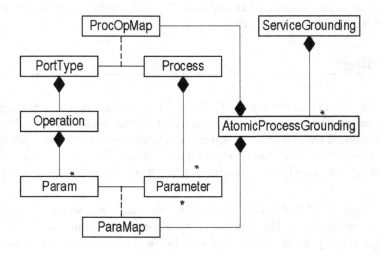

Figure 14. Conceptual architecture

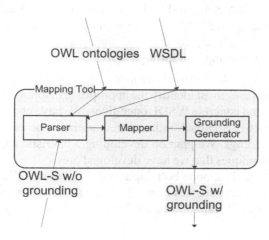

OWL ontologies   WSDL

Mapping Tool

| Parser | → | Mapper | → | Grounding Generator |

OWL-S w/o
grounding

OWL-S w/
grounding

We considered a number of alternatives for specifying groundings. We initially looked at a method that would allow users to specify groundings using UML instances but found that solution to be unwieldy, especially in those cases where either (or both) the Web service operation and the OWL-S atomic process have several parameters.

The conceptual architecture for the grounding tool is shown in Figure 14. The operations are essentially focused on three primary operations: parsing, interactive mapping, and grounding synthesis. The inputs to the system vary based on whether the user takes a top-down or bottom-up perspective on specification construction.

When taking the top-down perspective, the inputs are an OWL-S specification and either a list of WSDL specifications or a list of search criteria for locating the WSDL specifications. The intuition behind this perspective is that an architect has developed the description for a Semantic Web service and now wishes to locate an appropriate set of WSDL-specified services that implement the OWL-S specification. The output for the tool in this perspective is typically a complete OWL-S grounding, indicating that all the processes in the OWL-S specification are mapped to some WSDL operation. The specification can be incomplete if the mapping activity is either unfinished or the WSDL specifications do not cover all operations in the OWL-S specification. In this case, a user can rely on matchmaking or automated search to finish the grounding process.

When taking the bottom-up perspective, the inputs are an OWL-S specification and one or more WSDL specifications. The intuition behind the bottom-up perspective is that semantics are being added to WSDL specifications. In this case, the OWL-S specification can be optional as long as some mechanism exists to locate an appropriate OWL-S specification that matches the behavior of the WSDL operations. The other possibility is that an OWL-S specification (albeit one lacking semantics) is generated from the WSDL specification, as is the case with tools like WSDL2OWLS (Paolucci et al., 2003). The output for the tool in this perspective is an OWL-S grounding that is likely to be incomplete except in those cases that a single WSDL file completely covers all of the operations found in the OWL-S specifications provided as input or through search.

The mapping activity, controlled by the mapper component in Figure 14, is interactive in the sense that a user must identify the appropriate mappings between abstract OWL-S operations and concrete WSDL operations. We have chosen to develop the tool to use an interactive approach rather than automatic one as an initial solution for generating groundings. We plan on developing a heuristic approach based on the use of search techniques that we have developed previously (Gannod & Bhatia, 2004). Currently the tool supports both input perspectives and allows a user to create mappings for atomic processes in an OWL-S specification and single WSDL specifications. The search capabilities are being built into the system in a future revision.

Once a grounding has been completed using the tool, it is combined with an appropriate OWL-S specification, depending on the input context. In order to verify that the grounding is correct both syntactically and semantically (with respect to an ontology), we use the Protégé system (Gennari et al., 2002). Protégé will verify syntactic correctness as well as check that semantic constraints specified in the OWL-S specification are not violated by the generated grounding and that the entire OWL-S specification meets general constraints of the referenced ontologies.

Example

In this section we describe the PelicanSpellCheckService, an atomic process that specifies a spell-checking service. We developed this OWL-S specification as a demonstration of both the specification of processes using UML as well as the flexibility provided by groundings.

Specification

Figure 15 shows a class diagram that models the PelicanSpellCheck service with the OWL-S stereotypes described in Table 1. Specifically, it shows the specification for a PelicanSpellCheckservice class that allows a user to spell-check a word using a service interface. The class diagram represents the core structure of the OWL-S description as represented in the UML. Other classes, stereotypes, and tagged values are also needed in order to generate the corresponding OWL-S documents.

Figure 15. UML class diagram with OWL-S stereotypes

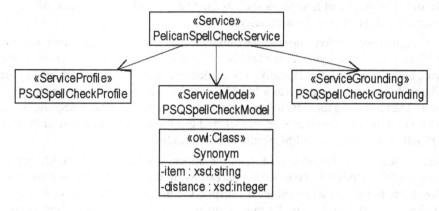

Figure 16. Specification of QuerySpellCheck operation

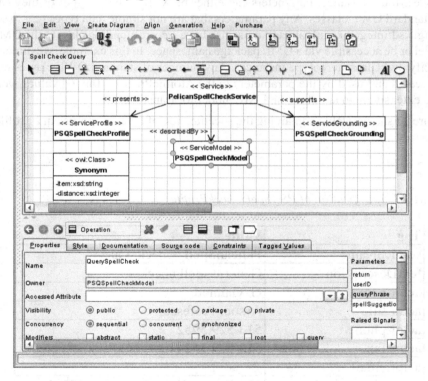

We consider a specification of this form to be far easier to construct than using XML or other graphical interfaces such as the OWL-S Editor (Scicluna, Abela, & Montebello, 2004) due to its simplicity.

The example contains five classes, one of which is an OWL class specified with the owl:Class UML stereotype. This class is a domain concept that is relevant to the service being specified. Specifically, it is an element of an ontology pertinent to the spell-checking domain and acts as a "type" for the input and output parameters of the service. The remaining four classes specify the top-level service (PelicanSpellCheck-Service) and its constituent profile, model, and grounding (PSQSpellCheckProfile, PSQSpellCheckModel, and PSQSpellCheckGrounding, respectively).

Figure 16 shows the Poseidon tool, with the upper part depicting the UML representation of the service and the bottom part showing the specification of a method. In Poseidon, there are many options for displaying methods. In this case, we chose for readability sake to display the method using the split view rather than the traditional method section of a class box due to the inability of the Poseidon tool to allow resizing of class boxes. Currently, only one Process instance is allowed per ServiceModel instance. Parameters can either be XML Schema types or they can be standard OWL classes. Any parameters that are not simple data types (e.g., xsd: string, xsd:integer, xsd:float, etc.) must also have a corresponding class in the UML model or be accessible via a UML package namespace. In this example, we directly specify owl:Class stereotype instances. Any number of standard OWL classes can be created and used by the parameters in the AtomicProcess. Tagged values were used extensively to annotate the UML model for transformation.

Figure 17 shows a table containing the specification of other properties in a profile.

Figure 17. Specification of PSQSpellCheckProfile

Tag	Value
serviceName	PelicanSpell_Check_Query
textDescription	Generic spell checker
actor:name	G. Gannod
actor:title	Assoc. Professor
actor:phone	513 529 5952
actor:fax	513 529 1524
actor:email	gannodg@muohio.edu
actor:physicalAddress	123 Kreger Hall, Oxford OH 45056
actor:webURL	http://www.users.muohio.edu/gannodg

Figure 18. Excerpt of XMI representation of Synonym class

```
<UML:Class xmi.id = '...' name = 'Synonym' visibility = 'public'
    isSpecification = 'false' isRoot = 'false'
    isLeaf = 'false' isAbstract = 'false' isActive = 'false'>
    <UML:ModelElement.stereotype>
        <UML:Stereotype xmi.idref = '...'/>
    </UML:ModelElement.stereotype>
    <UML:Classifier.feature>
        <UML:Attribute xmi.id = '...' name = 'item' visibility = 'private'
            isSpecification = 'false' ownerScope = 'instance'
            changeability = 'changeable'>
            <UML:StructuralFeature.type>
                <UML:DataType xmi.idref = '...'/>
            </UML:StructuralFeature.type>
        </UML:Attribute>
        <UML:Attribute xmi.id = '...' name = 'distance'
            visibility = 'private' isSpecification = 'false'
            ownerScope = 'instance' changeability = 'changeable'>
            <UML:StructuralFeature.type>
                <UML:DataType xmi.idref = '...'/>
            </UML:StructuralFeature.type>
        </UML:Attribute>
    </UML:Classifier.feature>
</UML:Class>
```

We had the option of specifying these options as either attributes or tagged values. We made the design decision to specify these properties, including the service name and contact information, as tagged values. These properties are embedded in the resulting XMI representation of the classes, and thus are not seen in the class directly on the class diagram, therefore making them more readable. Since the tagged values can be manipulated directly through the UML tool, their specification is easily supported. For example, all of the contact information for the service is implemented as a set of tagged values added to the class in the diagram with the ServiceProfile stereotype (PSQSpellCheck-Profile). Also, any preconditions in the process model are implemented as tagged values added to the single method in the class marked with the ServiceModel stereotype. Finally, any conditional outputs in the process model are implemented as tagged values added to the corresponding method parameters of the single method in the class marked with the ServiceModel stereotype.

Transformations

Figure 18 is an excerpt of an XMI specification of a UML class that would be used as input to the conversion tool. This represents the OWL class "Synonym," a parameter type in an OWL-S Process Model presented later. Specifications such as these are transformed using XSLT transformation rules such as the ones shown in Figure 14.

Figure 19. Excerpt of XSLT rule

```
<xsl:comment> OWL Classes </xsl:comment>
<xsl:for-each
  select =
  "//UML:Class[*//UML:Stereotype
                [@xmi.idref=$owlClassId]]">
  <xsl:variable name="className"
   select="current()/@name"/>
  <owl:Class rdf:ID="{$className}"/>
  <xsl:if test="current()//UML:Attribute">
    <xsl:for-each select="current()//UML:Attribute">
      <xsl:if test="current()//UML:Class">
        <xsl:variable name="cId"
            select="current()//UML:Class/@xmi.idref"/>
        <xsl:variable name="cName"
            select="//UML:Class[@xmi.id=$cId]/@name"/>
        <owl:ObjectProperty rdf:ID="{@name}">
          <rdfs:domain rdf:resource="#{$className}"/>
          <rdfs:range rdf:resource="#{$cName}"/>
        </owl:ObjectProperty>
      </xsl:if>
      <xsl:if test="current()//UML:DataType">
        <xsl:variable name="dtId"
            select="current()//UML:DataType/@xmi.idref"/>
        <xsl:variable name="dtName"
            select="//UML:DataType[@xmi.id=$dtId]/@name"/>
        <xsl:variable name="dataType">
          <xsl:choose>
            <xsl:when test="$dtName='xsd:string'">
            <xsl:value-of
            select="'http://.../XMLSchema#string'"/>
            </xsl:when>
            ...
          </xsl:choose>
        </xsl:variable>
        <owl:DatatypeProperty rdf:ID="{@name}">
          <rdfs:domain rdf:resource="#{$className}"/>
          <rdfs:range rdf:resource="{$dataType}"/>
        </owl:DatatypeProperty>
      </xsl:if>
    </xsl:for-each>
  </xsl:if>
</xsl:for-each>
```

Figure 19 contains an excerpt of the corresponding XSLT transformation rule for OWL classes. In this particular case, the transformation rule looks for all classes with the owl:Class stereotype and processes them one by one. An excerpt of a synthesized OWL-S specification is shown in Figure 20. The excerpt shows part of the result of applying the transformation rules in the conversion tool. The OWL class Synonym refers to a semantic concept that allows for an abstract notion of a synonym for a word to be associated with the concrete structures of a string and an integer. From the perspective of the user-architect, the entire transformation process is hidden behind the tools, allowing the user-architect to focus on graphical model construction.

Figure 20. Excerpt of synthesized OWL-S

```
<owl:Class rdf:ID="Synonym"/>
  <owl:DatatypeProperty rdf:ID="item">
    <rdfs:domain rdf:resource="#Synonym"/>
    <rdfs:range rdf:resource=
      "http://www.w3.org/2001/XMLSchema#string"/>
  </owl:DatatypeProperty>
  <owl:DatatypeProperty rdf:ID="distance">
    <rdfs:domain rdf:resource="#Synonym"/>
    <rdfs:range rdf:resource=
      "http://www.w3.org/2001/XMLSchema#integer"/>
  </owl:DatatypeProperty>
```

Figure 21. Protégé with loaded PelicanSpellCheck specification

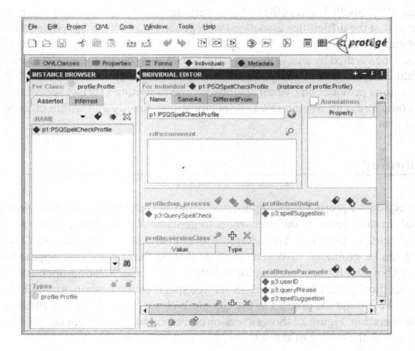

Discussion

Since there may be many possible groundings for any given Semantic Web service, the specification of the service grounding is left as an additional operation that is discussed in the next section. In order to identify any syntactic or semantic errors in generated OWL-S specifications, documents are loaded into the Protégé tool, which validates the OWL-S ontologies. A screenshot of Protégé with the PelicanSpell-Check ontology is shown in Figure 21. Protégé allows for further editing of the OWL-S ontology and other similar manipulation operations, but for our purposes it primarily serves as a validation tool for generated OWL-S descriptions. In the diagram, the lower middle section shows the name of the process specified in Figure 16 (QuerySpellCheck), the lower right section shows the inputs and outputs of the modeled service (userID, queryPhrase, and spell-Suggestion), while the instance browser on the left shows the name of the ServiceModel specified in the UML diagram (PSQSpellCheckProfile). Our experiences with this approach have demonstrated that the difficulties associated with generating OWL-S specifications can be isolated to making sure the UML specifications are complete, an operation that can easily be verified by analyzing synthesized OWL-S specifications with Protégé. Our future investigations include performing a user study to determine whether our technique provides an overall savings in time in writing OWL-S specifications when compared with writing OWL-S specifications directly and within other tools such as Protégé.

Grounding

In this section, we present an example demonstrating a usage scenario for the grounding tool. In this example, the user wants to generate a grounding for the OWL-S PelicanSpellCheckservice. This example demonstrates the fact that an OWL-S service can be grounded to WSDL services that on the surface may appear to be unrelated but after further examination result in a useful specification-operation pair. More specifically, the abstract OWL-S service specification describes a spell-check process. We ground the process to the Google Web service and the doSpellingSuggestion operation. Figure 22 shows a session corresponding to the PelicanSpellCheck example with the output of the session appearing in Figure 23.

The WSDL operation doSpellingSuggestion is identified in the WSDL tree view. The user clicks on the operation name in order to view the operation inputs, outputs, and parameters in the mapping area. The OWL-S operation QuerySpellCheck is identified and selected from the OWL-S tree view. The inputs, outputs, and parameters of QuerySpellCheck are shown in the mapping area.

Figure 22. User interface

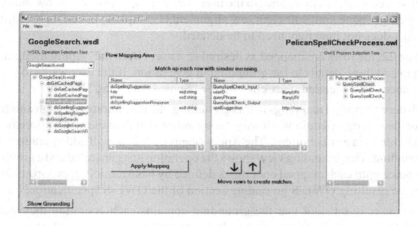

Figure 23. Excerpt of generated grounding

```
<grounding:WsdlAtomicProcessGrounding
            rdf:ID="WsdlGrounding_QuerySpellCheck">
    <grounding:wsdlDocument
        rdf:datatype=".../XMLSchema#anyURI">...GoogleSearch.wsdl
    </grounding:wsdlDocument>
    <grounding:owlsProcess
        rdf:resource="...PelicanSpellCheckProcess.owl#QuerySpellCheck"/>
    <grounding:wsdlOperation rdf:resource="#doSpellingSuggestion_operation"/>
    <grounding:wsdlInputMessage
        rdf:datatype="http://www.w3.org/2001/XMLSchema#anyURI">
        ...GoogleSearch.wsdl#doSpellingSuggestion_Input
    </grounding:wsdlInputMessage>
    <grounding:wsdlInput>
        <grounding:WsdlInputMessageMap>
            <grounding:owlsParameter
                rdf:resource="...PelicanSpellCheckProcess.owl#userID"/>
            <grounding:wsdlMessagePart
                rdf:datatype="http://www.w3.org/2001/XMLSchema#anyURI">
                ...GoogleSearch.wsdl#key
            </grounding:wsdlMessagePart>
        </grounding:WsdlInputMessageMap>
    </grounding:wsdlInput>
...
```

In order to map the WSDL operation doSpellingSuggestion operation with the OWL-S process QuerySpellCheck, the user needs to align the corresponding rows in the mapping area. For instance, in the left pane, the second row displays the WSDL parameter key. In the right pane, the second row displays the OWL-S parameter userID. Since these parameters are properly aligned, no adjustments are required by the user in our example. If there is a case where the parameters are not properly aligned, then rows in the right pane need to be moved so that the parameters in the left pane match in a way that makes semantic sense and creates a grounding that is correctly executable. In this scenario the user clicks the up and down arrow buttons under the right pane until sufficient row alignment is complete. In certain scenarios a row that does not map may need to be deleted.

In Figure 22, the rows are mapped as desired so a user clicks the "Apply Mapping" button to add these details to the grounding in generation. If the user wants to view the instance just generated, they click on the "Show Grounding" button.

To add more operation mappings to this grounding, the user iterates through another cycle of identifying operations, viewing the operation details in the mapping area and row matching via arrow buttons. The Apply Mapping button will add operations to the grounding. The grounding view shows the operation just generated and a grounding instance with each mapped operations defined by hasAtomicProcessGrounding tags in the resulting OWL-S grounding section of the OWL-S specification.

Once the user is satisfied that the grounding contains each operation they want mapped from GoogleSearch.wsdl and PelicanSpellCheckProcess.owl, they save the grounding with a specified name to a specified location.

Related Work

Protégé is a software tool that provides a visual environment for editing ontologies and knowledge bases (Gennari et al., 2002). The OWL plug-in for Protégé allows for visual editing of OWL-based ontologies, but does not specifically support the OWL-S ontology for services. Because the tool supports generic OWL ontologies, there is no mechanism to visualize OWL-S processes. Therefore, creating composite processes is difficult to achieve in a tool like Protégé. Protégé works well for general ontology development, but lacks features required to model specific OWL-S constructs and demands its own set of techniques. The learning curve for such a tool can be steep.

The OWL-S Editor supports visual editing of OWL-S descriptions (Scicluna et al., 2004). It provides a graphical user interface to create and modify an OWL-S description including all three parts: Service Profile, Service Model, and Service Grounding. The Visual Composer feature of the editor allows for the modeling of a composite process using a standard UML Activity Diagram. The OWL-S Editor also provides a mapping mechanism between WSDL and OWL-S. The OWL-S Editor is a good standalone tool, but is proprietary in nature and requires that the user become familiar with its user interface. Our approach leverages existing skills in UML modeling which can greatly improve the efficiency of the Semantic Web service development workflow.

Paolucci et al. (2003) developed the WSDL2OWLS system for automatically generating a one-shot OWL-S specification for a given WSDL file. As such, their approach generates a complete grounding, and incomplete profiles and process models. The approach works by translating a WSDL operation into OWL-S atomic processes and by translating XSD types into OWL-S concepts. Their original approach was developed for the DAML-S format (a precursor to OWL-S). From the perspective of the user, the WSDL2OWLS approach is a bottom-up technique. Our approach differs in that we use a top-down approach, preferring to develop high-level OWL-S specifications and then using the flexibility of OWL-S groundings to map the OWL-S services to any number of potential WSDL realizations of an OWL-S process.

A similar method of creating a one-shot OWL-S specification is taken by Shen, Yang, Zhu, and Wan (2005). In their approach a BPEL4WS specification is translated into an OWL-S specification. As with the approach by Paolucci et al. (2003), this technique generates a complete grounding. However, they also generate a complete process model using the BPEL composition operations as guidance. As a result, only the profile is incomplete since no semantic information is used. The shortcoming of this approach is that it is limited to a single process instance and a single set of groundings. That is, it takes a bottom-up approach. Our approach takes a top-down approach and thus supports development of more abstract OWL-S specifications.

Jaeger, Engel, and Geihs (2005) have proposed a methodology for developing semantic descriptions of Web services using OWL-S. They recognize the lack of tool support for the development of semantic descriptions. A three-step process is introduced in which their tools will create a template using existing software artifacts (e.g., software models, WSDL), automate the identification of relevant ontologies, and perform a classification based on those ontologies. Their methodology differs from ours in that it is focused around the use of a matchmaking algorithm to identify relevant ontologies and classify elements in the semantic description with those ontologies. Our work focuses on the creation of models, leveraging existing knowledge of UML and generating a partial OWL-S specification from those models.

The Object Management Group is creating a standard UML profile to support ontological development within UML tools via an ontology definition metamodel (OMG, 2005a). The OWL profile for OMG supports generic OWL constructs but does not address the issue of OWL-S-specific constructs. For our work, creating an OWL-S-specific UML profile turned out to be the only option to obtain the level of modeling granularity desired. In our approach, we have created a separate OWL-S profile which can be used in any UML modeling tool and allows a developer familiar with UML to efficiently create OWL-S specifications.

Conclusion and Future Investigations

OWL-S provides an ontology for Web services that can be used to describe the semantics of a Web service. Unfortunately, adopting a language like OWL-S can be difficult because of the learning curve and current state of tool support. The UML profile that we have created for OWL-S allows software developers to model OWL-S descriptions with a standard UML modeling tool. The conversion tool described in this chapter was created to take an XML representation of a UML model and convert it into an OWL-S specification. The grounding tool allows a developer to map the processes found in an OWL-S specification to operations in WSDL specifications.

The research issue of particular interest is that of automated composition of services. Currently service composition is performed at design-time. With semantic descriptions in place and mappings between the descriptions and the concrete realizations of the services, automated composition is possible. As part of our research, we are investigating how the use of a product-line approach that focuses on commonalities and variabilities can be used to develop OWL-S service specifications as commonalities and OWL-S service groundings as variabilities. In addition, we are developing an engine that will facilitate the execution of grounded OWL-S specifications.

Acknowledgment

G. Gannod is supported by the National Science Foundation CAREER grant No. CCR-0133956.

References

Akkiraju, R., Farrell, J., Miller, J., Nagarajan, M., Sheth, A., & Verma, K. (2005). *Web service semantics—wsdl-s*. Retrieved January 18, 2006, from *http://www. w3.org/Submission/WSDL-S/*

Andrews, T., Curbera, F., Dholakia, H., Goland, Y., Klein, J., Leymann, F., Liu, K., Roller, D., Smith, D., Thatte, S., Trickovic, I., & Weerawarana, S. (2003). *Specification: Business process execution language for Web services version 1.1*. Retrieved January 18, 2006, from *http://www-128.ibm.com/developer-works/library/ws-bpel/*

Berners-Lee, T., Hendler, J., & Lassila, O. (2001). The Semantic Web. *Scientific American,* (May), 34-43.

Christensen, E., Curbera, F., Meredith, G., & Weerawarana, S. (2001). *Web service description language 1.1.* Retrieved January 18, 2006, from *http://www.w3.org/TR/wsdl/*

Clark, J. (1999). *Xsl transformations version 1.0.* Retrieved January 18, 2006, from *http://www.w3c.org/TR/xslt*

Clarke, E.W., & Wing, J.M. (1996). *Formal methods: State of the art and future directions.* Technical Report CMU-CS-96-178, Carnegie Mellon University, USA.

Gannod, G.C., and Bhatia, S. (2004, July). Facilitating automated search for Web services. *Proceedings of the 2004 IEEE International Conference on Web Services* (pp. 761-764), San Diego, CA.

Gannod, G.C., Brodie, R.J., & Timm, J.T. (2005, September). An interactive approach for specifying OWL-S groundings. *Proceedings of the IEEE EDOC Enterprise Computing Conference* (pp. 251-260), Enschede, The Netherlands.

Gannod, G.C., Timm, J.T.E., & Brodie, R.J (2006). Facilitating the specification of Semantic Web services using model-driven development. *Journal of Web Services Research, 3*(3), 61-81.

Genesereth, M.R., & Fikes, R. (1998). *Knowledge interchange format (KIF).* Draft Proposed American National Standard, NCITS.T2/98-004, USA.

Gennari, J., Musen, M.A., Fergerson, R.W., Grosso, W.E., Crubezy, M., Eriksson, H., Noy, N.F., & Tu, S.W. (2003). The evolution of Protégé: An environment for knowledge-based systems development. *International Journal of Human-Computer Studies, 58*(1), 89-123.

Gentleware. (2005). *Poseidon for UML.* Retrieved January 18, 2006, from *http://www.gentleware.com/*

Horrocks, I., Patel-Scheider, P., Boley, H., Tabet, S., Groshof, B., & Dean, M. (2003). *SWRL: A Semantic Web rule language combining OWL and RuleML.* Retrieved January 18, 2006, from *http://www.daml.org/2003/11/swrl*

Jaeger, M.C., Engel, L., & Geihs, K. (2005, February). A methodology for developing OWL-S descriptions. *Proceedings of the 1st International Conference on Interoperability of Enterprise Software and Applications Workshop on Web Services and Interoperability,* Geneva, Switzerland.

Kiko, K., & Atkinson, C. (2005, September). Integrating enterprise architecture representation languages. *Proceedings of the Workshop on Vocabularies, Ontologies, and Rules for the Enterprise* (pp. 41-50), Enschede, The Netherlands.

Martin, D., Paolucci, M., McIlraith, S., Burstein, M., McDermott, D., McGuinness, D., Parsia, B., Payne, T., Sabou, M., Solanki, M., Srinivasan, N., & Sycara, K.

(2005). Bringing semantics to Web services: The OWL-S approach. *Proceedings of SWSWPC 2004* (pp. 26-42). Berlin: Springer-Verlag (LNCS 3387).

McDermott, D. (2004). *DRS: A set of conventions for representing logical languages in RDF.* Retrieved January 18, 2006, from *http://www.daml.org/services/owl-s/1.1/DRSguide.pdf*

Miller, J., & Mukerji, J. (Eds.). (2003). *MDA guide version 1.0.1.* Technical Report omg/2003-06-01, Object Management Group, USA.

OMG. (2005). *XML metadata interchange.* Technical Report formal/2005-09-01, Object Management Group, USA.

OMG. (2005a). *Ontology definition metamodel.* Technical Report OMG/RFP/ad/2003-03-40 (3rd revision), Object Management Group, USA.

OMG. (2005b). *Unified modeling language specification, version 1.4.2.* Technical Report formal/05-04-01, Object Management Group, USA. Retrieved from *http://www.omg.org/cgi-bin/doc?formal/05-07-04*

OMG. (2005c, June). *OCL 2.0 specification.* Retrieved from *http://www.omg.org/docs/ptc/05-06-06.pdf*

Paolucci, M., Srinivasan, N., Sycara, K., & Nishimura, T. (2003, June). Towards a semantic choreography of Web services: From WSDL to DAML-S. *Proceedings of the International Conference on Web Services* (pp. 22-26), Las Vegas, NV.

Scicluna, J., Abela, C., & Montebello, M. (2004, October). Visual modeling of OWL-S services. *Proceedings of the IADIS International Conference on the WWW/Internet,* Madrid, Spain.

Shen, J., Yang, Y., Zhu, C., & Wan, C. (2005, July). From BPEL4WS to OWL-S: Integrating e-business process definitions. *Proceedings of the 3rd International Conference on Services Computing* (SCC 2005) (pp. 279-286), Orlando, FL.

Smith, M.K., Welty, C., & McGuinness, D.L. (2004). *Owl Web ontology language guide.* Retrieved January 18, 2006, from *http://www.w3c.org/TR/owl-guide/*

Sycara, K., Paolucci, M., Ankolekar, A., & Srinivasan, N. (2003, September). Automated discovery, interaction and composition of Semantic Web services. *Journal of Web Semantics, 1*(1), 27-46.

About the Contributors

Peter Bertok is an academic staff member at the School of Computer Science, RMIT University in Australia. He has authored more than 90 refereed publications. Dr. Bertok also served on a number of program committees of international conferences. His main research areas are networked and distributed computing, Web services, and computer security.

Raynette J. Brodie is a software developer with the 41st Parameter. She earned a BS in computer science from Arizona State University. Her research interests fall in the areas of software engineering and service-oriented computing. The work described in this chapter was performed while Brodie was a student at Arizona State University.

Carsten Buschmann earned a master's degree in computer science from the Technical University of Braunschweig, Germany, in 2002. He is currently working towards his doctoral degree at the University of Lübeck in the area of wireless sensor networks. Within the SWARMS project, his task is to explore middleware support for application development for distributed pervasive computing.

Min Cai earned BS and MS degrees in computer science from Southeast University, China (1998 and 2001, respectively). In December 2006, he received a PhD in computer science from the University of Southern California. His research interests include P2P and Grid computing, network security, Semantic Web, and Web services technologies.

Jen-Yao Chung is the chief technology officer for IBM Global Electronics Industry, where he is responsible for identifying and growing new technologies into future businesses for IBM. Before that, he was senior manager of the Electronic Commerce and Supply Chain Department, and program director for the IBM Institute for Advanced Commerce Technology office. He has been involved in research on electronic commerce, electronic marketplaces, and Web application systems. Dr. Chung's current research is in the area of business process integration and management. He is the co-chair if the IEEE technical committee on e-commerce. He has published 120 technical papers and earned an IEEE Outstanding Paper award, two IBM Outstanding Technical Achievement awards, and an IBM Outstanding Contribution award. He is a senior member of IEEE and a member of ACM. Dr. Chung earned his MS and PhD degrees in computer science from the University of Illinois at Urbana-Champaign.

Stefan Fischer is professor of computer sciences at the University of Lübeck, Germany. Previously, he worked at the European Center for Network Research (ENC) of IBM in Heidelberg, at the University of Heidelberg where he received his doctoral degree in 1996, at the University of Montreal, the International University at Bruchsal, and the Technical University of Braunschweig. His current research activities focus on applications and supporting software for state-of-the-art distributed systems.

Shahram Ghandeharizadeh earned his PhD in computer science from the University of Wisconsin, Madison, in 1990. Since then, he has been on the faculty at the University of Southern California. In 1992, Dr. Ghandeharizadeh received the National Science Foundation Young Investigator Award for his research on the physical design of parallel database systems. In 1995, he received an award from the School of Engineering at USC in recognition of his research activities. His primary research interests include design and implementation of extensible storage systems that employ Web services as a building block. Microsoft and the National Science Foundation have been the primary sponsors of this research effort.

Gerald C. Gannod is an associate professor in the Department of Computer Science and Systems Analysis at Miami University in Oxford, Ohio. He earned his MS and PhD degrees in computer science from Michigan State University in 1994 and 1998, respectively. His research interests include service-oriented computing, software product lines, software reverse engineering, formal methods for software development, software architecture, and software for embedded systems. He is a recipient of a 2002 NSF CAREER Award.

Tobias Jäcker finished his studies at the Technical University of Braunschweig, Germany, with a diploma (equivalent to master's degree) in computer science in May 2005. He is currently working as a software developer at an IT consulting company, Auel EDV-Beratung GmbH, in Braunschweig, Germany.

Miroslaw Malek is a professor and chair of computer architecture and communication at Humboldt University, Berlin. His research focuses on high-performance responsive computing, including parallel architectures, real-time systems, networks, and fault tolerance. Dr. Malek earned his PhD in computer science from the Technical University of Wroclaw, Poland.

Nikola Milanovic is working as a researcher at the Berlin University of Technology. His research interests include component- and service-based environments, service composition, interoperability, model-driven software development, ubiquitous computing, ad-hoc networks, and wireless communication. He earned his PhD in computer science from the Humboldt University in Berlin, Germany.

Christos Papadopoulos is an associate professor at Colorado State University. He earned his PhD in computer science in 1999 from Washington University in St. Louis, Missouri. His interests include network security, router services, multimedia protocols, and reliable multicast. He is a member of the Network Security Lab at Colorado State University, which includes research on DDoS attacks, BGP, and secure DNS. In 2002 he received an NSF CAREER Award to explore router services as a component of the next-generation Internet architecture. He is currently working on an NSF-funded project to apply signal processing techniques to analyze and detect DDoS attacks. He participates in a multi-university collaborative project to fingerprint attacks and quickly distribute fingerprints to various IDSs. He also participates in a DHS-funded project to capture, store, and distribute network traces containing attacks to the research community. He participated on technical program committees of many major networking conferences and organized several workshops.

Francis Quek is a professor of computer science at Virginia Tech, as well as the director of the Center for Human-Computer Interaction. His current research interests center around computer vision (dynamic vision, color, object recognition), computational multimodal language analysis, human-computer interaction (HCI), medical imaging and visualization, video analysis for multimedia database access, and robot navigation. He earned his PhD in computer science in engineering from the University of Michigan, Ann Arbor in 1990. He is a senior member of IEEE and ACM.

Dusan Simic is a PhD student in the School of Engineering, RMIT University, Australia.

Zahir Tari is the head of the discipline "Distributed Systems & Networking Systems" at RMIT's School of Computer Science, Australia. His expertise is in the areas of system's performance (e.g., load balancing and caching), Web services (e.g., security and service discovery), and sensor networks. Dr. Tari wrote/edited several books and published in prestigious journals such as *ACM Transactions* and *IEEE Transactions on Distributed Systems*. He has been the program committee chair of several international conferences, including Distributed Object and Application symposiums, IFIP DS 11.3 on Database Security, and IFIP 2.6 on Data Semantics, and he has served as general chair of several international conferences.

John T.E. Timm is a PhD student at Arizona State University. He holds a BSE in computer systems engineering and an MCS in computer science from Arizona State University. His research interests include software engineering for embedded systems, software engineering for Web-based software applications, and semantic Web services. He has eight years of professional experience in the areas of Web-based software applications and embedded software engineering. Timm is working with Dr. Gerald Gannod at Arizona State University in the area of Semantic Web service composition and discovery.

Christian Werner is a scientific assistant at the University of Lübeck, Germany. He earned his diploma (equivalent to a master's degree) in computer science from the Humboldt University in Berlin in July 2002. He earned a doctoral degree from the University of Lübeck in August 2006. His main research activities are focused on technologies for enhancing Web service performance and using Web services on resource-constrained devices.

Jia Zhang is an assistant professor of computer science at Northern Illinois University, and a guest researcher of the National Institute of Standards and Technology (NIST). Her current research interests center around software trustworthiness in the domain of Web services, with a focus on reliability, integrity, security, and interoperability. She also has seven years of industrial experience as a software technical lead in Web application development. She earned her PhD in computer science from the University of Illinois at Chicago in 2000. She is a member of IEEE and ACM.

Liang-Jie Zhang is a research staff member and the founding chair of the Services Computing Professional Interest Community (PIC) at the IBM T.J. Watson Research Center. He is part of the business informatics research team, with a focus on SOA and Web services for industry solutions and business performance management services. He has filed more than 30 patent applications in the areas of e-commerce, Web services, rich media, data management, and information appliances, and he has published more than 80 technical papers in journals, book chapters, and conference proceedings. Dr. Zhang is an IEEE senior member and the chair of the IEEE Computer Society's Technical Steering Committee for Services Computing. He was the general chair of the 2004 IEEE International Conference on Web Services, the 2004 IEEE Conference on E-Commerce Technology, and the 2004 IEEE International Conference on Services Computing. He is the editor-in-chief of the *International Journal of Web Services Research*. Dr. Zhang earned a BS in electrical engineering from Xidian University in 1990, an MS in electrical engineering from Xi'an Jiaotong University in 1992, and a PhD in computer engineering from Tsinghua University in 1996.

Ning Zhang is a PhD candidate in the Department of Policy Analysis and Management of Cornell University. Her current research interests are health economics, labor economics, and Internet economics. She earned her master's degree from Cornell University and her bachelor's degree from Nanjing University, China.

Runfang Zhou earned her BS and MS degrees in computer science from Southeast University, China, in 1997 and 2001, and her PhD in computer science from the University of Southern California in May 2007. Her research interests include peer-to-peer reputation systems, overlay network design, Web services performance improvement, and trust and secure collaboration in grid computing.

Index

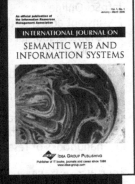